American Catholic Higher Education

Education

Essential Documents, 1967–1990

edited by
ALICE GALLIN, O.S.U.

UNIVERSITY OF NOTRE DAME PRESS
NOTRE DAME   LONDON

Library of Congress Cataloging-in-Publication Data

American Catholic higher education : essential docu-
ments. 1967–1990 / edited by Alice Gallin.
    p. cm.
    Includes index.
    ISBN 0-268-00634-2
    1. Catholic universities and colleges—United States
—History—20th century. 2. Catholic Church—
Doctrines. 3. Catholic Church—Education—United
States—Papal documents. I. Gallin, Alice.
LC501.A44 1992
377'.82'73—dc20   91-51113
                                     CIP

To the Presidents
of Catholic Colleges and Universities,
Past, Present, and Future

Contents

Preface

The genesis of this book is a very practical one. At the office of the Association of Catholic Colleges and Universities, we have received over the past ten years innumerable requests for the texts of these documents. College presidents, bishops, canon lawyers, historians, and newspaper editors need these documents in order to prepare their own speeches, magazine articles, news stories. We hope that this volume will therefore be a handy reference tool.

The years from 1965 to 1990 have been decisive in the history of Catholic colleges and universities in the United States. The changes in policies on the part of the federal and state governments made it possible for our institutions to expand and to improve in academic quality. At the same time, the changes in the church in the wake of Vatican II provided the freedom needed for such institutions to become more credible in the eyes of their colleagues in higher education.

But this did not occur without tension. The documents contained herein explicate the long dialogue that has gone between the Catholic universities around the world and the Congregation for Catholic Education in Rome (known variously as the Sacred Congregation for Catholic Education; the Congregation for Seminaries and Other Institutes; and the Congregation for Seminaries and Universities).

The dialogue was already underway before I came into my position with ACCU, but I have been intimately involved in it since 1980. The "giants" on whose shoulders I stood included Rev. Theodore Hesburgh, C.S.C., Rev. Paul Reinert, S.J., Ann Ida Gannon, B.V.M., and Msgr. John F. Murphy—to mention only the leaders. Archbishop William Borders and the many bishops who have served on the Bishops and Presidents' Committee during these important years contributed insights, skills, and patience to the task of articulating the relationship between colleges and the church community. To all of them, both presidents and bishops, we owe a debt of gratitude.

No product comes out of an office as the work of a single individual. At the ACCU office I have had the continual support and assistance of Paul Gallagher, Francine Simons, and Lynn O'Shea. Their work has been complemented by the editors at the University of Notre Dame

Press. It has been a pleasure working with all of them and benefiting from their special skills.

The texts of the documents are given here in English although the official language in some instances is Latin. They stand on their own for their authenticity. On the other hand, the interpretive comments and the historical background are the result of my participation in the process and are, I hope, informative and enlightening. I take full responsibility for them. In the years ahead others may write from different perspectives and thus add to our understanding.

Introduction

When historians attempt to reconstruct the history of Catholic higher education in the United States, they will note that the years from 1965 to 1990 were times of startling changes, significant soul-searching, and extraordinary maturing. Around the world the question, "What is a Catholic University?" became central to many discussions carried on by church and university officials, and nowhere was this more true than in the United States. It was a period of tremendous expansion in higher education of all kinds, a time when the civil-rights movement pushed toward opening paths of access for black Americans, the moment when we saw a shift to coeducation in many Catholic colleges, and a time when lay men and women assumed increasing responsibility in our institutions. With a more diverse student body, a decline in the number of religious, and the visible changes in discipline and social mores on campuses, the general public, as well as the various constituencies, found it hard to know what made the university "Catholic."

The twenty-five years following Vatican II witnessed some rather fundamental changes in the self-understanding of the Roman Catholic church. It is not surprising, therefore, that the Catholic college and university experienced a similar identity crisis. Two questions surfaced repeatedly: What does it mean to be a university or college, and what does it mean for that institution to be Catholic?

The documents that are presented in this volume speak of the efforts to answer those questions. For the most part they have been developed "in dialogue" between church officials and university presidents. In order that the impact of such dialogue on the final statement can be grasped, the various drafts of several of the documents are given. They are witnesses to the persistence, the clarity of vision, and the strong commitment to the importance of Catholic higher education on the part of many individuals. Running through all of the documents is the fundamental claim that a Catholic university has an important role as the mediator between faith and cultures, but the way in which the claim is actualized in and through the institution has proved harder to define with any specificity. Some persons, beginning from the point of view of the church, see the relationship as one of instrumentality—the university is an arm of the church and assists it in its task of preaching the gospel

1

to all nations and cultures; others begin with the broad understanding of the life and purpose of any university, and then struggle to express the way in which such a task might have a legitimate connection with the mission of the church.

Until 1965 there had been no attempt to make such a statement for the universities around the world. While the popes had often spoken of Catholic education in general and several had shown support for the foundation of various Catholic universities, none had attempted to articulate a special role for such universities in an ecclesial context.

The Code of Canon Law promulgated in 1917 passed over universities in silence, addressing only schools and seminaries. By that time most universities in Europe were secularized and were state institutions. Where that was the case, the church contented itself with securing the right to appoint the teachers of theology on faculties attached to state universities. This is the origin of the "canonical mission," to teach Roman Catholic theology. In the United States, on the other hand, colleges and universities had emerged from secondary schools and academies and, for the most part, were under the direction of men and women of the religious communities that had founded them in the late nineteenth and early twentieth centuries. Only a few were directly related to the local bishop, and only The Catholic University of America was founded under the patronage of the national hierarchy and the Vatican.

In the post-World War II years, a period of strong sentiment favoring international organizations, some leaders in Catholic universities, in response to a request from Pius XII and, in collaboration with the Sacred Congregation for Catholic Education, formed the International Federation of Catholic Universities. Official recognition was granted in 1949. Under Paul VI and with his blessing, it later became an independent association (1963) and moved forward under the leadership of Rev. Theodore Hesburgh, C.S.C., president of the University of Notre Dame. At its meeting in Tokyo in 1965, the IFCU decided to formulate a statement on the distinctive purposes of a Catholic university that would have as its context the Vatican II document, "The Church in the Modern World."

The story of the dialogue thus begun in 1965 which culminated in *Ex Corde Ecclesiae*, signed by Pope John Paul II on August 15, 1990, is encapsulated in the documents presented here. They are presented in four groupings: 1) the documents which fed into 1972's "The Catholic University in the Modern World"; 2) those which attempted to explicate and/or modify it (1973–1980); 3) those which dealt with the development of the revised Code of Canon Law (1977–1983); and 4) the many drafts of the apostolic constitution, *Ex Corde Ecclesiae* (1985–1990).

It is hoped that they will provide a handy reference tool for current leaders in both church and university and a basic resource for future historians of American Catholic higher education.

Part I

Toward a Universal Statement of the Nature of the Catholic University 1965–1973

With the advent of new international structures, the Catholic universities had organized into their own federation in 1949. Between 1949 and 1963 the International Federation of Catholic Universities had an interesting history, but for the purposes of this book the importance of this association lies in its initial efforts to describe the role of the Catholic university in the modern world. A decision was made in 1965 at a meeting of IFCU in Tokyo to organize regional conferences for the purpose of developing a statement on Catholic universities that would harmonize with the Vatican II document, "The Church in the Modern World." Such meetings were held at Buga (Colombia), Manila, Paris, and Land O' Lakes, Wisconsin, and the resultant documents were brought to the next IFCU Assembly at Kinshasa (Zaire) in September 1968. Since we are focusing on documents of American Catholic higher education, we present only the Land O' Lakes text (1967) and then point to its influence in the development of "The Catholic University in the Modern World" by including the drafts done at Kinshasa (1968) and Rome (1969).

The group that met at Land O' Lakes included some twenty-six persons representing nine major Catholic universities, members of the episcopacy, and well-known scholars and leaders of religious communities. The meeting was hosted by Rev. Theodore M. Hesburgh, C.S.C., president of the University of Notre Dame and the president of IFCU.

As will be seen, Land O' Lakes contained two phrases that became fundamental in the future dialogue: academic freedom and institutional autonomy. But it also stressed the fact that the Catholic university must be an institution " . . . in which Catholicism is perceptibly present and effectively operative." In fact, these concepts were carried over into the document developed at Kinshasa in September 1968, where the statement from Land O' Lakes was melded with those produced at Buga, Manila, and Paris. As could well be expected, this project was not completed at Kinshasa but was continued at further meetings in 1971 and 1972, culminating in a Congress held in Rome in November 1972. The final document was entitled "The Catholic University in the Modern World" and was disseminated in 1973. The document was well received in the United States because it acknowledged both academic freedom and institutional autonomy along the lines of Land O' Lakes and because it assumed that there were different ways by which an institution could be considered "Catholic." It described the characteristics of all Catholic universities in broad terms and contained no juridical norms.

It was not, however, accepted so easily by the Congregation for Catholic Education. Cardinal Garrone, Prefect of the Congregation, in a letter of April 25, 1973, which he asked to have attached to the document itself, spoke of the need for two further clarifications: 1) an explicit statement by each university of its character and commitment as Catholic; and 2) the development of efficacious instruments by the university so as to be able to put into effect proper self-regulation in the sectors of faith, morality, and discipline. It will be noted that this letter ended on a somewhat ambiguous note: " . . . although the document envisages the existence of university institutions without statutory bonds linking them to ecclesiastical authority, it is to be noted that this in no way means that such institutions are removed from those relationships with the ecclesiastical hierarchy which must characterize all Catholic institutions." What did this mean?

At this point no further document was attempted, and the assumption was that an acceptable statement was in place, even though there might be need for further clarification.

Land O'Lakes Statement:
The Nature of the Contemporary
Catholic University*

1. THE CATHOLIC UNIVERSITY: A TRUE
UNIVERSITY WITH DISTINCTIVE CHARACTERISTICS

The Catholic University today must be a university in the full modern sense of the word, with a strong commitment to and concern for academic excellence. To perform its teaching and research functions effectively the Catholic university must have a true autonomy and academic freedom in the face of authority of whatever kind, lay or clerical, external to the academic community itself. To say this is simply to assert that institutional autonomy and academic freedom are essential conditions of life and growth and indeed of survival for Catholic universities as for all universities.

The Catholic university participates in the total university life of our time, has the same functions as all other true universities and, in general, offers the same services to society. The Catholic university adds to the basic idea of a modern university distinctive characteristics which round out and fulfill that idea. Distinctively, then, the Catholic university must be an institution, a community of learners or a community of scholars, in which Catholicism is perceptibly present and effectively operative.

2. THE THEOLOGICAL DISCIPLINES

In the Catholic university this operative presence is effectively achieved first of all and distinctively by the presence of a group of scholars in all branches of theology. The disciplines represented by this theological group are recognized in the Catholic university, not only as legitimate intellectual disciplines, but as ones essential to the integrity

Reprinted from Neil G. McCluskey, S.J., *The Catholic University* (Notre Dame, Ind.: University of Notre Dame Press, 1970).

7

of a university. Since the pursuit of the theological sciences is therefore a high priority for a Catholic university, academic excellence in these disciplines becomes a double obligation in a Catholic university.

3. THE PRIMARY TASK OF THE THEOLOGICAL FACULTY

The theological faculty must engage directly in exploring the depths of Christian tradition and the total religious heritage of the world, in order to come to the best possible intellectual understanding of religion and revelation, of man in all his varied relationships to God. Particularly important today is the theological exploration of all human relations and the elaboration of a Christian anthropology. Furthermore, theological investigation today must serve the ecumenical goals of collaboration and unity.

4. INTERDISCIPLINARY DIALOGUE IN THE CATHOLIC UNIVERSITY

To carry out this primary task properly there must be a constant discussion within the university community in which theology confronts all the rest of modern culture and all the areas of intellectual study which it includes.

Theology needs this dialogue in order:

A) to enrich itself from the other disciplines;
B) to bring its own insights to bear upon the problems of modern culture; and
C) to stimulate the internal development of the disciplines themselves.

In a Catholic university all recognized university areas of study are frankly and fully accepted and their internal autonomy affirmed and guaranteed. There must be no theological or philosophical imperialism; all scientific and disciplinary methods, and methodologies, must be given due honor and respect. However, there will necessarily result from the interdisciplinary discussions an awareness that there is a philosophical and theological dimension to most intellectual subjects when they are pursued far enough. Hence, in a Catholic university there will be a special interest in interdisciplinary problems and relationships.

This total dialogue can be eminently successful:

A) if the Catholic university has a broad range of basic university disciplines;

B) if the university has achieved considerable strength in these disciplines; and

C) if there are present in many or most of the non-theological areas Christian scholars who are not only interested in, and competent in their own fields, but also have a personal interest in the cross-disciplinary confrontation.

This creative dialogue will involve the entire university community, will inevitably influence and enliven classroom activities, and will be reflected in curriculum and in academic programs.

5. THE CATHOLIC UNIVERSITY AS THE CRITICAL REFLECTIVE INTELLIGENCE OF THE CHURCH

Every university, Catholic or not, serves as the critical reflective intelligence of its society. In keeping with this general function, the Catholic university has the added obligation of performing this same service for the Church. Hence, the university should carry on a continual examination of all aspects and all activities of the Church and should objectively evaluate them. The Church would thus have the benefit of continual counsel from Catholic universities. Catholic universities in the recent past have hardly played this role at all. It may well be one of the most important functions of the Catholic university of the future.

6. THE CATHOLIC UNIVERSITY AND RESEARCH

The Catholic university will, of course, maintain and support broad programs of research. It will promote basic research in all university fields but, in addition, it will be prepared to undertake by preference, though not exclusively, such research as will deal with problems of greater human urgency or of greater Christian concern.

7. THE CATHOLIC UNIVERSITY AND PUBLIC SERVICE

In common with other universities, and in accordance with given circumstances, the Catholic university is prepared to serve society and all its parts, e.g., the Federal Government, the inner-city, etc. However, it will have an added special obligation to carry on similar activities, appropriate to a university, in order to serve the Church and its component parts.

8. SOME CHARACTERISTICS OF
UNDERGRADUATE EDUCATION

The effective intellectual presence of the theological disciplines will affect the education and life of the students in ways distinctive of a Catholic university.

With regard to the undergraduate—the university should endeavor to present a collegiate education that is truly geared to modern society. The student must come to a basic understanding of the actual world in which he lives today. This means that the intellectual campus of a Catholic university has no boundaries and no barriers. It draws knowledge and understanding from all the traditions of mankind; it explores the insights and achievements of the great men of every age; it looks to the current frontiers of advancing knowledge and brings all the results to bear relevantly on man's life today. The whole world of knowledge and ideas must be open to the student; there must be no outlawed books or subjects. Thus the student will be able to develop his own capabilities and to fulfill himself by using the intellectual resources presented to him.

Along with this and integrated into it should be a competent presentation of relevant, living, Catholic thought.

This dual presentation is characterized by the following emphases:

A) a concern with ultimate questions; hence a concern with theological and philosophical questions;
B) a concern for the full human and spiritual development of the student; hence a humanistic and personalistic orientation with special emphasis on the interpersonal relationships within the community of learners;
C) a concern with the particularly pressing problems of our era, e.g., civil rights, international development and peace, poverty, etc.

9. SOME SPECIAL SOCIAL CHARACTERISTICS OF
THE CATHOLIC COMMUNITY OF LEARNERS

As a community of learners, the Catholic university has a social existence and an organizational form.

Within the university community the student should be able not simply to study theology and Christianity, but should find himself in a social situation in which he can express his Christianity in a variety of ways and live it experientially and experimentally. The students and faculty can explore together new forms of Christian living, of Christian witness, and of Christian service.

The students will be able to participate in and contribute to a variety of liturgical functions, at best, creatively contemporary and experimental. They will find the meaning of the sacraments for themselves by joining theoretical understanding to the lived experience of them. Thus the students will find and indeed create extraordinary opportunities for a full, meaningful liturgical and sacramental life.

The students will individually and in small groups carry on a warm personal dialogue with themselves and with faculty, both priests and laymen.

The students will experiment further in Christian service by undertaking activities embodying the Christian interest in all human problems —inner-city social action, personal aid to the educationally disadvantaged, and so forth.

Thus will arise within the Catholic university a self-developing and self-deepening society of students and faculty in which the consequences of Christian truth are taken seriously in person-to-person relationships, where the importance of religious commitment is accepted and constantly witnessed to, and where the students can learn by personal experience to consecrate their talent and learning to worthy social purposes.

All of this will display itself on the Catholic campus as a distinctive style of living, a perceptible quality in the university's life.

10. CHARACTERISTICS OF
ORGANIZATION AND ADMINISTRATION

The total organization should reflect this same Christian spirit. The social organization should be such as to emphasize the university's concern for persons as individuals and for appropriate participation by all members of the community of learners in university decisions. University decisions and administrative actions should be appropriately guided by Christian ideas and ideals and should eminently display the respect and concern for persons.

The evolving nature of the Catholic university will necessitate basic reorganizations of structure in order not only to achieve a greater internal cooperation and participation, but also to share the responsibility of direction more broadly and to enlist wider support. A great deal of study and experimentation will be necessary to carry out these changes, but changes of this kind are essential for the future of the Catholic university.

In fine, the Catholic university of the future will be a true modern university but specifically Catholic in profound and creative ways for the service of society and the people of God.

NOTE

*Position paper adopted, July 20–23, 1967, at Land O'Lakes, Wisc., by the seminar participants: Gerard J. Campbell, S.J., President, Georgetown University; John Cogley, Center for the Study of Democratic Institutions, Santa Barbara, Calif.; Charles F. Donovan, S.J., Academic Vice President, Boston College; Most Rev. John J. Dougherty, Chairman, Episcopal Committee for Catholic Higher Education and President, Seton Hall University, South Orange, N.J.; Thomas R. Fitzgerald, S.J., Academic Vice President, Georgetown University; Rev. F. Raymond Fowerbaugh, Assistant to the President, Catholic University of America; Most Rev. Paul J. Hallinan, Archbishop of Atlanta; Robert J. Henle, S.J., Academic Vice President, Saint Louis University; Theodore M. Hesburgh, C.S.C., President, University of Notre Dame; Howard J. Kenna, C.S.C., Provincial, Indiana Province, Congregation of Holy Cross.

Robert D. Kidera, Vice President for University Relations, Fordham University; Germain-Marie Lalande, C.S.C., Superior General, Congregation of Holy Cross, Rome, Italy; Felipe E. MacGregor, S.J., Rector, Pontificia Universidad Católica del Peru, Lima, Peru; Right Rev. Theodore E. McCarrick, President, Catholic University of Puerto Rico, Ponce; Neil G. McCluskey, S.J., Secretary of the Seminar, University of Notre Dame; Leo McLaughlin, S.J., President, Fordham University; Vincent T. O'Keefe, S.J., Assistant General, Society of Jesus, Rome, Italy; Right Rev. Alphonse-Marie Parent, Laval University, Quebec, Canada; Paul C. Reinert, S.J., President, Saint Louis University.

M. L'abbé Lorenzo Roy, Vice Rector, Laval University; Daniel L. Schlafly, Chairman, Board of Trustees, Saint Louis University; George N. Shuster, Assistant to the President, University of Notre Dame; Edmund A. Stephan, Chairman, Board of Trustees, University of Notre Dame; M. L'abbé Lucien Vachon, Dean, Faculty of Theology, University of Sherbrook, Canada; John E. Walsh, C.S.C., Vice President for Academic Affairs, University of Notre Dame; Michael P. Walsh, S.J., President, Boston College.

Kinshasa Statement:
The Catholic University
in the Modern World*

The representatives of the Catholic universities of the world assembled at Lovanium University, Kinshasa, conscious of their responsibility to share in building a better and more human world, wish briefly to describe their specifically Catholic role in their fraternal collaboration with other institutions of higher learning.

In addition to the teaching, research, and service common to all universities, by institutional commitment the Catholic university brings to its task the inspiration and illumination of the Christian message. In the Catholic university, therefore, Catholic ideals, attitudes and principles penetrate and inform university activities in accordance with the nature and autonomy of these activities. Distinctively, then, the Catholic university must be an academic institution, a community of scholars, in which Catholicism is present and operative.

In the Catholic university, this operative presence is ideally and normally achieved first of all by the presence of a group of scholars in all branches of theology. The disciplines represented by this theologian group are recognized in the Catholic university, not only as legitimate intellectual disciplines, but as disciplines essential to the integrity of the Catholic university. Indeed, we believe that the science of religion by its very nature belongs to the task of any university. Since the pursuit of the theological sciences is, therefore, a high priority for a Catholic university, academic excellence in these disciplines becomes a double obligation.

At this period of social change when the mind questions the role of the university in society, when the Christian community itself is uncertain of the future of the Catholic university, we deem it essential to recall the reasons which justify in regard to society in general and to the Christian community in particular the objective which Catholic institutions of higher learning have to fulfill in the present time.

Reprinted from Neil G. McCluskey, S.J., *The Catholic University* (Notre Dame, Ind.: University of Notre Dame Press, 1970).

In practice there is a variety of activities proper to a Catholic university, which would include such endeavors as the following:

1. To contribute as much as possible to the integration of all knowledge in the light of the wisdom of Christian revelation, in accord with the university's mission of universality.

2. To make theology relevant to all human knowledge and all human knowledge relevant to theology itself.

3. To put at the disposal of the people of God and especially of those with responsibility for making serious decisions in the Church the discoveries of knowledge in every field.

4. To study and research problems of high Christian and human priority. For example:

  • respect for students' freedom during their formative years
  • enriching of culture and its profound human meaning
  • the problem of faith in a pluralistic society
  • the dignity of love and the stability of family life in an age where these values are being eroded

5. To create a Christian community of learning, in which, because of its authentic universality, non-Catholics as well as Catholics may participate and cooperate, thus bringing to the Catholic university the ideas and values of many traditions.

6. To create a true university community in which all members whether professors, students, or administrators, whether clerical or lay, participate authentically in its total life.

7. To promote ecumenism by forming thinkers fully equipped for dialogue through ecumenical studies at the highest level.

8. To serve society in general with dedication, in a Christian perspective, which especially focuses on the needs of the emerging nations and on the new world civilization now forming. To assist Catholic universities in the developing areas in the formulation of a theology suited to their cultures and ways of life.

9. To prepare graduates who can participate with all men in the continual development of every sector of our pluralistic society, especially in the achievement of social justice.

To these special tasks, Catholic universities are dedicated by an institutional commitment which includes a respect for and voluntary acceptance of the Church's teaching authority.

Thus, the Catholic university both in theory and in fact presents a rich potential of forms, modes, and activities. The Catholic universities of the world judge, therefore, that they have a specific contribution to make to university activity in general, and that they should respond in rich and creative ways to the needs of contemporary society.

To achieve any significant influence in contemporary society, an institution of higher learning must possess a certain quality of excellence recognizable throughout the academic world. Accordingly the International Federation of Catholic Universities urges careful planning before the foundation of universities and university colleges under Catholic sponsorship. Moreover, the Federation wishes to encourage the movement among Catholic institutions to affiliate both among themselves and with other private and state institutions of learning, as well as the movement toward sharing of resources.

The Catholic universities desire to be of service to their local communities as well as to the larger society, national and international. They feel, consequently that to achieve these goals they merit wide support not only from the general public, and philanthropic institutions, but also from governmental sources.

All are agreed that the essential note of a Catholic university consists, as Pope Paul VI has noted, in its existence as "a community of persons who are diverse in experience and in function, equal in dignity, occupied with scientific research and the integral formation of man, and who, whatever their task, draw inspiration from the light of revealed truth," rendering it therefore "a center for development and diffusion of an authentic Christian culture."

NOTE

*Position paper adopted by the delegates to the Eighth Triennial Congress of the International Federation of Catholic Universities, held September 10–17, 1968, at the Lovanium University, Kinshasa, Democratic Republic of the Congo. The delegates and participants were: Cardinal Gabriel-Marie Garrone, Prefect, Sacred Congregation for Catholic Education; Vittorino Veronese, Pontifical Commission for Justice and Peace; Ch. Vieyra, Chief, UNESCO Mission to the Democratic Republic of the Congo. CANADA: Paul Berry, St. Francis Xavier University, Antigonish; Msgr. Albert Louis Vachon, Université Laval; R. Brosseau, S.S., Université de Montréal; Germain Lesage, O.M.I., Université St. Paul, Ottawa; Roger Bernier, Université de Sherbrooke. U.S.A.: Robert Drinan, S.J., Boston College; Leo McLaughlin, S.J., Fordham University; John Felice, S.J., Loyola University, Chicago; Theodore M. Hesburgh, C.S.C., Neil G. McCluskey, S.J., Edmund A. Stephan, John E. Walsh, C.S.C., University of Notre Dame; Paul E. Waldschmidt, C.S.C., Portland University; Robert J. Henle, S.J., Paul C. Reinert, S.J., Daniel L. Schlafly, St. Louis University; Edmund W. Morton, S.J., Seattle University; Msgr. Theodore E. McCarrick, Universidad Catolica de Puerto Rico, Ponce. ARGENTINA: Ismael Quiles, S.J., Universidad del Salvador, Buenos Aires; Msgr. Octavio N. Derisi, Pontificia Universidad Argentina,

Buenos Aires; Fernando A. Storni, S.J., Universidad Católica de Córdoba, Argentina. BRAZIL: Rev. Irmao José Otao-Stefani, J. Girotto, Pontificia Universidade Católica de Rio Grande de Sul, Porto Alegre; Candido Mendes de Almeida, Pontificia Universidade Catolica de Rio de Janeiro. COLOMBIA: Antonio Osorio Isaza, Universidad Pontificia Bolivariana, Medellín. ECUADOR: Luis E. Orellana, S.J., Pontificia Universidad Católica del Ecuador, Quito. NICARAGUA: Cardenal, S.J., Universidad Centro Americana, Managua. PARAGUAY: Msgr. Juan Moleon Andreu, Universidad Católica, Asunción. PERU: Felipe E. MacGregor, S.J., Pontificia Universidad Católica del Peru, Lima. VENEZUELA: Carlos Plazza, S.J., Carlos Reyna, S.J., Universidad Católica, Caracas. CONGO: Antoine Bala, Enseignement Supérieur et Universitaire, Kinshasa; P. Ekwa, S.J., President, Bureau de l'Enseignement Catholique, Kinshasa; Louis-Paulin Mamanda, Ministère de l'Education Nationale, Kinshasa; Msgr. Tharcisse Tshibangu, Alphonse Elungu, Maurice Plevoets, Albert Mpase, Msgr. Luc Gillon, Université Lovanium. ETHIOPIA: Mother Maria Nora Onnis, Sister El Forces Berardi, University of Asmara. IRAQ: Richard J. McCarthy, S.J., Al-Hikma University, Bagdad. LEBANON: Abdallah Dagher, S.J., Université St. Joseph, Beirut. JAPAN: F. X. Oizumi, S.J., Sophia University, Tokyo. PHILIPPINES: James J. Meany, S.J., President, Philippine Accrediting Association of Schools, Colleges, and Universities; John Doherty, S.J., P. Ortiz, S.J., Ateneo de Manila University; Sylver Verhaeghe, Rev. Paul Zwaenepoel, St. Louis University, Baguio City; Rudolf Rahmann, S.V.D., University of San Carlos, Cebu City; Jesús Diaz, O.P., S. Molina, University of Santo Tomas, Manila; Luis F. Torralba, S.J., Xavier University, Cagayan de Oro City. BELGIUM: Msgr. A. Descamps, Rev. P. Lagrain, M. Vinck, M. Van Vindekens, Université Catholique de Louvain; Camille Joset, S.J., Facultés Universitaires, Namur. FRANCE: Msgr. Jean Honoré, M. l'Abbé Ecole, Melle Tremoulet, Université Catholique de l'Ouest, Angers; Msgr. Michel Descamps, President, Bureau International de l'Enseignement Catholique, Paris; Francois Russo, S.J., International Catholic Center of Coordination with UNESCO, Paris; Msgr. Pierre Haubtmann, M. L'Abbé Latour, Gilbert Olivier, Institut Catholique de Paris; Michel Falise, Msgr. Georges Leclercq, Canon Gerard Lepoutre, Facultés Catholiques de Lille. HOLLAND: J. Lammers, Katholieke Universitat Te Nijmegen, Nijmegen. ITALY: Sante Graciotti, Università Catolica del Sacro Cuore, Milano; John E. Blewett, S.J., Paolo Dezza, S.J., Jesuit Generalate, Rome; Hervé Carrier, S.J., Pontificia Università Gregoriana, Rome; Stanislas Morawski, Università Internazionale Pro Deo, Rome. POLAND: Stanislas Nagy, Katolicki Uniwersitet Lubelski, Lublin. SPAIN: Luis A. Sobreroca, S.J., Escuela Superior de Administración y Dirección de Empresas, Barcelona; Rev. Jaime Loring, Escuela Superior de Técnica Empresarial de Córdoba; Francisco Ponz, Universidad de Navarra, Pamplona; Tomás García Barberena, Francisco Martin, José Rodríquez Medina, Universidad Pontificia de Salamanca. SWITZERLAND: Norbert A. Luyten, O.P., Université de Fribourg.

Rome Statement:
The Catholic University
and the Aggiornamento*

SECTION I

A. Essential Characteristics of a Catholic University

Since the objective of the Catholic university, precisely as Catholic, is to assure in an institutional manner a Christian presence in the university world confronting the great problems of contemporary society, the following are its essential characteristics:

1. a Christian inspiration not only of individuals but of the community as well
2. a continuing reflection in the light of Christian faith upon the growing treasure of human knowledge
3. fidelity to the Christian message as it comes to us through the Church
4. an institutional commitment to the service of Christian thought and education

All universities that realize these conditions are Catholic universities, whether canonically erected or not. The purposes of the Catholic university can be pursued by different means and modalities according to diverse situations of time and place, and taking seriously into account the different natures of the disciplines taught in the university.

B. The Different Kinds of Catholic Universities

Given the different stages of development of higher education under Catholic auspices in various parts of the world, and even of institutions within the same country, it would be futile to attempt a univocal approach to the contemporary challenges and problems of our institutions of higher learning. Accordingly, the responses to the questionnaire

Reprinted from Neil G. McCluskey, S.J., *The Catholic University* (Notre Dame, Ind.: University of Notre Dame Press, 1970).

of the Congregation are simply the efforts of each institution to describe what it understands itself to be, how it understands its mission, and how it tries to achieve its objectives as a Catholic institution.

Since the meaning of the term "Catholic university" has been historically determined and conditioned by each historical and national situation, different institutions will have different relations to ecclesiastical authority relative to the magisterium, pastoral concern, and governance. As the following list indicates, there are various categories into which fall Catholic institutions of higher learning. Two basic categories can immediately be discerned: those institutions which have a juridical bond to Church authority in one form or another and those which do not.

According to the most reliable estimate, there are nearly 600 institutions of higher education in the world which are "Catholic" in some way or other.[1] Included in this figure are 143 universities; 240 separately organized university colleges; 86 separate faculties on a university level; over 80 university colleges which are constituent elements of state universities.

These institutions may be classified according to:

1. kind of instruction and research; e.g., almost exclusively theological-religious or not;
2. level of instruction and research and degrees conferred;
3. institutional complexity; i.e., one, several, many faculties, schools, departments, or institutes;
4. type of institutional governance; e.g., relative position of faculty, administration, students, and others in policy-making and executive work;
5. relationship to authority ecclesiastical or civil, whether expressed or not.

C. The Autonomy of the Catholic University and Its Relationships to Ecclesiastical Authority

The Catholic university today must be a university in the full modern sense of the word, with a strong commitment to and concern for academic excellence. To perform its teaching and research functions effectively the Catholic university must have a true autonomy and academic freedom. Nor is this to imply that the university is beyond the law: the university has its own laws which flow from its proper nature and finality. The following are the philosophical and theological principles which bear upon the meaning of autonomy in the university.

D. PHILOSOPHICAL AND THEOLOGICAL PRINCIPLES
RELATING TO THE AUTONOMY OF THE UNIVERSITY

1. Since the university is an institution for research and teaching at the center of society, it exists to serve the community which created and sustains it. This community can be the civil state, the Church, or a private group of persons. Rightfully then the university will depend upon its social sponsorship and cannot be completely autonomous but remains subject to the legitimate exigencies of the society which sustains it. For example, the preparation of civil servants or research in fields of high priority, etc.

2. However, this service to the community is valid only if the university is able without restrictions to follow the imperatives which flow from its very nature: pursuit of the truth without conditions. From hence flows its autonomy: freedom of research and of teaching. In other words, it is limited by no other factor than the truth it pursues. Every limitation imposed on the university which would clash with this unconditioned attitude for pursuing truth would be intolerable and contrary to the very nature of the university.

3. Because the universities themselves are best qualified to judge what is needed to pursue the truth, academic autonomy normally entails administrative autonomy in such things as the selection of faculty, the planning of academic programs, organization of teaching and research, the establishment of chairs, etc.

4. There is here a delicate balance which must be established between the self-government of the university and the right of accountability which belongs to the society from which the university takes its origin and exists. Public interest can make itself felt here in a way which does limit self-government provided that imperatives of unconditioned research for the truth are respected.

5. In the Catholic university there is a special element in the domain of academic autonomy including freedom of teaching and research. Though all natural truth is directly accessible to us through the exercise of our innate ability to grasp and to understand reality, the authentic Christian message is not available to us except with a guarantee of doctrinal authority, which is the magisterium of the Church. The datum from which theological reflection arises is not a datum of reality fully accessible to the human intelligence, but a revealed message entrusted to the Church. The freedom of the theological researcher, at the risk of basic self-destruction, rests on the foundation of revelation.

6. It follows from this that the magisterium as such can intervene only in a situation where the truth of the revealed message is at stake. Within these limitations, this means complete freedom of research and

of teaching must be guaranteed. In every case the intervention of the competent ecclesiastical authority should respect the statutes of the institution as well as the academic procedures and customs of the particular country.

E. Practical Considerations

With the foregoing principles in mind the following considerations should be stressed.

1. The Church has the right and the responsibility to determine Catholic belief and to define Catholic moral principles. To this authority all Catholics are subject, whether lay or cleric, preacher or theological scholar.

2. The theological scholar in taking his place in the university, must be able to pursue his discipline in the same manner as other research scholars. He must be allowed to question, to develop new hypotheses, to work toward new understandings and formulations, to publish and defend his views, and to approach the theological sources, including pronouncements of the teaching Church, with the free and full play of modern scholarship. His work should normally be reviewed and evaluated by his scholarly peers as is the case in other disciplines.

3. History teaches us how much the influence of the Church has been limited because of certain ecclesiastical or religious authorities who, overzealous to defend certain established positions, have precipitously and arbitrarily blocked the diffusion of scholarly research.

4. In teaching theology in the university, the theologian must of course present the authentic teaching of the Church, but he may and should form his students to an intelligent and critical understanding of the faith, prudent account being taken of the maturity and previous preparation of the students. As an individual he is bound to accept the authentic teaching of the Church and to submit to its legitimately exercised authority. As a theological scholar he is bound by the nature of his discipline to take into proper account the pronouncements of the Church. However, his relationship to ecclesiastical and religious authorities will vary in accordance with the types of Catholic universities.

5. In a university without statutory relationships with ecclesiastical or religious superiors, these authorities may deal with the theologian as an individual member of the Church. If they can make representation to the institutional authorities, any juridical intervention in university affairs must be excluded. In other institutions provision is made for appropriate action by designated ecclesiastical or religious superiors. In all cases, however, any action taken by ecclesiastical or religious superiors should conform exactly to their authority as established in the university

statutes and should be carried out according to those procedures of due process established in the statutes and recognized as general university common law in the geographical region of the particular university.

F. Pastoral Concern

The members of the community of a Catholic university constitute a special sort of community in which Christian professors and students are encouraged to live the Christian life together. Obviously, the ecclesial aspects of this common life—the Word, the sacraments, the eucharist liturgy—are subject to episcopal authority in the same way as any parish.

However, since the members of this community and its common interests are different, the style of Christian living should be appropriately different. Hence it is important that the relevant episcopal authority recognize this difference and not only allow for it but encourage it. The university community is especially appropriate for authorized experimentation, particularly concerning ways to make Christianity more relevant to their lives.

Since a university usually transcends the limits, the needs, and the conditions of a single diocese, it might be well to establish a bishop or a group of bishops for the university ministries—as is often done for the military chaplaincy. In any case the designated episcopal authority in directing the university ministries, both in Catholic and other type institutions, should rely on the advice of men trained in universities and experienced in the university ministry.

The relationship of university chaplains to episcopal authority and to religious superiors will vary according to the different constitutions of universities and the different agreements between universities and the episcopal or religious authorities.

SECTION II

A. the Contribution of the University
to the Common Good of Society

1. Objectives

a) The Catholic university, as a university, has an obligation to promote the progress of knowledge through scientific research, to assure its dissemination for the good of the society, and to form men of intelligence and action who will be able to serve society constructively.

Furthermore, as a Catholic university, it is a "public, stable, and universal institution of Christian ideas within the total, intellectual effort to promote a superior culture" in a Christian manner (*Gaudium et Spes*, 10). It is also a center for scientific study and for the dissemination of the Christian message.

b) Since the Catholic university is being integrated in local, regional, national, and international societies at a given time in history, this prospect for service ought to stimulate the university to be, through means within its competence, an instrument of progress for these diverse societies. The university should promote cultural values proper to the society in which it is located and it should concern itself with problems of developing countries which require a combined effort for their scientific, technological, and cultural progress.

c) The Catholic university's faithfulness to its scientific character and its objective search for truth render it particularly suitable for efficaciously influencing the changes of structure which existing political regimes require for both more human and more spiritual progress. The idea of "objectivity" is not incompatible with the idea of "service."

d) Although the Catholic university is dedicated to the service of society, it wishes to transcend the fluctuations of politics. It cannot link its activities to those of present or future political parties. Nor is it possible or desirable for the university to serve as the tool of any political party. It must in total independence propose and defend approaches to truth that seem most adequate to it, and it must be involved in current problems that lie within its competence.

2. Means

a) In carrying out its objectives, the Catholic university is convinced that the progress of society and the improvement of structures can only result through the efforts of groups of men who are well formed intellectually, spiritually, and morally, who are capable of influencing social structures and of becoming "eminent men of the faith in the world."

b) The university's admission policy should give preference to students who, because of their academic ability and other talents, are capable of making significant contributions to society. The admissions policy should help provide for the able student with financial difficulties.

c) The university should give its students the opportunity to become competent men in the exercise of their private or public profession; men capable of contributing to the progress of society by their presence and action; men of science, qualified to take responsibility in theoretical or applied scientific research or in teaching on different levels; men of moral integrity who are enlightened by their faith. The university should give to its Catholic students in particular the potential of becoming men who are capable of thoroughly examining and spreading the Christian faith at the university level in the context of the basic problems of the modern world.

d) In the choice of careers of teaching, research, or the social activities of its members, the university should present ideas for the progress of and service to contemporary society. Specifically, it should:

—Give its students factual information about the cultural, social, and economic realities of their milieu in its present condition, its foreseeable developments in its human and spiritual context, and information about the doctrines of the Church. This will help them in choosing their professions or acquaint them with the research needed for the development of their area of society.

—Propose to diverse societies observations, solutions, or partial solutions to obstacles to their progress. This is especially necessary in developing countries in regard to the problem of hunger, culture, the birthrate, housing, labor, and social legislation.

—Encourage its professors and students, to the fullest extent compatible with their academic functions, to engage in direct and specific social action resulting from scientific studies and research. Such action should be directed primarily toward the education of the underprivileged in the areas of culture, technology, health, and religion.

B. The Autonomy of a Catholic university in Regard to Civil and Economic Organizations

The importance of the autonomy of universities in relation to other authorities—especially political authority—is generally recognized in all universities, particularly among the faculty and academic authorities.

At the Fourth General Conference of the International Association of Universities, held in Tokyo in 1965, delegates clearly expressed their desire for a greater degree of university autonomy. This was not done from an attitude of self-defense or a reflex of auto-defense, nor from the standpoint of a quest for power, but in the sole conviction that through its autonomous nature a university is more capable of rendering to society the services that it should.

Catholic universities share the same viewpoint on autonomy, according to the differing circumstances of each university. The Tokyo Conference advocated full university autonomy in regard to these five specific points: selection of academic staff; freedom in its student admission policy; freedom in curriculum planning; freedom in research projects; and great freedom in apportioning its budget.

These objectives are similar to those of Catholic universities and they are restated here in a more general manner:

1) Juridical autonomy: The right to confer academic degrees and to set up programs of study which lead to these degrees. This autonomy is limited and subject to laws pertaining to certain civil and professional diplomas. It is desirable, however, that even these legal rules be as

flexible as possible, so that the universities may have real freedom of action, mainly to permit them to adapt their programs in accordance with scientific advancement.

2) Academic autonomy: Freedom in its student admission policy and in appointment of personnel; freedom in regard to subjects taught; and freedom of opinion in teaching, often referred to as academic freedom.

3) Administrative autonomy: The university must govern itself freely, especially in regard to the apportionment and the administration of its budgets, both regular and special.

4) Financial autonomy: This more properly can be called financial viability. It means that the Catholic university of today and tomorrow will often have to appeal for public financial support. It is not unreasonable to envision a process whereby, in regard to the preceding points, university autonomy will affirm itself increasingly while public financial aid continues to grow. The latter can certainly be doubled through proper supervision in the use of funds, but this supervision should not obstruct the university in the planning of its budget, and it should not have any influence on the exercise of the various forms of autonomy mentioned above.

The exercise of parallel autonomy clearly entails special obligations as the Tokyo report notes. It presupposes a high degree of responsibility on the part of all university personnel: its officials, teaching and administrative personnel, and students.

The autonomy of the universities is founded, in short, on the autonomy of knowledge. The latter is sovereign in its discipline. It is necessary, moreover, to distinguish it formally from all that does not pertain to it, political power included.

C. Relations with Other Universities and Cultural Organizations

The Catholic university has an obligation to associate itself with other public and private universities in order to participate in the scholarly life of the modern world. Active membership in local, regional, and international associations of universities widens the intellectual horizons of administrators, faculty, and students.

Collaboration with other universities in fields of common interest and research should be encouraged. The mutual exchange of professors, students, and academic credits between universities should be fostered so as to furnish the best academic experience for all. The larger and more experienced universities should lend their personnel, resources, experience, and guidance to newer universities whenever possible.

In like manner, the Catholic university should work with cultural organizations such as UNESCO, OAS, and other groups with whom the university shares a common commitment to serve the people of the world.

D. The Relationship of the University with Society

The relationships of the university with the society of which it forms a part are multiple. The main one may be described as the cultural stimulation that society needs for its dynamism and progress.

The university fulfills this function of stimulation by promoting knowledge, by forming the men that society needs, and by assisting in various tasks of research that the state or particular societies propose to it or that they themselves bring forth. An important part of cultural stimulation is the critical function in the light of scientific knowledge that the university exerts upon the environment in which it exists and upon the culture in which it grows. Catholic universities are able to play an important role in this context because they are not directly dependent on the state or a political regime.

By its nature the Catholic university favors a diversified system of higher education which is not made up exclusively of the state system of education but rather is enriched by the various systems and modes of organization of the nonofficial educational system. This is conducive to a climate of liberty and competition among various types of universities.

Besides its relationship with the state and political powers, the university is related to other organized societies in the national or international political community. Its relationship must always stem from its function as a useful institution within an autonomy and freedom that are irrevocable. Especially in regard to groups with economic power, the universities must maintain this close and yet remote relationship, leaving them free to fulfill their proper mission.

Universities today are regarded often as poles of economic development and local progress. It is for this reason that communities claim them more and more as avenues leading to cultural and social maturity. Catholic universities are civil institutions integrated within the society to which they belong. They live and grow according to the laws of each of the countries they serve. They must resist, therefore, any tendency to present them as parts of the supranational society that the Church is.

Finally, pontifical universities should take into account the needs of the society or community which they serve.

E. THE EXTERNAL ACTIVITY OF THE UNIVERSITY
UNDER THE ASPECT OF ITS RELIGIOUS DIMENSION

It is probably impossible to propose a precise series of actions to be undertaken by all Catholic universities, since conditions differ from country to country, region to region, and institution to institution. Thus ways and means of reaching essential purposes within these varied environments must remain completely open and relative to a specific institution at a specific time in its history.

It is imperative, however, that the Catholic university have competent Catholic administrators, scholars, and scientists as members of its staff. If the university has such competent people, they will study the environment within which the university is located; they will be aware of the essential purposes of the Catholic university; and they will then, through examination and study, devise and try ways and means to reach these purposes in their own particular religious environment.

The Catholic university, like any other university, is called to serve society in general in many different ways. As Catholic, it surely has a unique role to play for religious society in general and for Catholic and Christian society in particular—but this role cannot easily be defined a priori. The Catholic university undoubtedly also has a special role with respect to nonbelievers by making religion—including Catholicism—both a plausible and positive force for the world itself. Yet the specific means of doing this can only be worked out by starting from the exigencies of the university itself in its particular social setting.

The university community must endeavor to succeed in being witness to Christ. Although the Catholic university should not, properly speaking, be a center for indoctrination, yet its Catholic atmosphere should be such a living, palpable reality as to invite attention from non-Catholics and even nonbelievers. Possible forms of this witness might include the following:

1. With respect to religious sciences, the Catholic university should deepen its understanding and provide for the diffusion of commentaries on the doctrine of the Church. Beyond its primary academic obligation for an appropriate curriculum for its regular students, the Catholic university must make itself available for the service of people in general. Its undertaking continuing education programs, particularly in religious sciences, will give proof of its interest in and concern for basic religious needs of all men.

2. The Catholic university is an ideal setting for dialogue with nonbelievers and for ecumenical contacts of a high level. In its openness to collaboration in a vast array of cooperative programs with universities that are either non-Catholic or nonsectarian, as well as in its

participation in interdenominational activities within the community, the Catholic university can give ecumenical leadership that will have profound influence on all men of good will.

3. The Catholic university should serve as a laboratory to help the Church and the hierarchy by doing that type of research for which the university is particularly equipped, whether it be in the field of religious sciences or in allied fields of interest, such as education, sociology, etc.

4. The Catholic university must accept seriously its obligation to give testimony to the world around it. It must demonstrate that there is no incompatibility between science and faith. When given at the level of individuals, such testimony is not exclusive to the Catholic institution, since there are individual Catholic scholars in nonsectarian universities. When given at the level of a group, through the community of teachers and scholars in a Catholic university, such testimony is a unique contribution of Catholic higher education and, as such, it has special value. The most positive testimony of the Catholic university is in its being present to the world and giving a vision of life that has inner form and conviction.

Finally, in considering the essential purposes of a Catholic university in respect to its external religious milieu, it must be emphasized that the basic purpose of any university revolves around learning. The greatest liberty and freedom in the pursuit of truth must always be there, together with the responsibilities such a task involves. Professional competence must be the basis of all activity. The university pursues truth, inculcates basic respect for the dignity of man, and encourages a way of life consistent with this concept.

F. LONG-RANGE PLANNING OF THE UNIVERSITIES IN TODAY'S SOCIETY

1. Catholic universities should be conscious of the need for expert long-range planning if they are to develop as their responsible authorities hope they will, and if they are to be properly understood in the contemporary world. Modern methods of long-range planning are indispensable for probing the strengths and weaknesses of modern institutions.

2. Long-range planning is the projection, through diagnosis and prognostication of the reasonable aims and means by which an institution can fulfill its service to God and society. Such long-range planning should employ, in the case of Catholic universities, the advanced and more or less proven techniques and strategies utilized by knowledgeable and expanding governments, corporations, and academic institutions. This means that each institution must have a diagnosis and prognostication of its own. It must ask itself exactly what kind of university

it wants to become; the rate at which it can and should develop; the amount of duplication and competition with other universities and with itself which is justifiable; and where the revenues it requires are to be found.

If it is agreed that there can be expansion, and that this expansion will take the form of serving more students and establishing more faculties, centers, institutes, then planners must ask further what kind of students they are looking for. Such questions should be whether they are searching for paying or scholarship students, merely adequately or well prepared, socially predisposed for higher education or not. They should ask where they are going to get competent staff to teach them, how they are going to communicate their plans with their staff and students, with their constituency, and with the general public. They should inquire how their project is going to be affected by changes already in progress, e.g., loss of contributed services, student activism, attitude of society toward universities and their support. It should be asked how exactly the revenue is to be found to pay for them, whether from fees, contributed services, gifts from alumni, private benefactors, corporations, government, or Church sources. In every case, the projection must be based on publicly known figures so that all can determine who has and who has not been supporting the university, and what requires changing here if the planning is to be effective.

3. There should be collaboration and coordination among existing universities in a given region. Before deciding on a new university, already existing universities should be taken into account and competent authorities should be consulted. It may sometimes be best to consider the possibility of integrating available resources into a non-Catholic university. The development committee of the International Federation of Catholic Universities (IFCU) may eventually be helpful in the long-range planning of universities.

SECTION III

A. INTRODUCTION

The university world of today is characterized by a general and profound dissatisfaction with its professed functions and goals: the pursuit and communication of truth.

The reasons for this dissatisfaction, and the manner of its expression, may vary from university to university. Among the alleged causes of this state of affairs, the following deserve mention.

1) The tendency toward overspecialization. This has resulted in a feeling that knowledge has become too fragmented, and that truth has been dissociated from other values. In addition, there is an assumption

that truth must be sought in ways that are not necessarily cognitive or rational.

2) The greater awareness and maturity that today's students bring with them to the university. Modern methods of telecommunication give every viewer an immediate and vivid realization of the world around him, especially of its injustices and horrors; and this engenders, particularly among the young, a sense of the irrelevance and futility of what is supposed to absorb them at their universities.

3) There is a keener sense of competitiveness among university students today. Higher education is no longer the privilege of the affluent. Everyone wants a university degree today, to prepare him for a better living. A fear that the university is failing him in this regard often finds expression in violent disapproval of its goals.

4) Everywhere, but especially in developing countries, there is a feeling that a new age has begun. The age of unquestioning subservience, of colonial dependence, has passed. The times demand the assertion of individuality, the development of personality, the exercise of an inalienable right to equality of opportunity and status. From the obstruction of these ambitions there develops among some students a conviction that the universities are outdated embodiments of traditions which ignored these ambitions in the past, and that they are still too closely allied today with forms of government, or structures of society, that are violations of democracy in practice.

The malaise in university life today is obviously not peculiar to Catholic universities. We cannot therefore isolate the problems of a Catholic university from those of other universities. Our task is rather to grapple with the basic problems of the university in order to provide solutions for them in the light of our Christian faith, and to put them into practice first of all in our own universities.

B. TEACHER-STUDENT RELATIONSHIP IN THE CLASSROOM

The commission takes it for granted that a Catholic university should, in every respect, meet the requirements of a modern institution of higher learning for the pursuit and transmission of truth at all levels; that is to say, its faculty members should be of high competence, and that its structures should provide opportunities for the kind of teamwork rendered necessary today by the wide diversification of methods of investigation. Secondly, the commission interprets this part of the question as bearing on such relationships which belong intrinsically to the discovery and diffusion of knowledge.

The commission expresses its conviction that these relationships should be inspired by the following principles:

1) That although today's students demand from their universities, and from the individual staff members, a social, or even a political commitment, the pursuit of objectivity in the transmission of knowledge should at all costs be maintained.

This objectivity should be viewed by the university, and by its student body, not only as the testimony of the primary and profound commitment of universities to truth as such, but also, as the only possible guarantee on behalf of the university of its respect for the individual commitments, along different subjective parts, that may possibly be made by the individual members of the university community.

However, the pursuit of objectivity is not enough. The university should continually reexamine its curricular and research programs, to ensure their relevance both to the progress of knowledge and the practical needs of mankind.

2) That as producers of knowledge, universities are highly organized centers for the creation of culture. In all its aspects culture is created by communities through a process of intersubjective communication. Consequently, at the university, the organic units involved in the ongoing process of creating knowledge, should be composed of teams of professors and students, or of directors and collaborators, involved in reciprocally creative activity. This is another way of saying that knowledge, if it is to be universal, should also be universal in its becoming.

Therefore the university should, on the one hand, provide the organic structures that permit the effective participation of all its members at their specific levels of contribution; and on the other, reduce to a minimum the one-way transmission of ready-made knowledge, which can so easily degenerate into dogmatism, thus setting up another psychological barrier between professors and students. The foregoing is not intended as a general repudiation of the lecture method.

3) That Catholic universities should excel in the practical application of the above-mentioned principles; for objectivity and universality, rightly understood, are the forms which charity assumes in the intellectual sphere, thereby placing the highest value on the potential contribution of every human personality to the growth of knowledge, and to its integration with other values.

In this way, higher education at Catholic universities becomes the instrument of a truly self-controlled transformation and liberation of mankind.

C. CONCERN FOR HUMAN DEVELOPMENT

1) The root causes of student unrest should be carefully examined with the students themselves.

2) The university should create special institutes, if advisable, that will undertake to provide satisfactory solutions to the social problems that exert such a powerful impact on the psychological attitudes and behavior of students. The success of this attempt will be greatly enhanced by the collaboration of economists, sociologists, psychologists, moralists, etc., who would contribute their knowledge and experience to a correct enunciation and solution of the problem under study.

The Catholic university will especially examine the ethical dimensions of the social problems confronting mankind, such as poverty, discrimination, particularly insofar as they affect the students. Through the study of these moral issues, in the light of the gospel and of our Christian heritage, the students will have the opportunity to justify or modify their own moral stand or position on these issues.

The university that neglects this course of action in the face of the many problems that exercise the youth of our times, betrays one of its most serious responsibilities and sets itself up at odds with society, which it is its mission to serve.

3) The university must also endeavor to discover and identify the universal values that are present in the different national cultures, on the principle that the values of each culture complement one another.

4) The university is under a special obligation to initiate students in the correct methods of scientific research in the different areas of knowledge, according to their own personal aptitudes.

The university is also urged to provide opportunities to students to exercise academic and social responsibility. One way to achieve this objective would be to provide them with facilities to organize themselves into working teams to pursue their own research projects with the cooperation of the faculty.

D. The Governance of the University

The forms of governance of Catholic universities must be adaptive to their wide diversities, to the laws of the various states and to local conditions, and, therefore, no rigid patterns should be established. On the contrary, workable patterns will have to be determined according to specific needs. With this principle in mind, the commission recommends:

1) that the governance of the university be exercised within the just laws of the state;

2) that provisions be made in the structure of the university for all the members of the university community to participate, one way or another, according to the level and potentialities of each member, in the formulation of policy and in the decision-making process. It should be understood that such participation does not mean that all the members

necessarily have a deliberative power in decisions and policy-making actions of the university;

3) that the rights and obligations of all the members of the university community be clearly stated; and that a procedure for recourse be set up in case of conflicts regarding these rights;

4) that all the members of the university community have a right to be informed of the reasons for decisions made by the governance of the university, with due respect, however, for confidentiality and charity;

5) that a spirit of charity characterize the relationships within the university community, made especially manifest in a willingness on the part of all its members to engage in sincere dialogue. This dialogue will be ensured by the establishment of open, specific, and clearly defined channels of communication between the governance and all the members of the university community.

E. The Dialogue of the Academic
Disciplines with Philosophy and Theology

The commission has not considered it its task to discuss the differences and analogies between the different types of positive sciences: mathematics, physics, chemistry, biology, sociology, history, philology, etc. Nor has the commission thought it necessary to discuss profoundly the theoretical aspects of the dialogue between the positive sciences on the one hand and philosophy and theology on the other hand. The commission has confined itself to some general observations regarding the theoretical aspect of this dialogue. It has concentrated its efforts on indicating practical ways favoring this dialogue. By following this policy the commission has taken for granted that a Catholic university is the *locus naturalis* for such a dialogue.

1) The first principle governing the dialogue between science and theology is that if man wants to understand reality, it is necessary for him to make use of the methods and of the results of all types of knowledge available to him. History has taught us that there is not just one intellectual method, but several; not just one approach to reality, but several.

Using several methods to reach the truth does not imply that a real synthesis of knowledge is readily possible. The best we can hope for is perhaps a global vision, in which one type of knowledge complements another one. Much would be gained if we could prevent the trespassing of one discipline into the field of another. The mutual purification of theology, philosophy, and positive science is a condition for a sound dialogue. For without regard for the data of science and philosophy, theology cannot really be theology. Without criticism of theology and of philosophy, science is in danger of extrapolating its results into fields which are not its proper domain.

2) It would be wrong to see the dialogue between science and theology only in the perspective of "concordism" and of cheap apologetics. "Truth will liberate us," but only if we give it the chance to show itself to us.

3) An effective way in which science, philosophy, and theology can cooperate will be found in a concentration upon the concrete problems which confront mankind today. Each discipline as a specific approach to reality has the tendency to isolate itself, concentrating on the abstract problems as they appear in the perspective of the methodology of the science involved. The needs of mankind, however, are concrete. They invite an interdisciplinary approach in which each science can show its intrinsic value.

F. CONCRETE RECOMMENDATIONS

1) A dialogue is only possible when the participants know each other and are prepared to accept each other as they really are. This also applies to the dialogue between the different disciplines. For this reason it is necessary that the students of the different disciplines have the opportunity to get acquainted with the methodology of other disciplines. This is also a prerequisite for the reflection upon the methodology of one's own discipline. Without this reflection no correct view of the way in which a discipline approaches the truth is possible. Without this reflection no representative of a certain discipline can be a valuable participant in the dialogue. It must be stressed, however, that the acquaintance with the different methodologies of one's own discipline and of that of other participants, is not only a matter of the theory of knowledge. It is as important that each participant has a clear view of the different ways in which the different disciplines are able to contribute to the solutions of the practical needs of mankind. In sum, in each Catholic university opportunities should be provided for an introduction to the different disciplines and their methodologies. They should be available to students of each discipline.

2) It is already common practice in many countries that students of philosophy combine their studies with that of another discipline. Special curricula for such combined studies exist. As far as the commission knows, there is, however, hardly any opportunity to combine the study of theology with that of a positive science. Yet theologians prepared in this way are needed for a serious dialogue.

3) If there are philosophers or theologians who are acquainted with certain positive disciplines, it is of great importance that these

philosophers or theologians are not only members of their respective faculties, but are also associated with the faculty or department of the positive discipline involved.

4) When a Catholic university grows in a quantitative and a qualitative sense, the danger exists that it is so preoccupied with teaching and research in the different disciplines that it has hardly any time and energy left for those interdisciplinary problems which are of the greatest value for mankind. Nevertheless, these problems ought to be of the greatest concern for each university that calls itself a Catholic university.

In this situation it may be a good policy for a university to create a special instrumentality, consisting of both faculty members and students. The instrumentality could be a "higher institute," a commission, or whatever may be best according to local circumstances. The important point is that this mechanism should have the specific task of stimulating and organizing interdisciplinary research in all these problems in which a Catholic university ought to be interested.

NOTES

*Position paper adopted at the close of the congress of Catholic universities which met at the Vatican from April 25 to May 1, 1969. The elected delegates were: Guillermo Alba-Lopez, F.S.C., Universidad "LaSalle," Mexico; John E. Blewett, S.J., Sophia University, Tokyo; Msgr. Octavio N. Derisi, Pontificia Universidad Católica Argentina, Buenos Aires; Msgr. Albert-Louis Descamps, l'Université Catholique de Louvain, Belgium; Herbert DeSouza, S.J., St. Xavier's College, Ahmedabad, India; Laercio Dias de Moura, S.J., Pontifica Universidad Catolica do Rio de Janeiro, Brazil; Jesús Diaz, O.P., Santo Tomás University, Manila, Philippines; Rev Clarence W. Friedman, National Catholic Educational Association, Washington, D.C.; Msgr. Luc Gillon, l'Université de Lovanium, Kinshasa, Congo; Msgr. Pierre Hauptmann, l'Institut Catholique de Paris; Robert J. Henle, S.J., St. Louis University. Also: Theodore M. Hesburgh, C.S.C., International Federation of Catholic Universities; Maria-Joseph Heuts, l'Université Catholique de Louvain; Msgr. Georges LeClercq, International Federation of Catholic Universities; Felipe E. MacGregor, S.J., Universidad Católica del Peru, Lima; Neil G. McCluskey, S.J., University of Notre Dame, U.S.A.; Msgr. John J. McGrath, St. Mary's College, Notre Dame, U.S.A.; Rev. Jeremiah Newman, St. Patricks College, Maynooth, Ireland; Rev. Simon Nguyen Van Lap, Catholic University of Dalat, Vietnam; Br. Gregory Nugent, F.S.C., Manhattan College, Riverdale, N.Y.; José Stefani-Otao, Pontificia Universidad Catolica Rio Grande do Sul, Brazil. Also: most Rev. Candido Padin, Pontifica Universidad de Sao Paulo, Brazil; Leon Pallais, Universidad Centroamericana, Nicaragua; Rev. Marian Rechowicz, Catholic University of Lublin, Poland; Xavier Scheifler, S.J.,

Universidad Iberamericana, Mexico; Daniel L. Schlafly, St. Louis University, U.S.A., Rev. Laurence K. Shook, Institute of Medieval Studies, Toronto; Jean Sonet, S.J., Universidad Católica, Córdoba, Argentina; Aloysius Torralba, S.J., Xavier University, Cagayan de Oro, Philippines; Richard Tremblay, O.P., Laval University, Canada; Andreas G.M. Van Melsen, Nijmegen University, Holland; Rev. Pietro Zerbi, University of the Sacred Heart, Milano, Italy; Michael P. Walsh, S.J., Fordham University, New York; Most Rev. Roque Adames, Universidad Católica, Santiago, Dominican Republic.

The following were official observers and periti: José Bacelar e Oliveira, S.J., Universitas Catholica Lusitana, Lisbon; Florentino Idoate, S.J., Universidad José Canas, San Salvador; Nicanor Lana, University of San Augustine, Iloilo, Philippines; Edoardo Miras, Pontificia Universidad Católica, Buenos Aires; Thomas Pak, S.J., Sogang College, Seoul, Korea; Eugenio Veiga, Universidade Catolica San Salvador, Brazil; Rev. Umberto Betti, Pontificio Ateneo Antoniano, Rome; Rev. Luigi Calonghi, Pontificio Ateneo Salesiano, Rome; Paola Dezza, S.J., Curia Generaliza S.J., Rome.

1. Edward B. Rooney, S.J., "The Present Factual Situation of Catholic Universities in the World and What It Means," a paper prepared for the Eighth General Assembly of the International Federation of Catholic Universities at Kinshasa, Congo, September 1968, p. 14.

The Catholic University
in the Modern World

I. THE NATURE OF A CATHOLIC UNIVERSITY

A. Its Essential Characteristics

(1)   Since the objective of a Catholic university, precisely as Catholic, is to assure in an institutional manner a Christian presence in the university world confronting the great problems of contemporary society, the following are its essential characteristics:

1. a Christian inspiration not only of individuals but of the university community as such;
2. a continuing reflection in the light of the Catholic faith upon the growing treasury of human knowledge, to which it seeks to contribute by its own research;
3. fidelity to the Christian message as it comes to us through the Church;
4. an institutional commitment to the service of the people of God and of the human family in their pilgrimage to the transcendent goal which gives meaning to life.

All universities that realize these fundamental conditions are Catholic universities, whether canonically erected or not.

(2)   In the light of these four characteristics, it is evident that besides the teaching, research, and services common to all universities, by institutional commitment, a Catholic university brings to its task the inspiration and light of the Christian message. In a Catholic university, therefore, Catholic ideals, attitudes, and principles penetrate and inform university activities in accordance with the proper nature and autonomy of these activities. In a word, being both a university and Catholic, it must be both a community of scholars representing the various branches of human knowledge, and an academic institution in which Catholicism is vitally present and operative.

B. Its Objectives

(3)   In view of its own distinctive inspiration, a Catholic university strives to attain the following objectives.

Every university is intended to be a place where the various branches of human knowledge confront one another for their mutual enrichment. To this task of integration and synthesis, the Catholic university brings the light of the Christian message. This involves a profound conviction that the unity of truth makes necessary the search for a synthesis to determine the place and meaning of the various disciplines within the context of a vision of man and the world that is enlightened by the Gospel. This effort presupposes first a critical analysis of the epistemological bases and postulates of these scientific methods. Only then will it be possible to assign each discipline to its own sphere and to evaluate its significance. In this effort of synthesis, which will always remain imperfect, the Catholic university is called upon especially to show that there is no incompatibility between science and faith, but that these are two different approaches to the one truth, in which they meet without either losing its specific identity.

(4)   One of the principal tasks of a Catholic university, and one which it alone is able to accomplish adequately, will be to make theology relevant to all human knowledge, and reciprocally all human knowledge relevant to theology. Such an encounter, which excludes all facile concordism and postulates the respect of each discipline for the others, will help to delineate the domains of the various branches of knowledge, and prevent them from encroaching on one another. Such encroachment would in fact be an obstacle to a true integration of knowledge. In addition to this mutually beneficial setting of boundaries, a confrontation with philosophy and with positive and humane sciences can be extremely enriching for theology. Conversely, a confrontation with theology can open up new avenues and perspectives for other branches of knowledge.

(5)   Through its teaching and research the Catholic university is called on to witness to Christ. By insisting on the importance of the Christian message for the human community, and by giving expression to this conviction through its academic programs and scholarly research, it can render eloquent testimony to the truth and undying validity of the Gospel.

(6)   From a more practical standpoint, an important task of the Catholic university will be to make scholarly discoveries available to the people of God, and especially to those who have the responsibility for making important decisions, whether for the Church or for civil society.

Indeed all truth, even the most abstract, has a human impact and necessarily contributes to any global vision of man and the world. Likewise, since man is part of salvation history, which has been revealed to us by God, nothing which is human is outside the scope of the Christian understanding of reality.

(7)   Realizing that its own work of research is a part of human history, which in turn is a history of salvation, the Catholic university is conscious of its special obligation to contribute to the solution of the pressing problems that face mankind today. Scholarly disciplines, because each has its own methodology, have a tendency to isolate themselves from one another. This isolation can be overcome by focussing on the crucial problems that confront the whole of humanity, because the effort to find their solution usually calls for an interdisciplinary approach. Catholic universities should participate in, and thus add their own Christian inspiration to that effort of research where different disciplines meet and each makes it own contribution to the solution of these complex problems.

(8)   There is still another reason why a Catholic university is especially called upon to direct its attention to contemporary problems. Because of its institutional commitment to the service of the entire human family, it must be especially concerned with examining from a Christian point of view, the values and norms which are predominant in modern society. Thus it will try to respond to the urgent appeals of people who, in many different and sometimes aberrant ways, are crying out for values and ideals that will give meaning to their lives. A Catholic university must keep in mind the needs of developing nations, and of the new world civilization that is emerging. It will work for the promotion of the cultural values of the society of which it is a part. It will give special attention to those problems which are of the most vital interest to the faith, to morality, and to the life of the Church in the contemporary world.

(9)   In performing its task of preparing leaders both for civil society and for the Church, a Catholic university is called upon to give not only scientific and professional training but ethical teaching as well, based on the imperatives and principles of the Gospel. In this way it will contribute to the education of professional men who will be qualified to work with all others of good will for the advancement of all sectors of our pluralistic society, and especially for the achievement of social justice. Thus it will be an important factor in a progress that is truly human, and not material alone.

(10)   A university community with a Catholic atmosphere offers its students a milieu conducive to their integral development. In such a community they will find respect for intellectual life, for scholarly research, and also for religious values. They will experience a community that is open and receptive to truth from any quarter: a community which attempts to integrate all human knowledge into a vision of the world whose lines are drawn by faith as well as by reason.

In such a community, marked as it is by a spirit of universality, Catholics can participate and cooperate with those of other churches or religions, sharing ideas and values from many different traditions, not in a spirit of shallow eclecticism, but in an effort to see the whole of reality in the light of the truth which Christ came to reveal to us.

(11) Catholic universities can do much to promote Christian ecumenism and the ongoing dialogue with those of other religions and with non-believers, both by preparing persons qualified to participate in serious interfaith discussions, and by providing an atmosphere favorable to their success. Frank and open dialogue will do much to eliminate misunderstandings, highlight ideas and values that are held in common, and bring into sharper focus the meaning and impact of the Christian message for mankind.

It is especially when Catholic universities are located in countries whose culture has been deeply influenced by non-Christian religions, that they must be active promoters and centers of religious and cultural dialogue. They have a unique opportunity to help create a "language" in which the message of Christ can be made intelligible and relevant to those of other religious traditions.

(12) The Catholic university, as a research participant in the discovery of new knowledge and perspectives, will do what it can to encourage continuing education to aid in the assimilation of the growing body of knowledge. It will be equally concerned with providing opportunities for those not in the university to benefit from the wisdom it has discovered and to gain a knowledge of the Christian faith.

(13) The objectives that the Catholic university pursues have been summed up by Pope Paul VI in the following passage of his address to the council and committee of the International Federation of Catholic Universities, on the occasion of its 1971 meeting in Rome:

> Even in its research, a Catholic university should in the first place show that profound respect which the Church has for culture. In its studies and its teaching it should constantly be looking for the true, the good, the beautiful, whether it be in the realm of science, literature, art, or philosophy, with the method appropriate to each. In this search it must not be led astray by any apriori systems, which would jeopardize that genuine analysis and synthesis of which mankind has such great need. (*Gaudium et Spes*, 59, 2)

Culture thus understood is a stimulus for the believer, for it is the knowledge of the work of the Creator, and of His wisdom spread throughout creation and in the hearts of men. (ibid., 57, 4) Besides this contemplation, culture contributes to the development of man, to his mastery over the forces of nature, to his social progress. Finally, by initiating men to an ever wider knowledge of natural truth, it opens the way to a fruitful encounter with revealed truth. For the believer cannot afford not to seek for a harmonious synthesis between these two domains of truth. (ibid., 62) The Council explicitly recalled the contribution Catholic universities make in this effort "to make it more deeply understood how faith and reason give harmonious witness to the unity of all truth." (*Gravissimum Educationis*, 10)

The Catholic mission of these universities is fulfilled also in the cultural education they offer to their students, who will learn there how an intellectual life can be lived in a Christian manner. They will find themselves challenged by the demands of faith, and initiated into active and fraternal collaboration with others. In this atmosphere their desire will be enkindled to put at the service of their fellowman both their acquired human skills and their testimony to a deep and living faith. It is such men that Catholic universities strive to produce, without of course pretending to any monopoly of them. Granted that conditions differ greatly from country to country, who would dare to say that this task has lost its value or its urgency? As you are aware, it is of vital interest to the whole Church, and consequently is a primary concern of those who have the responsibility of leadership in it.[1]

C. THE VARIOUS KINDS OF CATHOLIC UNIVERSITIES

(14) Given the different types of institutions of higher learning under Catholic auspices in various parts of the world, and even in the same region, it would be futile to attempt a univocal approach to the contemporary situation of Catholic higher education. Consequently, each institution has to describe what it understands itself to be, how it perceives its objectives as a Catholic university, and how it tries to achieve them. (15) There are various categories into which Catholic institutions of higher learning will fall. While every Catholic university's fidelity to the Christian message as it comes to us through the Church involves a recognition of the teaching authority of the Church in doctrinal matters, nevertheless different institutions have different relations to ecclesiastical authority, since these relations have been determined and conditioned by many different historical and national situations. On this basis, various categories of Catholic universities can be discerned: some have been directly established or approved by ecclesiastical authority, while others have not; some have a statutory relationship with this authority, while others do not. The latter, provided that they maintain the essential characteristics of every Catholic university which were described above in Part I A, are no less Catholic, whether by a formal, explicit commitment on the part of their founders, trustees, or faculty, or by their implicit tradition of fidelity to Catholicism and their corresponding social and cultural influence.[2]

(16) Catholic universities also differ from one another by reason of the kind of relationship they have with civil society. Some of them enjoy full university status; others are subjected to restrictive conditions in comparison with state universities.

(17) Catholic universities likewise can be differentiated by the priorities which they give to various objectives, in accordance with their varying social milieus. In developing countries the primary role of a university may be to stimulate the emergence of new social classes, and to provide the professional training of the leaders whose contribution is so vitally needed for the progress of the nation. In other countries priority may be given to research, and to the analysis in depth of problems that are raised by the encounter of the Church and the modern world. These examples point out how necessary it is to take the variety of social, cultural, and economic situations into account, if one wishes to appreciate the plurality of services which Catholic universities are called upon to render.

(18) Finally, there is a great variety of Catholic institutions of higher learning, according to the various levels of university work at which they operate. Some have the fullest range of faculties, schools, and institutes in all branches of learning, with strong programs of both teaching and research. Others are specialized research institutes, while still others are professional schools (such as schools of law). Another category is made up of those which are primarily engaged in undergraduate education leading to a college degree (as in the United States) or the equivalent in other educational systems (e.g. the "first cycle" in French universities). Since all of these institutions engage, in various ways, in university activities, this document is intended to apply to all of them, with the necessary qualifications according to the particular kind of institution in question.[3]

II. THE GOVERNMENT OF THE UNIVERSITY

A. INTERNAL GOVERNMENT

(19) The internal government of Catholic universities must be adaptive to their wide diversities, to the laws of various states, and to local conditions. Workable patterns are determined according to specific needs. Provision should be made in the structure of the university for all the members of the university community to participate in some way, not necessarily deliberative, in the formulation of policy and in the decision-making process.

The rights and obligations of all members of the university community should be clearly stated and appropriate procedures established to deal with conflicts regarding these rights. Moreover, with all due regard for authority and for proper confidentiality, all members of the university community have the right to be informed about the basic decisions affecting the governance of the university and the reasons for these decisions.

Finally, it is vital that a spirit of charity characterize relationships within the university community, showing itself especially in a willingness on the part of all to engage in sincere dialogue. This dialogue will be facilitated by open and clearly defined channels of communication, especially between the administration and all the members of the university community.

B. AUTONOMY

(20) A Catholic university today must be a university in the full sense of the word, with a strong commitment to and concern for academic excellence. To perform its teaching and research functions effectively a Catholic university must have true autonomy and academic freedom. When we affirm the autonomy of the university we do not mean that it stands outside the law: we are speaking rather of that internal autonomy and integrity which flow from its very nature and purpose.

A university can render its own specific service to the community only if it is able to follow the imperatives which flow from its very nature, primary among which is the pursuit and transmission of truth. From this flows its autonomy, its freedom in teaching and research. This freedom is limited by no other factor than the truth which it pursues. Any limitation imposed on it which would clash with this unconditioned attitude for pursuing truth would be intolerable and contrary to the very nature of the university.[4]

Because the universities themselves are best qualified to judge what conditions are required for their research and their communication of truth, academic autonomy normally entails administrative autonomy in such matters as the selection of faculty, the planning of academic programs, organization of teaching and research, the establishment of chairs, and the like.

(21) The importance of the autonomy of universities vis-à-vis other authorities is generally recognized by all who are involved in university work, and particularly by faculty members and administrators. At the Fourth General Conference of the International Association of Universities, held in Tokyo in 1965, the delegates clearly expressed their desire for a greater degree of university autonomy. This was not done from an attitude of self-defense or quest for power, but with the conviction that through its autonomy a university is more capable of serving society as it should.[5]

The Tokyo Conference advocated full university autonomy in regard to these five points: selection of academic staff, student admission policy, curriculum planning, research projects, and apportionment of budget. Catholic universities share the need and desire for autonomy in these same areas, which can be described in somewhat greater detail under the following headings.

(a) *Juridical autonomy.* This includes the right to confer academic degrees and to set up programs of study which lead to these degrees. This autonomy is limited and subject to laws which govern the awarding of civil and professional diplomas. It is desirable, however, that even these laws be as flexible as possible, so that the universities may have real freedom of action to permit them to adapt their programs in accordance with scientific advancements.

(b) *Academic autonomy.* This means freedom in student admission policy, in appointment of personnel, in teaching (with regard both to subjects taught and to methods), and in research.

(c) *Administrative autonomy.* The university must govern itself freely, especially in regard to the apportionment and administration of its budgets, both regular and special.

(d) *Financial autonomy.* This more properly can be called financial viability. It means that even while Catholic universities come to need and depend more and more on public financial support, their autonomy must be the more zealously safeguarded.

As the Tokyo report also notes, the exercise of autonomy entails special obligations, and presupposes a high degree of responsibility on the part of all university personnel: its officials, trustees, administrators, professors, and students.

C. PLANNING

(22) Catholic universities should be conscious of the need for expert long-range planning if they are to develop as their responsible authorities hope they will, and if they are to be properly understood in the contemporary world. Modern methods of long-range planning are indispensable for probing the strengths and weaknesses of institutions.

Long-range planning for a Catholic university means the projection through diagnosis and prognosis of the reasonable aims and means by which it can fulfill its service to the Church and to civil society. Such long-range planning should employ the modern techniques and strategies utilized successfully by governments, corporations and other institutions. This means that each university must ask itself exactly what kind of an institution it wants to become, at what rate it can and should develop, how much duplication of facilities and competition with other universities is justifiable, and where the revenues it requires are to be found.

Planning should in a special way include provision for a program of productive research. For this purpose, constant consideration must be given to the promotion and support of research projects, whether they are carried on within the university or in collaboration with research being done elsewhere.

III. ACTIVITIES OF A CATHOLIC UNIVERSITY

(23) In the pursuit of their specific objectives, Catholic universities engage in those activities which are essential to any university: research, teaching, continuing education, and other services which universities are particularly qualified to provide. At the same time, they strive to impart a Catholic character to all their activities, and to provide an authentic human community for those who share in them. And finally, they have an important contribution to make to the vital task of promoting human and social development.

A. ACADEMIC ACTIVITIES

1. Research

(24) Scholarly research is the basis of university teaching, since teaching at this level must mean the initiation of the student into scientific method, which is an essential element of his intellectual formation.

When we speak of research here we mean to include individual research, group research within a given discipline, and interdisciplinary research.[6]

It is taken for granted that freedom is an indispensable condition for any authentic scholarly research. This freedom must be guaranteed both to the researcher and to the research policy that a university chooses to follow, taking its own social and political situation into account.[7]

It is our conviction that if a university wishes to fulfill its vocation to be an effective instrument of human progress, and not remain on the fringe of the dynamic forces of history, it must direct its research, and especially interdisciplinary research, to the urgent problems of social development. It must always keep in mind that the freedom of the human person is its goal, and that its contribution to progress will normally consist not so much in finding political solutions to problems, as in laying the scientific foundations for their solution.

(25) It is our hope, therefore, that in every Catholic university there be an office (or at least a person) responsible for stimulating and planning

research, especially interdisciplinary projects. Such an office, to be effective, must have appropriate facilities and an adequate share of the university budget.

Interdisciplinary research at a Catholic university should be organized in such a way as to avoid wasteful duplication of efforts. As far as possible it should aim at results which will have indisputable academic value and at the same time be of genuine service to the Church and the whole community. This postulates that an important place be given to research projects that will contribute to the promotion of a dialogue between the religious sciences and human culture. The first principle governing such a dialogue is that in order to understand reality one must use the methods and accept the findings of all branches of knowledge: no one single approach to reality suffices.

(26) Faculty members who belong to the Christian and Catholic tradition can bring to their research a further dimension of reality which often needs to be emphasized. They can in such research engage in a fruitful dialogue between theology and the other scholarly disciplines.

Complete intellectual openness requires the presence in the university of a group of scholars in theology and other religious studies. These scholars are not merely representatives of legitimate intellectual disciplines, but make an indispensable contribution to the integrity of the university, which, in order to embrace the fullness of human experience, must also take its religious dimension into account. Although the faculty of theology or department of religious studies in a Catholic university must search the full range and variety of man's religious experience, it should be preeminent in scholars of the Christian and Catholic tradition. A personal religious commitment, however it is specified denominationally, will characterize the member of such a department whose teaching and research probe in a vital way into the depths of his subject.

By its presence as an integral part of the university, the faculty of theology or department of religious studies can stimulate scholars of other disciplines, even nonbelievers, to take part in discussions that bear on the deepest human implications of their own sciences. Today such a dialogue is particularly important in the area of the behavioral and life sciences. Through such discussions the theologian too will be enriched by sharing the broader vision of man and the human condition which other disciplines provide.

(27) The deepening of their appreciation of the Christian message on the part of men who are thoroughly conversant with contemporary thought as well as with the sources of Christian doctrine and the lessons of history, should permit the Catholic university to make an important contribution to the creation of an authentic language of faith suited to our times.

Moreover, the program of research carried on at Catholic universities can be a valuable aid to the Church by providing its leaders with a better scientific basis for decisions regarding pastoral action in today's world. For this reason, those responsible for planning research at the universities should keep in close touch with those who have pastoral responsibility in the Church, for their mutual benefit.

2. Teaching

(28) University teaching aims at communicating the objectives, methods, and results of research. It should enable students to develop powers of critical judgment at a level of professional competence which will help them to be contributing members of society through their own research or the application of that done by others. The statement made above that teaching and research are both essential activities of universities is in no way intended to deny the importance either of institutions primarily engaged in the education of undergraduates, or of those which give priority to research.

It is taken for granted that academic freedom is an indispensable condition for genuine university teaching. The statutes of each institution should safeguard such freedom, taking due account of the religious inspiration which characterizes a university precisely as Catholic.[8]

(29) Teaching at a Catholic university, while respecting the nature and methods proper to each discipline, should be animated by a vital Christian spirit, and by a genuine respect for the dignity and freedom of each person. While engaged in the transmission of knowledge, teachers in a Catholic university should strive to point out how the application of that knowledge might be directed toward building a world of justice and peace.

In order that the university may provide its students the opportunity for an education of the highest quality, its faculty and administration must engage in regular and objective evaluation of its teaching methods. They should keep abreast of the contributions being made by research projects whose goal is to improve pedagogical methods.

(30) Through the presence in the university of a faculty of theology or department of religious studies, students of various disciplines are made aware of the question of God, and are confronted with values which, reaching beyond man's mortal limitations, challenge a more restricted view of reality. In their critical and reflective reaction to these values, students can force the scholar to a constant search for a more relevant and contemporary expression of his own science.

It is up to the members of a faculty of theology or department of religious studies to meet adequately the religious questions raised by the students, and to stimulate their interest in such questions where it is lacking. This task requires great flexibility. If effective work is to be done in this area, it is necessary to listen to the real needs and aspirations of the students.

(31) In every discipline the teachers in today's university must be willing to engage in an ongoing dialogue with students, recognizing that, if founded on mutual respect and understanding, dialogue is a normal means of cultural and human growth. In this spirit of dialogue, which is rooted in a deep sense of the liberty and dignity of the human person, Catholic teachers can share with students their own faith and values.

3. Continuing Education

(32) The Catholic university's role in continuing education can take several forms. It may be viewed as providing an opportunity for professional people to bring their knowledge and expertise up to date with the latest advances in their field, and with the changing needs of society. Continuing education can also be seen as expanding the educational services of the university beyond the limits of its campus. One example of this is the "Open University" initiated in England and rapidly being imitated in other countries.

(33) In the first sense the university may sponsor lecture series, courses, conferences, seminars, and the like, whose objective is to provide an opportunity for professional men and women to keep abreast of developments in their respective fields. A particular contribution of this kind of continuing education may be to offer to those professionally engaged in the promotion of human and social development, help toward a better understanding of the problems involved in such development and toward their solution, especially in the light of Christian faith. Here the emphasis is, therefore, on lifelong education. For this purpose the university will call upon both its own personnel and other experts who are available.

(34) In the second sense of continuing education, the university seeks to help people who have not had the advantage of a university background, and whose occupation or other responsibilities make full-time attendance impossible. By using modern means of communication, the university brings its services to these people wherever they happen to be, with the aim of enabling a larger proportion of the citizens to share in the cultural heritage of man and to participate in shaping the direction and development of human life. One objective of such education will be to enlarge the options available to people, and to help individuals and groups to learn how they can make institutions (whether governments, industries, businesses, or others) more responsive to their needs.

(35) A university that is conscious of its unique social role will creatively devise new ways and techniques to achieve a maximum impact in both senses of continuing education. To this end the university will not limit itself to lectures and conferences on the campus, but fully exploit the opportunities available through modern means of mass communication.

4. *Other Services to the Community*

(36) Other services which universities are particularly qualified to offer to the community at large include, but are not limited to, the following: provision of expert consultants to the Church, the government, and other public bodies; assistance in research projects, surveys, and the like; and various counselling and clinical services, depending on the kinds of faculties or professional schools in the university complex.

B. FOSTERING THE UNIVERSITY COMMUNITY

(37) A Catholic university pursues its objectives in two ways: it engages in academic activities such as research, teaching, and continuing education, and at the same time it strives to form an authentic human community. Its aim is to help all those who share in its activities to achieve human wholeness. The Catholic university community finds its unity in a vision of man and of the world which on the one hand flows from a common cultural heritage, and on the other, from the person and message of Christ. A spirit of freedom, charity, and respect for the particular character of the institution animates this community.

It is a fact that the educative process is carried on not only by academic activity but also by community life. The educational value of community life depends on two factors: the extent to which the individual joins in the community and opens himself to others, and the mutual respect which the members of the community show to one another. It is this respect that governs relationships among the various members of the community: professors, administrators, nonacademic staff, and students. This community spirit will be promoted by making sure that there are lines of communication open to everyone, and that everyone has an opportunity to contribute, according to his role and capacity, towards decisions which affect the community. To a great extent the human influence of the university will depend on the vitality of its community life.

(38) The *administrators* of such a university community will perform their duties in a spirit of service, paying special attention to the manifold needs of the various individuals and groups in the complex life of the university, so that a genuine community spirit may animate all who share its life.

(39) The *professors* will engage in a common and constant effort to improve their understanding of and collaboration with one another and with the students, especially those who come from other countries. They will aim not only to provide a sound humane and Christian education, but also to lead each student to discover his own aptitudes and vocation in life. In all the activities of the university, the ultimate goal is to form persons who are capable of effectively undertaking their responsibilities in the Church and in the world.

(40) *Students* will find, in their relationships with faculty and fellow students, a challenge that will test their desire and capacity to seek for the truth and live by it in every situation in which they find themselves. The experience of living in close association with people of different social, ethnic, and religious backgrounds, and sometimes of different nationalities, will give them a unique opportunity to learn to exercise responsibility in dealing with others, and to overcome any prejudices they may have.

(41) The *nonacademic staff* are an integral part of the university community, and make an indispensable contribution to the service which it renders. Their loyalty and competence, and their understanding of and dedication to the objectives of the university, are important factors in its achieving them.

(42) Since *those engaged in the pastoral ministry* play such a key role in fostering the Christian atmosphere of the university community, it is essential that they be especially well qualified and trained for this task. In addition to their own efforts, they will need the help of other individuals and groups who will share their responsibility to initiate and carry out pastoral programs adapted to the needs of the various categories of people in this community. Since these programs form part of the wider ecclesial ministry, they have to be carried out in harmony with the competent Church authorities. University administrators, conscious of the importance of this ministry, will provide it with adequate facilities and grant it the freedom of action which it needs.

Those engaged in the campus ministry cannot neglect the students of other faiths, but ought to offer them any spiritual assistance they may need, at the same time respecting their freedom to maintain and express their own religious convictions. To this end, it may be appropriate to invite ministers of other churches to participate in the university's pastoral program. Students of other religious traditions or of none at all should find at a Catholic university a living witness to Christianity that will attract them to want to know it better.

(43) Campus ministry, like the strictly academic activities of the university, must be inspired by a profound respect for human freedom, which is an indispensable basis for human and Christian growth of personality. It

is only on this basis that the Catholic university can form mature persons who will not tolerate a "divorce between the faith that they profess and the lives that they lead," but rather "will unite their human, domestic, professional, scientific, or technical endeavors into a vital synthesis with their religious values."[9]

C. CONTRIBUTION TO DEVELOPMENT

(44) The Catholic universities of today wish to commit themselves to the challenging tasks of development and social justice, as they have declared in the general assemblies of the I.F.C.U. held at Kinshasa (1968) and Boston (1970). All Catholic universities have to face together one of the gravest problems of our time, and realistically assess their responsibilities, so that they may become effectively involved in promoting "the development of those peoples who are striving to escape from hunger, misery, endemic diseases, and ignorance; of those who are looking for a wider share in the benefits of civilization and a more active improvement of their human qualities; of those who are aiming purposefully at their complete fulfillment."[10]

The Catholic university is concretely integrated in local, regional, national, and international societies, at a given time in history. This ought to stimulate the university to be an effective instrument of progress for these diverse societies, through means within its own competence as a center of education, learning, and research. The future role of universities will depend in large part on the answer that will be given to this crucial question: What is to be the contribution of institutions of higher learning to the urgent tasks of development in this modern world where want still prevails?

(45) In practice, the following points are to be noted.

1. If a special emphasis should be given to the needs of the developing countries of the Third World, due consideration must also be given to the marginal, or underprivileged, groups and regions of the modern nations.

2. Catholic universities should cooperate with one another in the formation of a theology suited to the cultures and ways of life of the emerging nations. Special institutes or centers of research on problems of development should be created and supported by the Catholic universities.

3. Professors and students should acquire a collective consciousness concerning the pressing needs of development, and be encouraged to participate in concrete projects in favor of the Third World, and take part in community services promoting welfare and social justice.

4. All these services should be undertaken in such a way that the proper mission of the university is respected. The university cannot allow its action to be exploited for political ends by factions within or outside the campus. Nor may the university become merely a technical instrument for development. It operates primarily on the level of education, and it is at this level that its action for human progress and social justice will be most efficient. Catholic universities, being inspired by Christian motivation and having such great potentialities for international cooperation, must recognize their particular responsibility with regard to world development and social justice.

IV. RELATIONSHIPS WITH OTHERS

A. COOPERATION WITH OTHER UNIVERSITIES

(46)   Coordinated and continuing research in an indispensable means to assure the effective growth of the Church's life and mission in the world today. For this reason it is urgent that Catholic universities study how best they can coordinate their research work, especially with regard to the most pressing problems that concern the entire Church, man's religious life, and human culture in general.

(47)   One fruitful method of such collaboration is the exchange of professors. Another is the establishment of research centers, which would encourage interdisciplinary research within the university, as well as promote and direct the collaboration of various universities toward the study of problems which are of general interest, problems chosen spontaneously by the universities themselves or proposed to them by those responsible for the pastoral activity of the Church. It should be noted that in many places there are, besides universities and research centers, various professional associations with a capacity for research and an expertise which can make a valuable contribution to the solution of such problems.

In this way, Catholic universities, in liaison with the Hierarchy, could contribute to the development of an organic and continuing research in the Church, a necessary factor in the continual renovation of its life and the effectiveness of its pastoral activity. They can serve as a kind of laboratory or resource to provide the Church that type of service for which they may be particularly well equipped, such as research in the field of religious studies, education, or sociology.

(48)   It is desirable that such collaboration include universities other than Catholic. It is particularly important that faculties or departments of theology cooperate ecumenically with other institutions in the same

field. By participating in research programs with other Christian faculties of theology, the theological faculties at Catholic universities will play an indispensable role in furthering the cause of ecumenism. In this way they will contribute on a university level to the mutual understanding and reconciliation of the Churches.[11]

(49)   Cooperation and coordination are indispensable among universities in the same region. Before a decision is made to create a new university, existing facilities should be assessed, and the competent authorities should be consulted. It may sometimes be preferable to consider the possibility of integrating available resources into an existing university, even one that is not Catholic. The International Federation of Catholic Universities may be helpful in such long-range planning.

B. Relations with the Catholic Hierarchy

(50)   Universities, as institutions for research and teaching, render a vital service to the communities which sustain them. Catholic universities, by assuring an effective presence of the truth of the Christian message at the level of university teaching and research, render a particular service to the Church and to mankind. They prepare leaders for civil and ecclesiastical society; they study the grave problems which today confront humanity and especially the Church; they seek solutions that will further human development and assure the wider and more effective spreading of the light of the Gospel.

(51)   Religious authorities, conscious of the importance of this contribution to the Church, will have a special concern for the welfare of the Catholic universities in their region. These universities represent a valuable resource for the accomplishment of their pastoral mission, in a world where problems are becoming ever more complex and technical.

For these reasons, Catholic universities can rightly expect inspiration, encouragement, and support from the Hierarchy in carrying out their difficult task. For their part, the universities will seek to promote a frank and confident collaboration with Church authorities, knowing that it is only in the context of the Church that they can accomplish their specifically Catholic mission.

(52)   There is a delicate balance to be maintained between the autonomy of a Catholic university and the responsibilities of the Hierarchy. Even at the level of civil society, public order and interest can entail limitations to the self-government of the university, provided that the requirements of unconditioned research for the truth are respected. *A fortiori* that community which is the Church will have its rights vis-à-vis Catholic universities. As the guardian of revealed truth, the Church is especially concerned where the truths of Catholic faith are at stake,

as well as where naturally known truths come into contact with them. This new dimension, namely, doctrinal authority with the right and duty to safeguard orthodoxy, creates a complicated and delicate situation by reason of the convergence of two sources of knowledge: revelation, a divine gift to be carefully protected, and science, the fruit of human reflection and research.

(53)   While the implications of the truths of salvation for the secular disciplines are usually indirect and remote, it is precisely in theology that the two sources of knowledge intersect.

It is the theologian's task to deepen the understanding of that faith which he shares and professes with all the people of God, to study its sources and implications, and to seek to express it in a way that is adapted to the needs of his times. In doing this, the theologian makes his special competence available to the Magisterium, while recognizing the latter's right to judge the value of his theology, its authentic catholicity, and its conformity with divine revelation.

(54)   This dialogue between theologians and the Hierarchy demands truth and sincerity from both parties, in a mutual love of Christ and a common desire to hand on His saving message.

As the report of the Doctrinal Commission of the First Synod of Bishops says: "One must assuredly grant to theologians due freedom both to explore new paths and to bring older positions up to date. . . . This due freedom must always remain within the limits of the Word of God, as this has been constantly preserved and as it is taught and explained by the living Magisterium of the Church, in the first place by that of the Vicar of Jesus Christ."[12]

(55)   It is Pope Paul VI himself who declared: "The Magisterium knows that without the help of theology it could no doubt preserve and teach the faith, but it would hardly attain to that degree of richness and depth which it needs in order to accomplish its task fully."[13]

As the Magisterium, in the person of Pope Paul VI, thus recognizes its need of the help of theology, so also every Catholic theologian who is true to the principles of his own discipline recognizes the dependence of theology on the Magisterium, to which, as Vatican II teaches, the task of authoritatively interpreting the Word of God has been entrusted.[14]

(56)   Teaching Catholic theology in the university, theologians must present the authentic doctrine of the Church. Taking prudent account of the maturity and previous preparation of the students, they should lead them to an intelligent understanding of the doctrinal pronouncements of the Church and of the principles according to which these are to be evaluated and interpreted.

Their teaching role is inseparable from their scholarly research. Fulfilling their function in the university, theologians must be able to pursue their discipline in the same manner as other research scholars, keeping in mind, as every researcher must, the particular nature of their own discipline. They must be free to question, to develop their hypotheses, to search for more adequate interpretations and formulations, to publish and defend their views on a scholarly level, and to study theological sources, including pronouncements of the teaching Church, with the full freedom of scholarly research.

(57) History shows us that it has not always been easy to reconcile the rights of Catholic scholars to academic freedom with the rights and responsibilities of the Hierarchy in matters of doctrine. Without in any way pretending to offer a complete solution to this complicated problem, we make the following statements in the conviction that it is of vital importance to the universities and to the whole Church that the respective limits of these equally undeniable rights be clearly delineated.

(58) The academic freedom which is essential if the science of theology is to be pursued and developed on a truly university level postulates that hierarchical authority intervene only when it judges the truth of the Christian message to be at stake.

Furthermore, the legitimate and necessary autonomy of the university requires that an intervention by ecclesiastical authority should respect the statutes and regulations of the institution as well as accepted academic procedures. The recognition of Church authority in doctrinal matters does not of itself imply the right of the Hierarchy to intervene in university government or academic administration.

(59) The form which a possible intervention of ecclesiastical authorities may take will vary in accordance with the type of Catholic institution involved. Where the university has statutory relationships with Church authorities, presumably these will spell out the conditions and modalities to be observed in any hierarchical intervention. If there are no such statutory relationships, Church authorities will deal with the individual involved only as a member of the Church.

While no one will deny to bishops the right to judge and declare whether a teaching that is publicly proposed as Catholic is in fact such, still the judgment concerning the product of a theologian's scholarly research will normally be left to his peers. The scholarly criticism of a theologian's views by his colleagues will in many cases constitute a kind of self-regulation of the Catholic academic community, which may well render unnecessary any direct intervention of ecclesiastical authority.

However, when bishops, after due consideration, are convinced that the orthodoxy of the people under their pastoral care is being endangered, they have the right and duty to intervene, by advising the person involved, informing the administration, and in an extreme case, declaring such a teaching incompatible with Catholic doctrine. However, unless statutory relationships permit it, this will not involve a juridical intervention, whether direct or indirect, in the institutional affairs of the university, whose responsibility it is to take the necessary and appropriate means to maintain its Catholic character.

(60)   There are, of course, many matters concerning the Catholic university, apart from those relating to such intervention, in which the Hierarchy has a deep and vital interest, and about which it has the right to make its views heard. Catholic universities, and their theological faculties in particular, share this vital interest in the pastoral welfare of the Church, especially insofar as it is affected by their work. Indeed, the entire pastoral field is one in which there is room and need for fruitful dialogue and collaboration between university personnel and the bishops.

CONCLUSION

(61)   In describing the nature and mission of the Catholic university, we have presented an image of what it aspires to be. Even if this ideal is not perfectly realized, it offers a valuable inspiration to every Catholic university, striving, despite limitations and deficiencies, to fulfill its distinctively Christian task in the university world. Here is the ideal of the Catholic university, here it finds its identity, here its *raison d'être*.

To be sure, this ideal, even considered as such, is not univocal. There is no one type of Catholic university which would be the model to be imitated everywhere in the world. The needs and aspirations of the various countries with their specific cultures and problems require that the idea of the Catholic university be adapted to each particular situation. For the Catholic university truly to fulfill its mission, it is necessary both that its Christian inspiration be real and efficacious, and that the university be deeply rooted in its own milieu.

Finally, the Catholic universities, recognizing that theirs is not the only way that Catholics are present in the university world, wish to pay homage to all those who by their Christian example and influence in other universities give a no less needed witness to the truth of Christ's message for mankind.

NOTES

1. Address of Pope Paul VI to the members of the Council and Committee of the International Federation of Catholic Universities. *L'Osservatore Romano*, May 7, 1971.

2. We prescind from the special situation of canonically erected faculties which grant ecclesiastical degrees. These are governed by the regulations contained in such documents as *Deus Scientiarum Dominus* (1913) and *Normae Quaedam* (1968) which spell out the extent of Church authority regarding such issues as the appointment of professors, requirements for obtaining degrees, and the contents of programs, in such faculties.

3. According to the best estimates there were in 1967 about 600 institutions of higher learning in the world which were considered to be Catholic. These included 143 universities, 240 independent university colleges, 86 autonomous faculties, and more than 80 university colleges attached to public universities. Cf. the report given by Edward B. Rooney, S.J., at the Kinshasa General Assembly of the I.F.C.U., published in *The Catholic University in the Modern World*, Paris, 1969, pp. 31–62.

More recent statistics, although they appear to use less exacting criteria, give the number of Catholic universities in the world as 198.

4. The question of the relationship between the autonomy of a Catholic university and the authority of the Hierarchy will be treated below in Part IV, B.

5. *Proceedings of the Fourth General Assembly of the International Association of Universities*, Paris, 1965.

6. The question of cooperation with other universities in research projects is treated below in Part IV, A.

7. See above, Part II, B.

8. The question of academic freedom at a Catholic university is treated more fully below in Part IV, B.

9. Vatican II, *Gaudium et Spes*, 43, 1.

10. *Populorum Progressio* 1, *AAS* 59 (1967) 257.

11. Cf. "Ecumenism in Higher Education, Part II of the *Directory for . . . Ecumenical Matters*, issued by the Secretariat for Promoting Christian Unity on April 16, 1970, and published in its *Information Services* n. 10 (June 1970) 3–10.

12. Report of the Doctrinal Commission, *Documentation Catholique* 64 (1967) 1986.

13. Discourse to the International Congress on the Theology of Vatican II, Oct. 1, 1966, *AAS* 58 (1966) 892–893.

14. Cf. Const. Dogm. de Divina Revelatione *Dei Verbum*, 10.

A Letter from Gabriel Marie
Cardinal Garrone, Prefect of the Sacred
Congregation for Catholic Education

April 25, 1973

To Presidents of Catholic Universities and Directors
of Catholic Institutions of Higher Learning

At the end of the Second International Congress of Delegates of Catholic Universities (Rome, November 20–29, 1972), this Sacred Congregation asked the International Federation of Catholic Universities (I.F.C.U.) to send to all Catholic universities a copy of the final document of the Congress, entitled "The Catholic University in the Modern World," pointing out at the same time that the document would have to undergo further consideration by the Plenary Assembly of the Congregation, consisting of thirty-seven cardinals and bishops, at a meeting set for April 2–3, 1973.

The Plenary Assembly having how taken place and the results of the Assembly having been duly approved by the Holy Father in an audience on April 6, 1973, this Sacred Congregation is now proceeding to execute these decisions.

First of all, it must be noted that it was the French version of the document that was studied by the Plenary Assembly and, therefore, it is to this version that the English and Spanish translations must be referred. This is the reason why English-speaking and Spanish-speaking Catholic universities are also being sent copies of the French version.

In faithful conformity to the expressed orders of the Fathers of the Assembly, this Sacred Congregation hereby sets out the following:

(1) The Fathers, gladly taking note of the praiseworthy task accomplished by the Catholic universities and their delegates, especially for taking account of the suggestions of the Plenary Assembly of 1969

Reprinted from National Catholic Educational Association, *College Newsletter* 35, no. 3 (March 1973), where it was published in conjunction with "The Catholic University in the Modern World."

in regard to the first version of the document (which came from the First Congress of 1969), noted that the document represents a considerable improvement on that of 1969. For this reason they consider the present document as "valid but needing improvement."

The document well defines and makes clear the purpose and characteristics of the Catholic university by setting out the consequences of fidelity to the Faith and to the Church. The Fathers point out, however, that, among other inevitable "lacunae" the document is not sufficiently explicit on two points:

(a) on the necessity for each Catholic university to set out formally and without equivocation, either in its statutes or in some other internal document, its character and commitment as "Catholic";

(b) on the necessity for every Catholic university to create within itself appropriate and efficacious instruments so as to be able to put into effect proper self-regulation in the sectors of faith, morality, and discipline.

(2) In order to avoid any false and damaging interpretations to which the text may give rise—as experience has shown already—the Fathers declare that:

(a) the document must be considered "as a whole," so that no single element can be extrapolated from its entirety and used out of context, especially regarding the treatment given to autonomy of teaching and research;

(b) although the document envisages the existence of university institutions without statutory bonds linking them to ecclesiastical authority, it is to be noted that this in no way means that such institutions are removed from those relationships with the ecclesiastical hierarchy which must characterize all Catholic institutions.

(3) Finally, the Fathers offer their cordial gratitude to the Catholic universities for the enlightened dedication with which they give so much to the Church and to society as a whole. The Fathers exhort them to do all that is possible to be sure that what is indicated in n. (1) of this letter is carried out, so that their Catholic character, which is described in the document, might be promoted and safeguarded.

Although this document was produced only by Catholic universities, it, nonetheless, commits the consciences of all who work in these universities to see to it that the conditions it sets out are satisfied in every university which calls itself or would be "Catholic."

The Sacred Congregation asks those in positions of responsibility in Catholic universities to be certain that, whenever this document is presented to anyone, the full contents of this letter are also presented at the same time.

Assuming that all who administer or work in Catholic universities will graciously understand and accept these remarks, the Sacred Congregation renews its sentiments of profound respect for these people, confident that this task we have undertaken together will be brought to a successful conclusion.

The Congregation is looking forward with satisfaction to further collaboration on matters of vital importance to the Church and is anticipating studying and solving those problems on which the Episcopacy and Catholic universities can fruitfully and mutually work.

Sincerely yours in Jesus Christ,

Gabriel Marie Cardinal Garrone
Most Rev. Joseph Schroeffer

Part II

Bilateral Dialogue Begins: The U.S.A. and the Vatican 1975–1980

In June 1975 there appeared a request from Rome for assistance in developing a new academic law for ecclesiastical faculties. The startling thing was that this request arrived on the desk of all Catholic university presidents, not just the few that might have been affected by it. The communication made it clear that the new academic law would apply only to ecclesiastical faculties; nevertheless, the concreteness of the norms and the suggestion that all departments of theology, even in universities that were not "canonically erected," should be interested in the "appropriate relationship between such study and the canon law," raised the level of anxiety. Concerned by this hint of a desire to forge a new relationship between non-ecclesiastical institutions and the Sacred Congregation, the Executive Committee of the College and University Department of the National Catholic Educational Association reflected on the complicated situation they found themselves in and embarked on a "white paper" to explain American Catholic higher education's distinctive character.

There is need to point out that in the 1970s some very important changes were taking place in American Catholic colleges and universities. New state and federal grants to higher education had enabled the colleges to undertake construction of campus facilities and to increase enrollments. The constitutionality of such grants to colleges that were church-related was being challenged in the courts, and some presidents feared that interference by Rome could easily undermine the legal case being made by the Catholic colleges. The desire to give greater visibility to the laity's role in the universities (already highlighted by Vatican II) and to make it clear that neither the official church nor the religious orders "controlled" these institutions, thus rendering them legally "sectarian," led an increasing number of institutions to move toward boards of trustees with predominantly lay trustees and to secure separate corporations and structures for these boards. In some cases, assets were transferred from religious communities to such boards without canonical approbation; thus, the Congregation for Catholic Education and the Congregation for Religious Institutes had grave misgivings about the whole American scene. Did this mean, Rome queried, that the institutions were no longer "Catholic"?

It was at this point that the Executive Committee of the College and University Department of NCEA, under the leadership of Msgr. John F. Murphy, attempted to answer that question by placing it in the context of American law regarding higher education. In 1976 a paper was developed and published entitled, *Relations of American Catholic Colleges and Universities with the Church.*

Meanwhile, work went forward on the academic law for ecclesiastical faculties, and on April 15, 1979, the apostolic constitution, *Sapientia Christiana*, was promulgated. Although it applied only to ecclesiastical faculties, the various drafts of it were widely circulated and inspired fear in the hearts of the non-ecclesiastical institutions. It gave a clue as to the intent of Rome which would later surface in the revision of the code of canon law (1983) and in the first schema for the document on all Catholic universities (1985), namely, that the use of the title, "Catholic University," had to have some juridical meaning.

In the fall of the same year, Pope John Paul II delivered a speech to a gathering of presidents of all Catholic colleges and universities at The Catholic University of America. The personal warmth of the papal allocution did much to offset the legalistic tone of the apostolic constitution. It also may have encouraged the American bishops to publish their own highly supportive document, *Catholic higher education and the pastoral mission of the Church*, the following year, a document that strongly affirmed the ministry of higher education and recognized the importance of Catholic colleges and universities as witnesses to the Catholic tradition of intellectual endeavor.

This document was, in part, the fruit of the ongoing dialogue between the episcopacy and the Catholic college presidents which had been initiated in 1974 with the establishment of a joint NCCB/NCEA Bishops' and Presidents' Committee. It was written only after extensive consultation, carried on by means of several drafts that were circulated for criticism. The use of such a methodology in the development of a document would serve as a pattern for later ecclesial dialogue.

First Draft of the Proposed Academic Law

Rome, June 1, 1975

Sacred Congregation for Catholic Education Prot. No 113/66/G
Preparation of *definitive* academic legislation on higher *ecclesiastical* studies

Gentlemen:

In the sixth and most recent circular letter which we sent you last year concerning the academic law of the Church, which is to be revised in accord with the *Normae quaedam* (see no. 113/66/F, March 25, 1974), we informed you that the time had arrived to develop a *new Apostolic Constitution* for the definitive promulgation of this academic law. In this connection, we were pleased to record, first, that in recent years you had worked with us readily and wisely—for which we now desire to express profound gratitude—and, second, that we have every confidence that you will also work generously in the completion of this important work.

On this account we address a *seventh* circular letter to you in order to request earnestly your careful cooperation in the suitable refinement, organization, and expression of this definitive legislation.

In a matter of this importance, the following should be kept in mind.

I. MATERIAL OBJECT OF THE WORK

The individual universities and autonomous faculties or higher institutes of ecclesiastical studies should be concerned with the *individual*

This is an unofficial translation of the cover letter to documents from the Sacred Congregation for Catholic Education, addressed to the rectors, deans, and similar officials of universities and faculties of ecclesiastical studies, taken from the Association of Catholic Colleges and Universities files. Since the documents were designed only for the ecclesiastical universities or faculties, we have chosen not to include them here. However, this cover letter suggests a highly juridical approach which surfaces later on in the documents leading to *Ex Corde Ecclesiae*.

regulations of the document *Normae quaedam* which is again to be revised but without neglecting in any way the norms of the Apostolic Constitution *Deus Scientiarum Dominus* (with the attached *Ordinationes*), which were *not* abrogated by the *Normae quaedam* (see Introduction, paragraph 2). As is evident, it is not a question of calling these norms into doubt, since the past years have clearly demonstrated that they have very well satisfied the current needs of universities. On the contrary, the question is rather to propose a better distribution of the matter, explication, integration, reformulation, etc. These questions will perhaps require further discussion. In any event, it will be good to examine and review everything methodically in order to achieve greater perfection.

The following may assist you in this task:

1) *Insert I* of 12 pages, accompanying this communication, which is entitled *"Summary of responses* given by academic centers of sacred studies, canonically erected or approved, of the entire world to the three most recent circular letters of the Congregation for Catholic Education." As is clear, this summary does not discuss the matter of future legislation but, since it offers the opinions of the universities and faculties in their responses, provides material for helpful investigation.

2) *Insert II* of 7 pages, also accompanying this communication. This document proposes *other* (*but not all*) *questions* pertaining to academic legislation, so that the *entire* mater of this legislation may be considered, so far as possible.

3) *Statutes and ordinances* of your universities or faculties which represent the happy outcome of your recent efforts, although limited to your own institutions. From these it will doubtless be possible to derive some regulations of a *general* legislative order which may be necessary or useful for all academic centers of the Church.

II. METHODS

1) Since the academic legislation of the Church is to be observed by all categories of persons (*"university components"*) which participate in the governance of a university or faculty (with the rights and obligations proper to each recognized or conceded), all categories of this kind are bound to express their opinion in the preparation of the responses. (As is customary everywhere, in order to proceed more expeditiously and effectively, the first phase of the work may be entrusted to a special commission of a few experts by the rector, dean, etc.; this commission shall then seek the judgment of the university components concerning the document it has prepared.)

2) Since it is foreseen that the definitive legislation will be issued in two separate and distinct documents (as was done in the case of the Apostolic Constitution *Deus Scientiarum Dominus* and the attached *Ordinationes*), a very careful distinction will have to be made between the norms that are to be inserted in the Constitution and the norms of the *Ordinationes* (depending upon their nature, as being of greater or less universality or weight).

3) We expect that such texts *will be formulated with special* exactitude, expressing neither more nor less than necessary. (In this connection we have been pleased already to notice excellent examples in some of your statutes.)

4) Scientific rigor demands that suggestions which are proposed (whether definitively formulated or not) should be based upon valid reasons. (In the proposal of sound and lawful regulations, it is not a question of the number of voters but rather of the validity and *authority* of the arguments advanced.) Therefore we earnestly request that when matters are in dispute *you propose explicit reasons* in favor of your position, adding reasons which weaken or even invalidate contrary positions.

III. FURTHER STEPS IN COMMON COLLABORATION

1) We strongly urge you to be generous in the carrying out of this task and that you *send to us* the results of your work *by November 30, 1975*. The reason is that the Congregation will need at least the entire month of December to prepare a synthesis of your responses and promptly to inform the 34 cardinals and bishops (who will assemble for a plenary meeting in March 1976) of this synthesis and of further work prepared with your help.

2) After this plenary session has considered the matters pertaining to it, it will be our responsibility to convene the *Second International Congress* of delegates of all universities and faculties of *ecclesiastical* studies (in the same way as was done for the First Congress, held in Rome, November 20–30, 1967). This will probably take place in Rome, November 20–30, 1976. Everything will be communicated to you in sufficient time and the drafts of documents to be considered at the Congress will be transmitted.

IV. NATURE OF ACADEMIC CENTERS TO
WHICH THIS CIRCULAR LETTER IS SENT

As indicated at the beginning of this letter, it is a question of redacting the academic law of the Church concerning higher *ecclesiastical* studies: first of all, *sacred* studies, namely, theology (with its special-izations), biblical and ancient oriental studies, missiology, ecclesiastical history, Christian archaeology, canon law (and comparative civil law), etc.; next, *certain profane studies* directly connected with sacred studies, namely, philosophy, education (especially pedagogy and psychology), sociology, etc. Thus there is no question here of *merely profane studies which are not directly connected with sacred studies.*

Consequently the academic centers which are considered here are per se the universities, faculties, schools, and higher institutes which engage in sacred or ecclesiastical studies in a *strictly academic manner*, have been canonically erected or explicitly approved by the Apostolic See, have statutes approved by that Apostolic See, and thus confer aca-demic, scientific, or professional degrees in the name of the Apostolic See. Among these are also included faculties or higher institutes of *ecclesias-tical* studies (especially theology) which have been canonically erected in *Catholic* universities (that is, in universities which, whether or not they were erected by the Apostolic See, are primarily intended for the instruction of *lay* young people in *profane* letters and sciences), including as well those which exist in *state* universities but have been expressly or equivalently recognized by the Church by force of concordats.

Certainly *it is strongly hoped* that *other schools* of theology or sacred or religious studies (institutes, departments, etc.) which exist in many universities which are *Catholic* either canonically or in fact (es-pecially in the United States of America) but up to now have had no relationship with the Congregation for Catholic Education with regard to their programs of studies will freely and willingly offer their assistance in the preparation of suitable academic legislation for the Church, offer-ing their judgment and recommendations to us openly and confidently in order to achieve an appropriate relationship of programs of study with the canon law. There is no one who would not recognize that it is entirely irregular for academic degrees in sacred studies to be conferred by Catholic faculties or schools which are not governed by the academic law of the Church. This is most certainly a matter of an important good of the Church which no one may neglect or minimize.

While we express our very sincere gratitude, we dare to draw your attention once again to the significance of the present endeavor. Since the efforts of all are necessary for the satisfactory completion of this work, we urge you to afford us your valuable cooperation with concern and willingness. This Congregation will undertake its own careful study along with you, making use of its own consultors in the certain hope that through united effort and counsel valid laws with firm authority may be prepared.

With gratitude we salute you fraternally, send best wishes, and remain

Yours devotedly in Jesus Christ,

Gabriel Marie Cardinal Garrone
J. Schrôffer, Secretary

Relations of American Catholic Colleges and Universities with the Church

Position Paper of the College and University Department, National Catholic Educational Association

I. INTRODUCTION

In recent years a continuing dialogue has flourished across the world on the nature and role of Catholic institutions of higher learning. Participants have included scholars and administrators, bishops and representatives of the Holy See. The conversations have been fruitful, resulting in new statements of mission to guide college and university leaders in their labors to serve the Church and contemporary society.

In June of 1975 some colleges and universities were invited to contribute to the formulation of a "new academic law of the Church," even though, as His Eminence, Cardinal Gabriel Garrone stated in a letter of January 10, 1976, the new Constitution "will not concern the generality of Catholic Universities as such nor those seminaries which have not been canonically erected into Faculties."

Cardinal Garrone accepted the offer of service of the College and University Department, National Catholic Educational Association, to prepare a "national response" for those institutions which so wished, so long as the right of institutions to respond directly to the Congregation for Catholic Education was respected.

Reprinted from *Occasional Papers on Catholic Higher Education*, vol. 2, no. 1, ed. Msgr. John F. Murphy (Washington, D.C.: National Catholic Educational Association, 1976). The designation of "College and University Department" was replaced in 1978 by the title "Association of Catholic Colleges and Universities," the original name at the time it was founded (1899).

II. CATHOLIC COLLEGES AND UNIVERSITIES IN THE U.S.

A. VARIETY AND NUMBER

Catholic colleges and universities of the United States are as varied in their size and programs as are other American institutions of higher learning. Catholic institutions have five characteristics in common: 1) they are chartered by the state as public trusts, a basic condition of their existence and operation, and they are granted tax-free status by the states; 2) they are privately supported and under independent rather than state control; 3) they sustain their Catholic commitment by an institutional profession of Catholic identity; 4) they maintain a Catholic presence through their departments of religion and theology, the many Catholic administrators and faculty who are associated with them, their official policies and institutional concerns, the impact of theological and philosophical reflection on the various disciplines, and their programs of pastoral ministry; 5) their "ultimate goal is to form persons who are capable of effectively undertaking their responsibilities in the Church and in the world."[1]

Even these characteristics do not apply uniformly to all Catholic colleges and universities. For example, almost all participate in some form of government support either through student aid or through federal contracts. Universities and larger colleges are more likely to receive research support from the government. As for the Catholic "presence," some of the smaller Catholic institutions may have a higher proportion of their personnel from the sponsoring religious congregation. Larger institutions, on the other hand, will not only have more laity in their faculty, they are more likely to have invited those of other faiths to join in the enterprise.

The scope and variety of these institutions is evident from the fact that some institutions are large, urban universities with enrollments of 10,000–20,000 students, with many graduate and professional schools and programs of teaching, research, and service similar to their public university counterparts. Others are primarily colleges offering the baccalaureate degree, and serving a more local or regional constituency. Many colleges which are located in urban areas have large continuing education or adult education programs to serve the needs of part-time students. Following the typical pattern of American higher education, most are coeducational, although fifty of the colleges are for women only. A small number are two-year institutions—called "junior colleges" or "community colleges," which concentrate on liberal arts and/or terminal programs with a career orientation.

These diverse Catholic colleges and universities number 250, enrolling approximately 425,000 students. The percentage of students and faculty who are Catholic varies widely. The institutions perceive and carry out their educational and religious mission in various ways and according to different models. However, all strive vigorously to maintain a Catholic presence on campus and manifest the four characteristics listed in "The Catholic University in the Modern World":

1. a Christian inspiration not only of individuals but of the university community as such;
2. a continuing reflection in the light of the Christian faith upon the growing treasury of human knowledge, to which it seeks to contribute by its own research;
3. fidelity to the Christian message as it comes to us through the Church;
4. an institutional commitment to the service of the people of God and of the human family in their pilgrimage to the transcendent goal which gives meaning to life.[2]

None of these colleges and universities is a seminary.

B. Origin and Legal Structure of Control

The vast majority of American Catholic colleges and universities were founded at the initiation of religious communities of men or women. Twelve are sponsored by dioceses.

Charters for United States colleges and universities are granted by the authority of the several states. Hence, each of the institutions is legally incorporated, with the ultimate authority residing in Boards of Trustees. Determination of programs, of curricula, and of faculty appointments lies with the institution. Degrees are awarded by authority of the trustees and faculty.

C. Regional Accreditation Associations and Other Professional Associations

American higher educational institutions have grouped themselves according to regions (six in number) into voluntary accrediting associations which establish minimum standards of academic quality as well as professional standards governing personnel policies and managerial practices. Colleges and universities uniformly seek admittance to these associations. An institution's ability to attract faculty and students, community support and needed funding, both from government and from private sources, is contingent upon fulfillment of the academic and professional standards set by the accrediting bodies. Thus the accreditation process imposes certain limitations on institutional autonomy.

Professional educational associations in the United States exercise large influence and power—whether they represent the colleges or universities themselves or other interest groups, for example, the faculty. It is important to recognize the role of these associations in the life of American higher education. The government does not accredit institutions. There is no government ministry of control. The control is exercised basically by the educators themselves.

Unionization of faculty and collective bargaining are new and growing phenomena on the American campuses. Some Catholic institutions are unionized, and it seems inevitable that more will be in the future, resulting in still further limitations on institutional autonomy.

This brief summary of the Catholic college and university scene in the United States may serve to reveal, albeit sketchily, the variety and complexity of these institutions as they seek to implement their educational mission in a pluralistic society.

III. IDENTITY AS CATHOLIC

A. SERVICE TO SOCIETY AND THE CHURCH

Tens of thousands of Catholic men and women give their lives to this apostolate which the Holy Father recently termed "of irreplaceable importance, especially in our day."[3] They share the view of the American bishops who wrote in *To Teach As Jesus Did*:

> Everything possible must be done to preserve the critically important contribution made by Catholic institutions through their commitment to the spiritual, intellectual, and moral values of the Christian tradition. Their students have a right to explore the distinctively Catholic intellectual patrimony which affirms, among other things, the existence of God and His revelation in Jesus Christ as ontological facts and the essential elements in seeking and sharing truth. The Church itself looks to its colleges and universities to serve it by deep and thorough study of Catholic beliefs in an atmosphere of intellectual freedom and according to canons of intellectual criticism which should govern all pursuit of truth. The Catholic community should fully support practical efforts to assure the continued effective presence of distinctively Catholic colleges and universities in our nation.[4]

The colleges and universities provide a service to the country and to the Church by their involvement in the significant human enterprise of the higher education of American citizens (and numerous foreigners)— a noble tradition traceable to Paris, Bologna, and earlier, to the first schools under Church sponsorship. The kind of service includes all the categories proper to the variety of institutions previously outlined.

B. THEOLOGICAL STUDIES

All Catholic colleges and universities provide courses and curricula in theology and religious studies. At the undergraduate level, a major thrust is to help young people to reflect upon their faith at an intellectual level consonant with their scientific and humanistic growth in other disciplines. The larger universities have, in addition, degree programs at the graduate level in the wide spectrum of theological and related sciences. The departments of theology concur in their commitment to present authentic Catholic doctrine, "taking prudent account of the maturity and previous preparation of the students."[5] In the graduate programs in American universities, "the characteristic strength," as the bishops pointed out, "appropriately lies in the presence of scholars whose professional competence and personal commitment are rooted in the Catholic tradition."[6]

The institutions offer many courses, workshops, and programs in religious education, liturgy, and spirituality for diverse groups of clergy, religious, and laity, in order to help in the Church renewal mandated by the Vatican Council, and by the American bishops in their pastoral, *To Teach As Jesus Did*.[7] Most of the teachers in the Catholic elementary and secondary system have been trained in the summer programs of Catholic colleges and universities.

C. LEADERSHIP IN ECUMENISM

Also, in direct response to the Vatican Council and subsequent initiatives of the Holy See, the colleges and universities are making serious and successful efforts in the area of ecumenism in many ways: 1) sponsorship of ecumenical gatherings, workshops, and seminars; 2) support of Catholic scholars for interdenominational research and reflection; 3) faculty exchange programs in theological sciences with institutions of other denominations; 4) courses offered in theological traditions other than Catholicism.[8]

To this most delicate work of the Spirit, which is ecumenism, the Catholic institutions bring a theology that is truly Catholic, because, as Pope Paul observed, "even those who do not share the position of the Church request from us an exacting clarity of position so that they may be able to establish a constructive and loyal dialogue."[9]

D. Pastoral Ministry on the Campus

The institutions are seriously committed to pastoral ministry for the members of the college or university community. Under the heading of "campus ministry" falls a wide variety of activities and programs that assist the students and faculty in their faith commitment, such as liturgies, retreats, spiritual direction, penance services, catechetical instruction of children, and organization of student service to the aged and the poor. There is a complete unanimity of opinion regarding the importance of this ministry. New projects and programs seek to transform this conviction into ever more effective forms of ministry.[10]

E. Theological and Ethical Reflection on Secular Disciplines

The institutions engage the attention of their students and faculty in interdisciplinary programs, lectures, seminars, etc., which seek to interface theological and ethical insights with those of other disciplines. The goal is to enlighten the mind with the eternal truths of revelation.[11]

F. The Worshipping Community

Every college and university celebrates the mysteries of the Risen Christ through community worship on campus. The most persistent and successful efforts in the country to keep the college-age generation participating in Catholic life and worship are centered on the nation's campuses.

There is a conscious effort to establish an atmosphere on campus that is friendly to the search for truth, supportive of Catholic faith and identity, and productive of a genuinely experienced Christian community. The aim is indeed to make "the Catholic university... the privileged place where the young person can be helped to find a way to work out a global synthesis, which will be for him and for others a bountiful source of light for a whole lifetime."[12]

G. Forum for Dialogue in the Church

Encouragement is given to discussions which seek to focus attention on areas where Catholic scholars and thinkers can provide a unique service to the Christian community. Programs are fostered which establish a forum where scholars and teachers can interact with other members of the Church: bishops, clergy, religious, and laity. Scholarly research, writing, and publication give impetus to the dialogue by probing and illuminating issues facing the Christian community in the contemporary world.

H. The National Association

Catholic colleges and universities have grouped themselves voluntarily as a national association—The National Catholic Educational Association, College and University Department—which is explicitly concerned with the issue of Catholic identity and service. The N.C.E.A., founded in 1904, plans national and regional meetings and establishes commissions and committees directed to helping the members realize their Catholic purpose.

IV. CONCERNS

A. Survival of U.S. Catholic Colleges and Universities

In the last decade and a half, Catholic and other independent institutions in the United States have witnessed a rapid expansion of public tax-supported institutions that provide education to large numbers of students at a low cost. In our highly inflationary economy, tuitions at Catholic institutions have increased to many times the cost of attending public institutions. For the vast majority of Catholic colleges and universities, endowments are small and religious contributions are proportionately less than they were when the institutions were able to depend on the "living endowment" of contributed services of clergy and religious.

This situation has adverse effects on educational quality as well as on enrollments. Balanced budgets have often been achieved at the cost of quality, a problem which afflicts all of higher education, but especially the independent sector.

B. Public Support

1. Changing Enrollment and Financial Patterns

In the desire to remain competitive in allowing students an economic choice to enroll in Catholic institutions, colleges and universities are obliged to seek funds from sources other than constantly escalating tuitions. Because of our public service, we feel government has an obligation to help. The continued inflation spiral in the U.S. and the decline of higher education as an accepted national priority by executive and legislative branches of government have combined to produce support programs inadequate to the need. Additionally, we recognize that constitutionally the federal and state governments are prohibited from supporting Churches and from assisting some forms of church-related schools. Yet financial assistance of some sort is necessary to survive.

2. Dimensions of the Constitutional Law Issue

The American constitution and the constitutions of the individual states have sections prohibiting both governmental establishment of religion and governmental interference with the free exercise of religion. These clauses, commonly designated "separation of church and state," have always been interpreted by the courts as prohibiting government financial support of churches. There has been an unrelenting series of court challenges to every kind of law passed by state and national legislatures to aid church-sponsored schools financially. Most support programs for elementary and secondary schools have been found unconstitutional.

At the higher education level, some support programs have survived court challenge, but only with delicate distinctions and qualifications. The most important Supreme Court decision affecting church-related colleges and universities was the *Tilton v. Richardson* case (1971). By the narrowest of margins (5-4) the Court ruled that the Higher Education Facilities Act (providing grants and loans for building construction to colleges and universities, including those that are church-related) did not violate the United States Constitution. The decision was based principally on the answers to three questions: "First, does the Act reflect a secular legislative purpose? Second, is the primary effect of the Act to advance or inhibit religion? Third, does the administration of the Act foster an excessive entanglement with religion?"

Although the challenge was struck down, the opinion of the Court (written by the Chief Justice of the United States) leads to the conclusion that the only church-related institutions which are eligible for aid have the following characteristics:

- Persons other than Catholics are admitted to the student body and given faculty appointments.
- Attendance at religious services is not required of students.
- Religion courses are not limited to the religion of the sponsoring body.
- There is no effort by the college to proselytize.
- The college adheres to established principles of academic freedom.[13]

The Supreme Court of the United States has pending before it a case involving state aid to Catholic colleges. A negative decision would have significant adverse effects on church-related higher education. If the federal Constitution is interpreted so as to prevent Catholic colleges and universities from participating in tax-supported programs at the state and federal levels, the vast majority of them nay not survive. Without opportunity for their students to obtain grants and loans for tuition and other costs, enrollment would be possible only to the children of the wealthy, or the costs of student aid would fall back on the severely restricted resources of the institution.

Thus, the future of Catholic presence in higher education in the United States is linked to a successful withstanding of constitutional challenges to certain forms of tax support. Hence, the relationship of Catholic colleges and universities to the Church would best be handled in ways that would not invite court challenge.

3. The Church's Recognition of Constitutional Problems

The leadership in the American Church recognizes the delicacy and the importance of these matters, and stands confidently behind the educational leaders as they attempt to work out the problems. Any indication of interference in the institutions' proper autonomy by representatives of the official Church would only assist the attempt to deprive church-related institutions of equal treatment before the law with other institutions. American bishops widely recognize that any insensitivity to the dimensions of the problem of juridical relationships with the Church could effectively destroy the good presently being done by our institutions. A cooperative relationship of people who are recognized as having genuine responsibilities—Bishops, Trustees, President—maintains a Catholic identity within the limitations imposed by American law, and thus fosters the noble purpose of Catholic higher education.

C. CATHOLICITY OF THE INSTITUTIONS

The previous points seriously concern American colleges and universities because of their absolute commitment to the survival of academically strong and authentically Catholic centers of higher learning. The leadership of these institutions endeavors to foster the principles of Catholic tradition and the recent statements of the Vatican Council, the Synods, the statements of the American hierarchy—all as they can be applied in the context of the American society in which the institutions exist. Illustrative of this dedication are the following activities:

a) Cooperation in preparation of the Rome '72 document and subsequent discussions about it on the campuses and at national Catholic conferences.

b) Encouragement of papers and discussions on Catholic identity and purpose at the national and regional meetings of the N.C.E.A. as well as through publications.[14]

c) Establishment of permanent committees in the N.C.E.A. on (1) Catholic Purpose and Identity; (2) Relations with Sponsoring Religious Bodies; (3) Campus Ministry.

d) Joint committee of presidents and American bishops, the U.S.C.C./Higher Education Committee.

e) Participation in the International Federation of Catholic Universities.

f) Establishment of an inter-university research council in conjunction and cooperation with the United States Catholic Conference.[15]

g) Designation by the bishops of several Catholic universities as institutes for liturgical research.

h) Multiple examples of cooperation with the local Church in providing various programs, especially in religious studies, to meet local needs. Our bishops in their recent pastoral have issued a particularly cordial invitation to the departments of theology to collaborate in the pastoral ministry of the bishops.[16]

The opportunities for service have certainly not been exhausted. The climate in the Church in the United States has never been more favorable to encourage various initiatives and, on the part of the colleges and universities, to respond with enthusiasm.

It is inevitable that in trying to define and act upon Catholic identity, mistakes can occur, but they should be seen in the context of the sincere dedication to the Church which is so evident. The Church, the university and college, American society—all are dynamic forces interrelating. Patience, trust, confidence, respect for tradition, hope for the future, cooperation—these are the elements that characterize the leadership which administrators and faculty are attempting to give United States Catholic colleges and universities in these challenging times.

American Catholic educators note with sorrow the weakening, if not the disappearance of independent Catholic higher education in many other parts of the world. The fact that the principal strength of Catholic higher learning has now shifted to the United States provides added incentive, if such were needed, to maintain our colleges and universities despite the pressures of severe problems.

It is not the educators alone who carry the burden for preserving Catholic institutions and maintaining their historic mission and heritage. Living alumni of our Catholic colleges and universities number between 1,500,000 – 2,000,000 men and women, and are to be found in every walk of American and international life. They are loyal and grateful to their colleges. Among them are counted many of our bishops and clergy, and countless religious whose higher learning now enables them to give distinguished service to nation and Church. As the Catholic population has grown in size and influence, the colleges and universities see their alumni in positions of prominence throughout American society, in politics and business, in the professions of every kind, giving witness to their Catholic heritage. They are the rich harvest of American Catholic higher education.

V. RELATIONSHIP WITH THE CHURCH

A. Role of the Bishops

The American bishops have evidenced their recognition and support of the nature of Catholic higher education by writing in a recent statement: "The Catholic college or university must of course be an institution of higher education according to sound contemporary criteria. It will therefore be strongly committed to academic excellence and the responsible academic freedom required for effective teaching and research."[17]

The bishops also recognize the existence of a new stage in the relationships between Catholic higher education and the American Church:

> At present, cordial, fruitful, and continuing dialogue on the complex questions of the relationship of the Catholic college or university to the Church is proceeding between representatives of such schools and others officially concerned with Catholic education. The entire Catholic community stands to benefit from this continued exploration.[18]

It is indeed the spirit of Vatican II—at once reconciling and vivifying— that animates this relationship. What the Congress of Rome called for in November 1972 has already begun to assume form in the United States. "Catholic universities can rightfully expect inspiration, encouragement, and support from the Hierarchy in carrying out their difficult task. For their part, the universities will seek to promote a frank and confident collaboration with Church authorities, knowing that it is only in the context of the Church that they can accomplish their specifically Catholic mission."[19]

A joint committee of American bishops and college and university representatives, which has been chaired by Archbishop William D. Borders of Baltimore, is a new and already successful forum for fruitful dialogue on issues of common concern. In an atmosphere of candor and mutual understanding, both bishops and presidents recognize the peculiarly American aspects of the colleges and universities, and the need to consider and implement Catholic principles of higher learning within that cultural reality.

B. Type of Relationships

Since the colleges and universities in the United States have received their charters from the respective state governments and have independent legal existence as private, non-profit educational institutions, the notion of canonical establishment by the Holy See has never been thought of as typical or standard in the United States. In the spirit of Vatican Council II and with the long history we have had in providing a genuine Catholic educational experience in an American framework, we believe the word "cooperation" or the phrase "mutual respect and support" best characterizes the kind of relationship that should exist between institution and Church.

"The Church has always had the duty of scrutinizing the signs of the times," we are admonished in *Gaudium et Spes*.[20] This warning has special relevance to our present discussion. If it is difficult for us to envision new relationships between Church and university, "it happens," according to one perceptive analyst, "because we remain captive of a mentality that knew only one form of being a Catholic university; it was the form of jurisdictional relationship to the hierarchy."[21] This writer, Father Ladislas Orsy, S.J., in his memorable address at the N.C.E.A. annual meeting in 1974, called for the relationship between Church and university to be described as a *communio*, which would allow for both healthy distance and the needed closeness. The *communio* would be a "union, not imposed by any one, wanted by everyone."[22]

Indeed, this direction seems to be the one pointed out by the Council Fathers if their vision of the Church and its relations with the world is applied to the present subject. Several statements from *Gaudium et Spes* reflect this new vision of reality:

> The human race has passed from a rather static concept of reality to a more dynamic, evolutionary one.[23]

> Only in freedom can man direct himself towards goodness. Our contemporaries make much of this freedom and pursue it eagerly; and rightly so, to be sure. . . . For its part, authentic freedom is an exceptional sign of the divine image within man.[24]

In speaking of a rightful independence of earthly affairs, the Fathers state, "We cannot but deplore certain habits of mind, sometimes found too among Christians, which do not sufficiently attend to the rightful independence of science.[25]

The language of "juridical relationship" and "canonical establishment" found in recent documents from the Congregation for Catholic Education does not seem to find focus in the vocabulary and the substance—and, indeed, the spirit—of Vatican Council documents and declarations. The former appears to conceive of the university as "an arm of the Church," rather than the locus for interplay between Church and world, a canonical and juridical concept rather than the dialogue approach of *Gaudium et Spes*.

We do not think a juridical relationship between the Church and Catholic institutions in the exercise of their proper autonomy is desirable or even possible at this stage of American history, given the prominence of church-state issues. Since we have been asked to comment on the forthcoming conference in Rome in 1976 concerning "an academic law of the Church," we do not consider appropriate nor legally feasible the extension of jurisdiction over noncanonically established institutions, at the expense of existing rights of local bishops or the institutions themselves.

It is our collective experience that the Rome 1972 document clearly identifies the essential characteristics of American Catholic colleges and universities. We concur that "all universities [and colleges] that realize these fundamental conditions are Catholic universities, whether canonically erected or not."[26] We cannot speak for Catholic institutions in other lands; their circumstances and cultures differ from ours. We can only say that juridical, canonical, statutory relationships which would infringe upon proper institutional autonomy are not in keeping with our circumstances, and would make no positive contribution to our efforts to maintain and strengthen Catholic higher education and its service to the American Church.

C. ATTITUDE OF THE COLLEGES AND UNIVERSITIES

The leadership in American colleges and universities is devoted to the teaching of authentic Catholic doctrine as it is authoritatively defined and proclaimed by the magisterium.[27] We acknowledge the value of close and trusting relationships among the bishops, the theologians, and the administrative heads of the institutions. We support the responsibility of the magisterium to guide through its proclamation of the faith those who teach theology and related disciplines, as our bishops have pointed out in *To Teach As Jesus Did*, and the Council Fathers noted in the *Decree on the Apostolate of the Laity*.[28] We recognize that at times a bishop may need to issue warnings (even publicly) as a last resort if he discovers after careful study and consultation that doctrine is taught inconsistent with that presented for our belief by the magisterium.[29] It is unlikely that this would often be necessary if bishops and theologians maintain dialogue about theological teachings. It is also possible that representatives of the bishops and of Catholic higher education could be called upon to conciliate where differences arise between a particular institution and a local bishop.

In other words, the members of the Church who are engaged in the higher education apostolate do not wish to have the role and responsibility of the bishop diminished or circumscribed. These Catholic leaders do not want the role of the academy compromised either. Infringements on the freedom of college and university faculty to teach the results of their study and research would destroy the opportunity for the college to make its contribution to the Church. Freedom from outside constraints is the very breath of life for a college and university. An authentic Catholic institution of higher learning must be free to be Catholic.[30] If the integrity and freedom of the academy is attacked, undermined by "an academic law of the Church," the Church will be the first to suffer. Its enemies will contend derisively that truth cannot be upheld and defended without resort to penalties and outside sanctions, confirming for some the suspicion that Catholic institutions cannot be true universities. Catholic colleges and universities in the United States cannot deprive faculty members of their civil rights as defined by American law, nor limit their academic rights which are supported by accrediting and other professional associations, without severe penalty to the institutions, not least of which would be the loss of prestige and influence in American society and particularly in the American intellectual community.

We hope it is evident that it is precisely our loyalty to the Church and our dedication to its doctrine that leads us to prefer a relationship of service to a juridical relationship with the official Church as the recommended way to relate Church to university and college in the United States at this point in our history. What we are claiming is that there is a way to maintain intact the Catholic character of the university and to witness the faith, a way for bishops to exercise leadership in the field of higher education, a way to serve the Church through service rather than through mechanisms of control which are out of character with the American experience and out of character for American scholars and teachers. Inappropriate control and supervision procedures could weaken if not destroy the very institutions which are seeking to strengthen their unique service to the Church and to American society.

VI. CONCLUSION

We propose to find in close collaboration with our bishops and the American Church, contemporary models of relationships which will serve the Church community effectively in our times. Cooperation in an atmosphere of trust and respect will enable us to respond to the serious problems of secularization which afflict our age and exert pressures on Catholic higher education.[31]

At issue is not whether orthodoxy and Christian standards of behavior (among both faculty and students) should prevail, but rather how they are to be achieved without destruction of institutional and personal freedoms, in accord with the mission the Church has given itself through the Vatican Council documents and its recent policies.

We propose in the United States to make a new effort to improve our colleges and universities in every way, not least in the quality and extent of service given to the Church and the world. We believe that a newly vitalized Catholic college and university can evolve from the sincere efforts of loyal sons and daughters of the Church to cooperate with American episcopal leaders. We dedicate ourselves to this task, and we are confident that we have the support of the vast majority of the American bishops as we do so. Our joint efforts will be made easier with the support of the Congregation for Catholic Education, recognizing our fidelity to the Church and, particularly, our knowledge of how to administer Catholic institutions in the context of the American system of higher education and in close collaboration with the American bishops.

NOTES

1. "The Catholic University in the Modern World," document of the Second Congress of Delegates of the Catholic Universities of the World, Rome, November, 1972. Published in the *College Newsletter*, National Catholic Educational Association, vol. XXXV, no. 3, March, 1973, paragraph #39.

2. Ibid., paragraph #1.

3. Pope Paul VI to the Jesuit presidents, Rome, August 6, 1975 (translation provided by the Association of Jesuit Colleges and Universities, Washington, D.C.), paragraph #64.

4. Pastoral Message on Catholic Education, National Conference of Catholic Bishops, November 1972. Published 1973 by Publications Office, United States Catholic Conference, entitled *To Teach As Jesus Did*.

5. "The Catholic University in the Modern World," op. cit., paragraph #56.

6. *To Teach As Jesus Did*, op. cit., paragraph #81.

7. Ibid., paragraph #80.

8. Cf. "The Catholic University in the Modern World," paragraphs #10–11.

9. To the Jesuits, loc. cit., p. 4.

10. ". . . the pastoral care of the university youth is a matter of extreme urgency." Pope Paul VI, loc. cit., p. 5. Also *To Teach As Jesus Did*, op. cit., paragraphs #66–72. Also "The Catholic University in the Modern World," op. cit., paragraphs #42–43.

11. Cf. Vatican Council *Declaration on Christian Education*, paragraph #10.

12. Pope Paul VI, loc. cit.

13. Cf. Charles H. Wilson, *Tilton v. Richardson, The Search for Sectarianism in Education*, Washington, D.C., The Association of American Colleges, 1971, p. 44.

14. For example, the 1974 annual meeting of the College and University Department, N.C.E.A.—"Interaction Between University and Church," Ladislas Orsy, S.J., *Delta Epsilon Sigma Bulletin*, Loras College, Dubuque, Iowa, vol. XIX, no. 2, May 1974. Also, 1973 annual meeting of the College and University Department, N.C.E.A.—Two papers on "How Is a College or University Catholic in Practice?", James Hitchcock and Frederick Crosson, *Delta Epsilon Sigma Bulletin*, vol. XX, no. 2, May 1975.

15. The Rome 1972 document, frequently referred to, has several excellent sections on the need for research in Catholic universities to provide a distinctive service to the Church. Cf. paragraphs #25, 26, 27, 47.

16. *To Teach As Jesus Did*, paragraph #80.

17. Ibid., paragraph #74.

18. Ibid., paragraph #76.

19. Ibid., paragraph #51.

20. Vatican Council, *Declaration on the Church and the Modern World*, paragraph #4.

21. Orsy, op. cit., p. 49.

22. Ibid., p. 48.

23. *Gaudium et Spes*, paragraph #5.

24. Ibid., paragraph #17.

25. Ibid., paragraph #36.

26. "The Catholic University in the Modern World," paragraph #1.

27. Cf. Ibid., paragraph #56.

28. "Theological research and speculation which are entirely legitimate and commendable enterprises, deal with divine revelation as their source and material, and the results of such investigation are therefore subject to the judgment of the magisterium." *To Teach As Jesus Did*, paragraph #75. *Declaration on the Apostolate of the Laity*, paragraph #24.

29. Cf. "The Catholic University in the Modern World," op. cit., paragraph #58–59.

30. Cf. Ibid., paragraph #20–21.

31. "In some Catholic universities in recent years an opinion gained ground that they could respond better to the questionings of modern man and the world if their mark and stance as Catholic were glossed over. And the consequences? We saw a fading of Christian values and their substitution by a humanism that was then transformed into a true and proper secularization. We saw also a lowered tone of behavior in the ambit of the university campus, to the point that young people were losing sight of the appeal of many Christian virtues." Pope Paul VI, loc. cit.

Sapientia Christiana, John Paul II

with the Norms of Application of the Sacred Congregation for Catholic Education

FOREWORD

I

Christian wisdom, which the Church teaches by divine authority, continuously inspires the faithful of Christ zealously to endeavour to relate human affairs and activities with religious values in a single living synthesis. Under the direction of these values all things are mutually connected for the glory of God and the integral development of the human person, a development that includes both corporal and spiritual well-being.[1]

Indeed, the Church's mission of spreading the Gospel not only demands that the Good News be preached ever more widely and to ever greater numbers of men and women, but that the very power of the Gospel should permeate thought patterns, standards of judgment, and norms of behavior; in a word, it is necessary that the whole of human culture be steeped in the Gospel.[2]

The cultural atmosphere in which a human being lives has a great influence upon his or her way of thinking and, thus, of acting. Therefore, a division between faith and culture is more than a small impediment to evangelization, while a culture penetrated with the Christian spirit is an instrument that favors the spreading of the Good News.

Furthermore, the Gospel is intended for all peoples of every age and land and is not bound exclusively to any particular culture. It is valid for pervading all cultures so as to illumine them with the light of divine revelation and to purify human conduct, renewing them in Christ.

For this reason, the Church of Christ strives to bring the Good News to every sector of humanity so as to be able to convert the consciences of human beings, both individually and collectively, and to fill with the light of the Gospel their works and undertakings, their entire lives, and, indeed, the whole of the social environment in which they are engaged. In this way the Church carries out her mission of evangelizing also by advancing human culture.[3]

II

In this activity of the Church with regard to culture, Catholic universities have had and still have special importance. By their nature they aim to secure that "the Christian outlook should acquire a public, stable, and universal influence in the whole process of the promotion of higher culture."[4]

In fact, as my predecessor Pope Pius XI recalled in the preface to the Apostolic Constitution *Deus Scientiarum Dominus,*[5] there arose within the Church, from her earliest period, *didascaleia* for imparting instruction in Christian wisdom so that people's lives and conduct might be formed. From these houses of Christian wisdom the most illustrious Fathers and Doctors of the Church, teachers and ecclesiastical writers drew their knowledge.

With the passing of centuries schools were established in the neighborhood of cathedrals and monasteries, thanks especially to the zealous initiatives of bishops and monks. These schools imparted both ecclesiastical doctrine and secular culture, forming them into one whole. From these schools arose the universities, those glorious institutions of the Middle Ages which, from their beginning, had the Church as their most bountiful mother and patroness.

Subsequently, when civil authorities, to promote the common good, began and developed their own universities, the Church, loyal to her very nature, did not desist from founding and favoring such kinds of centers of learning and institutions of instruction. This is shown by the considerable number of Catholic universities established in recent times in nearly all parts of the world. Conscious of her worldwide salvific mission, the Church wishes to be especially joined to these centers of higher learning and she desires that they flourish everywhere and work effectively to make Christ's true message present in the field of human culture and to make it advance in that field.

In order that Catholic universities might better achieve this goal, my predecessor Pope Pius XII sought to stimulate their united activity when, by his Apostolic Brief of 27 July 1949 he formally established the International Federation of Catholic Universities. It was "to include all Athenaea which the Holy See either has canonically erected or will in the future erect in the world, or will have explicitly recognized as following the norms of Catholic teaching and as completely in conformity with that teaching."[6]

The Second Vatican Council, for this reason, did not hesitate to affirm that "the Church devotes considerable care to schools of higher learning," and it strongly recommended that Catholic universities should "be established in suitable locations throughout the world" and that "the students of these institutions should be truly outstanding in learning, ready to shoulder duties of major responsibility in society and to witness to the faith before the world."[7] As the Church well knows, "the future of society and of the Church herself is closely bound up with the development of young people engaged in higher studies."[8]

III

It is not surprising, however, that among Catholic universities the Church has always promoted with special care *ecclesiastical faculties and universities,* which is to say those concerned particularly with Christian revelation and questions connected therewith and which are therefore more closely connected with her mission of evangelization.

In the first place, the Church has entrusted to these faculties the task of preparing with special care students for the priestly ministry, for teaching the sacred sciences, and for the more arduous tasks of the apostolate. It is also the task of these faculties "to explore more profoundly the various areas of the sacred disciplines so that day by day a deeper understanding of sacred revelation will be developed, the heritage of Christian wisdom handed down by our ancestors will be more plainly brought into view, dialogue will be fostered with our separated brothers and sisters and with non-Christians, and solutions will be found for problems raised by doctrinal progress."[9]

In fact, new sciences and new discoveries pose new problems that involve the sacred disciplines and demand an answer. While carrying out their primary duty of attaining through theological research a deeper grasp of revealed truth, those engaged in the sacred sciences should therefore maintain contact with scholars of other disciplines, whether these are believers or not, and should try to evaluate and interpret the latters' affirmations and judge them in the light of revealed truth.[10]

From this assiduous contact with reality, theologians are also encouraged to seek a more suitable way of communicating doctrine to their contemporaries working in other various fields of knowledge, for "the deposit of faith, or the truths contained in our venerable doctrine, is one thing; quite another is the way in which these truths are formulated, while preserving the same sense and meaning."[11] This will be very useful so that among the People of God religious practice and uprightness of soul may proceed at an equal pace with the progress of science and technology, and so that, in pastoral work, the faithful may be gradually led to a purer and more mature life of faith.

The possibility of a connection with the mission of evangelization also exists in faculties of other sciences which, although lacking a special link with Christian revelation, can still help considerably in the work of evangelizing. These are looked at by the Church precisely under this aspect when they are erected as ecclesiastical faculties. They therefore have a particular relationship with the Church's Hierarchy.

Thus, the Apostolic See, in carrying out its mission, is clearly aware of its right and duty to erect and promote ecclesiastical faculties dependent on itself, either with a separate existence or as parts of universities, faculties destined for the education of both ecclesiastical and lay students. This See is very desirous that the whole People of God, under the guidance of their Shepherds, should cooperate to ensure that these centers of learning contribute effectively to the growth of the faith and of Christian life.

IV

Ecclesiastical faculties—which are ordered to the common good of the Church and have a valuable relationship with the whole ecclesial community—ought to be conscious of their importance in the Church and of their participation in the ministry of the Church. Indeed, those faculties which treat of matters that are close to Christian revelation should also be mindful of the orders which Christ, the Supreme Teacher, gave to his Church regarding this ministry: "Go therefore and make disciples of all nations, baptizing them in the name of the Father and of the Son and of the Holy Spirit, teaching them to observe all that I have commanded you" (*Mt* 28: 19–20). From this it follows that there must be in these faculties that adherence by which they are joined to the full doctrine of Christ, whose authentic guardian and interpreter has always been through the ages the Magisterium of the Church.

Bishops' Conferences in the individual nations and regions where these faculties exist must diligently see to their care and progress, at the same time that they ceaselessly promote their fidelity to the Church's doctrine, so that these faculties may bear witness before the whole community of the faithful to their wholehearted following of the above-mentioned command of Christ. This witness must always be borne both by the faculty as such and by each and every member of the faculty. Ecclesiastical universities and faculties have been constituted in the Church for the building up and perfecting of Christ's faithful, and they must always bear this in mind as a criterion in the carrying out of their work.

Teachers are invested with very weighty responsibility in fulfilling a special ministry of the word of God and in being instructors of the faith for the young. Let them, above all, therefore be for their students, and for the rest of the faithful, witnesses of the living truth of the Gospel and examples of fidelity to the Church. It is fitting to recall the serious words of Pope Paul VI: "The task of the theologian is carried out with a view to building up ecclesial communion so that the People of God may grow in the experience of faith."[12]

V

To attain these purposes, ecclesiastical faculties should be organized in such a way as to respond to the new demands of the present day. For this reason, the Second Vatican Council stated that their laws should be subjected to revision.[13]

In fact, the Apostolic Constitution *Deus Scientiarum Dominus,* promulgated by my predecessor Pope Pius XI on 24 May 1931, did much in its time to renew higher ecclesiastical studies. However, as a result of changed circumstances, it now needs to be suitably adapted and altered.

In the course of nearly fifty years great changes have taken place not only in civil society but also in the Church herself. Important events, especially the Second Vatican Council, have occurred, events which have affected both the internal life of the Church and her external relationships with Christians of other churches, with non-Christians, and with nonbelievers, as well as with all those in favor of a more human civilization.

In addition, there is a steadily growing interest being shown in the theological sciences, not only among the clergy but also by lay people, who are attending theological schools in increasing numbers. These schools have, as a consequence, greatly multiplied in recent times.

Finally, a new attitude has arisen about the structure of universities and faculties, both civil and ecclesiastical. This is a result of the justified desire for a university life open to greater participation, a desire felt by all those in any way involved in university life.

Nor can one ignore the great *evolution* that has taken place in pedagogical and didactic methods, which call for new ways of organizing studies. Then too there is the closer connection that is being felt more and more between various sciences and disciplines, as well as the desire for greater cooperation in the whole university environment.

To meet these new demands, the Sacred Congregation for Catholic Education, responding to the mandate received from the Council, already in 1967 began to study the question of renewal along the lines indicated by the Council. On 20 May 1968, it promulgated the *Normae quaedam ad Constitutionem Apostolicam "Deus Scientiarum Dominus" de studiis academicis ecclesiasticis recognoscendam,* which has exercised a beneficial influence during recent years.

VI

Now, however, this work needs to be completed and perfected with a new law. This law, abrogating the Apostolic Constitution *Deus Scientiarum Dominus* and the Norms of Application attached to it, as well as the *Normae quaedam* published on 20 May 1968 by the Sacred Congregation for Catholic Education, includes some still valid elements from these documents, while laying down new norms whereby the renewal that has already successfully begun can be developed and completed.

Nobody is unaware of the difficulties that appear to impede the promulgation of a new Apostolic Constitution. In the first place, there is the "passage of time" which brings changes so rapidly that it seems impossible to lay down anything stable and permanent. Then there is the "diversity of places" which seems to call for a *pluralism* which would make it appear almost impossible to issue common norms, valid for all parts of the world.

Since however there exist ecclesiastical faculties throughout the world, which are erected and approved by the Holy See and which grant academic degrees in its name, it is necessary that a certain substantial unity be respected and that the requisites for gaining academic degrees be clearly laid down and have universal value. Things which are necessary and which are foreseen as being relatively stable must be set down by law, while at the same time a proper freedom must be left for introducing into the statutes of the individual faculties further specifications, taking into account varying local conditions and the university customs obtaining in each region. In this way, legitimate progress in academic studies is neither hindered nor restricted, but rather is directed through right channels towards obtaining better results. Moreover, together with the legitimate differentiation of the faculties, the unity of the Catholic Church in these centers of education will also be clear to everyone.

Therefore, the Sacred Congregation for Catholic Education, by command of my predecessor Pope Paul VI, has consulted, first of all, the ecclesiastical universities and faculties themselves, then, the departments of the Roman Curia and the other bodies interested. After this, it established a commission of experts who, under the direction of the same Congregation, have carefully reviewed the legislation covering ecclesiastical academic studies.

This work has now been successfully completed, and Pope Paul VI was about to promulgate this Constitution, as he so ardently desired to do, when he died; likewise Pope John Paul I was prevented by sudden death from doing so. After long and careful consideration of the matter, I decree and lay down, by my apostolic authority, the following laws and norms.

PART ONE: GENERAL NORMS

SECTION I: NATURE AND PURPOSE OF ECCLESIASTICAL UNIVERSITIES AND FACULTIES

Article 1. To carry out the ministry of evangelization given to the Church by Christ, the Church has the right and duty to erect and promote universities and faculties which depend upon herself.

Article 2. In this Constitution the terms *ecclesiastical universities and faculties* mean those which have been canonically erected or approved by the Apostolic See, which foster and teach sacred doctrine and the sciences connected therewith, and which have the right to confer academic degrees by the authority of the Holy See

Article 3. The purpose of ecclesiastical faculties are:
§1. through scientific research to cultivate and promote their own disciplines, and especially to deepen knowledge of Christian revelation and of matters connected with it, to enunciate systematically the truths contained therein, to consider in the light of revelation the most recent progress of the sciences, and to present them to the people of the present day in a manner adapted to various cultures;
§2. to train the students to a level of high qualification in their own disciplines, according to Catholic doctrine, to prepare them properly to face their tasks, and to promote the continuing permanent education of the ministers of the Church;
§3. to collaborate intensely, in accordance with their own nature and in close communion with the Hierarchy, with the local and the universal Church, in the whole work of evangelization.

Article 4. It is the duty of Bishops' Conferences to follow carefully the life and progress of ecclesiastical universities and faculties, because of their special ecclesial importance.

Article 5. The canonical erection or approval of ecclesiastical universities and faculties is reserved to the Sacred Congregation for Catholic Education, which governs them according to law.[14]

Article 6. Only universities and faculties canonically erected or approved by the Holy See and ordered according to the norms of this present Constitution have the right to confer academic degrees which have canonical value, with the exception of the special right of the Pontifical Biblical Commission.[15]

Article 7. The statutes of each university or faculty, which must be drawn up in accordance with the present Constitution, require approval by the Sacred Congregation for Catholic Education.

Article 8. Ecclesiastical faculties erected or approved by the Holy See in nonecclesiastical universities, which confer both canonical and civil academic degrees, must observe the prescriptions of the present Constitution, account being taken of the conventions signed by the Holy See with various nations or with the universities themselves.

Article 9. §1. Faculties which have not been canonically erected or approved by the Holy See may not confer academic degrees having canonical value.

§2. Academic degrees conferred by such faculties, if they are to have value for some canonical effects only, require the recognition of the Sacred Congregation for Catholic Education.

§3. For this recognition, to be given for individual degrees for a special reason, the conditions laid down by the Sacred Congregation must be fulfilled.

Article 10. For the correct carrying out of the present Constitution, the Norms of Application issued by the Sacred Congregation for Catholic Education must be observed.

SECTION II: THE ACADEMIC
COMMUNITY AND ITS GOVERNMENT

Article 11. §1. Since the university or faculty forms a sort of community, all the people in it, either as individuals or as members of councils, must feel, each according to his or her own status, co-responsible for the common good and must strive to work for the institution's goals.

§2. Therefore, their rights and duties within the academic community must be accurately set down in the statutes, to ensure that they are properly exercised within correctly established limits.

Article 12. The Chancellor represents the Holy See to the university or faculty and equally the university or faculty to the Holy See. He promotes the continuation and progress of the university or faculty and he fosters its communion with the local and universal Church.

Article 13. §1. The Chancellor is the Prelate Ordinary on whom the university or faculty legally depends, unless the Holy See established otherwise.

§2. Where conditions favor such a post, it is also possible to have a Vice-Chancellor, whose authority is determined in the statutes.

Article 14. If the Chancellor is someone other than the local Ordinary, the statutory norms are to establish how the Ordinary and the Chancellor carry out their respective offices in mutual accord.

Article 15. The academic authorities are personal and collegial. Personal authorities are, in the first place, the Rector or President and the Dean. The collegial authorities are the various directive organisms or councils of the university or faculty.

Article 16. The statutes of the university or faculty must very carefully set out the names and offices of the academic authorities, determining the way they are designated and their term of office, taking into account both the canonical nature of the individual university or faculty and the university practice in the local area.

Article 17. Those designated as academic authorities are to be people who are truly knowledgeable about university life and, usually, who come from among the teachers of some faculty.

Article 18. The Rector and the President are named, or at least confirmed, by the Sacred Congregation for Catholic Education.

Article 19. §1. The statutes determine how the personal and the collegial authorities are to collaborate with each other, so that, carefully observing the principle of collegiality, especially in more serious matters and above all in those of an academic nature, the persons in authority will enjoy that exercise of power which really corresponds to their office.

§2. This applies, in the first place, to the Rector, who has the duty to govern the entire university and to promote, in a suitable way, its unity, cooperation, and progress.

Article 20. §1. When faculties are parts of an ecclesiastical university, their governance must be coordinated through the statutes with the governance of the entire university in such a way that the good of the single faculties is assured, at the same time that the good of the whole university is promoted and the cooperation of all the faculties with each other is favored.

§2. The canonical exigencies of ecclesiastical faculties must be safeguarded even when such faculties are inserted into nonecclesiastical universities.

Article 21. When a faculty is joined to a seminary or college, the statutes, while always having due concern for cooperation in everything pertaining to the students' good, must clearly and effectively provide that the academic direction and administration of the faculty is correctly distinct from the governance and administration of the seminary or college.

SECTION III: TEACHERS

Article 22. In each faculty there must be a number of teachers, especially permanent ones, which corresponds to the importance and development of the individual disciplines as well as to the proper care and profit of the students.

Article 23. There must be various ranks of teachers, determined in the statutes, according to their measure of preparation, their insertion into the faculty, their permanence, and their responsibility to the faculty, taking into account the university practice of the local area.

Article 24. The statutes are to define which authorities are responsible for hiring, naming and promoting teachers, especially when it is a question of giving them a permanent position.

Article 25. §1. To be legitimately hired as a permanent teacher in a faculty, a person must:
1) be distinguished by wealth of knowledge, witness of life, and a sense of responsibility;
2) have a suitable doctorate or equivalent title or exceptional and singular scientific accomplishment;
3) show documentary proof of suitability for doing scientific research, especially by a published dissertation;
4) demonstrate teaching ability.
§2. These requirements for taking on permanent teachers must be applied also, in proportionate measure, for hiring nonpermanent ones.
§3. In hiring teachers, the scientific requirements in current force in the university practice of the local area should be taken into account. .

Article 26. §1. All teachers of every rank must be marked by an upright life, integrity of doctrine, and devotion to duty, so that they can effectively contribute to the proper goals of an ecclesiastical faculty.
§2. Those who teach matters touching on faith and morals are to be conscious of their duty to carry out their work in full communion with the authentic Magisterium of the Church, above all, with that of the Roman Pontiff.[16]

Article 27. §1. Those who teach disciplines concerning faith or morals must receive, after making their profession of faith, a canonical mission from the Chancellor or his delegate, for they do not teach on their own authority but by virtue of the mission they have received from the Church. The other teachers must receive permission to teach from the Chancellor or his delegate.

§2. All teachers, before they are given a permanent post or before they are promoted to the highest category of teacher, or else in both cases, as the statutes are to state, must receive a declaration of *nihil obstat* from the Holy See.

Article 28. Promotion to the higher ranks of teachers is to take place only after a suitable interval of time and with due reference to teaching skill, to research accomplished, to the publication of scientific works, to the spirit of cooperation in teaching and in research, and to commitment to the faculty.

Article 29. The teachers, in order to carry out their tasks satisfactorily, must be free from other employment which cannot be reconciled with their duty to do research and to instruct, according to what the statutes require for each rank of teacher.

Article 30. The statutes must state:

a) when and under which conditions a teaching post ends;

b) for what reasons and in which ways a teacher can be suspended, or even deprived of his post, so as to safeguard suitably the rights of the teachers, of the faculty or university, and, above all, of the students and also of the ecclesial community.

SECTION IV: STUDENTS

Article 31. Ecclesiastical faculties are open to all, whether ecclesiastics or laity, who can legally give testimony to leading a moral life and to having completed the previous studies appropriate to enrolling in the faculty.

Article 32. §1. To enroll in a faculty in order to obtain an academic degree, one must present that kind of study title which would be necessary to permit enrollment in a civil university of one's own country or of the country where the faculty is located.

§2. The faculty, in its own statutes, should determine what, besides what is contained in §1 above, is needed for entrance into its course of study, including ancient and modern language requirements.

Article 33. Students must faithfully observe the laws of the faculty about the general program and about discipline—in the first place about the study program, class attendance, and examinations—as well as all that pertains to the life of the faculty.

Article 34. The statutes should define how the students, either individually or collectively, take part in the university community life in those aspects which can contribute to the common good of the faculty or university.

Article 35. The statutes should equally determine how the students can for serious reasons be suspended from certain rights or be deprived of them or even be expelled from the faculty, in such a way that the rights of the students, of the faculty or university, and also of the ecclesial community are appropriately protected.

SECTION V: OFFICIALS AND STAFF ASSISTANTS

Article 36. §1. In governing and administering a university or faculty, the authorities are to be assisted by officials trained for various tasks.

§2. The officials are, first of all, the Secretary, the Librarian, and the Financial Procurator.

Article 37. There should also be other staff assistants who have the task of vigilance, order, and other duties, according to the needs of the university or faculty.

SECTION VI: STUDY PROGRAM

Article 38. §1. In arranging the studies, the principles and norms which for different matters are contained in ecclesiastical documents, especially those of the Second Vatican Council, must be carefully observed. At the same time account must be taken of sound advances coming from scientific progress which can contribute to answering the questions being currently asked.

§2. In the single faculties let that scientific method be used which corresponds to the needs of the individual sciences. Up-to-date didactic and teaching methods should be applied in an appropriate way, in order to bring about the personal involvement of the students and their suitable, active participation in their studies.

Article 39. §1. Following the norm of the Second Vatican Council, according to the nature of each faculty:

1) just freedom[17] should be acknowledged in research and teaching so that true progress can be obtained in learning and understanding divine truth;

2) at the same time it is clear that:

a) true freedom in teaching is necessarily contained within the limits of God's Word, as this is constantly taught by the Church's Magisterium;

b) likewise, true freedom in research is necessarily based upon firm adherence to God's Word and deference to the Church's Magisterium, whose duty it is to interpret authentically the Word of God.

§2. Therefore, in such a weighty matter one must proceed with prudence, with trust, and without suspicion, at the same time with judgment and without rashness, especially in teaching, while working to harmonize studiously the necessities of science with the pastoral needs of the People of God.

Article 40. In each faculty the curriculum of studies is to be suitably organized in steps or cycles, adapted to the material. These are usually as follows:

a) first, a general instruction is imparted, covering a coordinated presentation of all the disciplines, along with an introduction into scientific methodology;

b) next, one section of the disciplines is studied more profoundly, at the same time that the students practice scientific research more fully;

c) finally, there is progress toward scientific maturity, especially through a written work which truly makes a contribution to the advance of the science.

Article 41. §1. The disciplines which are absolutely necessary for the faculty to achieve its purposes should be determined. Those also should be set out which in a different way are helpful to these purposes and, therefore, how these are suitably distinguished one from another.

§2. In each faculty the disciplines should be arranged in such a way that they form an organic body, so as to serve the solid and coherent formation of the students and to facilitate collaboration by the teachers.

Article 42. Lectures, especially in the basic cycle, must be given, and the students must attend them, according to the norms to be determined in the statutes.

Article 43. Practical exercises and seminars, mainly in the specialization cycle, must be assiduously carried on under the direction of the teachers. These ought to be constantly complemented by private study and frequent discussions with the teachers.

Article 44. The statutes of the faculty are to define which examinations or which equivalent tests the students are to take, whether written or oral, at the end of the semester, of the year, and especially of the cycle, so that their ability can be verified in regard to continuing in the faculty and in regard to receiving academic degrees.

Article 45. Likewise the statutes are to determine what value is to be given for studies taken elsewhere, especially in regard to being dispensed from some disciplines or examinations or even in regard to reducing the curriculum, always, however, respecting the prescriptions of the Sacred Congregation for Catholic Education.

Section VII: Academic degrees

Article 46. §1. After each cycle of the curriculum of studies, the suitable academic degree can be conferred, which must be established for each faculty, with attention given to the duration of the cycle and to the disciplines taught in it.

§2. Therefore, according to the general and special norms of this Constitution, all degrees conferred and the conditions under which they are conferred are to be determined in the statutes of the individual faculties.

Article 47. §1. The academic degrees conferred by an ecclesiastical faculty are: baccalaureate, licentiate, and doctorate.

§2. Special qualifications can be added to the names of these degrees according to the diversity of faculties and the order of studies in the individual faculties.

Article 48. Academic degrees can be given different names in the statutes of the individual faculties, taking account of the university practice in the local area, indicating, however, with clarity the equivalence these have with the names of the academic degrees above and maintaining uniformity among the ecclesiastical faculties of the same area.

Article 49. §1. Nobody can obtain an academic degree unless properly enrolled in a faculty, completing the course of studies prescribed by the statutes, and successfully passing the examinations or tests.

§2. Nobody can be admitted to the doctorate unless first having obtained the licentiate.

§3. A requisite for obtaining a doctorate, furthermore, is a doctoral dissertation that makes a real contribution to the progress of science, written under the direction of a teacher, publicly defended and collegially approved; the principal part, at least, must be published.

Article 50. §1. The doctorate is the academic degree which enables one to teach in a faculty and which is therefore required for this purpose; the licentiate is the academic degree which enables one to teach in a major seminary or equivalent school and which is therefore required for this purpose.

§2. The academic degrees which are required for filling various ecclesiastical posts are to be stated by the competent ecclesiastical authority.

Article 51. An honorary doctorate can be conferred for special scientific merit or cultural accomplishment in promoting the ecclesiastical sciences.

SECTION VIII: MATTERS RELATING TO TEACHING

Article 52. In order to achieve its proper purposes, especially in regard to scientific research, each university or faculty must have an adequate library, in keeping with the needs of the staff and students. It must be correctly organized and equipped with an appropriate catalogue.

Article 53. Through an annual allotment of money, the library must continually acquire books, old and new, as well as the principal reviews, so as to be able effectively to serve research, teaching of the disciplines, instructional needs, and the practical exercises and seminars.

Article 54. The library must be headed by a trained librarian, assisted by a suitable council. The librarian participates opportunely in the council of the university or faculty.

Article 55. §1. The faculty must also have technical equipment, audiovisual materials, etc., to assist its didactic work.

§2. In relationship to the special nature and purpose of a university or faculty, research institutions and scientific laboratories should also be available, as well as other apparatus needed for the accomplishment of its ends.

SECTION IX: ECONOMIC MATTERS

Article 56. A university or faculty must have enough money to achieve its purposes properly. Its financial endowments and its property rights are to be carefully described.

Article 57. The statutes are to determine the duty of the financial procurator as well as the part the rector or president and the university or faculty council play in money matters, according to the norms of good economics and so as to preserve healthy administration.

Article 58. Teachers, officials, and staff assistants are to be paid a suitable remuneration, taking account of the customs of the local area, and also taking into consideration social security and insurance protection.

Article 59. Likewise, the statutes are to determine the general norms that will indicate the ways the students are to contribute to the expenses of the university or faculty, by paying admission fees, yearly tuition, examination fees, and diploma fees.

SECTION X: PLANNING AND COOPERATION OF FACULTIES

Article 60. §1. Great care must be given to the distribution, or as it is called, the planning of universities and faculties, so as to provide for their conservation, their progress, and their suitable distribution in different parts of the world.

§2. To accomplish this end, the Sacred Congregation for Catholic Education is to be helped by advice from the Bishops' Conferences and from a commission of experts.

Article 61. The erection or approval of a new university or faculty is decided upon by the Sacred Congregation for Catholic Education when all the requirements are fulfilled. In this the Congregation listens to the local Ordinaries, the Bishops' Conference, and experts, especially from neighboring faculties.

Article 62. §1. Affiliation of some institution with a faculty for the purpose of being able to grant the bachelor's degree is approved by the Sacred Congregation for Catholic Education, after the conditions established by that same Sacred Congregation are fulfilled.

§2. It is highly desirable that theological study centers, whether diocesan or religious, be affiliated to a faculty of sacred theology.

Article 63. Aggregation to a faculty and incorporation into a faculty by an institution for the purposes of also granting higher academic degrees is decided upon by the Sacred Congregation for Catholic Education, after the conditions established by that same Sacred Congregation are fulfilled.

Article 64. Cooperation between faculties, whether of the same university or of the same region or of a wider territorial area, is to be diligently striven for. For this cooperation is of great help to the scientific research of the teachers and to the better formation of the students. It also fosters the advance of interdisciplinary collaboration, which appears ever more necessary in current times, as well as contributing to the development of complementarity among faculties. It also helps to bring about the penetration by Christian wisdom of all culture.

PART TWO: SPECIAL NORMS

Article 65. Besides the norms common to all ecclesiastical faculties, which are established in the first part of this Constitution, special norms are given hereunder for certain of those faculties, because of their particular nature and importance for the Church.

SECTION I: FACULTY OF SACRED THEOLOGY

Article 66. A faculty of sacred theology has the aim of profoundly studying and systematically explaining, according to the scientific method proper to it, Catholic doctrine, derived with the greatest care from divine revelation. It has the further aim of carefully seeking the solution to human problems in the light of that same revelation.

Article 67. §1. The study of sacred scripture is, as it were, the soul of sacred theology, which rests upon the written Word of God together with living Tradition, as its perpetual foundation.[18]

§2. The individual theological disciplines are to be taught in such a way that, from their internal structure and from the proper object of each as well as from their connection with other disciplines, including philosophical ones and the sciences of man, the basic unity of theological instruction is quite clear, and in such a way that all the disciplines converge in a profound understanding of the mystery of Christ, so that this can be announced with greater effectiveness to the People of God and to all nations.

Article 68. §1. Revealed truth must be considered also in connection with contemporary, evolving, scientific accomplishments, so that it can be seen "how faith and reason give harmonious witness to the unity of all truth."[19] Also, its exposition is to be such that, without any change of the truth, there is adaptation to the nature and character of every culture, taking special account of the philosophy and the wisdom of various peoples. However, all syncretism and every kind of false particularism are to be excluded.[20]

§2. The positive values in the various cultures and philosophies are to be sought out, carefully examined, and taken up. However, systems and methods incompatible with Christian faith must not be accepted.

Article 69. Ecumenical questions are to be carefully treated, according to the norms of competent Church authorities.[21] Also to be carefully considered are relationships with non-Christian religions; and problems arising from contemporary atheism are to be scrupulously studied.

Article 70. In studying and teaching Catholic doctrine, fidelity to the Magisterium of the Church is always to be emphasized. In the carrying out of teaching duties, especially in the basic cycle, those things are, above all, to be imparted which belong to the received patrimony of the Church. Hypothetical or personal opinions which come from new research are to be modestly presented as such.

Article 71. In presenting doctrine, those norms are to be followed which are in the documents of the Second Vatican Council,[22] as well as those found in more recent documents of the Holy See[23] insofar as these pertain to academic studies.

Article 72. The curriculum of studies of a faculty of sacred theology comprises:

a) the first cycle, fundamentals, which lasts for five years or ten semesters, or else, when a previous two-year philosophy course is an entrance requirement, for three years. Besides a solid philosophical formation, which is a necessary propaedeutic for theological studies, the theological disciplines must be taught in such a way that what is presented is an organic exposition of the whole of Catholic doctrine, together with an introduction to theological scientific methodology.

The cycle ends with the academic degree of baccalaureate or some other suitable degree as the statutes of the faculty determine.

b) the second cycle, specialization, which lasts for two years or four semesters. In this cycle the special disciplines are taught corresponding to the nature of the diverse specializations being undertaken. Also seminars and practical exercises are conducted for the acquisition of the ability to do scientific research.

The cycle concludes with the academic degree of a specialized licentiate.

c) the third cycle, in which for a suitable period of time scientific formation is brought to completion, especially through the writing of a doctoral dissertation.

The cycle concludes with the academic degree of doctorate.

Article 73. §1. To enroll in a faculty of sacred theology, the student must have done the previous studies called for in accordance with article 32 of this Constitution.

§2. Where the first cycle of the faculty lasts for only three years, the student must submit proof of having properly completed a two-year course in philosophy at a faculty of philosophy or at an approved institution.

Article 74. §1. A faculty of sacred theology has the special duty of taking care of the scientific theological formation of those preparing for the priesthood or preparing to hold some ecclesiastical office.

§2. For this purpose, special courses suitable for seminarians should be offered. It is also appropriate for the faculty itself to offer the "pastoral year" required for the priesthood, in addition to the five-year basic cycle. At the end of this year, a special diploma may be conferred.

SECTION II: FACULTY OF CANON LAW

Article 75. A faculty of canon law, whether Latin or Oriental, has the aim of cultivating and promoting the juridical disciplines in the light of the law of the Gospel and of deeply instructing the students in these, so as to form researchers, teachers, and others who will be trained to hold special ecclesiastical posts.

Article 76. The curriculum of studies of a faculty of canon law comprises:

a) the first cycle, lasting at least one year or two semesters, in which are studied the general fundamentals of canon law and those disciplines which are required for higher juridical formation;

b) the second cycle, lasting two years or four semesters, during which the entire Code of Canon Law is studied in depth, along with other disciplines having an affinity with it;

c) the third cycle, lasting at least a year or two semesters, in which juridical formation is completed and a doctoral dissertation is written.

Article 77. §1. With regard to the studies prescribed for the first cycle, the faculty may make use of the studies done in another faculty and which it can acknowledge as responding to its needs.

§2. The second cycle concludes with the licentiate and the third with the doctorate.

§3. The statutes of the faculty are to define the special requirements for the conferring of the academic degrees, observing the Norms of Application of the Sacred Congregation for Catholic Education.

Article 78. To enroll in a faculty of canon law, the student must have done the previous studies called for in accordance with Article 32 of this Constitution.

SECTION III: FACULTY OF PHILOSOPHY

Article 79. §1. An ecclesiastical faculty of philosophy has the aim of investigating philosophical problems according to scientific methodology, basing itself on a heritage of perennially valid philosophy.[24] It has to search for solutions in the light of natural reason and, furthermore, it has to demonstrate their consistency with the Christian view of the world, of man, and of God, placing in a proper light the relationship between philosophy and theology.

§2. Then, the students are to be instructed so as to make them ready to teach and to fill other suitable intellectual posts as well as to prepare them to promote Christian culture and to undertake a fruitful dialogue with the people of our time.

Article 80. In the teaching of philosophy, the relevant norms should be observed which are contained in the documents of the Second Vatican Council[25] and in other recent documents of the Holy See concerning academic studies.[26]

Article 81. The curriculum of studies of a faculty of philosophy comprises:

a) the first cycle, basics, in which for two years or four semesters an organic exposition of the various parts of philosophy is imparted, which includes treating the world, man, and God. It also includes the history of philosophy, together with an introduction into the method of scientific research;

b) the second cycle, the beginning of specialization, in which for two years or four semesters through special disciplines and seminars a more profound consideration is imparted in some sector of philosophy;

c) the third cycle, in which for a suitable period of time philosophical maturity is promoted, especially by means of writing a doctoral dissertation.

Article 82. The first cycle ends with the degree of baccalaureate, the second with the specialized licentiate, and the third with the doctorate.

Article 83. To enroll in a faculty of philosophy, the student must have done the previous studies called for in accordance with Article 32 of the Constitution.

SECTION IV: OTHER FACULTIES

Article 84. Besides the faculties of sacred theology, canon law, and philosophy, other faculties have been or can be canonically erected, according to the needs of the Church and with a view to attaining certain goals, as for instance:

a) a more profound study of certain sciences which are of greater importance to the theological, juridical, and philosophical disciplines;

b) the promotion of other sciences, first of all the humanities, which have a close connection with the theological disciplines or with the work of evangelization;

c) the cultivation of letters which provide a special help either to a better understanding of Christian revelation or else in carrying on the work of evangelizing;

d) finally, the more exacting preparation both of the clergy and laity for properly carrying out specialized apostolic tasks.

Article 85. In order to achieve the goals set down in the preceding article, the following faculties or institutions "ad instar Facultatis" have already been erected and authorized to grant degrees by the Holy See itself:

- Christian archaeology
- Biblical studies and ancient Eastern studies
- Church history
- Christian and classical literature
- Liturgy
- Missiology
- Sacred music
- Psychology
- Educational science or pedagogy
- Religious science
- Social sciences
- Arabic studies and Islamology
- Medieval studies
- Oriental ecclesiastical studies
- "Utriusque Iuris" (both canon and civil law).

Article 86. It belongs to the Sacred Congregation for Catholic Education to set out, in accordance with circumstances, special norms for these faculties, just as has been done in the above sections for the faculties of sacred theology, canon law, and philosophy.

Article 87. The faculties and institutes for which special norms have not yet been set out must also draw up their own statutes. These must conform to the General Norms established in the first part of this Constitution, and they must take into account the special nature and purpose proper to each of these faculties or institutes.

TRANSITIONAL NORMS

Article 88. This present Constitution comes into effect on the first day of the 1980–1981 academic year or of the 1981 academic year, according to the scholastic calendar in use in various places.

Article 89. Each university or faculty must, before 1 January 1981, present its proper statutes, revised according to this Constitution, to the Sacred Congregation for Catholic Education. If this is not done, its power to give academic degrees is, by this very fact, suspended.

Article 90. In each faculty the studies must be arranged so that the students can acquire academic degrees according to the norms of this Constitution, immediately upon this Constitution coming into effect, preserving the students' previously acquired rights.

Article 91. The statutes are to be approved experimentally for three years so that, when this period is completed, they may be perfected and approved definitively.

Article 92. Those faculties which have a juridical connection with civil authorities may be given a longer period of time to revise their statutes, provided that this is approved by the Sacred Congregation for Catholic Education.

Article 93. It is the task of the Sacred Congregation for Catholic Education, when, with the passage of time, circumstances shall require it, to propose changes to be introduced into this Constitution, so that this same Constitution may be continuously adapted to the needs of ecclesiastical faculties.

Article 94. All laws and customs presently obtaining which are in contradiction to this Constitution are abrogated, whether these are universal or local, even if they are worthy of special or individual mention. Likewise completely abrogated are all privileges hitherto granted by the Holy See to any person, whether physical or moral, if these are contrary to the prescriptions of this Constitution.

It is my will, finally, that this my Constitution be established, be valid, and be efficacious always and everywhere, fully and integrally in all its effects, that it be religiously observed by all to whom it pertains, anything to the contrary notwithstanding. If anyone, knowingly or unknowingly, acts otherwise than I have decreed, I order that this action is to be considered null and void.

Given at Saint Peter's in Rome, the fifteenth day of April, the Solemnity of the Resurrection of our Lord Jesus Christ, in the year 1979, the first of my Pontificate.

Joannes Paulus PP. II

NOTES

1. Cf. Second Vatican Ecumenical Council, Pastoral Constitution on the Church in the Modern World *(Gaudium et Spes)*, 43ff.: *AAS* 58 (1966), pp. 1061ff.

2. Cf. Apostolic Exhortation *Evangelii Nuntiandi*, 19–20: *AAS* 68 (1976), pp. 18f.

3. Cf. *ibid.*, 18: *AAS* 68 (1976), pp. 17f. and also Pastoral Constitution on the Church in the Modern World *(Gaudium et Spes)*, 58: *AAS* 58 (1966), p. 1079.

4. Cf. Second Vatican Ecumenical Council, Declaration on Christian Education *(Gravissimum Educationis)*, 10: *AAS* 58 (1966), p. 737.

5. *AAS* 23 (1931), p. 241.

6. *AAS* 42 (1950), p. 387.

7. Declaration on Christian Education *(Gravissimum Educationis)*, 10: *AAS* 58 (1966), p. 737.

8. Ibid.

9. Ibid. 11: *AAS* 58 (1966), p. 738.

10. Pastoral Constitution on the Church in the Modern World *(Gaudium et Spes)*, 62: *AAS* 58 (1966), p. 1083.

11. Cf. Pope John XXIII, Allocution at the opening of the Second Vatican Ecumenical Council: *AAS* 54 (1962), p. 792 and also the Pastoral Constitution on the Church in the Modern World *(Gaudium et Spes)*, 62: *AAS* 58 (1966), p. 1083.

12. Pope Paul VI, Letter *(Le transfert à Louvian-la-Neuve)* to the rector of the Catholic University of Louvain, 13 September 1975 (cf. *L'Osservatore Romano*, 22–23 September 1975). Also cf. Pope John Paul II, Encyclical Letter *Redemptor Hominis*, 19: *AAS* 71 (1979), pp. 305ff.

13. Declaration on Christian Education *(Gravissimum Educationis)*, 11: *AAS* 58 (1966), p. 738.

14. Cf. Apostolic Constitution *(Regimini Ecclesiae Universae)*, 78: *AAS* 59 (1967), p. 914.

15. Cf. Motu Proprio *(Sedula Cura): AAS* 63 (1971), pp. 665ff. and also the Decree of the Pontifical Biblical Commission *(Ratio Periclitandae Doctrinae):AAS* 67 (1975), pp. 153ff.

16. Cf. Second Vatican Ecumenical Council, Dogmatic Constitution on the Church *(Lumen Gentium)*, 25: *AAS* 57 (1965), pp. 29–31.

17. Second Vatican Ecumenical Council, Pastoral Constitution on the Church in the Modern World *(Gaudium et Spes)*, 59: *AAS* 58 (1966), p. 1080.

18. Second Vatican Ecumenical Council, Dogmatic Constitution on Divine Revelation *(Dei Verbum)*, 24: *AAS* 58 (1966), p. 827.

19. Second Vatican Ecumenical Council, Declaration on Christian Education *(Gravissimum Educationis)*, 10: *AAS* 58 (1966), p. 737.

20. Second Vatican Ecumenical Council, Decree on the Missionary Activity of the Church *(Ad Gentes)*, 22: *AAS* 58 (1966), pp. 973ff.

21. See the Ecumenical Directory, Second Part: *AAS* 62 (1970), pp. 705–724.

22. See especially Second Vatican Ecumenical Council, Dogmatic Constitution on Divine Revelation *(Dei Verbum): AAS* 58 (1966), pp. 713ff.

23. See especially the Letter of Pope Paul VI *Lumen Ecclesiae*, about Saint Thomas Aquinas, of 20 November 1974: *AAS* 66 (1974), pp. 673ff. Also see the circular letters of the Sacred Congregation for Catholic Education: on the Theological Formation of Future Priests, 22 February 1976; on Canon Law Studies in Seminaries, 1 March 1975; and on Philosophical Studies, 20 January 1972.

24. See Second Vatican Ecumenical Council, Decree on Priestly Formation *(Optatam Totius)*, 15: *AAS* 58 (1966), p. 722.

25. Especially see the Second Vatican Council, Decree on Priestly Formation *(Optatam Totius): AAS* 58 (1966), pp. 713ff., and the Declaration on Christian Education *(Gravissimum Educationis): AAS* 58 (1966), pp. 728ff.

26. See especially the letter of Pope Paul VI on Saint Thomas Aquinas *Lumen Ecclesiae* of 20 November 1974: *AAS* 66 (1974), pp. 673ff., and the Circular letter of the Sacred Congregation for Catholic Education, On the Study of Philosophy in Seminaries, of 20 January 1972.

Norms of Application

Of the Sacred Congregation for Catholic Education
for the Correct Implemenation of the
Apostolic Constitution SAPIENTIA CHRISTIANA

The Sacred Congregation for Catholic Education, according to article 10 of the Apostolic Constitution *Sapientia Christiana*, presents to the ecclesiastical universities and faculties the following Norms of Application and orders that they be faithfully observed.

PART ONE: GENERAL NORMS

SECTION I: NATURE AND PURPOSE OF ECCLESIASTICAL UNIVERSITIES AND FACULTIES
(Apostolic Constitution, articles 1–10)

Article 1. By the term *university or faculty* is understood also those athenaea, institutes, or academic centers which have been canonically erected or approved by the Holy See with the right to confer academic degrees by the authority of the same See.

Article 2. With a view to promoting scientific research, a strong recommendation is given for specialized research centers, scientific periodicals and collections, and meetings of learned societies.

Article 3. The tasks for which students can be prepared can be either strictly scientific, such as research or teaching, or else pastoral. Account must be taken of this diversity in the ordering of the studies and in the determining of the academic degrees, while always preserving the scientific nature of the studies for both.

Article 4. Active participation in the ministry of evangelization concerns the action of the Church in pastoral work, in ecumenism, and in missionary undertakings. It also extends to the understanding, defense, and diffusion of the faith. At the same time it extends to the whole context of culture and human society.

Article 5. Bishops' Conferences, joined to the Apostolic See in these matters also, are thus to follow carefully the universities and faculties:

1. together with the Chancellor they are to foster their progress and, while of course respecting the autonomy of science according to the mind of the Second Vatican Council, they are to be solicitous for their scientific and ecclesial condition;

2. with regard to common problems which occur within the boundaries of their own region, they are to help, inspire, and harmonize the activity of the faculties;

3. bearing in mind the needs of the Church and the cultural progress of their own area, they are to take care that there exist an adequate number of such faculties;

4. to do all this, they are to constitute among themselves a commission for this purpose, which could be helped by a committee of experts.

Article 6. In preparing the statutes and study program, the norms in Appendix I of these directives must be kept in mind.

Article 7. §1. The canonical value of an academic degree means that such a degree enables one to assume an office in the Church for which a degree is required. This is, first of all, for teaching sacred sciences in faculties, major seminaries, or equivalent schools.

§2. The conditions to be fulfilled for the recognition of individual degrees mentioned in article 9 of the Apostolic Constitution, concern, first of all, besides the consent of the local or regional ecclesiastical authorities, the college of teachers, the study program, and the scientific helps used.

§3. Degrees thus recognized, for certain canonical effects only, may never be considered simply as equal to canonical degrees.

SECTION II: THE ACADEMIC COMMUNITY AND ITS GOVERNMENT
(Apostolic Constitution, articles 11–21)

Article 8. The duty of the Chancellor is:

1. to promote continually the progress of the university or faculty, to advance scientific progress, to ensure that Catholic doctrine is integrally followed, and to enforce the faithful implementation of the statutes and the prescriptions of the Holy See;

2. to help ensure close relationships between all the different ranks and members of the community;

3. to propose to the Sacred Congregation for Catholic Education the names of those who are to be nominated or confirmed as Rector and

President, as well as the names of the teachers for whom a *nihil obstat* is to be requested;

4. to receive the profession of faith of the Rector and President;

5. to give to or take away from the teachers the canonical mission or permission to teach, according to the norms of the Constitution;

6. to inform the Sacred Congregation for Catholic Education about more important matters and to send to that Congregation every three years a detailed report on the academic, moral, and economic condition of the university or faculty.

Article 9. If the university or faculty depends upon a collegial entity (for instance, on an Episcopal Conference), one designated member of the group is to exercise the office of Chancellor.

Article 10. The local Ordinary, if he is not the Chancellor, since he has the pastoral responsibility for his diocese, is, whenever something in the university or faculty is known to be contrary to doctrine, morals, or ecclesiastical discipline, to take the matter to the Chancellor so that the latter may take action. In case the Chancellor does nothing, the Ordinary may have recourse to the Holy See, without prejudice to his own obligation to provide personally for action in those cases which are more serious or urgent and which carry danger for his diocese.

Article 11. What is contained in article 19 of the Constitution must be explained further in the proper statutes of the individual faculties, giving more weight, as the case may require, either to collegial or else to personal government, while always preserving both forms. Account should be taken of the university practice of the region where the faculty is located or of the religious institute on which the faculty may depend.

Article 12. Besides the university council (academic senate) and the faculty council, both of which must everywhere exist even if under different names, the statutes can suitably establish other special councils or commissions for scientific learning, teaching, discipline, finances, etc.

Article 13. §1. According to the Constitution, a rector is one who presides over a university; a president is one who presides over an institute or a faculty which exists separately; a dean is one who presides over a faculty which is a part of a university.

§2. The statutes are to fix a term of office for these persons (for instance, three years) and are to determine how and how many times their term can be renewed.

Article 14. The office of the rector or president is:

1. to direct, promote, and coordinate all the activity of the academic community;

2. to be the representative of the university or of the institute or faculty existing separately;

3. to convoke the council of the university or of the institute or faculty existing separately and preside over the same according to the norms of the statutes;

4. to watch over the administration of temporalities;

5. to refer more important matters to the Chancellor;

6. to send, every year, a statistical summary to the Sacred Congregation for Catholic Education, according to the outline provided by that same Congregation.

Article 15. The dean of the faculty is:

1. to promote and coordinate all the activity of the faculty, especially matters regarding studies, and to see to providing with due speed for their needs;

2. to convoke the faculty council and preside over it;

3. to admit or exclude students in the name of the rector according to the norms of the statutes;

4. to refer to the rector what is done or proposed by the faculty;

5. to see that the instructions of higher authorities are carried out.

SECTION III: TEACHERS
(Apostolic Constitution, articles 22–30)

Article 16. §1. Teachers who are permanently attached to a faculty are, in the first place, those who are assumed in full and firm right and who are called ordinary professors; next come extraordinary professors. It can also be useful to have others according to university practice.

§2. Besides permanent teachers, there are other teachers who are designated by various titles, in the first place, those invited from other faculties.

§3. Finally, it is also opportune to have teaching assistants to carry out certain academic functions.

Article 17. By a suitable doctorate is meant one that corresponds to the discipline that is being taught. If the discipline is sacred or connected with the sacred, the doctorate must be canonical. In the event that the doctorate is not canonical, the teacher will usually be required to have at least a canonical licentiate.

Article 18. Non-Catholic teachers, co-opted according to the norms of competent ecclesiastical authority,[1] require permission to teach from the Chancellor.

Article 19. §1. The statutes must establish when a permanent status is conferred in relationship with the obtaining of the *nihil obstat* that must be procured in accordance with article 27 of the Constitution.

§2. The *nihil obstat* of the Holy See is the declaration that, in accordance with the Constitution and the special statutes, there is nothing to impede a nomination which is proposed. If some impediment should exist, this will be communicated to the Chancellor who will listen to the teacher in regard to the matter.

§3. If particular circumstances of time or place impede the requesting of the *nihil obstat* from the Holy See, the Chancellor is to take counsel with the Sacred Congregation for Catholic Education to find a suitable solution.

§4. In faculties which are under special concordat law the established norms are to be followed.

Article 20. The time interval between promotions, which must be at least three years, is to be set down in the statutes.

Article 21. §1. Teachers, first of all the permanent ones, are to seek to collaborate with each other. It is also recommended that there be collaboration with the teachers of other faculties, especially those with subjects that have an affinity or some connection with those of the faculty.

§2. One cannot be at one and the same time a permanent teacher in more than one faculty.

Article 22. §1. The statutes are to set out with care the procedure in regard to the suspension or dismissal of a teacher, especially in matters concerning doctrine.

§2. Care must be taken that, first of all, these matters be settled between the rector or president or dean and the teacher himself. If they are not settled there, the matters should be dealt with by an appropriate council or committee, so that the first examination of the facts be carried out within the university or faculty itself. If this is not sufficient, the matters are to be referred to the Chancellor, who, with the help of experts, either of the university or the faculty or from other places, must consider the matter and provide for a solution. The possibility remains open for recourse to the Holy See for a definitive solution, always allowing the teacher to explain and defend himself.

§3. However, in more grave or urgent cases for the good of the students and the faithful, the Chancellor can suspend the teacher for the duration of the regular procedure.

Article 23. Diocesan priests and religious or those equivalent to religious from whatever institute, in order to be teachers in a faculty or to remain as such, must have the consent of their proper Ordinary or religious superior, following the norms established in these matters by competent Church authority.

SECTION IV: STUDENTS
(Apostolic Constitution, articles 31–35)

Article 24. §1. Legal testimony, according to the norm of article 31 of the Constitution:

1) about a moral life is to be given, for clergy and seminarians, by their own Ordinary or his delegate; for all other persons by some ecclesiastic;

2) about previous studies is the study title required in accordance with article 32 of the Constitution.

§2. Since the studies required before entry into a university differ from one country to another, the faculty has the right and duty to investigate whether all the disciplines have been studied which the faculty itself considers necessary.

§3. A suitable knowledge of the Latin language is required for the faculties of the sacred sciences, so that the students can understand and use the sources and the documents of the Church.[2]

§4. If one of the disciplines has been found not to have been studied or to have been studied in an insufficient way, the faculty is to require that this be made up at a suitable time and verified by an examination.

Article 25. §1. Besides ordinary students, that is, those studying for academic degrees, extraordinary students can be admitted according to the norms determined in the statutes.

§2. A person can be enrolled as an ordinary student in only one faculty at a time.

Article 26. The transfer of a student from one faculty to another can take place only at the beginning of the academic year or semester, after a careful examination of his academic and disciplinary situation. But in any event nobody can be given an academic degree unless all the requirements for the degree are fulfilled as the statutes of the faculty demand.

Article 27. In the norms which determine the suspension or the expulsion of a student from a faculty, the student's right to defend himself must be safeguarded.

SECTION V: OFFICIALS AND STAFF ASSISTANTS
(Apostolic Constitution, articles 36–37)

Article 28. In the statutes or in some other suitable document of the university or faculty, the right and duties of the officials and staff assistants should be determined, as well as their participation in the community life of the university.

SECTION VI: STUDY PROGRAM
(Apostolic Constitution, articles 38–45)

Article 29. The statutes of each faculty must define which disciplines (principal and auxiliary) are obligatory and must be followed by all, and which are free or optional.

Article 30. Equally, the statutes are to determine the practical exercises and seminars in which the students must not only be present but also actively work together with their colleagues and produce their own expositions.

Article 31. The lectures and practical exercises are to be suitably distributed so as to foster private study and personal work under the guidance of the teachers.

Article 32. §1. The statutes are also to determine in what way the examiners are to make their judgments about candidates.

§2. In the final judgment about the candidates for the individual academic degrees, account is to be taken of all the marks received in the various tests in the same cycle, whether written or oral.

§3. In the examinations for the giving of degrees, especially the doctorate, it is also useful to invite examiners from outside the faculty.

Article 33. The statutes are to indicate the permanent curricula of studies which are to be instituted in a faculty for special purposes and indicate the diplomas which are conferred at their conclusion.

SECTION VII: ACADEMIC DEGREES
(Apostolic Constitution, articles 46–51)

Article 34. In ecclesiastical universities or faculties which are canonically erected or approved, the academic degrees are given in the name of the Supreme Pontiff.

Article 35. The statutes are to establish the necessary requisites for the preparation of the doctoral dissertations and the norms for their public defense and publication.

Article 36. A copy of the published dissertation must be sent to the Sacred Congregation for Catholic Education. It is recommended that copies also be sent to other ecclesiastical faculties, at least those of the same region, which deal with the same science.

Article 37. Authentic documents regarding the conferring of degrees are to be signed by the academic authorities, according to the statutes, and then are to be countersigned by the secretary of the university or faculty and have the appropriate seal affixed.

Article 38. Honorary doctorates are not to be conferred except with the consent of the Chancellor, who, having listened to the opinion of the university or faculty council, has obtained the *nihil obstat* of the Holy See.

SECTION VIII: MATTERS RELATING TO TEACHING
(Apostolic Constitution, articles 52–55)

Article 39. The university or faculty must have lecture halls which are truly functional and worthy and suited to the teaching of the disciplines and to the number of students.

Article 40. There must be a library open for consultation, in which the principal works for the scientific work of the teachers and students are available.

Article 41. Library norms are to be established in such a way that access and use is made easy for the students and teachers.

Article 42. Cooperation and coordination between libraries of the same city and region should be fostered.

SECTION IX: ECONOMIC MATTERS
(Apostolic Constitution, articles 56–59)

Article 43. To provide for continuous good administration, the authorities must inform themselves at set times about the financial situation and they must provide for careful, periodic audits.

Article 44. §1. Suitable ways should be found so that tuition fees do not keep from academic degrees gifted students who give good hope of one day being useful to the Church.

§2. Therefore care must be taken to set up forms of assistance for scholars, whatever their various names (scholarships, study burses, student subsidies, etc.), to be given to needy students.

SECTION X: PLANNING AND COOPERATION OF FACULTIES
(Apostolic Constitution, articles 60–64)

Article 45. §1. In order to undertake the erection of a new university or faculty, it is necessary that:

a) a true need or usefulness can be demonstrated, which cannot be satisfied either by affiliation, aggregation, or incorporation;

b) the necessary prerequisites are present, which are mainly:

1) permanently engaged teachers who in number and quality respond to the nature and demands of a faculty;

2) a suitable number of students;

3) a library with scientific apparatus and suitable buildings;

4) economic means really sufficient for a university or faculty;

c) the statutes, together with the study program, be exhibited, which are in conformity to the Constitution and to these Norms of Application.

§2. The Sacred Congregation for Catholic Education—after listening to the advice first of the Bishops' Conference, mainly from the pastoral viewpoint, and next of experts, principally from nearby faculties, mainly from the scientific viewpoint,—will decide about the suitability of a new erection. This is commonly conceded at first experimentally for a period of time before being definitively confirmed.

Article 46. When, on the other hand, the approval of a university or faculty is undertaken, this is to be done:

a) after the consent of both the Episcopal Conference and the local diocesan authority is obtained;

b) after the conditions stated in article 45, §1, under *b)* and *c)* are fulfilled.

Article 47. The conditions for affiliation regard, above all, the number and qualification of teachers, the study program, the library, and the duty of the affiliating faculty to help the institution being affiliated. Therefore, this is usually granted only when the affiliating faculty and the affiliated institution are in the same country or cultural region.

Article 48. §1. Aggregation is the linking with a faculty of some institute which embraces only the first and second cycle, for the purpose of granting the degrees corresponding to those cycles through the faculty.

§2. Incorporation is the insertion into a faculty of some institute which embraces either the second or third cycle or both, for the purpose of granting the corresponding degrees through the faculty.

§3. Aggregation and incorporation cannot be granted unless the institute is specially equipped to grant degrees in such a way that there is a well-founded hope that, through the connection with the faculty, the desired ends will be achieved.

Article 49. §1. Cooperation is to be fostered among the ecclesiastical faculties themselves by means of teacher exchanges, mutual communication of scientific work, and the promoting of common research for the benefit of the People of God.

§2. Cooperation with other faculties, even those of non-Catholics, should be promoted, care always however being taken to preserve one's own identity.

PART TWO; SPECIAL NORMS

SECTION I: FACULTY OF SACRED THEOLOGY
(Apostolic Constitution, articles 66–74)

Article 50. The theological disciplines are to be taught in such a way that their organic connection is made clear and that light is shed upon the various aspects or dimensions that pertain intrinsically to the nature of sacred doctrine. The chief ones are the biblical, patristic, historical, liturgical, and pastoral dimensions. The students are to be led to a deep grasp of the material, at the same time as they are led to form a personal synthesis, to acquire a mastery of the method of scientific research, and thus to become able to explain sacred doctrine appropriately.

Article 51. The obligatory disciplines are:
1. in the first cycle:
a) the philosophical disciplines needed for theology, which are above all systematic philosophy together with its main parts and its historical evolution;
b) the theological disciplines, namely:
• Sacred Scripture, introduction and exegesis
• fundamental theology, which also includes reference to ecumenism, non-Christian religions, and atheism
• dogmatic theology
• moral and spiritual theology
• pastoral theology
• liturgy
• Church history, patrology, archaeology
• canon law

c) the auxiliary disciplines, namely, some of the sciences of man and, besides Latin, the biblical languages insofar as they are required for the following cycles.

2. in the second cycle: the special disciplines established in various sections, according to the diverse specializations offered, along with the practical exercises and seminars, including written work.

3. in the third cycle: the statutes are to determine if special disciplines are to be taught and which ones, together with practical exercises and seminars.

Article 52. In the five-year basic cycle, diligent care must be exercised that all the disciplines are taught with order, fullness, and with correct method, so that the student receives harmoniously and effectively a solid, organic, and complete basic instruction in theology, which will enable him either to go on to the next cycle's higher studies or to exercise some office in the Church.

Article 53. Besides examinations or equivalent tests for each discipline, at the end of the first and of the second cycle there is to be a comprehensive examination or equivalent test, so that the student proves that he has received the full and scientific formation demanded by the respective cycle.

Article 54. It belongs to the faculty to determine under which conditions students who have completed a normal six-year philosophy-theology course in an ordinary seminary or in some other approved institution of higher learning may be admitted into the second cycle, taking account of their previous studies and, where necessary, prescribing special courses and examinations.

SECTION II: FACULTY OF CANON LAW
(Apostolic Constitution, articles 76–79)

Article 55. In a faculty of canon law, whether Latin or Oriental, there must be a careful setting forth both of the history and texts of ecclesiastical laws and of their disposition and connection.

Article 56. The obligatory disciplines are:
1. in the first cycle:
a) the general fundamentals of canon law;
b) the elements of sacred theology (especially of ecclesiology and sacramental theology) and of philosophy (especially ethics and natural law) which by their very nature are prerequisites for the study of canon

law. It is useful to add elements from the sciences of man which are connected with the juridical sciences.

2. in the second cycle:

a) the Code of Canon Law with all its various parts and the other canonical laws;

b) the connected disciplines, which are: the philosophy of law, the public law of the Church, fundamentals of Roman law, elements of civil law, the history of canon law. The student must also write a special dissertation.

3. in the third cycle: the statutes are to determine which special disciplines and which practical exercises are to be prescribed, according to the nature of the faculty and the needs of the students.

Article 57. §1. Whoever successfully completes the philosophy-theology curriculum in an ordinary seminary or in some other approved institution of higher learning, or who has already successfully completed the studies of the first cycle, may be admitted directly into the second cycle.

§2. A person who has already earned a doctorate in civil law, may be allowed, according to the judgment of the faculty, to abbreviate the course, always maintaining however the obligation to pass all the examinations and tests required for receiving academic degrees.

Article 58. Besides examinations or equivalent tests for each discipline, at the end of the second cycle there is to be a comprehensive examination or equivalent test, whereby the student proves that he has received the full and scientific formation demanded by the cycle.

SECTION III: FACULTY OF PHILOSOPHY
(Apostolic Constitution, articles 79–83)

Article 59. §1. Philosophy is to be taught in such a way that the students in the basic cycle will come to a solid and coherent synthesis of doctrine, will learn to examine and judge the different systems of philosophy, and will also gradually become accustomed to personal philosophical reflection.

§2. All of the above is to be perfected in the second cycle, which begins specialization. In this cycle there is to be a deeper grasp of the determined object of philosophy and of the proper philosophical method.

Article 60. The obligatory disciplines are:

1. in the first cycle:

a) systematic philosophy (preceded by a general introduction) with its principal parts: philosophy of knowledge, natural philosophy,

philosophy of man, philosophy of being (including natural theology), and moral philosophy;

b) history of philosophy, especially of modern philosophy, with a careful study of the systems which are exercising a major influence;

c) the auxiliary disciplines, namely selected natural and human sciences.

2. in the second cycle: the special disciplines established in various sections, according to the diverse specializations offered, along with practical exercises and seminars, including written work.

3. in the third cycle: the statutes are to determine if special disciplines are to be taught and which ones, together with the practical exercises and seminars.

Article 61. Besides examinations or equivalent tests for each discipline, at the end of the first and second cycle there is to be a comprehensive examination or equivalent test whereby the student proves that he has received the full and scientific formation demanded by the respective cycle.

Article 62. It belongs to the faculty to determine under what conditions students who have done a biennium of philosophy in an approved institution, or who have done a six-year philosophy-theology course in an ordinary seminary or equivalent school, may be admitted to the second cycle, taking account of their previous studies and, where necessary, prescribing special courses and examinations.

SECTION IV: OTHER FACULTIES
(Apostolic Constitution, articles 84–87)

Article 63. In accordance with article 86 of the Constitution, the Sacred Congregation for Catholic Education will gradually give special norms for the other faculties, taking account of the experience already gained in these faculties and institutes.

Article 64: In the meantime, in Appendix II there is a list of the areas or divisions of ecclesiastical studies—besides the theological, canonical, and philosophical ones treated of in the three previous sections of these Norms of Application—which at the present time in the Church are ordered academically and are in existence as faculties, institutes *ad instar*, or specialization sections. The Sacred Congregation for Catholic Education will add to the list of these sections when appropriate, indicating for these sections their special purposes and the more important disciplines to be taught and researched.

His Holiness John Paul II, by divine Providence Pope, has ratified, confirmed, and ordered to be published each and every one of these Norms of Application, anything to the contrary notwithstanding.

Given from the offices of the Sacred Congregation for Catholic Education in Rome, 29 April, the memorial of Saint Catherine of Siena, Virgin and Doctor of the Church, in the year of our Lord 1979.

Gabriel-Marie Cardinal Garrone
Prefect

ANTONIO MARÍA JAVIERRE ORTAS
TITULAR ARCHBISHOP OF META
Secretary

NOTES

1. See the Ecumenical Directory, Second Part: *AAS* 62 (1970), pp. 705ff.

2. The Second Vatican Ecumenical Council, Decree on Priestly Formation *(Optatam Totius)*, 13: *AAS* 58 (1966), p. 721 and the Chirograph of Pope Paul VI *Romani Sermonis: AAS* 68 (1976), pp. 481ff.

Appendix I: According to article 6 of Norms of Application

NORMS FOR DRAWING UP STATUTES

Taking into account what is contained in the Apostolic Constitution and in the Norms of Application—and leaving to their own internal regulations what is of a particular or changeable nature—the universities or faculties must mainly deal with the following points in drawing up their statutes:

1. *The name, nature, and purpose* of the university or faculty (with a brief history in the foreword).

2. *The government*—the Chancellor, the personal and collegial academic authorities: what their exact functions are; how the personal authorities are chosen and how long their term of office is; how the collegial authorities or the members of the councils are chosen and how long their term is.

3. *The teachers*—what the minimum number of teachers is in each faculty; into which ranks the permanent and nonpermanent are divided; what requisites they must have; how they are hired, named, promoted, and how they cease functioning; their duties and rights.

4. *The students*—requisites for enrollment and their duties and rights.

5. *The officials and staff assistant*—their duties and rights.

6. *The study program*—what the order of studies is in each faculty; how many cycles it has; what disciplines are taught; which are obligatory; attendance at them; which seminars and practical exercises; which examinations and tests are to be given.

7. *The academic degrees*—which degrees are given in each faculty and under what conditions.

8. *Matters relating to teaching*—the library; how its conservation and growth are provided for; other didactic helps and scientific laboratories, if required.

9. *Economic matters*—the financial endowment of the university or faculty and its economic administration; norms for paying the staff assistants, teachers, and officials; student fees and payments, burses, and scholarships.

10. *Relationships with other Faculties and Institutes, etc.*

Appendix II: According to article 64 of the Norms of Application

DIVISIONS OF ECCLESIASTICAL STUDIES
AS NOW (1979) EXISTING IN THE CHURCH

LIST

Note: These individual study sectors are listed alphabetically (according to their *Latin* names) and in parenthesis is noted the academic organizational form (whether a faculty or an institute *ad instar* or a sector of specialization) in which it now exists in some ecclesiastical academic center. Not listed are the studies of a theological, philosophical, or canonical kind which are treated in articles 51, 56, and 60 of the Norms of Application.

1. *Arabic-Islamic* studies (an institute *ad instar*, a specialized sector in a theology faculty).

2. *Christian Archaeology* studies (an institute *ad instar*).

3. Studies in *Atheism* (a specialized sector in a theology and/or philosophy faculty).

4. *Biblical* studies (a faculty of biblical science, a specialized sector in a theology faculty).

5. *Catechetical* studies (a specialized sector in a theology or education faculty).

6. *Ecclesiastical Oriental* studies (a faculty of ecclesiastical Oriental studies).

7. *Education* studies (a faculty of education).

8. *Church History* studies (a faculty of church history, a specialized sector in a theology faculty).

9. *Comparative Canonical-Civil Juridical* studies (a faculty of comparative civil law).

10. *Classical and Christian Literary* studies (a faculty of Christian and classical letters).

11. *Liturgical* studies (a faculty, a specialized sector in a theology faculty).

12. *Mariological studies* (a specialized sector in a theology faculty).

13. *Mediaeval studies* (an institute *ad instar*, a specialized sector in a faculty of theology or canon law or philosophy).

14. *Missiological* studies (a faculty of missiology, a specialized sector in a theology faculty).

15. *Moral* studies (a specialized sector in a theology faculty).

16. Studies in *Sacred Music* (an institute *ad instar*, a specialized sector in a theology faculty).

17. *Ecumenical* studies (a specialized sector in a theology faculty).

18. *Ancient Oriental* studies (a faculty of Eastern antiquity, a specialized sector in a theology or philosophy faculty).

19. *Pedagogical* studies (a faculty of pedagogy, a specialized sector in a philosophy or education faculty).

20. *Pastoral* studies (a specialized sector in a theology faculty).

21. *Patristic* studies (a specialized sector in a theology faculty).

22. Studies in *Psychology* (an institute *ad instar*, a specialized sector in a faculty of philosophy, or pedagogy, or education).

23. Studies in *Religion and Religious Phenomenology* (a specialized sector in a theology or philosophy faculty).

24. Catholic *Religious* studies (a higher institute of religious science).

25. *Sociological* studies (a faculty of social science, a specialized sector in a faculty of education).

26. *Spirituality* studies (a specialized sector in a theology faculty).

27. Studies in the *Theology of Religious Life* (a specialized sector in a theology faculty).

Address, Pope John Paul II to the Presidents of Catholic Colleges and Universities

October 7, 1979

Catholic University of America

Dear brothers and sisters in Christ,

1. Our meeting today gives me great pleasure, and I thank you sincerely for your cordial welcome. My own association with the university world, and more particularly with the Pontifical Theological Faculty of Cracow makes our encounter all the more gratifying for me. I cannot but feel at home with you. The sincere expressions with which the Chancellor and the President of The Catholic University of America have confirmed, in the name of all of you, the faithful adherence to Christ and the generous commitment to the service of truth and charity of your Catholic Associations and Institutions of higher learning are appreciated.

Ninety-one years ago Cardinal Gibbons and the American bishops requested the foundation of The Catholic University of America, as a university "destined to provide the Church with worthy ministers for the salvation of souls and the propagation of religion and to give the republic most worthy citizens." It seems appropriate to me on this occasion to address myself not only to this great institution, so irrevocably linked to the bishops of the United States, who have founded it and who generously support it, but also to all the Catholic universities, colleges, and academies of postsecondary learning in your land, those with formal and sometimes juridical links with the Holy See, as well as all those who are "Catholic."

2. Before doing so, though, allow me first to mention the ecclesiastical faculties, three of which are established here at The Catholic University of America. I greet these faculties and all who dedicate their best talents in them. I offer my prayers for the prosperous development and the

---

From the files of the Association of Catholic Colleges and Universities.

unfailing fidelity and success of these faculties. In the Apostolic Constitution *Sapientia Christiana*, I have dealt directly with these institutions in order to provide guidance and to ensure that they fulfill their role in meeting the needs of the Christian community in today's rapidly changing circumstances.

I also wish to address a word of praise and admiration for the men and women, especially priests and religious, who dedicate themselves to all forms of campus ministry. Their sacrifices and efforts to bring the true message of Christ to the university world, whether secular or Catholic, cannot go unnoticed.

The Church also greatly appreciates the work and witness of those of her sons and daughters whose vocation places them in non-Catholic universities in your country. I am sure that their Christian hope and Catholic patrimony bring an enriching and irreplaceable dimension to the world of higher studies.

A special word of gratitude and appreciation also goes to the parents and students who, sometimes at the price of great personal and financial sacrifice, look toward the Catholic universities and colleges for the training that unites faith and science, culture and the Gospel values.

To all engaged in administration, teaching, or study in Catholic colleges and universities I would apply the words of Daniel: "They who are learned shall shine like the brightness of the firmament and those that instruct many in justice as stars for all eternity" (Dan 12:3). Sacrifice and generosity have accomplished heroic results in the foundation and development of these institutions. Despite immense financial strain, enrollment problems, and other obstacles, divine Providence and the commitment of the whole People of God have allowed us to see these Catholic institutions flourish and advance.

3.   I would repeat here before you what I told the professors and students of the Catholic universities in Mexico when I indicated three aims that are to be pursued. A Catholic university or college must make a specific contribution to the Church and to society through high quality scientific research, in-depth study of problems, and a just sense of history, together with the concern to show the full meaning of the human person regenerated in Christ, thus favoring the complete development of the person. Furthermore, the Catholic university or college must train young men and women of outstanding knowledge who, having made a personal synthesis between faith and culture, will be both capable and willing to assume tasks in the service of the community and of society in general, and to bear witness to their faith before the world. And finally, to be what it ought to be, a Catholic college or university must set up, among its faculty and students, a real community which bears witness to a living and operative Christianity, a community where sincere commitment to

scientific research and study goes together with a deep commitment to authentic Christian living.

This is your identity. This is your vocation. Every university or college is qualified by a specific mode of being. Yours is the qualification of being Catholic, of affirming God, his revelation, and the Catholic Church as the guardian and interpreter of that revelation. The term "Catholic" will never be a mere label, either added or dropped according to the pressures of varying factors.

4.   As one who for long years has been a university Professor, I will never tire of insisting on the eminent role of the university, which is to instruct but also to be a place of scientific research. In both these fields, its activity is closely related to the deepest and noblest aspiration of the human person: the desire to come to the knowledge of truth. No university can deserve the rightful esteem of the world of learning unless it applies the highest standards of scientific research, constantly updating its methods and working instruments, and unless it excels in seriousness, and therefore, in freedom of investigation. Truth and science are not gratuitous conquests, but the result of a surrender to objectivity and of the exploration of all aspects of nature and man. Whenever man himself becomes the object of investigation, no single method, or combination of methods, can fail to take into account, beyond any purely natural approach, the full nature of man. Because he is bound by the total truth on man, the Christian will, in his research and in his teaching, reject any partial vision of human reality, but he will let himself be enlightened by his faith in the creation of God and the redemption of Christ.

The relationship to truth explains therefore the historical bond between the university and the Church. Because she herself finds her origin and her growth in the words of Christ, which are the liberating truth (cf. Jn 8:32), the Church has always tried to stand by the institutions that serve, and cannot but serve the knowledge of truth. The Church can rightfully boast of being in a sense the mother of universities. The names of Bologna, Padua, Prague, and Paris shine in the earliest history of intellectual endeavor and human progress. The continuity of the historic tradition in this field has come down to our day.

5.   An undiminished dedication to intellectual honesty and academic excellence are seen, in a Catholic university, in the perspective of the Church's mission of evangelization and service. This is why the Church asks these institutions, your institutions, to set out without equivocation your Catholic nature. This is what I have desired to emphasize in my Apostolic Constitution *Sapientia Christiana*, where I stated: "Indeed, the Church's mission of spreading the Gospel not only demands that the Good News be preached ever more widely and to ever greater numbers of men and women, but that the very power of the Gospel should

permeate thought patterns, standards of judgment, and the norms of behavior; in a word, it is necessary that the whole of human culture be steeped in the Gospel. The cultural atmosphere in which a human being lives has a great influence upon his or her way of thinking and, thus, of acting. Therefore, a division between faith and culture is more than a small impediment to evangelization, while a culture penetrated with the Christian spirit is an instrument that favors the spreading of the Good News" (*Sapientia Christiana*, I). The goals of Catholic higher education go beyond education for production, professional competence, technological and scientific competence; they aim at the ultimate destiny of the human person, at the full justice and holiness born of truth (cf. Eph 4:24).

6.   If then your universities and colleges are institutionally committed to the Christian message, and if they are part of the Catholic community of evangelization, it follows that they have an essential relationship to the hierarchy of the Church. And here I want to say a special word of gratitude, encouragement, and guidance for the theologians. The Church needs her theologians, particularly in this time and age so profoundly marked by deep changes in all areas of life and society. The bishops of the Church, to whom the Lord has entrusted the keeping of the unity of the faith and the preaching of the message—individual bishops for their dioceses; and bishops collegially, with the successor of Peter for the universal church—we all need your work, your dedication, and the fruits of your reflection. We desire to listen to you and we are eager to receive the valued assistance of your responsible scholarship.

But true theological scholarship, and by the same token theological teaching, cannot exist and be fruitful without seeking its inspiration and its source in the word of God as contained in Sacred Scripture and in the Sacred Tradition of the Church, as interpreted by the authentic Magisterium throughout history (cf. *Dei Verbum*, 10). True academic freedom must be seen in relation to the finality of the academic enterprise, which looks to the total truth of the human person. The theologian's contribution will be enriching for the Church only if it takes into account the proper function of the bishops and the rights of the faithful. It devolves upon the bishops of the Church to safeguard the Christian authenticity and unity of faith and moral teaching, in accordance with the injunction of the Apostle Paul: "Proclaim the message and, welcome or unwelcome, insist on it. Refute falsehood, correct error, call to obedience . . . " (2 Tim 4:2). It is the right of the faithful not to be troubled by theories and hypotheses that they are not expert in judging or that are easily simplified or manipulated by public opinion for ends that are alien to the truth. On the day of his death, John Paul I stated: "Among the rights of the faithful, one of the greatest is the right to receive God's word in all its entirety and purity . . . " (September 28, 1979). It behooves the theologian to be free, but with the freedom that is openness to the truth and the light that comes from faith and from fidelity to the Church.

In concluding I express to you once more my joy in being with you today. I remain very close to your work and your concerns. May the Holy Spirit guide you. May the intercession of Mary, Seat of Wisdom, sustain you always in your irreplaceable service of humanity and the Church. God bless you.

Catholic Higher Education and the Pastoral Mission of the Church

Statement of the National Conference of Catholic Bishops

PART ONE: THE MINISTRY OF CATHOLIC HIGHER EDUCATION

As we enter the twentieth decade of Catholic higher education in the United States, we wish to express in a formal fashion our profound gratitude and esteem for those in this ministry. They serve the entire American people in every field of learning. They also serve the Church in three indispensable ways. Catholic colleges and universities strive to bring faith and reason into an intellectually disciplined and constructive encounter. In addition, they are called to be communities of faith and worship that provide the young men and women of our country and Church with opportunities to mature in mind, body, heart, and soul. Without that maturity, they cannot function effectively as the future leaders of American business, government, culture, and religion. Finally, our schools are serving increasingly the educational needs of adults as they seek to advance their learning at various stages of their lives.

During his recent visit in the United States, our Holy Father, Pope John Paul II, emphasized the importance of these functions of Catholic colleges and universities. Speaking to representatives of these institutions at The Catholic University of America, he stated that Catholic colleges and universities

> must train young men and women of outstanding knowledge, who, having made a personal synthesis between faith and culture, will be both capable and willing to assume tasks in the service of the community and of society in general, and to bear witness to their faith before the world.[1]

Catholic colleges and universities of the United States have been a significant part of the Catholic community and of American higher

---

education since Georgetown University was founded in 1789 by the first Bishop of Baltimore, John Carroll. Their growth since then has been extraordinary. They constitute the largest group of Catholic institutions of higher education in the world, a striking testimonial to the generosity and commitment of the clergy, religious, and laity in our country. They have produced great numbers of American leaders both in public life and in the Church.

From the schools at Antioch and Alexandria, the monastic and cathedral schools, to the medieval universities of Paris and Bologna, the Church has fostered schools dedicated to the integration of the Christian faith and culture. This same concern led to the creation of such institutions in the New World as the University of Santo Domingo in 1533 and the many others which followed it.

The Second Vatican Council clarified the reason for the Church's commitment to higher education when it said that people who devote themselves to the various disciplines of philosophy, history, science, and the arts can help elevate the human family to a better understanding of truth, goodness, and beauty, and to the formation of judgments which embody universal values.[2]

The world is good because it reflects its Creator. Human culture is good to the extent that it reflects the plan and purpose of the Creator, but it bears the wounds of sin. The Church wishes to make the Gospel of Jesus Christ present to the world and to every sector of humanity at every stage of history. The Catholic college or university seeks to do this by educating men and women to play responsible roles in the contemporary world in the framework of that most important historical fact: the sending of the Son by the Father to reconcile, to vivify, to spread the Good News, to call all the world to a restoration in Christ Jesus.[3]

The Catholic Church is, of course, not the only religious body in the United States to recognize the enormous importance of colleges and universities that seek to broaden human knowledge and understanding as part of their commitment to a particular religious faith. We note the ongoing contribution of Jewish and Protestant colleges and universities. At the recent National Congress of Church-Related Colleges and Universities, delegates of twenty-three churches and their affiliated colleges came to a deeper understanding of their need for each other. They discovered that they have many of the same problems and challenges, and can assist one another in facing them.

During the decade of the 80s, all church-related colleges and universities will meet new challenges and new pressures. The burdens of inflation and of excessive governmental regulation will probably increase.[4] Moreover, the number of men and women of traditional college age will decline at a rate of almost half-a-million a year,[5] placing great economic stresses on all colleges and universities. Finally, there will be the continuing need for a clear definition by each institution of its religious identity and mission. All who are dedicated to the vitality of church-related higher education must work to surmount these challenges.

The future of church-related education is essential to the preservation of pluralism in higher education. The historic vitality of American Catholic colleges and universities has been indispensable to that pluralism.

A distinctive contribution to that pluralism has been the significant role played by women. To have so many women as presidents, major administrators, and faculty of Catholic colleges has been unique in the annals of American higher education.

PART TWO: A PASTORAL MESSAGE TO CATHOLIC COLLEGES AND UNIVERSITIES

Our statement is intended as a pastoral message addressed first of all to those engaged in the ministry of Catholic higher education and then to the Church at large. It speaks about the pastoral dimension of the life of the Catholic college and university.

This dimension is only one aspect of Catholic higher education. The Church attaches great importance to higher learning, both for its own sake and for the life of the Church. This was acknowledged in "The Catholic University in the Modern World," issued by the Second Congress of Delegates of the Catholic Universities of the World, convened in November of 1972 by the Sacred Congregation of Catholic Education.[6] The document "Relations of American Catholic Colleges and Universities with the Church," issued in 1976 by the Association of Catholic Colleges and Universities[7] describes how Catholic colleges and universities function in the American context. This pastoral message need not restate all that in detail but it does reaffirm the intellectual importance of Catholic colleges and universities in the modern world.

IDENTITY AND MISSION

One of our expectations is that Catholic colleges and universities continue to manifest, with unmistakable clarity, their Catholic identity and mission. The Holy Father has said that their character must be safeguarded,[8] and that the term "Catholic" should never be "a mere label, either added or dropped according to the pressures of varying factors."[9]

The Catholic identity of these institutions should be evident to faculty, students, and the general public. Policies, practices, programs, and general spirit should communicate to everyone that the institution is a community of scholars dedicated to the ideals and values of Catholic higher education.

Trustees and administrators have an extremely important role to discharge in maintaining fidelity to the nature of the institution and the kind of education the students experience. We look in a special way, however, to faculties for the leadership to accomplish this.

The many faculty members who come from other religious traditions can make a special contribution to the breadth of your students' experience. However, those faculty members who completely share the Catholic vision and heritage of faith carry the greatest responsibility to maintain the Catholic character of these institutions. The recruitment and retention of committed and competent Catholic faculty are essential.

Many Catholic colleges and universities are making serious efforts to renew their Catholic identity and mission within the guidelines provided by the Second Vatican Council, and thus remain true to their heritage while they adapt to modern circumstances. Academic freedom and institutional independence in pursuit of the mission of the institution are essential components of educational quality and integrity; commitment to the Gospel and the teachings and heritage of the Catholic Church provide the inspiration and enrichment that make a college fully Catholic.

LIBERAL ARTS

The Catholic identity of a college or university is effectively manifested only in a context of academic excellence. Policies, standards, curricula, governance, and administration should accord, therefore, with the norms of quality accepted in the wider academic community.

A necessary, though not sufficient, element in the identity of undergraduate programs in Catholic institutions is the provision of a liberal education of high quality. But that education must go beyond secular humanism which also emphasizes the liberal arts. Catholic institutions of higher learning can uniquely fuse the traditional study of arts and sciences with the light of Faith in the synthesis we call Christian and Catholic humanism. That synthesis provides an integral view of human existence—one that gives true meaning, purpose, and value to the study of all the disciplines. Indeed the Christian and Catholic view of human nature is a sound guide through the moral dilemmas that are so frequent in contemporary society and technology.

We are concerned that the erosion in the teaching of the liberal arts in American higher education today might compromise their important part in teaching the ideals of Christian humanism. That is why we urge

Catholic colleges and universities to preserve and strengthen the teaching of the liberal arts in undergraduate and preprofessional education. Particularly in professional and graduate programs the faculty and students should address human and religious issues that are intrinsic to a humane education. An institution's Catholic identity is largely expressed in a curriculum that shows how the values of the Judaeo-Christian view of life illuminate all fields of study and practice.

THEOLOGY

Theological education is a major concern of the bishops since we are responsible before God and before His people for

> A heritage of faith that the Church has the duty of preserving in its untouchable purity, and of presenting...to the people of our time in a way that is as understandable and persuasive as possible.[10]

For its part,

> One of the principal tasks of a Catholic university, and one which it alone is able to accomplish adequately, will be to make theology relevant to all human knowledge and reciprocally all human knowledge relevant to theology.[11]

The early American Catholic colleges were founded, in part, to protect the faith of students. The mission of Catholic institutions has broadened considerably since that time. They are full partners in the higher education community of the nation, offering wide diversity of academic programs and degrees. With all this diversity, however, theological education has maintained a role that is central to their mission. We are grateful for this continued emphasis and take note of the improvement of education in theology and religious studies in Catholic colleges since the Second Vatican Council. Recent progress in exegesis and patristic research has enriched biblical, liturgical, and historic theology, and has contributed to progress in systematic, pastoral, and moral theology. We also appreciate the efforts to pursue the ecumenical and inter-religious directives of the Council by providing students with the opportunity to learn of other religious traditions.

Theology is not the same as faith or spirituality or holiness. These, too, are important values of Catholic education, but here we want to emphasize that the distinguishing mark of every Catholic college or university is that, in an appropriate academic fashion, it offers its students an introduction to the Catholic theological heritage. This is a moral obligation owed to Catholic students. In fulfilling this obligation a theological faculty should take "prudent account of the maturity and previous preparation of the students,"[12] and should be cautious about private speculation of a kind that might undermine the students' foundations of faith in God's revealed truth. It is advisable, however, that students be encouraged to cope with their personal problems of faith and to consider the religious dimensions of the major issues in our contemporary culture and society. Theology should enable students to think and to act within a vision of life that includes religious values. A truly liberating and elevating education is incomplete without the study of theology or religion.

For this reason, scholars in theology and other religious studies

> ...make an indispensable contribution to the integrity of the university, which in order to embrace the fullness of human experience, must take its religious dimension into account.[13]

Although the majority of Catholic institutions are undergraduate colleges, some are universities with graduate and professional programs of theology. Graduate teachers and students, enriched by sacred scripture, the traditions of the Church, and the Church's magisterium, can utilize the professional tools of their discipline to explore Catholic teaching in depth and to discern its applicability to the problems of our times. Because many of the graduates of these programs in theology will be engaged in the ministry of teaching religion, the faculty will have special reason to show respect to the authentic teaching of the Church.

CHRISTIAN FORMATION OF TEACHERS

The Christian formation of teachers has always been basic to the educational mission of the Church. Until a few years ago, Catholic schools were staffed almost exclusively by men and women, priests and religious, who had not only received training in a formal Christian formation program, but who also had available ongoing opportunities for growth and development in their spiritual and professional lives.

Today lay persons have become the overwhelming majority in virtually every Catholic school. They come to Catholic schools with a variety of teacher preparation backgrounds, motivations, and perspectives. Usually, this formation is achieved at secular universities where the prospective teacher is exposed to either a theological pluralism, or receives no special training at all in this field. This is in stark contrast to those who previously were formed in a specifically Catholic environment and emerged certain and secure in their understanding of Catholic tradition and practice.

Therefore, teacher preparation programs adequate for public schools are inadequate for teachers in Catholic schools. They omit the necessary spiritual and ministerial formation which must be an integral part of the professional preparation of the Catholic school teacher. This need is urgent and can best be met by the Catholic colleges and universities who alone possess the unique resources and desire to be of service to the Catholic community.

Catholic institutions of higher education which have teacher preparation programs are urged to provide Christian formation programs for educators who are evangelizers by call and covenant and mission. Only those teachers who have been formed theologically and spiritually can respond adequately to the call of professional ministry in Christian education according to the vision of Jesus Christ and His Church.

THEOLOGIANS AND BISHOPS

We bishops, for our part, look to biblical scholars and theologians for assistance in understanding and explicating the Gospel message within the framework of the Church's theological traditions, and for helping the Church's judgment to mature on current questions.[14] In the words of the Second Vatican Council,

> Furthermore, while adhering to the methods and requirements proper to theology, theologians are invited to seek continually for more suitable ways of communicating doctrine to the men and women of their times. For the deposit of faith or revealed truths are one thing; the manner in which they are formulated without violence to their meaning and significance is another.[15]

The Holy Father, when speaking at The Catholic University of America, said:

> I want to say a special word of gratitude, encouragement, and guidance for the theologians. The Church needs her theologians, particularly in this time and age so profoundly marked by deep changes in all areas of life and society. The bishops of the Church, to whom the Lord has entrusted the keeping of the unity of the faith and the preaching of the message—individual bishops for their dioceses; and bishops collegially, with the successor of Peter for the universal Church—we all need your work, your dedication and the fruits of your reflection. We desire to listen to you and we are eager to receive the valued assistance of your responsible scholarship.[16]

Tension sometimes occurs as we seek to satisfy the respective claims of faith and reason, and to distinguish the doctrinal and pastoral responsibilities of bishops from the particular tasks of theologians. The Pope alluded to this tension when he said

> The theologian's contribution will be enriching to the Church only if it takes into account the proper function of the bishops and the rights of

the faithful. It devolves upon the bishops of the Church to safeguard the Christian authenticity and unity of faith and moral teaching. . . [17]

Bishops and the theological community share a mutual but not identical responsibility to the Church. Like theology, the ecclesiastical magisterium is subject to the word of God, which it serves.[18] As Pope John Paul II has reminded us,

> In putting themselves at the service of the truth, the magisterium and the theologians are joined together by common ties, namely by the word of God, by the *sensus fidei*, which has been alive in the Church in the past and is alive today, by the documents of tradition in which the faith of the people in general is set forth, and finally by pastoral and missionary considerations.[19]

Conscious of our different roles in the Church, and also of our mutual responsibilities, we seek a fruitful cooperation with theologians. Together we must work to build up the body of Christ and to bring the truth and power of the Gospel to our society and culture with due respect for the legitimate autonomy of culture and of the sciences.[20]

We encourage the universities to develop ways which will bring bishops and theologians together with other members of the Church and the academy to examine theological issues with wisdom and learning, with faith, and with mutual charity and esteem. We shall all need to recall and to work for that "delicate balance . . . between the autonomy of a Catholic university and the responsibilities of the hierarchy."[21] There need be no conflict between the two.

PHILOSOPHY

Another major concern of ours is the study of philosophy. We do not see philosophy as merely one more subject area in the field of liberal arts, nor as an academic luxury for those of speculative bent, but rather as an essential component of any education worthy of the name. It is philosophy which familiarizes the student with the laws and patterns of human thought. It brings the student to face, in a disciplined academic fashion, the great questions about God, the world, and humanity. It brings with itself an ever-increasing sense of the proportion and relationship that exist between the various aspects of reality and learning. Without solid philosophical grounding, both teachers and students in all fields of study cannot avoid the risk of superficiality and fragmentation.

ETHICS

Catholic colleges and universities have the obligation to study and teach the moral and ethical dimensions of every discipline. They must guarantee that the moral considerations of the Catholic tradition are related to all programs of study and that the ethical implications of new findings are probed in what Pope John Paul II called a "proportionate development."[22] This is especially urgent in professional and technical studies because in a technologically oriented society it is often the professional who in fact makes many decisions involving human values.

JUSTICE

Education for justice is a significant element in the general call to Gospel holiness. We issued a call to justice on the occasion of our nation's bicentennial in 1976 and we repeat now that "we must expand and improve our programs of education for justice."[23]

Those who enjoy the benefits of Catholic higher education have the obligation to provide our society with leadership in matters of justice and human rights.

Knowledge of economics and politics will not in itself bring about justice, unless it is activated by human and religious ideals. However, religious ideals without the necessary secular expertise will not provide the kind of leadership needed to influence our complex society.

Many Catholic colleges and universities integrate social justice teaching with field education and experience. Students and faculty are encouraged to become personally aware of problems of injustice and their responsibility to be involved in the social process. These are responses we should expect from institutions which take the Gospel seriously.

For the college or university to be an authentic teacher of social justice, it must conduct its own affairs in a just way.[24] "Modern man listens more willingly to witnesses than to teachers, and if he does listen to teachers, it is because they are witnesses."[25] It is important that Catholic institutions of higher education continually review their policies and personnel practices in order to ensure that social justice is a reality on campus. Fidelity to the social teachings of the Church in this basic witness means there is no contradiction between practice and theory.

MINORITY CONCERNS

Another aspect of justice is the treatment of minority concerns. For much of it history, the Catholic Church in the United States bore the title of the "Church of the Immigrants," and these same immigrants frequently found opportunities for higher education in the Catholic colleges and universities. As new minority groups seek educational opportunities, Catholic institutions should strive to respond to their legitimate needs, providing student aid and an education which respects their culture while offering the benefits of the Christian heritage. We have in mind Blacks, Native Americans, Orientals, and other minorities, but, especially, Hispanic-Americans, whose own Catholic culture is so rich and whose numbers are so great. We encourage our colleges and universities to institute precollege programs for disadvantaged persons. We ask that attention be given to the need for the presence of minority persons on boards of trustees and faculties of these institutions.

THE INTERNATIONAL VIEWPOINT

Because the unity of all people under God our Father is a fundamental principle of Catholic theology, an international point of view should be evident on the Catholic campus. Modern means of transportation and communication make possible a closer union of the peoples of the world by diminishing the distances that separate us. The way is thus being prepared for the familial closeness, the mutuality of service, and the union of hearts which lie at the core of the Gospel and to which the human family is called. The present climate of competition, hostility, and violence must be replaced by a constructive sharing of the earth's goods in a secure and peaceful environment. This suggests that international studies have an important place in the curriculum. It is also important and beneficial for students from other nations to be present on Catholic campuses. Their presence provides an opportunity for close associations which make possible an increased appreciation of others' culture and point of view.

CAMPUS MINISTRY

This pastoral document envisions a Catholic university or college as an enterprise wholly committed to evangelical ministry. To relegate this ministry to the institution's periphery in an isolated department or office of "campus ministry" is to fault the university's or college's essential Catholic identity.

Trustees, administrators, faculties, parents, and, above all, students need to see their whole college or university experience as a unique opportunity for the discovery of God's abiding presence and influence in the lives of people and in the signs of the times. At most and at best an office of campus ministry can be a catalyst to spark and to energize the total institution's involvement in a gospel-oriented evangelism. This office is badly degraded if it is regarded only as something like a bookstore or student union, some sort of a convenience for those students who want a little religion on the side of their higher education.

A university or college which has an ongoing, dynamic program to clarify its Catholic identity will expect the office of campus ministry to have a voice on a policy-making level and to insist in season and out of season on the preservation and enrichment of the institution's religious traditions.

Because campus ministry normally includes elements of parish ministry, e.g., counseling, preparation for the sacraments, preaching, liturgical worship, and cooperation with diocesan activities, we are obliged to grant appropriate jurisdiction and authority to duly approved campus ministers at institutions of higher education in our dioceses. We see this duty not as one needlessly to restrict the highly commendable pastoral practices in campus ministry but rather as one to give our official support, and, as far as possible, our assistance to a ministry for which we have a share of responsibility. For this reason, we believe it to be of utmost importance that those who are selected for this important ministry, whether they be clergy, religious, or lay, be prepared for this kind of apostolate theologically and philosophically. They should present the authentic teaching of the Church in a pastoral manner in the context of the academic communities in which they serve.

We would like university and college students to feel that they are not mere visitors in our diocese but are temporary residents for whose spiritual welfare we pray and work. There is merit, therefore, in a growing trend for bishops personally to visit university and college campuses for the celebration of liturgies and, on occasion, for closeup dialogue with students. Pope John Paul II has set a good example for our face-to-face conversations with students.

Though much progress lately has been made in improving the quality and extent of campus ministry on Catholic campuses there still is vast room for upgrading this important element of Catholic higher education. To a large extent, we fear, campus ministry still suffers badly from inadequate budgets and from too limited a staff. A very encouraging development, however, is team ministry in which laity, religious, and priests combine their talents and experience for efficacious ministry.

In this ministry the gospel adage is controlling: "I know mine, and mine know me." To do the work of the Lord Jesus Himself on a Catholic university or college campus is to have close personal contact with students who are ready to share their intimate hopes and anxieties with a person who truly can say, "I know you, and you know me." Obviously, this ministry should not and cannot be limited to persons formally designated as campus ministers even though they rightfully are expected to take the lead.

We bishops, as best we can, wish to pledge our active cooperation with this kind of ministry on the campuses in our dioceses.

A COMMUNITY OF FAITH

Pope John Paul II has repeatedly called for the Catholic campus to be a community of faith. In Mexico and in Poland, in Rome and in Washington, he has again and again returned to the same theme.[26] No more fitting ideal can be sought than to build a community which encourages intellectual growth and which calls to and supports a personal religious commitment.[27]

Growth in Christ is never an easy task. Indeed, in our times, it is exceedingly difficult to live a fully Christian life. We honor those persons—especially young people—who reject the patterns of behavior which surround them and, as "children of light"[28] attempt to respond with fidelity to the grace of their Baptism. It is that very grace which calls us to support one another as a company of believers.

All Catholic activity must of necessity be pointed to an objective that is ultimately religious: how to know God better and serve Him more faithfully. The goals of a Catholic college are specified by its very nature as a place of learning. But learning itself does not constitute the perfect and fulfilled life. It needs to be integrated with our search for the Lord and in our living with our neighbor a life of faith in Him and fidelity to His way. Our concern, then, is that students and faculty find on our campuses the community of faith which can encourage and support them in reaching for that goal. Unless a Catholic institution of higher learning fosters such a faith community it contradicts its own mission.

Residential students can more easily experience a campus-based community. For commuter students the formation of community is more difficult. We encourage dedicated persons to develop new ways to draw more students and faculty into communities of friends who help one another live strongly religious lives.

ADULT LEARNERS

Our concern for the welfare of the younger college students does not exclude the growing number of older students. These men and women seek education for new careers, to complete an interrupted education, or for the pleasure of learning. They constitute a growing proportion of the student body on our campuses. Their needs for an integrated Catholic education are similar to those of the younger students, but they must be addressed in different ways.

We appreciate the many programs developed by Catholic institutions to provide theological renewal and training for ministry to Catholic adults in the years since the Second Vatican Council. These programs illustrate a distinct form of service to the Church community, which we hope will grow as we learn how to use the many resources of our institutions more effectively.

THE CAMPUS AND ECUMENISM

The Second Vatican Council called for strong ecumenical initiatives. The Catholic colleges have been responding not only with courses designed to acquaint Catholic students with other religious traditions, but with faculty members drawn from those traditions who have added a rich new dimension to departments of theology and religious studies. The Catholic college or university can be a fertile environment for further ecumenical activity, and we encourage cooperative work with the local (and national) Church to that end. Catholic faculty trained in biblical and theological sciences can offer leadership in the explorations and study in which we join with others outside the Catholic community.

RESEARCH

The Church has always encouraged the advancement of human knowledge, because the more we know of truth the closer we come to God in Whom truth ultimately resides. Catholic scholars, as Pope John Paul II urged, should examine all the fundamental questions in human culture with the highest degree of intellectual rigor. These scholars also have a special obligation to undertake research closely related to human and spiritual needs.[29] It is for this reason that the bishops of America in their 1976 Bicentennial Conference *A Call to Action* urged scholars to undertake research in areas of pastoral concern, especially in issues of justice and peace.[30] In these efforts the Church would be materially assisted if cooperative efforts could be organized to mobilize the combined research capabilities of the Catholic universities of this country. We shall work with the universities to find the resources necessary for research of high quality and utility.

PART THREE: SUPPORT FOR CATHOLIC HIGHER EDUCATION

We have addressed in particular those who work and study in Catholic colleges and universities; now we want to urge upon all in the Church a firm support for this important ministry.

RELIGIOUS CONGREGATIONS

The entire Church owes much to those generations of sisters, brothers, and priests who provided higher education to their students, financed by their own labors, and often by their own funds.

Today the numbers of clergy and religious are smaller at many Catholic colleges and universities. This is due, in part, to the decline in religious vocations, and, in part, to entry into other fields of ministry. It is important that the mission of Catholic higher education remain a high priority among religious communities. The nurturing of tomorrow's leadership through service in Catholic colleges and universities is an effective way of building the Christian community and of preparing the next generation of leaders for our society.

PARENTS

We join with Pope John Paul II to offer gratitude and appreciation . . . to the parents . . . who, sometimes at the price of great personal and financial sacrifice, look toward the Catholic universities and colleges for the training that unites faith and science; cultures and the Gospel values.[31]

Combinations of federal, state, and institutional student aid programs make it possible, although not without sacrifice, for parents to encourage and support the attendance of their sons and daughters at Catholic institutions. These programs narrow the tuition gap between the independent college and the state institution which is heavily subsidized by all taxpayers. Consequently, some exercise of choice is possible for many students. In helping a son or daughter select a college, parents should give a priority, where possible, to the Catholic institution. Adult Catholic leaders need adult Catholic education. The religious learning of the child will not suffice for the religious needs and demands of the adult.

THE AMERICAN CHURCH AT LARGE

We appeal, finally, to the entire American Church for support of Catholic higher education. Catholic foundations, as well as Catholic individuals and families, should see generous and long-term support of Catholic institutions as one of the top priorities in our Church. The stability of institutions of higher learning in America in our time is based on a firm underpinning of endowment funds. The Catholic colleges and universities have relied through their history on the "living endowment" of religious and clergy, as well as on the generous assistance of lay persons. The day has now come when we American Catholics of the present must reciprocate the gifts we have received from the past. To all Catholics who believe with us that Catholic higher education is important for the life of the Church, we appeal for financial support, so that the benefits we have enjoyed will be preserved for the next generation of Catholic Americans.

We conclude by noting once again the historic interest of the Catholic Church in higher education. We thank the clergy and religious, and laity in ever increasing numbers, who staff the colleges and universities of our country. We commend all who are undertaking the renewal of Catholic higher education as part of that renewal to which the Holy Spirit through the Vatican Council has called the whole Church.[32]

NOTES

1. Pope John Paul II, "Excellence, Truth and Freedom in Catholic Universities," *Origins: NC Documentary Service*, vol. 9, no. 19 (October 25, 1979): 307.

2. Second Vatican Council, *Gaudium et Spes* (Constitution on the Church in the Modern World), par. 57.

3. Pope John Paul II, *Sapientia Christiana, Origins: NC Documentary Service*, vol. 9, no. 3 (June 7, 1979): 37.

4. Indeed, during the past decade some colleges and universities, founded by Catholics, lay or clerical or religious, which have long presumed and styled themselves to be Catholic, have found themselves required to refrain from such designation as a condition for government aid to the institution. We regret the presence of such pressures and look to their removal in a timely fashion.

5. U.S. Bureau of the Census, Current Population Reports, Series P–25, no. 704, 1977, pp. 38–60 and no. 721, 1978, pp. 9–11, as cited in Exhibit 3. *Policy Analysis Service Reports*, vol. 4, no. 2 (Washington, DC: American Council on Education, December 1978).

6. "The Catholic University in the Modern World," *College Newsletter* of the National Catholic Educational Association, Washington, DC, vol. XXXV, no. 3 (March 1973). Cf. also the letter to Presidents of Catholic Universities from Cardinal Garrone, then Prefect of the S. Congregation for Catholic Education, and dated April 25, 1973, appearing in the same issue of *College Newsletter*, pp. 11–12.

7. "Relations of American Catholic Colleges and Universities with the Church," *Occasional Papers on Catholic Higher Education*, vol. II, no. 1 (Washington, DC: Association of Catholic Colleges and Universities, April 1976).

8. Pope John Paul II, "Catholic Universities for an Apostolate of Culture . . ." Address to members of the Council of the International Federation of Catholic Universities, and Rectors of the Catholic Universities of Europe, Rome, February 24, 1979, *L'Osservatore Romano*, English edition (March 5, 1979): 6.

9. Pope John Paul II, "Excellence, Truth and Freedom in Catholic Universities" loc. cit.

10. Pope Paul VI, *Evangelii Nuntiandi (On Evangelization in the Modern World)*, Apostolic Exhortation (December 8, 1975): par. 3.

11. "The Catholic University in the Modern World," op. cit., pp. 2–3.

12. Ibid., p. 9. Cf. also Pope Paul VI, *Evangelii Nuntiandi*, op. cit., par. 78.

13. Ibid., p. 6.

14. Second Vatican Council, *Dei Verbum* (Constitution On Divine Revelation) (November 18, 1965), par. 12.

15. Second Vatican Council, *Gaudium et Spes* (Constitution on the Church in the Modern World), op. cit., par. 9.

16. Pope John Paul II, "Excellence, Truth and Freedom in Catholic Universities," loc. cit.

17. Ibid., p. 308.

18. Second Vatican Council, *Dei Verbum* (Constitution On Divine Revelation), par. 10.

19. Pope John Paul II, "Papal Address to International Theological Commission," *Origins: NC Documentary Service*, vol. 9, no. 24 (November 29, 1979): 394–395.

20. Second Vatican Council, *Gaudium et Spes* (Constitution on the Church in the Modern World), par. 59.

21. "The Catholic University in the Modern World," op. cit., p. 9.

22. Pope John Paul II, *Redemptor Hominis* (*The Redeemer of Man*), (March 4, 1979), par. 15.

23. The National Conference of Catholic Bishops, *To Do the Work of Justice*, (Washington, DC: United States Catholic Conference, 1978), p. 5.

24. Carnegie Council on Policy Studies in Higher Education, *Fair Practices in Higher Education* (Washington, DC: Jossey-Bass Publishers, 1979).

25. Pope Paul VI, "Address to the Members of the Concilium de Laicis," October 2, 1974, as cited in the Apostolic Exhortation "On Evangelization in the Modern World," op. cit., 41.

26. "To be what it ought to be, a Catholic college or university must set up, among its faculty and students, a real community which bears witness to a living and operative Christianity, a community where sincere commitment to scientific research and study goes together with a deep commitment to authentic Christian living." Pope John Paul II, "Excellence, Truth and Freedom in Catholic Universities," loc. cit.

27. "The Catholic University in the Modern World," op. cit., p. 3.

28. *Ephesians* 5:8.

29. Cf. Pope John Paul II, "Excellence, Truth and Freedom in Catholic Universities," loc. cit.

30. The National Conference of Catholic Bishops, *To Do the Work of Justice*, loc. cit.

31. Pope John Paul II, "Excellence, Truth and Freedom in Catholic Universities," op. cit., p. 307.

32. Since this message has addressed exclusively Catholic higher education, we were unable to speak of the excellent intellectual and pastoral leadership of many Catholics engaged as teachers, administrators, and campus ministers in the colleges and universities which are not Catholic. We hope for a future opportunity to speak of their invaluable contribution to the intellectual life of our country.

Construction of the Code
of Canon Law of 1983
1977–1983

Although chronologically this section overlaps with the preceding one, it seems advisable to group all the drafts of the proposed canon law together. In addition, the fact that in the Revised Code of Canon Law there was to be a special section dealing with Catholic universities can probably only be understood in the light of the ongoing conversations about the proper role of the Catholic university in the modern world. In the Code of 1917 there had been canons dealing with Catholic schools and seminaries but none that referred to universities. As mentioned above, the oversight of the Vatican with regard to universities where theology was taught was exercised by means of the "canonical mission" provided for by Concordats with specific European governments. Such agreements required that approval be given by the bishop to all who were to teach Catholic theology in the university; the university itself was secular and state controlled. In the United States, on the other hand, the appointment of theologians was left up to the normal channels of faculty hiring since the presidents and trustees were most often members of a religious community. As the situation changed, the assumption of orthodoxy was not as simple, and Rome now proposed new canons that would have as their object the assurance of the "Catholicity" of the universities.

A typescript of a draft of the new canons was circulated to a limited group in 1976, but the first official draft arrived in 1978. A critique of this was prepared by some noted American canon lawyers at the request of the ACCU and submitted to Cardinal Garrone, then Prefect of the Congregation of Catholic Education. A revision was received in 1980 but there were still unsatisfactory aspects. Hence another critique was submitted. In 1981 a meeting of the Commission for the Revision of Canon Law was held in Rome and at that time only some minor modifications were made. Consequently, the ACCU Board asked for a personal visit with Pope John Paul II, and a committee of five was received by him on March 18, 1982. Finally, the Revised Code was promulgated in 1983 with the relevant canons numbered 807–814.

Proposed Revision of Canon Law: The 1976 Draft

Canons Regarding Universities (Canons 17–22)

17   The Church holds in high esteem universities and faculties in which diverse scientific disciplines are studied and taught. These institutions, while contributing to a more elevated human culture and the progress of the human person, also benefit the spiritual welfare of men and women. In addition, as they seek more profound knowledge, they may help in the better understanding of revealed truth. (See II Vatican Council, declaration *Gravissimum Educationis*, no. 10.)

18   No university may bear the name, "Catholic university," unless it has been erected by the Apostolic See or the conference of bishops or has been granted this name by the Apostolic See or the conference of bishops.

19   1. Wherever they judge it possible or expedient, in view of all the circumstances, the conferences of bishops should see that there are universities, suitably spread throughout their territory. In these the various disciplines should be taught in such a way that, while their legitimate autonomy is preserved, the universal presence of a Christian mentality may be made effective in the whole study of culture and that account may be taken of revealed truth as this has been declared by the Church's magisterium. (See *Gravissimum Educationis*, no. 10.)

2. The conferences of bishops and the interested diocesan bishops should be solicitous that the principles of Christian doctrine be faithfully maintained in Catholic universities.

20   1. So that theological inquiry may be more closely related to contemporary questions and may also help students of various disciplines to reach a fuller knowledge of faith and a universal understanding of the created order, the conferences of bishops

---

From the files of the Association of Catholic Colleges and Universities

should see that in Catholic universities and, where this is expedient and possible, in other universities as well, there be erected a faculty or institute of sacred theology or at least a chair of theology, so that courses also accommodated to lay students may be given. (See *Gravissimum Educationis*, no. 10; constitution *Gaudium et Spes*, no. 57.)

2. In the individual faculties of a Catholic university, there should be courses in which the principal theological questions related to the disciplines of these faculties are treated. (See *Gravissimum Educationis*, no. 10; *Gaudium et Spes*, no. 35.)

3. Those who give the theological courses mentioned in 1 and 2 require a canonical mission.

21   The administrators and professors of such universities should see that the various faculties collaborate among themselves and cooperate with other universities, participating in and promoting international meetings, working together in scientific research, exchanging professors on a temporary basis, and fostering whatever means will contribute to the greater increase of knowledge. (See *Gravissimum Educationis*, no. 12.)

22   The conference of bishops of the region and the local Ordinary should provide that adults be also given the opportunity for more profound instruction in the Christian religion. They should therefore arrange courses and colloquies about religious questions and, where possible, establish advanced schools or academies of religious studies where the theological disciplines and others pertinent to Christian culture may be taught.

Proposed Revision of Canon Law: The 1978 Draft

Canons Regarding Universities (Canons 58–64)

58 [Exactly the same as 17 above]

59 [Exactly the same as 18 above]

60 1. Wherever they judge it possible or expedient, in view of all the circumstances, the conferences of bishops should see that there are universities, suitably spread throughout their territory. In these universities, the various disciplines should be taught in such a way that, while their legitimate autonomy is preserved, the universal presence of a Christian mentality may be made effective in promoting the entire study of culture and that account may be taken of revealed truth as this has been declared by the Church's magisterium.

2. The conferences of bishops and the interested diocesan bishops have the right and the duty to be vigilant that the principles of Christian doctrine be faithfully maintained in Catholic universities.

61 1. [Same as 20 above with the exception that "competent ecclesiastical authority" is substituted for "the conferences of bishop."]

2. [Same as in 20]

3. [Deleted (appears as #64)]

62 [Same as 21]

63 [Same as 22 with a slight change in language] The conference of bishops of the region and the local diocesan bishop should provide that Christian adults be also given the opportunity for more profound instruction in the Christian religion. They should therefore see to the planning of courses and colloquies about religious questions and, where possible, the establishment of advanced schools or academies of religious studies where the theological

---

From the files of the Association of Catholic Colleges and Universities

disciplines and others disciplines pertinent to Christian culture may be taught.

64   Those who, in any kind of institute of higher studies, give courses in theology or courses related to theology require a canonical mission.

Revision of the Code of Canon Law: Canons On Higher Education

Critique endorsed by the Board of the Association of Catholic Colleges and Universities and the Bishops and Presidents' Committee.

The following is a report of consultations with canonists concerning the projected canons on higher education in the revision of the Code of Canon Law. The Board of Directors of the Association of Catholic Colleges and Universities has asked that such a report be made for the information of the member institutions.

INTRODUCTION

The present canons, still in draft form, were prepared by the Pontifical Commission for the Revision of the Code of Canon Law. They have been submitted to the episcopal conferences for the comments of the bishops and to others such as the canonically established institutions, associations, etc. Recommendations are to be sent to the Commission by the end of October 1978.

The observations in this report are concerned exclusively with the projected canons on higher education in those institutions which are not canonically or pontifically established or recognized. An English version of the canons is appended to this report.

The pertinent canons are preceded by canons dealing with Christian education in general and with schools. They are followed by a series of canons treating the canonically established institutions, namely, the universities and faculties of ecclesiastical studies.

From the files of the Association of Catholic Colleges and Universities

GENERAL COMMENTS

1. It should be noted that the references in the Latin text are exclusively to "universities." This terminology seems clearly to embrace also what are called colleges in the United States. For purposes of this critique, therefore, references to universities should be so understood.

2. A careful and technical critique of the canons does not seem necessary or appropriate for the purposes of the member institutions. The latter are presumed to be interested directly only in those canons which may create difficulties and which should be brought to the attention of bishops and others who may be submitting comments to the Roman Commission.

3. It may be argued that there is no genuine necessity for this chapter of canons, which constitutes an addition to the codification, since no similar section appeared in the 1917 Code of Canon Law. The specific criticisms below do not consider this question. The canons on institutions of higher learning might well be omitted from the codification and the same purpose served by a discursive treatment of the matter in an apostolic exhortation or similar document. If the canons are to be included in the codification, however, the criticisms given below need to be taken into account.

4. Several of the canons are simply statements of principle or somewhat general exhortations. Some of these are derived in part from conciliar documents. See canons 58; 60, §1; 61, §1, §2; 62; 63. No commentary is given on these canons.

It may or may not be desirable that canons of this kind, which are statements of principle or general exhortations, be included in the canon law, but they need not be a source of concern for the institutions of higher education. Perhaps a general recommendation should be offered: canons of this sort should be carefully distinguished from others, and possibly be included only as a preamble to the preceptive norms.

5. With regard to the canons that are partially derived from conciliar documents (above), there are some departures from the conciliar language and intent, for example:

a) Canon 58, on the study and teaching of diverse disciplines, is partially derived from n. 10 of the declaration *Gravissimum Educationis*, but the emphatic reference to academic freedom in the conciliar document is omitted from the proposed canon and should be included: "in accord with their own principles, method, and freedom of scientific inquiry" [. . . propriis principiis, propria methodo atque propria inquisitionis scientificae libertate ina excolantur].

It is not possible to include verbatim texts of the conciliar documents (which were not framed as disciplinary canons or decrees), but the stress placed upon the legitimacy of distinct principles, method, and freedom of inquiry or research (*"propriis* principiis, *propria* methodo atque *propria* . . . libertate"*) should not be tendentiously neglected in the canon.

b) Canon 60, §1, is likewise dependent in part upon n. 10 of *Gravissimum Educationis*. Again, while there is no objection to the reference in the canon to the promotion of study with account taken of "revealed truth as this has been declared by the Church's magisterium," the conciliar statement is preferable; it speaks of the formation of students "truly outstanding in learning, prepared to undertake serious responsibilities in society, and witnesses of the faith in the world" [doctrina vere praestantes, gravioribus in societate obeundis parati atque fidei in mundo testes].

6. The canons which speak of principles are, as already noted, somewhat dependent upon conciliar texts. If such material is to be redacted as canons, whether descriptive, hortatory, or introductory, it would be preferable to follow n. 53–62 of the pastoral constitution *Gaudium et Spes*, which deals with cultural and educational questions with a breadth and openness not evident in the proposed canons.

CANON 59

Text: "No university may bear the name, 'Catholic university,' unless it has been erected by the Apostolic See or by the conference of bishops or has been granted this name by the Apostolic See or by the conference of bishops."

1. There should be a presumption that an institution established by Catholics, lay or clerical or religious, with Christian purposes, is indeed Catholic and may so style itself. The canon conceives the use of "Catholic" according to an ecclesiology which considers the Church to consist only of the hierarchy or the episcopate.

2. Granted that there may be some point at which ecclesiastical authority, in an extreme case, may have to declare an institution to be no longer authentically Christian or Catholic, such action should occur only when the presumption of asserted Catholicity has been certainly disproved.

3. It is clear that the canon also weakens ecclesiastical subsidiarity, since the local church or diocese should be able to act in these matters unless, for cause, it proves necessary for the higher authority of the episcopal conference or the Apostolic See to intervene.

4. There is a special problem in the failure of the canon to consider the many institutions of higher education which are established by religious institutes.

5. In its present form, the canon suggests that the many universities and colleges in the United States which call themselves "Catholic" or which express their Christian and Catholic identity in equivalent terms are somehow less than Catholic without the formality of canonical erection, approbation, or recognition. It will have an adverse effect on institutions that attempt to bring a Christian and Catholic influence into the life of society to learn that, without the canonical status demanded by canon 59, they are not "Catholic" universities or colleges.

6. It is desirable that neither this formulation nor one which might take place (below) specify any juridical relationships. The latter may be neither useful nor necessary.

Recommendation: If indeed this matter needs to be considered in the canons, an appropriate formulation would be the following:

"An institution of higher studies which is established by Catholics for the pursuit of learning in the light of Christian faith shall be considered to be a Catholic institution and may so designate itself unless for grave cause the legitimate ecclesiastical authority declares that the contrary has been proved."

[Institutum studiorum superiorum a catholicis erecta ad doctrinam et scientiam colendam sub luce fidei christianae institutum catholicum habeatur et nomen "Universitatis catholicae" gerere potest nisi, decreto auctoritatis ecclesiasticae competentis gravi de causa lato, constiterit Institutum de quo agitur catholicum reapse non esse.]

CANON 60, §2

Text: "The conference of bishops and the interested diocesan bishops have the right and duty to be vigilant that the principles of Christian doctrine be faithfully maintained in Catholic universities."

1. The expression *officium et ius invigilandi* is needlessly harsh and authoritarian. It is sufficient that there be a general expression of the obligation of concern and solicitude.

2. The canon is seriously defective inasmuch as it neglects the responsibility incumbent upon the whole Christian community in witness to faith.

3. More important, the canon fails to acknowledge a co-responsibility, and indeed an immediate and primary responsibility, within the academic community itself in any institution of higher education. This responsibility was recognized in a footnote to the *Normae quaedam* in the case of the canonically established institutions; it should not be neglected or denied in the present context of all Catholic institutions of higher education.

Recommendation: "The responsibility for the protection of the doctrine of the Church, which is the concern of the whole community of believers, resides individually and collectively in the faculty and administration of Catholic institutions of higher studies, while preserving the right and duty of the bishop of the local church and other legitimate ecclesiastical authorities."

[Responsabilitas doctrinam Ecclesiae tuendi, quae ad totam communitatem fidelium spectat, omnibus et singulis docentibus et directoribus Institutorum incumbit, salvis iure, et officio Epsicopi Ecclesiae particularis et aliorum competentium acutoritatem ecclesiasticarum.]

CANON 64

Text: "Those who, in any kind of institute of higher studies, give courses in theology or courses related to theology require a canonical mission."

1. It is very doubtful whether the expression, "canonical mission," which has various meanings, should be employed at all in this context. As stated, it is anachronistic, since a genuine and authentic "mission of teaching," which is presumably meant by the canon, is exercised by many in the Church without any formality of expressed or implied mission beyond that of baptism.

2. In addition, the requirement of a canonical mission by way of prior approbation of the local bishop would be an intolerable intrusion into the ordinary academic governance of Catholic institutions of higher studies. Its introduction would immediately render suspect the legitimate freedom of professors and would weaken gravely the reputation of institutions within the academic community.

3. In the United States, to condition an academic appointment upon the prior reception of a canonical mission is unrealistic. It could not be carried out as in some other countries.

4. The canon is defective in not distinguishing between (a) research, legitimate theological speculation, and their communication and (b) the teaching of the Christian faith in the manner of catechesis.

5. The language "aut [lectiones] cum theologia conexas" is much too broad and subject to misinterpretation, entirely apart from the question of the need for the canon.

6. It is quite possible, without resorting to the formality of prior approbation or canonical mission, for the ecclesiastical authorities to indicate in extreme cases that an individual is unsuitable for the teaching of the Catholic faith. Such means should be invoked, however, only as a last resort, after the fact, and upon proof certainly established with

all the safeguards of due canonical process. It is unnecessary to mention such a possibility in the canons on institutions of higher studies; it can be left to other parts of the canon law which refer to disqualification for teaching the Catholic faith by reason of heterodoxy.

Recommendation: It is preferable that the canon be deleted. If something must be retained, perhaps the following formulation would be appropriate:

"Those who exercise the mission of teaching the Christian faith in institutions of higher studies should always perform that ministry in full communion of faith with the holy Catholic Church."

[Qui in studiorum superiorum Institutis missionem fidem christianam docendi exercent ministerium huius modi in plena communione fidei cum Ecclesia catholica semper adimpleant.]

Proposed Revision of Canon Law: The 1980 Draft

Canons Regarding Universities (Canons 762–770)

762 The Church has the right to establish and direct universities which work toward the advance of human culture, the greater progress of the human person, and the fulfillment of the Church's office of teaching.

763 No university may bear the name Catholic University unless it is conceded by the Apostolic See.

764 The conferences of bishops should see to it that, if possible and expedient, there be universities or at least faculties, suitably distributed within their territory, in which the various disciplines are investigated and taught in the light of Catholic understanding and truth.

765 It is the duty of the competent authority, as determined in the statutes, to name teachers in Catholic universities who, over and above their scientific and pedagogical qualifications, are outstanding in integrity of doctrine and probity of life and, in the absence of such requisites, to remove them from office, observing the procedure determined in the statutes.

The respective conferences of bishops and diocesan bishops have the right and duty to exercise vigilance that the principles of Catholic doctrine be faithfully observed in these universities; and likewise to require that teachers be removed from office if reasons of faith or morals demand.

766 The competent ecclesiastical authority should see to it that in Catholic universities, and indeed in other universities if expedient and possible, a faculty or institute of theology or at least a chair of theology be established in which courses are also given to lay students.

In each Catholic university, courses should be given in which

From the files of the Association of Catholic Colleges and Universities

theological questions which are related to the disciplines of these faculties are chiefly treated.

767 In any kind of institute of higher studies, those who give theological courses or courses related to theology require a canonical mission.

768 The diocesan bishop should exercise serious pastoral care for students, even by means of the establishment of a parish or at least through priests appointed for the purpose on a stable basis; and he should provide that at universities, including non-Catholic universities, there be Catholic university centers to offer assistance, especially spiritual assistance, to young people.

769 The prescriptions established for universities apply in the same way to other institutions of higher studies.

770 The conference of bishops and the diocesan bishop should provide that, where possible, higher institutes of religious studies be founded in which theology and other disciplines pertinent to Christian culture are taught.

Canons 762–770
on Catholic Higher Education
Recommendations

A Response from the Association of Catholic Colleges and Universities

INTRODUCTION

The following recommendations are submitted by the Association of Catholic Colleges and Universities of the United States (ACCU), a body which includes 211 postsecondary degree-granting institutions. These are founded, sponsored by, or otherwise related to the Church; committed in their aims to the Church's ministry within higher education; chartered by authority of the several states of the United States; recognized by the American academic community and its voluntary associations, including accrediting agencies. All but thirty of the colleges (chiefly very small institutions) are members of ACCU, which embraces a great diversity: small and large, liberal arts colleges, major universities with a range of doctoral programs and professional schools, sponsored by religious institutes and by dioceses, etc.; the Jesuit colleges and universities are members of ACCU and have in addition their own association. The Catholic colleges and universities now have some 535,000 students at postsecondary school level; they constitute an entirely unique development, in size, breadth, and academic quality, within the Church's educational ministry.

The present and traditional relationships of the Catholic colleges and universities to the local churches and the religious institutes largely avoid the formalities of direct juridical or canonical bonds. Over several generations the present relationships have proved to be practically desirable and exceptionally fruitful. In the past few years these relationships have been strengthened, and the service of the institutions to the Church

From the files of the Association of Catholic Colleges and Universities

167

and their communion with the Church have been deepened. This has come about because of the clearer definitions of purpose and identity and the greater dialogue with the bishops, both in the local churches or provinces or states and at the national level, in the Committee of Bishops (from the National Conference of Catholic Bishops) and Presidents (from the ACCU).

The strength and Catholic commitment of the colleges and universities have been warmly recognized and supported by the November 1980 pastoral letter of the National Conference of Catholic Bishops, "Catholic Higher Education and the Pastoral Mission of the Church." This letter incorporates by reference two other documents which embrace our understanding of the best relationship of Church and higher education, namely, "The Catholic University in the Modern World" (1972) and "Relations of American Catholic Colleges and Universities with the Church" (1976).

PROPOSED CANONS ON CATHOLIC
HIGHER EDUCATION

In the light of this background and their history, the Catholic colleges and universities are extremely concerned with the proposed chapter of canons on this subject in the latest (1980) schema. Such a chapter of canons is an innovation in the law and, whatever their need or usefulness in other countries, would gravely jeopardize the integrity, academic standing, and even the survival of the American institutions. They would weaken, diminish, or destroy what has been and continues to be an extraordinary contribution of these Catholic institutions in the service of the Gospel.

The first recommendation of the ACCU remains, as stated in 1978 with reference to an earlier schema, that the canons on this topic not be included in the Code of Canon Law. For those countries or regions where such ecclesiastical legislation can be shown to be certainly necessary or useful, particular laws should suffice. Failing this, canons expressing the broad goals and responsibilities of Catholic higher education (such as canons 764, 768, and 770 of the schema) are certainly sufficient.

It is the conviction of the ACCU that the entire academic enterprise of its 211 member institutions—and thus their Christian and Catholic witness and presence in American society—will be needlessly placed in jeopardy by the proposed chapter of canons. The basic problem is the new, formal, and direct interventions in the internal governance of the institutions which is proposed in these canons. Such interventions, or their appearance, might well have the following harmful results:

1. Harm to the educational integrity and quality of the colleges and universities in relation to the rest of the Catholic community. The canons can be expected to place the institutions at the greatest disadvantage in the attraction and retention of qualified Catholic faculty members and students—all of whom have, in the United States, the opportunity to choose state and independent institutions with assured and legitimate academic autonomy.

2. Similar danger to the status and reputation of the Catholic institutions in relation to the rest of the academic community, especially the voluntary associations and accrediting agencies. These bodies will perceive a grave threat to academic excellence in the intervention of ecclesiastical authority.

3. Perhaps most serious of all, the danger of loss of governmental support—at both the federal and state levels. About 60 percent of the students in the Catholic institutions depend upon governmental grants and loans for assistance. Without this assistance to students the Catholic colleges and universities could not survive. The assistance is provided without governmental control of academic programs; it is provided under the condition of legitimate institutional autonomy, with serious Constitutional implications.

On the other hand, it should be added most emphatically that the absence of the formal juridical requirements of the proposed canons—in other words, the present relationship of Church and institutions—in no way weakens the authentically Catholic mission or witness of the colleges and universities. The latter see no problem in, and indeed welcome, the statements and principles of the Second Vatican Council on higher education (in *Gravissimum Educationis* and *Gaudium et Spes*), of Pope John Paul II (especially in his address to the members of ACCU in Washington in 1979), and of the National Conference of Catholic Bishops (pastoral letter referred to above). The Catholic colleges and universities would insist upon their institutional commitment to the ministry of higher education within the Catholic Church community.

INDIVIDUAL CANONS

Not all the proposed canons present equal difficulties to the American Catholic higher education community. Three, however, are seen as having the gravest consequences if retained in their present form.

Canon 763   Nulla studiorum Universitas nomen *Universitatis catholicae* gerat, nisi ex concessione Apostolicae Sedis.

1. If this text is interpreted in the strictest manner, as applicable only to the use of the word "Catholic" in the name or title of Catholic universities and colleges, it would not be of concern to the members of ACCU, only one of which employs the word itself in its name. The application of the canon to institutions which style themselves Catholic (for example, in their statements of purpose or by their membership in ACCU or IFCU) is a possibility which, at the very least, calls for clarification.

2. It is unnecessary and undesirable to reserve the recognition of such institutions to the Apostolic See. As in canon 686, §1, of the schema, and following the intent of the conciliar decree *Apostolicam Actuositatem*, n. 24, the reference should be to the competent ecclesiastical authority, namely, to the authority at the appropriate level, as demanded by ecclesial subsidiarity.

3. In the United States, experience demonstrates that the purposes of Catholic higher education can best be served by implicit recognition of the Catholic nature of the institutions by the local church or churches. It is always understood that such implicit recognition can yield, for cause and in some extreme case, to a formal pronouncement by the competent ecclesiastical authority that an institution has lost its Catholic character.

The following might be an alternative reading of canon 763:

> Nulla studiorum universitas nomen vel titulum *catholica* gerat nisi ex concessione vel agnitione, saltem implicita pro diversis regionis adiunctis, auctoritatis ecclesiasticae competentis.

Canon 765, §2 Episcoporum Conferentiae et Episcopi dioecesani quorum interest officium habent et ius invigilandi ut in iisdem Universitatibus principia doctrinae catholicae fideliter serventur; itemque evigendi ut, si ratio fidei morumve id requirat, docentes a munere removeantur.

1. The proposed text of §2 of this canon introduces a direct and formal intervention of extrinsic ecclesiastical authority into the internal governance of an academic institution in order to dismiss a professor from office, without any indication of a procedure, administrative or judicial, to be followed. In the United States (and in countries with similar academic systems) such interventions would violate institutional autonomy and would be potentially destructive of the institutions themselves.

2. It is recognized that professors, including those who enjoy continuous or permanent tenure, must sometimes be removed for incompetence, dishonesty, moral turpitude, or other grave and adequate cause. It is necessary, however, that this be done according to established academic procedures (which already exist in the United States). This was explicitly acknowledged in the 1972 statement: "In all cases, however,

any action taken by ecclesiastical or religious superiors should conform exactly to their authority as established in the university statutes and should be carried out according to those procedures of due process established in the statutes and recognized as general university common law in the geographical region of the particular university."

3. As drafted, the canon fails to respect the diversity of academic customary law, which in the United States determines in great detail the procedures to be followed and the responsibilities of faculty members, administrators, boards of trustees, etc. in this connection. Even in the case of the ecclesiastical faculties—for which more rigid canonical requirements may be expected if they are to give canonical degrees by papal authority—regional diversity has been recognized. See the introduction to the apostolic constitution *Sapientia Christiana*: "ratione habita regionum adiunctorum et universitatum usus in unaquaque regione vigentis."

In harmony with canon 765, §1, which acknowledges that the proper statutes of an institution should determine the right to appoint professors, the following text of §2 should be considered:

Espiscoporum Conferentiae . . . serventur; itemque exigendi ut, si ratio fidei morumve id requirat, docentes a munere removeantur, servata tamen procedura propriis statutis definita ad normam universitatum usus in unaquaque regione vigentis.

Canon 767   Qui in studiorum superiorum Institutis quibuslibet lectiones tradunt theologicas aut cum theologia conexas missione egent canonica.

1. The proposed canon introduces an unnecessary innovation which will immediately create all the problems referred to above. It is not in harmony, moreover, with what has already been established in canon 765, §1, namely, that the appointment of professors—of which the conferral of a canonical mission is an integral part in the case of teachers of theology—should follow the proper statutes of the individual institution.

2. In circumstances, both academic and civil, such as those which prevail in the United States, it is preferable and sufficient that the recognition or acknowledgement of the legitimacy or mission of Catholic professors remain entirely implicit and without canonical formality, as at present.

3. In 1978 ACCU proposed that the purpose of the *missio canonica* could be better achieved by imposing upon professors of theology or religious studies the obligation of maintaining orthodoxy within the full communion of the Catholic Church:

Qui in superiorum studiorum Institutis missionem fidem catholicam docendi exercent ministerium huiusmodi in plena communione fidei cum
Ecclesia catholica semper adimpleant.

4. Alternatively, since it is evident that the teaching of Catholic
doctrine at every educational level takes place and has taken place in
past centuries without the formality of *missio canonica*—whether in
universities, seminars, colleges, or schools—the purpose of the introduction of canon 767 should be considered, namely, the opportunity it
provides for the orthodoxy of Catholic teachers to be examined and, in
an extreme and extraordinary case, for their dismissal from teaching by
withdrawal of the *missio*. This purpose can be equally well achieved by
deleting canon 767 and relying upon the provision of canon 765, §2, as
considered above.

The Revised Code of Canon Law

Canons Regarding Universities (Canons 807–814)

807 The Church has the right to erect and to *supervise* universities which contribute to a higher level of human culture, to a fuller advancement of the human person and also to the fulfillment of the Church's teaching office.

808 *Even if it really be Catholic,* no university may bear the *title* or name Catholic university without the consent of the *competent ecclesiastical authority.*

809 If it is possible and advantageous, the conferences of bishops are to see to it that universities or at least faculties are established, suitably distributed throughout their territory, in which the various disciplines are to be investigated and taught *with due regard for their academic autonomy,* and *with due consideration for Catholic doctrine.*

810 1. It is the responsibility of the authority who is competent *in accord with* the statutes *to provide for the appointment* of teachers to Catholic universities who besides their scientific and pedagogical suitability are also outstanding in their integrity of doctrine and probity of life; when those requisite qualities are lacking they are to be removed from their positions in accord with the procedure set forth in the statutes.

2. The conference of bishops and the diocesan bishops concerned have the duty and right of being vigilant that in these universities the principles of Catholic doctrine are faithfully observed.

811 1. The competent ecclesiastical authority is to provide that at Catholic universities there be erected a faculty of theology, an institute of theology, or at least a chair of theology so that classes may be given for lay students.

2. In the individual Catholic universities classes should be given

From the files of the Association of Catholic Colleges and Universities

which treat in a special way those theological questions which are connected with the disciplines of their faculties.

812 It is necessary that those who teach *theological disciplines* in any institute of higher studies have a *mandate* from the competent ecclesiastical authority.

813 The diocesan bishop *is to have serious pastoral concern* for students by erecting a parish for them or by assigning priests for this purpose on a stable basis; he is also to provide for Catholic university centers at universities, even non-Catholic ones, to give assistance, especially spiritual to young people.

814 The prescriptions established for universities are equally applicable to other institutes of higher studies.

Code of Canon Law

Commentary on Canons 807–814

CATHOLIC UNIVERSITIES AND OTHER
INSTITUTES OF HIGHER STUDIES [cc. 807–814]

A preliminary question of a very serious nature must be raised about this set of canons on higher education, namely, whether or not they are applicable to most of the Catholic colleges and universities in the United States. Our Catholic institutions of higher learning are both distinctive and diverse in character, and they are the most numerous—with the largest number of students—in the world.

Both historically and in contemporary practice, the Catholic colleges and universities of the United States are considered as related to or affiliated with the Church rather than as "canonically Catholic." Except in the case of the very few diocesan colleges and The Catholic University of America, ties with the institutional Church have generally been informal and implicit at most; even diocesan colleges have been incorporated civilly, and the sponsorship and church responsibility, although of the greatest moral weight and significance, have not ordinarily been made a matter of canonical formality or determination. The vast majority of the colleges and universities in the United States have been sponsored by religious institutes of women or of men; these have been characterized by the proportion of religious, very great in the past, who serve as members of the governing boards, faculty, and administration. Generally these institutions have been without canonical ties to the local church or diocese, although again the moral weight and significance of their relationship to the church community cannot be overestimated.

The diversity among the Catholic colleges and universities in the United States further underlines a basic difference from the patterns in European countries and in countries whose educational systems are

---

Reprinted from *The Code of Canon Law, Text and Commentary*, ed. James Coriden et al. (Mahwah, N.J.: Paulist Press, 1985).

under European influence. This diversity ranges from small four-year liberal arts colleges to major universities with a comprehensive offering of graduate, professional, and undergraduate programs. There are many variations and combinations, for example, colleges with baccalaureate programs and one or more graduate programs added at the master's degree level.

In the United States there are some institutions that are considered *nonsectarian* at civil law, despite their original and continuing Catholic sponsorship and their present and continuing maintenance of the Catholic educational tradition, the presence of strong departments of religious studies, including Roman Catholic theology, close collaboration with the diocesan bishop, etc. Other institutions lack a formal policy affirming their Christian and Catholic nature, but de facto perpetuate, as a result of their foundation and sponsorship, a strong Christian and Catholic presence. Still others, and perhaps the considerable majority, express official policies—differing greatly in language and style—that assert their Catholic mission. It is difficult if not impossible to apply the canons as such to such divergent situations of the Catholic colleges and universities in the fifty states of the United States.

The Catholic character and mission of all these American institutions are not at question. The character and mission have been maintained in different ways, but any kind of formalization of canonical status has been generally avoided, the recognition of the Catholic character and mission by church authorities has been implicit, and the relationships of the institutions to the total church community and to church authorities have instead been cooperative and collaborative. (Unlike the institutions sponsored by some other religious bodies in the U.S., the Catholic colleges and universities do not enter into formal covenants or the like with ecclesiastical authorities nor do they, with certain exceptions, receive any direct church support.)

The question of the applicability of the canons to Catholic colleges and universities in the United States has other important facets:

First, it is evident that the canons are designed for systems of higher education in situations considerably different from those in North America. The pattern of postsecondary institutions which are publicly chartered but still retain their private and independent character is not known in most countries. Similarly, academic acceptance by private accrediting associations and other professional agencies and by voluntary educational associations is not significant elsewhere; in the United States it is of primary significance for the evaluation of institutions of higher learning and indeed for their impact upon human society, that is, for that very "public, persistent, and universal presence [of the Christian mind] in the whole enterprise of advancing human culture" of which

Vatican II spoke (*GE*, 10). Again, the location of the ultimate institutional authority in a governing board or board of trustees, which holds a public trust under the charter of incorporation, is a distinctive feature of institutions that is not contemplated in the canons.

The Catholic institutions in the United States, in order to satisfy the nature and purpose of higher education, follow the distinctive American pattern. At the same time they remain completely free to conduct instructional and research programs in the light of Catholic faith and with the interaction of all academic disciplines. This pattern differs so greatly in style of academic governance and in cultural and social dimensions from the European system of higher education that it is seriously questionable whether the canons are indeed applicable in the United States.

A second and related element is the purpose of canons 810, §2 and 812, which seek to assure the integrity of Catholic teaching. The historical background of such legislation, and specifically the background of the "canonical mission," which in turn is related to the mandate required of teachers of theological disciplines (c. 812), is found in nineteenth-century efforts to protect the Church's teaching office and the freedom of teachers of theology from the hostile interference of civil states and secular political control. To the extent that this is the purpose of the law, it has no application at all in the United States. In this country both ecclesiastical authorities and teachers of theological disciplines are protected by the provisions of the First Amendment, prohibiting a governmental establishment of religion and protecting the free exercise of religion, and by similar provisions in the constitutions of the fifty states. In other words, the absence of this rationale for the law, a rationale which may remain a genuine concern in some countries today, makes the law inapplicable in the United States. The other evident purpose of the law, namely, the safeguarding of doctrine within the church community, appears to be adequately assured by the exercise of moral rather than canonical authority.

Still another, and third, consideration has already been suggested by the absence of formal juridical or canonical ties—in most instances—between the American Catholic post-secondary institutions and church authorities. The revised Code of Canon Law has refined the definitions of institutions which are considered as having juridical personality at canon law, namely, as subjects of canonical rights and obligations (see c. 113, §2). The determination whether an individual institution is a juridical person would have to be made. None of the Catholic colleges and universities would be considered a public juridical person, that is, with the capacity of acting "in the name of the Church" (c. 116, §1). In other matters also, even apart from the canons on Catholic higher education, the institutions are not touched directly by the canon law. For example,

see canon 1257, §2 concerning property: this is not governed by the
canon law even in the case of those institutions which might have been
constituted as private juridical persons. These principles hold despite the
fact that the canon law is understood as applicable to Catholic members
of the college or university community, whether faculty members or
administrators or students.

This point is made because in fact the canons concerning Catholic
colleges, universities, and other institutions of higher studies—when read
carefully—appear to avoid imposing norms or obligations upon the
institutions as such, beyond stating what would be otherwise evident
from the nature of their identity, precisely because without juridical
personality the institutions do not have any standing in the canon law.
This becomes especially important in the case of canon 812, which is
later commented upon at some length.

The aforementioned considerations about applicability are sound
and have led some to the conclusion that the canons are inapplicable to most American institutions of higher education. They do not,
however, diminish either the need to examine the canons carefully or
the significance of the ministry of higher education within the Church.
Such a ministry demands that, in accord with the fundamental purpose of the canons, those Catholics who teach or who exercise other
positions of responsibility in Catholic colleges and universities act in
full communion with the Church. This does not contravene in any way
the right to academic freedom, which the canons expressly uphold in
accord with the explicit teaching of Vatican II (see cc. 809 and 218).
(These observations on the applicability of the canons are derived from
a memorandum drawn up by Frederick R. McManus with the assistance
of other canonists and circulated to Catholic college presidents on 3 Aug.
1983 by the Association of Catholic Colleges and Universities.)

Canon 807—The Church has the right to erect and to supervise
universities which contribute to a higher level of human culture, to a
fuller advancement of the human person and also to the fulfillment of
the Church's teaching office.

The opening canon both reasserts the Church's right to be involved
in higher education and offers a brief rationale for that involvement. The
Church may establish and run colleges and universities; in so doing, they
contribute to: (1) the advancement of culture; (2) the development of the
human person; and (3) the fulfillment of the Church's teaching office.
Gravissimum Educationis, 10, from which this canon is drawn, speaks
eloquently of the Church's intention to have the individual disciplines
studied according to their own principles and methods and with proper

freedom of scientific investigation (cf. c. 218) so that a deeper understanding may result, and so that faith and reason will be seen to be at
one in the harmony of truth.

Pope John Paul II said to the presidents of Catholic colleges and
universities in the United States:

> As one who for long years has been a university professor, I will never tire
> of insisting on the eminent role of the university, which is to instruct but
> also to be a place of scientific research. In both these fields, its activity
> is closely related to the deepest and noblest aspiration of the human
> person: the desire to come to the knowledge of truth. No university can
> deserve the rightful esteem of the world of learning unless it applies the
> highest standards of scientific research, constantly updating its methods
> and working instruments, and unless it excels in seriousness, and therefore,
> in freedom of investigation (Oct. 7, 1979; *Pilgrim of Peace*, USCC, p. 165).

No authority is designated for the establishment or governance of
these institutions; per se they do not require the intervention of any
ecclesiastical authority. *Gravissimum Educationis*, 8 and canon 1375 of
the 1917 Code are also among the sources for this canon; canon 800 of
the revised Code is its parallel.

Canon 808—Even if it really be Catholic, no university may bear
the title or name *Catholic university* without the consent of the competent ecclesiastical authority.

Anyone in the Catholic Church can establish a Catholic college or
university. The action of a church authority is required if it is canonically
erected as a public juridic person (c. 116; cf. 1981 *Rel* 181). But for the
college or university to bear the *title* or *name "Catholic"* the permission
of a competent ecclesiastical authority must be received, even though the
institution is already really Catholic (Cf. the remarks at the beginning of
this chapter of the Code about the applicability of these canons to U.S.
institutions.)

This preoccupation with the use of the name "*Catholic*," both here
and in reference to elementary and secondary schools in canon 803, §3,
is difficult to understand. It goes beyond the restrictions on the canonical
establishment of Catholic universities and faculties and the approval of
statutes by the Holy See called for in canon 1376 of the 1917 Code. It
is echoed in canon 300 on associations of the faithful and canon 216 on
apostolic enterprises. Its root is in *Apostolicam Actuositatem*, 24, which
is far removed from higher education. It may reflect a desire to prevent
the use of the title "*Catholic*" by institutions which are perceived not
to be authentically Catholic. But the words of Pope John Paul II to the

presidents of Catholic colleges and universities place the concern in a more positive light:

> A Catholic university or college must make a specific contribution to the Church and to society through high quality scientific research, in-depth study of problems, and a just sense of history, together with the concern to show the full meaning of the human person regenerated in Christ, thus favoring the complete development of the person. Furthermore, the Catholic university or college must train young men and women of outstanding knowledge who, having made a personal synthesis between faith and culture, will be both capable and willing to assume tasks in the service of the community and of society in general, and to bear witness to their faith before the world. And finally, to be what it ought to be, a Catholic college or university must set up, among its faculty and students, a real community which bears witness to a living and operative Christianity, a community where sincere commitment to scientific research and study goes together with a deep commitment to authentic Christian living.
>
> This is your identity. This is your vocation. Every university or college is qualified by a specific mode of being. Yours is the qualification of being Catholic, of affirming God, his revelation and the Catholic Church as the guardian and interpreter of that revelation. The term "Catholic" will never be a mere label, either added or dropped according to the pressures of varying factors (Oct. 7, 1979; *Pilgrim of Peace*, USCC, pp. 164–165).

No definition of a Catholic college or university is given in the Code; the following canon (c. 809) and the place in *Gravissimum Educationis*, 10 from which it is drawn, and the foregoing words of Pope John Paul II help us to understand what the Church considers them to be.

Who are the ecclesiastical authorities competent to give permission for a college or university to call itself "Catholic"? Earlier drafts of this same canon mentioned the Apostolic See and the episcopal conference, and surely both of them are included here; diocesan bishops who are given the right and duty of vigilance in canon 810 could also grant permission, personally or through a delegate, for institutions within the diocesan territory. It might be argued that major superiors of clerical religious communities devoted to the educational apostolate might also grant such permission for an institution founded and operated by their community, based on their status as ordinaries (c. 134) and their communities' special participation in the teaching office of the Church (cc. 758, 801). Normally the executive authority of such ordinaries is limited to the members of their communities.

It is difficult to imagine very many Catholic colleges or universities in the United States actually requesting the permission suggested in this canon. Most such institutions are already confident in their Catholic identity. And the canons do not have retroactive effect (c. 9); an institution which used *"Catholic"* in its title or description before November 27, 1983, is not subject to the new provision of this canon.

Canon 809—If it is possible and advantageous the conferences of bishops are to see to it that universities or at least faculties are established, suitably distributed throughout their territory, in which the various disciplines are to be investigated and taught with due regard for their academic autonomy, and with due consideration for Catholic doctrine.

This canon, echoing the teaching of *Gravissimum Educationis*, 10 and canon 1379, §2 of the 1917 Code, obliges the bishops' conference to be concerned about the establishment of Catholic colleges and universities and their appropriate distribution throughout the territory of the conference. The conference is to see to their establishment if it is judged possible and expedient. The brief statement of the purpose of these institutions of higher learning also reflects *Gravissimum Educationis*, 10: the various disciplines may be investigated and taught, observing the scientific autonomy of each, and with due regard for Catholic teaching. Their proper educational function is given clear priority.

As Pope John Paul II said,

> The relationship to truth explains therefore the historical bond between the university and the Church. Because she herself finds her origin and her growth in the words of Christ, which are the liberating truth (cf. Jn 8:32), the Church has always tried to stand by the institutions that serve, and cannot but serve the knowledge of truth (Oct. 7, 1979; *Pilgrim of Peace*, USCC, p. 165).

Canon 810—§1. It is the responsibility of the authority who is competent in accord with the statutes to provide for the appointment of teachers to Catholic universities who besides their scientific and pedagogical suitability are also outstanding in their integrity of doctrine and probity of life; when those requisite qualities are lacking they are to be removed from their positions in accord with the procedure set forth in the statutes.

§2. The conference of bishops and the diocesan bishops concerned have the duty and right of being vigilant that in these universities the principles of Catholic doctrine are faithfully observed.

In treating of the appointment and removal of teachers in Catholic colleges and universities in paragraph one, the revised Code *canonizes* the statutes of the institution. It respects the legitimate autonomy of each academic setting. These critical and sensitive processes are to be governed by the internal regulations of each school. The authorities responsible and the procedures to be followed are those which the institution has established for itself; this paragraph simply recognizes those statutes as the law to be applied. The statutes should embody the standards of fairness and good practice which are accepted in the academic community of the country or culture. The institutional authority is addressed in the first paragraph; the second paragraph speaks to episcopal responsibilities.

In addition, paragraph one gives an indication of the qualities to be sought in those who are candidates for teaching positions in Catholic colleges or universities: (1) capability in knowledge and in teaching; and (2) integrity of doctrine and uprightness of life. These are very general guidelines; they simply point in the direction of the kind of scholarly excellence and personal example which should characterize Catholic college faculty members. They cannot be applied to teachers employed because of their doctrinal divergence (e.g., for ecumenical reasons) or where the discipline is devoid of doctrinal implications.

In its 1981 *Relatio* (pp. 182–183) it is clear that the Code Commission feels that this paragraph applies to administrators as well as to the teaching faculty.

The duty and right of vigilance over Catholic colleges and universities stated in the second paragraph is concurrent, that is, it belongs both to the episcopal conference and to the diocesan bishop. The interested diocesan bishop (presumably the one in whose territory the college or university is located) acts by his own authority and not as the agent for the conference, but his action does not prevent the conference from also exercising vigilance, that is, from also overseeing the same institution. The canon does not provide for the resolution of the possible conflicts which could arise out of this double concession of authority (but cf. cc. 1732–1739 on administrative recourse).

What is the duty and right of vigilance? It does *not* imply ownership, governance, jurisdiction, control, intervention, or even visitation— all of those levels of authority and responsibility are distinct from the "ius invigilandi." It does mean a pastoral watchfulness, a benign surveillance, a solicitous oversight. It implies information and communication, inquiry, advice, sharing of concerns, even perhaps friendly persuasion. But it is not an adversarial relationship; it is neither inquisitorial nor authoritarian.

What is the *scope* of this duty and right of vigilance over Catholic colleges and universities? "That . . . the principles of Catholic doctrine are faithfully observed," says the canon. It is an interest which stems from the bishop's teaching office, a concern which is related to the ministry of the word in his diocese (cf. c. 386). The scope of vigilance is limited then to the basics of Catholic teaching and the way they are communicated and witnessed in the context of and in accord with the methods of an institution of higher education.

The bishop or the conference may exercise this duty of vigilance by delegation.

Earlier drafts of the second paragraph provided that bishops could remove teachers for reasons of faith or morals. The deletion of that provision is most worthy of note. It was removed as both unnecessary and inappropriate, an improper external intervention in the internal affairs of an institution of higher education.

Canon 811—§1. The competent ecclesiastical authority is to provide that at Catholic universities there be erected a faculty of theology, an institute of theology, or at least a chair of theology so that classes may be given for lay students.

§2. In the individual Catholic universities classes should be given which treat in a special way those theological questions which are connected with the disciplines of their faculties.

The first paragraph of this canon makes it incumbent upon ecclesiastical authorities to promote the teaching of theology in Catholic colleges and universities, especially so that lay students will benefit from it. It is taken directly from *Gravissimum Educationis*, 10, and it is also related to *Gaudium et Spes*, 57, which is concerned with the necessary dialogue between faith and culture. The bishops of the United States spoke to the value of theological studies in this context in 1980:

> It is advisable, however, that students be encouraged to cope with their personal problems of faith and to consider the religious dimensions of the major issues in our contemporary culture and society. Theology should enable students to think and to act within a vision of life that includes religious values. A truly liberating and elevating education is incomplete without the study of theology or religion. ("Catholic Higher Education and the Pastoral Mission of the Church," USCC, 1981, p. 5).

The competent ecclesiastical authority is not specified, but it would include the Holy See, episcopal conferences, diocesan bishops, and might possibly extend to major religious superiors of clerical congregations which are devoted to Catholic higher education. Three forms of theological presence are suggested in the canon: a faculty (i.e., a school or department), an institute, or at least a chair; the choice depends on the situation within the college or university and the funds which can be raised to support the theological enterprise.

Paragraph two is an attempt to promote the dialogue between theology and the other disciplines on campus, and to promote theological reflection on the issues raised by those disciplines. The canon is drawn from *Gravissimum Educationis*, 10, and *Guadium et Spes*, 36; both insist on the value of genuine scientific investigation in all branches of learning. Catholic colleges and universities are to stimulate the exchange between theology and the other disciplines by seeing that the theological questions related to those other disciplines are publicly discussed.

Canon 812—It is necessary that those who teach theological disciplines in any institute of higher studies have a mandate from the competent ecclesiastical authority.

This terse, new canon caused more apprehension and provoked more opposition during the drafting stages of the revised Code than probably any other provision of the law. The requirement of an ecclesiastical mandate to teach theology is found nowhere in the 1917 Code nor in the teachings of the Second Vatican Council. It originated in Germany in 1848 when the hierarchy was struggling to retain some control over the teaching of religion in the newly secularized schools. The German bishops ruled that no one could teach the Catholic religion at any level of the educational system unless he or she had a "canonical mission" from the local bishop. This provision was later included in the various concordats between the Vatican and the German State. It was taken over into the regulations for "pontifical faculties" (i.e., those erected or approved by the Holy See) in the Apostolic Constitution *Deus Scientiarum Dominus* (24 May 1931; *AAS* 23 [1931], 241). This authorization ("missio canonica") to teach was to be given and could be withdrawn by the chancellor of the pontifical university (acts. 21, 22). When these norms for pontifical schools were reissued in 1979 (Apostolic Constitution *Sapientia Christiana*, 15 Apr. 1979; *ASS* 71 [1979], 469) this provision was retained (art. 17). Now, with this present canon, the ecclesiastical authorization process is extended to all teachers of theology in all Catholic colleges and universities. (Cf. what was said at the outset of this chapter of the Code on the applicability of these canons to the North American context.)

When the canon was proposed in the 1977 draft of the revised Code, it raised a storm of opposition in North America. The Association of Catholic Colleges and Universities, the Catholic Theological Society of America, and the "Bishops and Presidents Committee" all made strong representations for its deletion. The grounds for their opposition, briefly, were these: (1) this mode of ecclesiastical control would have a chilling and stifling effect on theological investigation; (2) it represents an unwelcome intrusion into the normal academic procedures by an outside authority, i.e., a violation of the legitimate autonomy of educational institutions; (3) this sort of control may well cause conflicts with teachers' unions or government regulations; (4) this new form of church involvement might jeopardize financial assistance from the government; (5) the canon contains no provision for the customary procedures in cases of removal of professors; (6) it may cause a major administrative burden on some bishops; (7) the purpose which the law seeks is presently being accomplished within the academic institutions by the judgment of peers and by conscientious administrators; and (8) the canon is superfluous because adequate provision is already made in canon 810. This concern was carried by prelates from Canada and the United States to the Code Commission (cf. 1981 *Rel*, p. 183), and in person to Pope John Paul II by delegates of the Association of Catholic Colleges and Universities (audience of March 18, 1982). Concern remains at such a level in North America that the United States and Canadian bishops are being urged to request an indult dispensing these territories from the obligation of canon 812.

The canon proposed by the Code Commission in 1977 and again in 1980 was changed significantly but not essentially when it was presented to the plenary meeting of October 1981. The earlier version read: "Those who teach courses in theology or courses related to theology in any kind of institute of higher studies require ("egent") a canonical mission." Four significant changes appear in the present canon 812: (1) the level of exigency was moderated from "require" ("egent") to "should have" ("habeant oportet"); (2) the authorization was changed from a "canonical mission" ("missio canonica") to a "mandate" ("mandatum")—the Code Commission said that it was not the same as a real canonical mission (*Rel*, p. 184); (3) the granting authority is named, at least generically, the "competent ecclesiastical authority"; and (4) it is limited to "theological disciplines"—the "courses related to theology" are omitted.

As it now stands, what institutions are referred to by the canon? All and only Catholic colleges and universities are included, that is, all Catholic institutions of postsecondary education, including academies, institutes, etc., but excluding seminaries because they are specifically regulated by another section of the Code, namely, canons 232–264. Institutions erected or approved by the Holy See, "ecclesiastical universities and faculties," are included by canon 818. But the canon is not directed to the institutions; its obligation falls upon the individual teacher to have a mandate.

Which instructors in those institutions are covered by this regulation? Those who will be added to faculties to teach theology on a full-time basis as their chief faculty responsibility. One-time, part-time, or occasional theology teachers are probably not included because the canon is concerned with ongoing, long-term instruction. Since the Code is not retroactive (cf. c. 9), those who held academic appointments at the time it became effective are not affected. Similarly not affected are those who are teaching or will teach theology who are not Catholics or not in the Latin Church; they are not bound by the Code (cf. cc. 1, 11). Finally, what is meant by "theological disciplines"? Since the law is clearly restrictive of the "free exercise of rights" it is subject to strict interpretation (c. 18). The "theological disciplines" certainly refer to dogmatics or systematics as well as historical, moral, and sacramental theology. Church history, liturgical studies, canon law, and sacred scripture, while not—strictly speaking—"theology," are probably included in the meaning of "theological disciplines" (cf. c. 252). However, catechetics, many areas of pastoral studies, comparative religions, history or sociology of religion are not considered "theological disciplines."

Who is the "competent ecclesiastical authority"? The Apostolic See and the local diocesan bishop are surely capable of granting the mandate to teach theology. Probably the other ordinaries listed in canon 134 could also do so, and it might be argued that the major religious superiors of clerical communities which own and operate Catholic colleges could give mandates for their own members teaching in their own institutions. The episcopal conference is probably not included.

The "mandate" is simply a recognition that the person is properly engaged in teaching the theological discipline. It is not an empowerment, an appointment, or a formal commission. It is disciplinary, not doctrinal. It does not grant approval of what is taught nor is it a formal association with the Church's mission or ministry of teaching. There is no requirement that the mandate be in writing or even explicit, nor that it be received more than once.

Those ordinaries who are competent to grant the mandate may delegate that authority to others (e.g., an administrative officer of the college, the faculty of a department, etc.). Before issuing any such mandates for teaching theology (if a dispensation from the law is not obtained), it might be well to consider the following: (1) delegating an academic administrator within each institution to grant such mandates, following the school's usual procedures for appointments of and, when necessary, removal of instructors; and (2) establishing procedural safeguards so that the customary peer review and due process protection are afforded and all appearances of arbitrary action avoided.

Canon 813—The diocesan bishop is to have serious pastoral concern for students by erecting a parish for them or by assigning priests for this purpose on a stable basis; he is also to provide for Catholic university centers at universities, even non-Catholic ones, to give assistance, especially spiritual to young people.

This canon fixes on the diocesan bishop the pastoral responsibility for providing campus ministry. It is taken directly from *Gravissimum Educationis*, 10, where the motivation is stated: "the lot of society and of the Church itself is intimately connected with the development of those young people who are engaged in higher studies." The pastoral concern is for students at both Catholic and non-Catholic colleges and universities, and the bishop is instructed to set up a parish for their benefit or at least permanently assign priests for their ministry. Colleges and universities, both Catholic and non-Catholic, are to have "Catholic university centers," like the Newman Foundations, for the aid, especially spiritual help, of the young people studying there. The Second Vatican Council spoke of the "carefully selected and prepared priests, religious and lay persons providing both intellectual and spiritual assistance" to the students. It is indeed a critical apostolate.

Canon 814—The prescriptions established for universities are equally applicable to other institutes of higher studies.

This canon simply clarifies terminology. In the foregoing canons the term "universities" was used to stand for all sorts of postsecondary educational institutions: colleges, universities, academies, institutes, etc. (but not seminaries; they are separately regulated by cc. 232–264). The canon states that what was prescribed for universities applies to the other institutions as well.

Part IV

Point and Counterpoint:
Ex Corde Ecclesiae
1985–1990

The documents in this section address the development of the apostolic constitution, *Ex Corde Ecclesiae*. Beginning in 1980, the Congregation for Catholic Education undertook the task of formulating a document that would define a Catholic University. With the promulgation of the Code of Canon Law in 1983, the explanation for the new document was that it would "flesh out" the new canons (807–814). The first draft circulated for consultation was that done in the same year, 1983; it went only to certain "periti" for their review. Following some revision in the text, a draft was then circulated to all bishops and university presidents in 1985; this draft became known as the "Schema." In the United States the responses from the presidents were synthesized and reported to the Congregation by ACCU and the bishops' responses were collated by USCC. During the process of the consultation, bishops and presidents exchanged views and opinions through the medium of the Bishops' and Presidents' Committee which had been organized in 1974. This proved to be a helpful instrument of dialogue. The critiques were submitted to Rome in February, 1986.

In the following year (1987), Pope John Paul II was received by the Catholic colleges and universities assembled at Xavier University of Louisiana. Once again, his genuine appreciation of the work of universities dissipated many of the fears that the Schema had aroused. Meanwhile, the Congregation, having received over 650 responses worldwide, collated these and distributed them to all the participants in the consultation. Further responses were invited. At the same time, the Congregation drew up another draft and circulated it in 1988 in preparation for a meeting to be convened in Rome in April, 1989.

This process of extensive consultation was appreciated by the institutions to be affected by the final document. In April, 1989, ninety rectors or presidents of universities and forty bishops chosen by their national conferences met in Rome for eight days of discussion and debate. Eighteen of the delegates were from the United States, chosen by the Board of Directors of ACCU, and four bishops from the United States were designated by the NCCB. In addition to the delegates, about forty persons were there as periti or guests of the Congregation.

The final voting on the recommendations was limited to the elected delegates. There was unanimous approval for most of the recommendations but there were a few negative votes on one or two of them. The group then voted to have a small delegation of fifteen persons elected from among the participants in this meeting return to Rome in September 1989, to give final assistance in writing the draft to be given to the Plenarium of the congregation and then to the pope. His holiness addressed the meeting on April 25th and expressed gratitude for the work of Catholic universities. A revised text, based on the changes proposed by the delegates to the April meeting, was issued in August so that the opportunity for response was kept open.

This extensive process was in itself a source of confidence in the outcome. For this reason each of the drafts is an important document and so we include them here. When the final apostolic constitution, *Ex Corde Ecclesiae*, was issued in September 1990, such confidence was rewarded. Apart from the norms (already in the Code of 1983), there was little to cause anxiety and much to enable and inspire those in higher education. The implementation of the "norms" was handed to the national conferences of bishops. Thus, it will be many years before the process will be completed. The last document in this collection, therefore, is *Ex Corde Ecclesiae.*

Draft Schema of a Pontifical Document on Catholic Universities

April 1985

PRELIMINARY OBSERVATIONS AND QUERIES CONCERNING THE SCHEMA

1. Course of the Schema

Previous to the present Schema there were two international congresses of representatives of Catholic universities throughout the world, convoked in Rome by the Congregation for Catholic Education in 1969 and 1972. At the conclusion of the second, a booklet composed by the participants was issued. The booklet "L'Université Catholique dans le Monde Moderne" was approved by the same Congregation in its letter of 23 April 1973. It contains the fundamental elements of the identity of a Catholic university.

Following the publication on 15 April 1979 of the Apostolic Constitution *Sapientia Christiana* for *ecclesiastical* universities and faculties (= faculties of sacred studies or secular studies connected with the sacred), the Supreme Pontiff John Paul II entrusted to the Congregation the task of advancing the preparation—in collaboration with all other interested parties—a pontifical document on *Catholic* universities (= faculties of secular studies, with or without faculties of sacred studies). The Plenary Assembly of the Fathers of the Congregation, 25 March 1981, was occupied for the first time with a rudimentary draft of such a document, which, reworked in accordance with their observations, was then submitted by the Congregation on 1 March 1982 to a restricted number of experts for a first study.

In execution of the Plenarium of 9 March 1983—which had examined the results of the experts' study—the Congregation extended the consultation, *ever informal*, to a greater number of interested and

---

Sacred Congregation for Catholic Education, from *Origins* 15, no. 43 (April 10, 1986): 706–711.

competent parties. A notably modified Schema resulted from this, and was brought for examination by the Fathers of the Congregation in the Plenarium of 4 April 1984. The Fathers, ordering further revisions, have enjoined that the resulting Schema be sent now, *for official consultation, to all interested parties,* namely Catholic universities, episcopal conferences, bishops of dioceses in which there are Catholic universities, religious families and similar institutes or canonical entities managing Catholic universities, some other competent Roman Dicasteries, executives of the International Federation of Catholic Universities and of other associations of Catholic universities, as well as experts of sound competence.

2. Brief Description of the Schema

a) Concerning Its Content

It is to be borne in mind that its content is only the *fruit of certain informal consultations,* even though the Fathers of the Congregation have provisionally expressed themselves on them. The Schema therefore is to be considered *a simple respectful synthesis of suggestions* made so far, subject therefore to all the changes which the various examiners will want to propose on the basis of their specific competence.

b) Concerning Its Form

The Schema is divided into two parts, Proemium and Norms, as is generally expected of pontifical documents of this kind. Subdivisions are introduced, bearing appropriate subheadings.

In the Proemium the subdivisions have been made through the sequence of roman numerals, though adjoined on the left-hand side and in parentheses is the indication of the material treated. It is clear however that such subheadings are purely functional, and may be modified or even eliminated. To facilitate citation of the Proemium, each paragraph has been numbered, and observations may be made on the matter by simply referring to the number.

In the Norms the "chapters" and their "headings" are foreseen to remain. For these too, though, you have full freedom to propose changes of any kind.

3. Queries Addressed to Examiners

In execution of the mandate it has received, the Congregation for Catholic Education invites *a thorough examination* of the present schema. The matter certainly merits the greatest attention whether on account of the subject itself or on account of the variety of situations existent in the Church in this respect.

The Congregation invites an examination *in full freedom and frankness*, without preclusions of any sort. It is and wants to be a pure *working instrument*, to be assessed with impartiality from every point of view. Particular care is to be given to the *structure* both of the Proemium and of the Norms and, within each of the two parts, to the validity of their contents.

Consequently, we would like the examiners' opinions on the *effective suitability* of the Schema, proposing additions, suppressions, substitutions and changes of any kind, with particular attention to the *ideal motivations* contained in the Proemium.

The Congregation earnestly asks that the *most concrete possible suggestions* be made, rewriting if need be chapters, paragraphs, or articles, without limiting oneself to a simple indication of not liking this or that step. Evidently, for each suggestion the *reasoning* which justifies it is important.

4. DATE FOR PRESENTATION OF RESPONSES

The Congregation for Catholic Education asks that responses be sent *before and not later than 30 November 1985*.

As is necessary in these cases, the Congregation will prepare a reasoned synthesis of responses with a view to presenting them in advance to the future participants of an *International Congress*, which we hope to be able to call in the course of 1986.

5. FINAL NOTE

As is said expressly in a note at the beginning of the Proemium, the pontifical document on Catholic universities is directed also to *Catholic institutes of higher studies* which confer academic degrees.

PROEMIUM

I. REASONS FOR A PONTIFICAL DOCUMENT

(1) The Catholic Church greatly values Catholic universities.* In fact, while rendering to truth the service expected of every university, they perform an irreplaceable task in the work of sowing the Gospel of Christ in the culture of our time and in the culture of individual peoples. They do it through scientific research, university teaching, and the higher education of her members. Such a task appears today to be all the more necessary and urgent, considering the complexity of modern civilization,

great technical progress, the enormous possibilities for human activity, the problem of fundamental values, the multiple currents of thought, and the various threats confronting mankind.

(2)   For this reason the ecclesial community wants her universities to be more effective and more numerous in order to offer to mankind the content and dynamism of Catholic thought.[1] The ecclesial community feels the need that the Catholic character of her universities be more evident and powerful in order to respond better to their duty because it is precisely this character which constitutes their fundamental *raison d'être* and which explains the trust accorded to them.

(3)   The present pontifical document, taking different situations and experiences into account, proposes to contribute to the strengthening of Catholic universities in the firm conviction that their greater promotion will be to the benefit of society, both ecclesial and civil.

II. CHURCH AND UNIVERSITY

(4)   In the courses of centuries the Catholic Church has shown great consideration for universities. She has the credit of being involved in the very foundation of the university as such.[2]

Indeed from the beginning of her existence the Church has cultivated knowledge and has created numerous teaching centers. In her monasteries and through her more illustrious members, she has long been a point of reference for culture. When universities began to be formed she gave them all her support and interest, putting at their disposal her own experience, guidance, personnel, cultural resources, and economic means. Indeed, she herself founded the majority of them. With the passage of time civil society has taken responsibility for the university world and the Church has felt the need to have Catholic universities as such.[3]

(5)   The Catholic Church is fully conscious of the right which she has to create freely Catholic universities. A long historical tradition demonstrates and confirms the natural rights of Catholics to establish her own formative system.

III. ACTUAL SITUATION OF THE CATHOLIC UNIVERSITIES

1. Positive Factors

(6)   In our time there are in existence numerous Catholic universities which by reason of scientific commitment enjoy great prestige and the trust of society. There is satisfaction in the fact that their number is growing and their activity developing further. Other forms of Catholic

higher education are also prospering: institutes of university formation of various kinds and levels, professional schools, scientific research centers. (7)   Other than these institutions, there is the great number of Catholic teachers and scientists who, in the various universities and institutions of higher education, bear splendid Christian witness in their work.

All these facts are a source of optimism about a qualified and public presence of Catholic thought in the modern world.

2. Negative Factors

(8)   On the other hand, one notes that Catholic universities encounter various difficulties. The insufficiency of economic means, the temptation of pragmatism, the tendency to secularization, the influence of extraneous ideologies, the weakening of the Catholic character lead to situations of hesitation and in some cases bewilderment.
(9)   Then, it is necessary to reveal that in some parts of the world abnormal situations persist in which Catholic universities cannot be established or are forcibly subject to the elimination of their Catholic character, or are exposed to multiple administrative restrictions, or to ideological manipulations by the holders of power who champion different visions of the world.

3. Pluralist Situation

(10) Today the Catholic university lives and functions in a society profoundly pluralistic. For its existence and activity the Catholic university claims an appropriate space and freedom.

She declares a sincere collaboration with civil society and its institutions, above all with those of higher education in order to contribute to the common good and to the integral development of man and of society.
(11) Moreover, by reason of the same pluralism and of equality in dialogue, the Catholic university firmly requests respect for its proper Catholic identity and for equal treatment with all institutions of higher education, including the help and facility conceded by civil authority because the Catholic university too contributes to the common good.

IV. NATURE OF THE CATHOLIC UNIVERSITY

(12) The Catholic university, like every university, is a higher institution of research, teaching, and of every other educational service at university level. More specifically, it is the place in which, at a scientific level, aspects of reality are examined and scrutinized, the various disciplines and sciences are taught, and persons are educated in an adequate manner; all

in order to promote continuously the development and the good of man. As "Catholic", it seeks to enrich with the values of the Gospel, as the Catholic Church proposes them, the knowledge acquired, the disciplines taught, and the other aspects of its activity.

(13) As a "universitas scientiarum" the Catholic university is a place of encounter where the various branches of human knowledge continuously confront one another for their mutual enrichment in the light of the gospel message.[4]

(14) As a "universitas scholarum" it educates men and women suited for work in the professions or specific careers, in possession of the Christian ethic adequate to the problems to be confronted, eager to serve the human family in helping it in its growth, understanding, and solidarity.

(15) Its professors, "universitas magistrorum" must be people who are competent in their disciplines and in possession of that educative wisdom which has always distinguished Catholic teaching.

(16) Thus, as a whole it constitutes a communal committed witness of the Catholic faith lived out in the world of science;[5] it finds "its ultimate and profound significance in Christ, in his message of salvation that embraces man in his totality, and in the teaching of the Church."[6]

V. THE ECCLESIAL FUNCTION OF THE CATHOLIC UNIVERSITY

1. Catholic Character and Its Implications

(17) The Catholic university is an expression and a presence of the Church in the world of culture and higher education.[7] It exists within the Church and is part of it. Although it exists within a specific local Church, by reason of its nature and activity it exercises an influence at a universal level because neither science nor faith are limited and are for the benefit of everyone.

(18) Its Catholic character is derived from the ordering of the university to integral truth which is put before mankind by the Catholic Church and the members of the university take on this truth as their own. This ordering implies a particular relationship with the pastors of the Church who have the task of being authentic teachers of the faith for their faithful.[8]

(19) On the one hand, such Catholic character takes on an ecclesial function which must be reflected in all activities of those working in the university so that their Christian witness be clear. Furthermore the university is called to respond to the expectations of the People of God who see in it a more mature, more responsible and a higher assumption of the Christian vocation in the world.

(20) On the other hand, the Catholic character generates obligations on the part of the whole Church with regard to the universities themselves. In various parts of the world new initiatives are to be planned and taken to found such universities. Then, it is necessary to sustain and promote those already existing. The pastors of the Church have the task of acknowledging and encouraging the difficult mission of Catholic universities, in particular of their teachers and researchers, and at the same time to assist them in every possible way in the various difficult situations. They invite the faithful to sustain their own university institutions whether by protecting their just rights in civil matters or by contributing economic means.

(21) The promotion and the safeguard of the "Catholic" character of the Catholic university is certainly the duty of the members of the University itself and of those who direct it or who support it in any way. It is equally the special task of the pastors of the Church who are responsible for the faith in their own particular churches. Pope Paul VI said in this regard: "Today as yesterday, the Magisterium is still the authentic guarantor of your inspiration in the fidelity freely given to the living tradition received from the apostles.[9]

2. Contribution of the Catholic University to the Mission of the Church

(22) Being part of the Church, the Catholic university participates in her mission and takes on in accordance with her nature a part of the responsibility for it.[10] "The Church, precisely because she is ever more conscious of her salvific mission in this world, wants to feel close to these centers: she wants to have them present and operating in the spreading of the authentic message of Christ."[11]

(23) The Catholic university can be considered in fact a particular place for the carrying out of the salvific mission of the Church. It is its duty to operate so that the Christian message may be easily understood, accepted, and seen in the vast world of human culture.

(24) Furthermore, the immense progress in the natural and human sciences, recent studies and investigations bring forth new questions and present new difficulties. The specific task of the Catholic university will be to accept these challenges and to make its contribution towards a solution that safeguards and promotes the spiritual and transcendent vision of man.

(25) Educating people at the highest cultural and professional level, the Catholic university deepens in them a living Catholic faith, so that they are thus prepared to take up their proper posts in society, giving with

their life's work an authentic Christian witness, becoming in their turn evangelizers of their environment.

(26) The Catholic university offers to non-Catholics the possibility of knowing in the most profound manner the message of salvation announced by Christ.

(27) In this way the Catholic university inserts itself in the life of the evangelizing mission and proper service of the Church,[12] participating at its level in the "diakonia" of the whole Church to mankind.

3. The Catholic University as a Place of Christian Education

(28) The Catholic university, by virtue of its university and Catholic character, is called first of all to make available a suitable environment for a solid intellectual education, integrated with Christian education. The latter is not to be considered something added from without, but rather as an internal, profound dimension, thanks to which "the academic institution is, so to speak, specified and lived."[13]

(29) Therefore, there must be offered to the students the possibility of being able to realize "a more and more harmonious synthesis between faith and reason, between faith and culture, between faith and life" (ibid.) They must be helped to understand "how intellectual research can be done in a Christian manner."[14]

(30) It is evident that such purposes can only be accomplished if the Catholic university be a truly intellectual community in which Catholicity be present and active.[15]

(31) According to Paul VI, the professors and principally the students need this. "Religious teaching is not enough—though obviously it should be attended to with scientific seriousness and in fidelity to the teaching of the Church—it is necessary also to create that atmosphere in which the young feel sincerely drawn to follow Christ, to love Him and to bring Him to others. Right in the university itself the young must acquire or, if they have acquired it already, promote an authentic Christian style of life, feel the seriousness of their future profession, the enthusiasm of being tomorrow's qualified leaders, witnesses to Christ in those places where they must go about their professions."[16]

VI. ROLE OF THE CATHOLIC UNIVERSITY IN SOCIETY

1. The Catholic University as a Place of Dialogue between Faith and Science

(32) A particular importance clothes the problem of the relationship between faith and science. It has been present throughout the history of the Church and has taken various turns, even to a radical antithesis of the

two terms. In reality a contradiction cannot exist between them because the truth is always 'one' and comes from only one source. Vatican Council II affirms "methodical research in all branches of knowledge, provided it is carried out in a truly scientific manner and does not override moral laws, can never conflict with the faith, because the things of the world and the things of faith derive from the same God."[17] And John Paul II adds, "It is certain that science and faith represent two orders of diverse knowledge autonomous in their process but finally converging in the discovery of reality as a whole which has its origin in God."[18]

(33) This "unity of truth" means that the search for a *synthesis* is rendered possible and necessary, a synthesis which strives to determine the place, the meaning of the acquisitions, ever partial, of the different sciences and of the various conquests with regard to the essential truths. It is evident that with the development of science such a synthesis remains ever open to further progress.[19]

(34) Contributing to the accomplishment of this is a fundamental task of the Catholic university. In this way it demonstrates in a concrete way that an incompatibility between faith and science does not exist, but that faith and science constitute two different approaches to the one truth. Rather, science and faith encounter and are open to each other for a reciprocal dialogue which becomes enriching for both.

(35) In this perspective of reciprocal dialogue, science meets the mystery of existence, particularly the mystery of man, and it recognizes its limits, glimpses spiritual values, and better directs scientific progress for the authentic good of humanity. Faith, for its part, with a contribution from the sound results of science, is enriched such that it is rendered more understandable to man and to different cultures. Then it shows how the eternal truth is reflected in the partial truths discovered progressively by man.

2. The Catholic University as a Place of Dialogue between Faith and Culture

(36) Another great reality which faith must necessarily encounter in dialogue is culture of which science is a part. Every culture has the right to be respected, but at the same time must be confronted with the Gospel of Christ. Just as the power of the Gospel transforms and regenerates every reality, so too it corrects and elevates so many aspects of culture, achieving its evangelizing. The Gospel itself is expressed in anthropological language and in symbols of a particular culture, giving place for its inculturation in the life of a given people.[20]

(37) Such dialogue is rendered all the more necessary with regard to modern culture, characterized by industrial civilization and by freedom

of thought. Serious anticulture phenomena are manifested which threaten man and reduce him to only one material dimension. Therefore, there is the urgent need to identify them and eliminate them in the light of a healthy anthropology and Gospel principles.[21]

(38) Thus faith, in order to be really dynamic and operative and to have a decisive force on human realities in order to elevate them, must become culture: "a faith which does not become culture is a faith not fully accepted, not wholly thought, not faithfully lived."[22]

The Catholic university presents itself as a place particularly adapted and fully suited to contribute to this dialogue between culture and faith.[23]

3. The Catholic University Promoter of Values

(39) The Catholic university, in constant dialogue with science and, in general, with culture, makes herself promoter and bearer of values in the life of the individual and of society. It becomes the place in which are sought the ways through which one can arrive at that *wisdom* which is able to help man "to measure according to criteria of truth the means to the ends, the projects to the ideals, the actions to the moral parameters which permit the reestablishment of the balance of values."[24]

(40) In the various kinds of research and discussion that are carried out and promoted, the Catholic university strives to demonstrate that science and technology cannot be separated from ethical values. It insists on affirming that scientific and technological advances must incline to the promotion of man in his wholeness, by his very nature a spiritual being open to trascendence. The Catholic university makes it known that ethics has priority over technology, the person has primacy over things, being prevails over having and doing, spirit is superior to matter, and so that "intelligence and conscience (predominate) over materialistic processes that threaten to annul the value of the person and the meaning of life,"[25] thus contributing to the auspicious affirmation of the "logos" over praxis.

(41) The Catholic university being an integral part of human society, fully shares all its discoveries and difficulties. With its scientific and educative work it contributes to progress as a whole. In this engagement it is in direct contact with the various problems affecting man and the social sphere. It seeks to understand them in their depth and complexity, going to their roots and their causes, and bringing the Christian light towards their solution. According to the principles of the Gospel, it strives to see, to evaluate, and to propose ways and means to overcome the sources of the crises.

(42) In a particular way the Catholic university is called to cooperate in the more delicate and vulnerable sectors, that is, in the problems of life and its quality, in the promotion of human rights, including those of social justice, in the affirmation of the culture of peace and of international order.[26]

(43) The Catholic university in this way becomes cultivator of the "human sense", promoter of human dignity, and carries out its specific contribution to the complete truth about man.

(44) This task involves the promotion of an anthropology which, necessarily projecting light on man in the totality of his being and acting, ought to be illumined by the faith and developed in coherence with faith, bringing into relief the actuality and fecundity of creation and redemption.[27]

VII. Opportuneness of Some Fundamental Norms for Catholic Universities

(45) With the Apostolic Constitution *Sapientia Christiana* on 15 April 1979 (28), norms for ecclesiastical universities and faculties were issued. These are the academic centers concerned with the study and teaching of the sacred sciences and the subjects of study connected with them. The time is now opportune for the provision of a new pontifical document for the issuing of analogous norms for Catholic universities and faculties by which are meant centers of secular studies, including those that also have faculties of ecclesiastical studies.

(46) It is necessary to point out that the situation of Catholic universities differs from region to region. The religious, political, and social conditions of the nations in which they exist differ. Civil university legislation similarly differs; it is necessary to take this into account so that Catholic universities can be recognized and so that the academic degrees which they confer can have civil value. Also, the ecclesial conditions of Catholic universities differ from place to place. Some in fact have been canonically erected and approved, and others, though being really Catholic, do not have such a juridical status.

(47) Furthermore, there exist Catholic universities that contain faculties or institutes of secular studies only, and others which as well as such studies also contain ecclesiastical faculties, erected in accordance with the Constitution *Sapientia Christiana*.

(48) In such diversity of situation a precise law for application uniformly to all Catholic universities appears impossible.

(49) However, some elements necessarily common by virtue of Catholic identity do exist and can be emphasized. It is precisely this which involves

the possibility of establishing norms concerning the nature and purposes of Catholic universities and the indispensable means for accomplishing them.

(50) For this reason the present pontifical document on Catholic universities, including autonomous faculties and institutes and higher schools which confer degrees and titles, treats them in as much as they are *Catholic* and establishes the necessary requirements so that they can be truly such and can be clearly recognized as such.

(51) The document does not therefore treat them inasmuch as they are universities, because under this aspect the same laws apply to them as apply to every university.

NOTES

*When the expression "university" or "Catholic university" appears in the draft, it is to be understood that *Catholic institutes of higher studies* are included (cf. last paragraph of the Proemium and art. 20 of the Norms).

1. Vatican Council II, Declaration on Catholic Education (*Gravissimum Educationis*), n. 10, *AAS* 58 (1966), 737.

2. John Paul II, Message to the University World, nn. 1–2 (7 March 1983): Teaching of John Paul II, VI, 1 (1983), 640–641; John Paul II, *Ad Academicas Auctoritates*, n. 2 (5 May 1980): *AAS* 72 (1980), 454–455.

3. John Paul II, To the University Professors of the Atheneum of the Sacred Heart, Milan, n. 4 (22 May 1983): Teaching of John Paul II, VI, l (1983), 1330.

4. International Federation of Catholic Universities (FIUC), "L'Université Catholique dans le Monde Moderne," n. I, B (1972).

5. FIUC, "L'Univ. Cath.," n. I, B (5).

6. John Paul II, To the Students and Professors of the Catholic Universities of Mexico, n. 2 (31 January, 1979): *AAS* 71 (1979, I), 236.

7. John Paul II, To the University Professors of the Atheneum of the Sacred Heart, Milan, n. 5 (22 May 1983): Teaching of John Paul II, VI, I (1983), 133.

8. Vatican Council II, Dogmatic Constitution on the Church (*Lumen Gentium*), n. 25: *AAS* 57 (1965), 29–31; John Paul II, To the Catholic University of America, Washington, n. 6 (7 October 1979): *AAS* 71 (1979, II), 1263.

9. Paul VI, To the Delegates of Catholic Universities (26 April 1969): Teaching of Paul VI, VII (1969), 237.

10. John Paul VI, To the Catholic University of America, Washington, n. 5 (7 October 1979); *AAS* 71 (1979, II), 1262–1263.

11. Paul VI, *Allocutio Moderatoribus Studiorum Universitatum Societatis Jesu,* n. 2 (6 August 1975); *AAS* 67 (1975), 533.

12. John Paul II, To the Catholic University of America, Washington, nn. 5–6 (7 October 1979): AAS 71 (1979, II), 1262–1263.

13. John Paul II, To the Students and Professors of the Catholic Universities of Mexico, n. 2 (31 January 1979): AAS 71 (1979, I), 237; cf. John Paul II, To the Council of FIUC (24 February 1979): Teaching of John Paul II, II, I (1979), 445–446.

14. Paul VI, *Allocutio Consociationi Catholicarum Studiorum Universitatum* (7 May 1971): AAS 63 (1971), 460.

15. FIUC, Declaration of the General Assembly at Kinshasa (10–16 September 1968).

16. Paul VI, *Allocutio Moderatoribus Studiorum Universitatum Societatis Jesu*, n. 4 (6 August 1975); AAS 67 (1975), 535.

17. Vatican Council II, Pastoral Constitution on the Church in the Modern World (*Gaudium et Spes*), n. 36: AAS 58 (1966), 1054.

18. John Paul II, *Ad eos qui Conventui Romae habito de "scientia Galileiana" interfuerunt*, n. 3 (9 May 1983): AAS 75 (1983), 690.

19. FIUC *l'Univ. Cath. dans le Monde Moderne*, n. 1, B (3); Pius XII, To the Executives, Professors and Students of the Catholic Institutes of France (21 September 1950): Discourses and Radio Messages of Pius XII. 220. Vatican Poliglot Press.

20. John Paul II, *Ad Nigeriae Episcopos Locupoli Locutio Habita* n. 3 (15 February 1982): AAS 74 (1982), 616; John Paul II, Encounter with the natives of Ecuador, Aspirations, nn. 1–3 (31 January 1985): *L'Osservatore Romano*, 2 February 1985, p. 4.

21. John Paul II, To University Professors and Men of Culture at Coimbra, n. 6 (15 May 1982): Teaching of John Paul II, V, 2 (1982), 1696–1697; 1703–1704; John Paul II, To the Pontifical Council for Culture, n. 8 (16 January 1984): Teaching of John Paul II, VII, I (1984), 106.

22. John Paul II, To the Participants at the National Congress of the Church Movement for Cultural Commitment, n. 2 (16 January 1982): Teaching of John Paul II, V, I (1982), 131; cf. John Paul II, *Epistola qua Pont. Consilium pro hominum cultura instituitur: AAS* 74 (1982), 685.

23. FIUC, *L'Univ. Cath. dans le Monde Moderne*, n. I, B (11).

24. John Paul II, To the Participants at the 2nd National Congress of the Church Movement for Cultural Commitment, n. 4: *L'Osservatore Romano* 10 February 1985.

25. John Paul II, ibid., n. 5; cf. John Paul II, *Litterae Encyclicae Redemptor Hominis*, n. 16: AAS 71 (1979, I), 290.

26. FIUC, *L'Univ. Cath. dans le Monde Moderne*, n. I, B (nn. 7–9).

27. John Paul II, To the Members of the Council of FIUC (24 February 1979); Teaching of John Paul II, II, I (1979), 446.

28. *AAS* 71 (1979), 469–521.

NORMS[1]

CHAPTER I. NATURE AND OBJECTIVES
OF THE CATHOLIC UNIVERSITY

Art. 1 - §1.　The Catholic university, as 'Catholic,' is a university which by reason of its constitutional bond or by a common decision between those concerned animates its research and teaching, as well as its other activities, with a genuine Catholic spirit.

§2.　The Catholic university is distinguished by the following characteristics:[2]

a) its Christian inspiration not only of individuals but of the university community as such;

b) a continuing reflection in the light of the Catholic faith upon the growing treasury of human knowledge, to which it seeks to contribute by its own research;

c) fidelity to the Christian message as it comes to us through the Church in conformity with the Magisterium;

d) an institutional commitment to the service of the people of God and of the human family in their pilgrimage to the transcendent goal which gives meaning to life.

Art. 2 -　In view of the particular nature of the faculties, the objectives of the Catholic university [3] are principally the following:

§1.　To promote scientific investigation in seeking and disseminating truth. In order to achieve this the Catholic university:

a) shall evaluate the achievements of the various disciplines through philosophical and theological reflection in order to come to a clearer understanding of the meaning of life, of mankind, and of the world.

b) shall dedicate itself to the structuring of a vital synthesis of the various disciplines in order to promote and illustrate the concept of man in his wholeness.

c) shall bring to bear the principles of the Gospel and the results of experience in the debates on contemporary questions.

d) shall seek ways and means of bringing out into the

open the truths and ethical values to be found in a study of various cultures.

§2. To educate men and women so that after completing their higher studies they will duly undertake their professions, tasks, and services, and in so doing be authentic witnesses of the Catholic faith.

§3. To offer appropriate aid to the Church primarily in spreading the message of Christ in the world of culture.

§4. To create in its midst an environment permeated with the evangelical spirit thanks to which all the members of the university community may be helped to perfect their personal and spiritual development and each, according to his or her condition, may enrich with Catholic values the knowledge of the world, of life, and of man which one is acquiring or gradually deepening.

Art. 3 -   The statutes or other equivalent document shall establish in every Catholic university the manner in which these objectives shall be sought and attained, in accordance with this present document.

CHAPTER II. THE CATHOLIC UNIVERSITY WITHIN THE CHURCH[4]

Art. 4 -   The Church has the right to establish and to govern universities, which serve to promote the deeper culture and fuller development of the human person, and to complement the Church's own teaching office.[5]

Art. 5 - §1. The Catholic university touches the Church herself and hence it cannot be considered as a purely private institution. It is for this reason that the relationship between the Catholic university and the Church as a whole, and with its pastors, must be seen as an internal requirement of the university insofar as it is Catholic, i.e., to the degree that this component distinguishes and animates the whole activity of the university.

§2. This relationship should be constantly fostered in order to protect the identity of the Catholic university for the good of both the university and the Church.

Art. 6 -   No university, even if it is in fact Catholic, may bear the title "Catholic University" except by the consent of the competent ecclesiastical authority.[6]

Art. 7 -   A Catholic university may be honored by the Congregation for Catholic Education with the designation "Pontifical" in special circumstances.

Art. 8 - §1. Episcopal conferences and diocesan bishops shall foster and assist Catholic universities in view of their importance so that they may contribute ever more to the good of the Church. Episcopal conferences, then should create an episcopal commission for such universities.

§2. On their part Catholic universities shall maintain strict and faithful relations with diocesan bishops and episcopal conferences because this communion with the pastors of the Church is required of its nature for the attainment of their goals.

Art. 9 - §1. The episcopal conferences and the diocesan bishops concerned have the duty and the right of seeing to it that, in these universities, the principles of Catholic doctrine are faithfully observed.[7]

§2. Should problems arise concerning the Catholic identity of the university, whether doctrinal or disciplinary, the ecclesiastical authority will confer with the authorities at the university in order to find satisfactory solutions taking into account the university's statutes or equivalent document.

§3. If the Catholic character of the university continues to be compromised in a serious way the competent ecclesiastical authority may declare the university to be no longer Catholic.

Art. 10 - §1. The autonomy proper to universities belongs also to Catholic universities.[8] This autonomy is never absolute but is inspired and disciplined by truth and the common good.

§2. Likewise due freedom in research, in accordance with the norms of Vatican II,[9] shall be recognized in order that genuine progress may be made.

CHAPTER III. VARIOUS TYPES OF CATHOLIC UNIVERSITY[10]

Art. 11 -   There are universities which are Catholic because they have been erected or approved by the Holy See.

Art. 12 -   This erection or approval requires on the part of the Congregation for Catholic Education the approbation of the statutes and the establishment of the office of Chancellor.

Art. 13 - §1. The Chancellor is the Ordinary Prelate on whom the university depends unless the Holy See otherwise decrees.

      §2. If the Chancellor is not the local Ordinary norms shall be drawn up so that the Chancellor and the Ordinary may be able to carry out their respective responsibilities in mutual accord and to ensure that the rights of the local Ordinary are fully respected.

Art. 14 -   The Chancellor
      §1. represents the Holy See in relations with the university and the university vis-à-vis the Holy See,
      §2. fosters the preservation and progress of the university,
      §3. defends and promotes the Catholic character of the university and facilitates its close links with the local and universal Church.

Art. 15 -   In the case of a canonically erected or approved university the nomination of rector/president needs to be confirmed by the Holy See, or by another ecclesiastical authority delegated by it.

Art. 6 - §1. There are also universities which are Catholic because they are approved by episcopal conferences in accordance with the norms drawn up by the Holy See.

      §2. This approbation shall be given in the form of a written document especially in the case of a university that wishes to include the term "Catholic" in its name.

Art. 17 -   There are universities which are Catholic because they depend on, or are administered by, a religious family or some other canonical entity.

Art. 18 -   There are universities which are Catholic by reason of a common decision by those concerned on condition that these universities have a juridical connection with the diocesan Ordinaries concerned.

Art. 19 -   All the universities referred to here shall define accurately their Catholic identity in their statutes or in some equivalent document in such a way that all that has been prescribed in this pontifical document is clearly indicated and applicable.

Art. 20 - §1. There are also various kinds of Catholic institutes of higher studies legally equivalent to universities either in their full structure or in part thereof.

§2. What is decreed in this pontifical document concerning Catholic universities shall have congruous application to such institutes.[11]

Art. 21 -   Every five years Catholic universities and other Catholic institutes of higher education shall send to the Congregation for Catholic Education a statistical report and information on their academic state and educational activity.

Art. 22 -   "Ecclesiastical faculties" within Catholic universities shall be governed by the Apostolic Constitution *Sapientia Christiana* and its annexed Norms.

CHAPTER IV. THE ACADEMIC COMMUNITY[12]

Art. 23 -   As a University constitutes a community of persons, all who belong to this community, whether considered as individuals or as members of academic moral bodies, shall accept responsibility—according to each one's situation—both for the common good and for the Catholic identity of the university, and therefore they shall cooperate diligently in their efforts to assist the university to attain its proper goals.[13]

Art. 24 - §1. To encourage this sense of co-responsibility all those involved in the university should share the same vision of man and of the world, should be animated by the same spirit of love, and shall share reciprocally in a sincere dialogue.

§2. In a special way spiritual values in relation to the person and the Christian community must be coherently shared and properly fostered by all members of the university community.

§3. The authorities of the university shall render effective this co-responsibility by appropriate means such as participation in the councils of the university, consultations with members of the university community, and the creation of suitable university associations.

Art. 25 - The Rector of the university, who shall be chosen and named in accordance with the university's statutes, shall be a Catholic and shall possess those qualities that will enable him or her to promote the academic life of the university and its Catholic identity.

Art. 26 - §1. All teachers who are to be chosen, nominated, and promoted in accordance with the statutes are to be distinguished by academic and pedagogic ability as well by doctrinal integrity and uprightness of life so that they may cooperate effectively to achieve the goals of the university.[14]

§2. Teachers who lack these requirements are to be dismissed, observing the procedures established in the statutes, or equivalent document.[15]

§3. In accordance with Art. 19 of these Norms every Catholic university shall establish such a juridical procedure.

Art. 27 - §1. Catholic teachers and researchers shall carry out their tasks faithfully observing the principles of Catholic doctrine.[16]

§2. In view of their accepting appointments to teach in Catholic universities, non-Catholic teachers shall loyally respect the Catholic character of the universities.

Art. 28 - §1. Catholic students shall be educated in such a way that their learning and general development as well as their continuing formation are always marked by sound Catholic doctrine and practices so that they be evident in their everyday lives.

§2. Non-Catholic students shall be expected to respect the Catholic character of their university and opportunities shall be provided for them to learn about the Catholic faith while their freedom of conscience shall be always fully respected.

CHAPTER V. CATHOLIC ORIENTATION
OF THE CURRICULUM

Art. 29 - §1. Scientific research and academic teaching shall be carried out according to methods and principles that are properly scientific.

§2. The research and teaching shall always take Catholic teaching into account.[17]

Art. 30 - §1. The competent ecclesiastical authority is to ensure that in Catholic universities there is established a faculty or institute or at least a chair of theology in which lectures are given to lay students also, so that they may deepen their understanding of Catholic doctrine.[18]

§2. There are also to be lectures on the theological questions particularly connected with the sciences and disciplines cultivated in the university, and in which both the Christian vision of the world and of man, and the professional ethic, will be expounded so that the students will be prepared to exercise rightly their future professions.[19]

§3. In the measure of their importance, ecumenical questions are also to be treated, according to the norms of the competent ecclesiastical authority; relations with non-Christian religions and the problems arising from modern atheism should also be treated.[20]

Art. 31 - Those who teach theological subjects in any institute of higher studies must have a mandate from the competent ecclesiastical authority.[21]

Art. 32 - In conferring the doctorate "honoris causa" on persons for scientific, cultural, or ecclesial merits, the Catholic character of the university is to be taken into account.

CHAPTER VI. UNIVERSITY PASTORAL CARE[22]

Art. 33 - §1. Very special attention shall be given to the pastoral care of the university so that the Christian life may be promoted and practiced.[23]

§2. Suitable opportunities shall be provided for teachers and students to deepen their understanding of the Word of God and to participate in the sacraments.

§3. Free initiatives are to be encouraged to help to deepen Christian life and its free exercise in a manner consonant with contemporary mentality.

§4. A zealous apostolic spirit shall be encouraged among the members of the university community in order to foster a genuine Christian community spirit in the university milieu.

Art. 34 - §1. In view of serious social problems facing human society, possibilities to know the social teaching of the Church are to be offered.

§2. Various suitable initiatives inspired by a true Christian spirit and directed towards helping those in need, both within the university milieu and more particularly among the masses of deprived and impoverished people in society at large, shall be encouraged and facilitated.

Art. 35 - §1. Diocesan bishops in accord with the competent university authorities shall promote pastoral care within the university.[24]

§2. To achieve this, appropriate initiatives are to be taken such as the setting up of various associations and even of the establishment of a university parish if there be need.(ibid.)

§3. The university pastoral apostolate shall always be carried on in harmony with the Church's pastoral ministry on the local and universal levels in order that, in reciprocal coordination, apostolic action may be efficaciously accomplished in society.

Art. 36 - Chaplains and other pastoral collaborators who are full of zeal, experts in pastoral care, capable of dialogue with teachers and students, and outstanding valiant helpers from among them, shall be appointed by agreement between the local Ordinary and the university authorities.[25]

Art. 37 - Wherever Catholic universities are situated in non-Catholic countries or areas, the university pastoral apostolate shall take due account of the local religious situation.

CHAPTER VII. PLANNING AND COOPERATION

Art. 38 -   Due attention shall be taken to ensure that Catholic universities are well distributed in various parts of the world through well-informed planning.[26]

Art. 39 -   §1. It is primarily the responsibility of the episcopal conferences[27] to carry out this plan, because they know effectively the apostolate needs and financial possibilities of their region, it is also the responsibility of religious orders dedicated to the university apostolate.

            §2. The Congregation for Catholic Education, assisted by experts, presides over the planning.

Art. 40 -   Cooperation on the national and international levels between Catholic universities shall be promoted in order that through mutual help the desired goals may be more easily attained.[28]

Art. 41 -   To achieve this cooperation the following forms of collaboration shall be used:
            a) exchange of information, academic initiatives, publications, etc.;
            b) exchange and interchange of teachers and students;
            c) sponsoring conferences in various academic fields;
            d) collaboration in research on various problems of interest to the Church and society.

Art. 42 -   Cooperation shall be encouraged with other universities including non-Catholic universities firstly through associations of teachers and through contacts with organizations that are not university based, especially to accomplish interdisciplinary research, in order to study important issues of society and to apply humanely the fruits of knowledge.

Art. 43 -   §1. In order to facilitate the cooperation and collaboration it is useful to have university associations functioning on the national, regional, and international levels.

            §2. Firstly the International Federation of Catholic Universities, erected by the Holy See for a more effective pursuit of their aims, is to be promoted.[29]

CHAPTER VIII. OTHER ECCLESIAL ACTIVITIES
IN THE UNIVERSITY AND CULTURAL MILIEU

Art. 44 -   A harmonious form of pastoral care of intellectuals ("pastoralis intelligentiae") shall also be encouraged and extended throughout the world of culture. This kind of apostolate shall be regarded as of prime importance and urgent need in today's world.

Art. 45 -   Other kinds of Catholic institute of higher studies which will have a salutary influence on education and on the cultural apostolate shall be established.[30]

Art. 46 - §1. Eminent Catholic scholars are to be encouraged to undertake scientific research and teaching in non-Catholic universities.

§2. Special interest should be taken in very talented students, whether Catholic or not, who show evidence of being well suited to research or teaching, so that they be qualified to undertake various university appointments.

Art. 47 -   Where it is possible faculties of Catholic theology or institutes, or chairs of Catholic theology, should be established in non-Catholic universities too on condition that orthodoxy of teaching be safeguarded.

Art. 48 -   Special care is to be taken of Catholic students in non-Catholic universities or institutes. To this end, it will be helpful to establish at or near such universities or institutes residences or colleges in which well chosen and qualified priests and laity offer spiritual assistance to the students as well as doctrinal and civil advice.[31]

Art. 49 -   Opportunities should be available to university students for financial support in the form of bursaries, accommodation, social security, etc.[32]

NOTES

1. Quite a number of these Norms have been suggested in the booklet "The Catholic University in the Modern World," edited by the International Federation of Catholic Universities in 1972. They are cited "IFCU: Cath. Univ."

2. Cf. "IFCU: Cath. Univ."

3. Cf. ibid. n. I, B.

4. Cf. "IFCU: Cath. Univ." n. IV, B.

5. Cf. Can. 807, CIC.

6. Can. 808, CIC.

7. Can. 810, CIC.

8. Cf. "IFCU: Cath. Univ.," n. II, B.

9. Cf. *Gaudium et Spes*, n. 59.

10. Cf. "IFCU: Cath. Univ.," n. I, C.

11. Cf. Can. 814, CIC.

12. Cf. "IFCU: Cath. Univ.," n. III, B.

13. Cf. ibid., n. II, A and B.

14. Cf. Can. 810, §1, CIC.

15. Cf. ibid.

16. Cf. Can. 810, §2, CIC.

17. Cf. Canons 809 and 810, §2, CIC.

18. Cf. Can. 811, §1, CIC.

19. Cf. ibid., §2, CIC.

20. Cf. "Directorium Oecumenicum," Pars. II.

21. Cf. Can. 812, CIC.

22. Cf. "IFCU: Cath. Univ.," n. III, B.

23. Cf. Can. 813, CIC.

24. Cf. ibid.

25. Cf. Can. 813 CIC.

26. Cf. Can. 809, CIC and *Grav. Educ.*, n. 10.

27. Cf. Can. 809, CIC.

28. Cf. "IFCU: Cath. Univ., n. IV, A.

29. Pius XII, Apost. Lett. "Catholicas studiorum universitates," 27.7.1949, *AAS* 42 (1950), 387.

30. Cf. Can. 813, CIC.

31. Cf. Can. 813, CIC.

32. Ibid.

Empowered by the Spirit: Campus Ministry Faces the Future

A Pastoral Letter on Campus Ministry
Issued by the National Conference of
Catholic Bishops (November 15, 1985)

INTRODUCTION

1.   "I pray that he will bestow on you gifts in keeping with the riches of his glory. May he strengthen you inwardly through the working of his Spirit. May Christ dwell in your hearts through faith and may charity be the root and foundation of your life" (Eph 3:16–17). For over a century, Catholic campus ministry in our country, empowered by the Spirit, has been forming communities of faith which witness to the presence of the risen Christ. Now we are at the beginning of a new era filled with opportunities to build up the faith community on campuses and to promote the well-being of higher education and society as a whole. In this pastoral letter addressed to the Catholic Church in the United States and especially to the Church on campus, we offer our prayerful support, encouragement, and guidance to the men and women who are committed to bringing the message of Christ to the academic world. In preparing this letter, we have consulted with many of them and have come to a deeper appreciation of their dedication and achievements, as well as their concerns and frustrations. This new era, which is filled with promise, challenges campus ministry to respond creatively to the promptings of the Spirit for the well-being of the Church and higher education.

2.   Our 1981 statement on Catholic higher education concluded by noting "the excellent intellectual and pastoral leadership of many Catholics engaged as teachers, administrators, and campus ministers in the colleges and universities which are not Catholic."[1] We said at that time

---

that "we hope for a future opportunity to speak of their invaluable contribution to the intellectual life of our country."[2] In this pastoral letter, we fulfill that hope and turn our attention primarily to the ministry of the Church on these public and private campuses, where each year millions of Catholics are being prepared as future leaders of society and Church.[3] We are mindful of our previous comments on the crucial importance of Catholic higher education, especially the distinctive task of campus ministry on Catholic campuses to call the total institution to spread the Gospel and to preserve and enrich its religious traditions.[4] In addition, the suggestions for this document made by those who serve at Catholic institutions affirmed that all who minister in the world of higher education have certain common concerns and similar desires for cooperation. Collaboration among all colleges and universities within a diocese enhances the Church's ministry to higher education. Mutual support, joint sponsorship of programs, and sharing of resources improve the total efforts of campus ministry. Many of the perspectives, suggestions, and directions in this pastoral letter should be helpful to those who serve so well in our Catholic institutions of higher education.

3.   Campus ministry is best understood in its historical, sociological, and theological context. Thus, the first section discusses our hopes for the Church on campus in the light of its previous history. The next section locates campus ministry within the relationship between the Church and the world of higher education, highlighting the need for renewed dialogue. Campus ministry derives its life from the persons who bring the Gospel of Christ to the academic world. Therefore, the third section focuses on the members of the Church on campus, emphasizing the call of all the baptized to collaborate in the work of the Church, as well as the special responsibility of professional campus ministers to empower others for this task. The fourth section examines six aspects of campus ministry that flow from the nature of the Church and the situation on campus. Here we state principles and suggest strategies for carrying out this ministry. The epilogue notes our own responsibilities as bishops to serve the Church on campus and calls the Church to an exciting new phase in the history of campus ministry in our country.

I. HISTORY AND CURRENT OPPORTUNITIES

A. HISTORY AND CONTEMPORARY DEVELOPMENTS

4.   The Church's response to current opportunities on campus will benefit from an awareness of the history of the Newman Movement in the United States.[5] This ministry began in 1883 at the University of Wisconsin with the founding, through lay initiative, of the Melvin Club

which was designed to keep Catholics on campus in touch with their religious heritage. A decade later the first Newman Club was established at the University of Pennsylvania, with much the same purpose. It was named after John Henry Cardinal Newman, who was the English leader in the nineteenth-century intellectual renewal in the Church and later was chosen the great patron of campus ministers in our country. During this initial stage, farsighted leaders recognized that the growing number of Catholic collegians attending public institutions needed support and instruction in their religious heritage. They responded by establishing clubs for Catholic students, with their own chaplains and residence halls.

5.   In 1908, the second stage began with the establishment of the first association of Catholic clubs in state universities. What would become the National Newman Club Federation replaced this first effort about the time of World War I. This phase, which lasted until 1969, was often characterized by a defensive and even hostile attitude on the part of Catholic students and their chaplains toward the academic world, which was perceived as dominated by a secularist philosophy. During this period, many students and chaplains in the Newman Movement felt estranged from the rest of the Church and decried the lack of support from the hierarchy.

6.   The third stage, begun in 1969 in response to the Second Vatican Council and continuing until the present, has produced some healthy new developments. First, the Church as a whole has grown in appreciation and support of campus ministry. It is true there are still problems: some colleges and universities lack officially appointed campus ministers and many others are understaffed and suffer from financial problems. At times, there are misunderstandings between the Church on campus and local parishes and diocesan offices. However, progress has clearly been made in integrating campus ministry into the life of the Church. Today, there are over two thousand Catholics ministering on campuses throughout the country—a significant increase over a couple of decades ago. There is an increased commitment to providing well-trained campus ministers who appreciate the need for continued professional and theological development. Student groups at all levels collaborate with official representatives of the Church. Diocesan directors of campus ministry help keep campus concerns before the whole Church. More Catholics appreciate the importance of campus ministry and support diocesan funding of this work. Through this pastoral letter, we affirm these positive developments and pledge to work with others to build on them. We bring to the attention of the whole Church the importance of campus ministry for the future well-being of the Church and society. Our goal is to foster a closer relationship and a greater spirit of cooperation between campus ministry and the rest of the local Church. Campus

ministry is an integral part of the Church's mission to the world and must be seen in that light.

7.   Second, we endorse the improving relationship between the Church on campus and the academic community. While problems remain, Catholics have developed a greater understanding of the positive values and legitimate concerns of higher education. Many campus ministers have established good working relationships with administrators, faculty, and staff. There is greater appreciation of the way the Church benefits from the teaching, research, and service carried on by colleges and universities. Similarly, many administrators view campus ministry as an ally in the common effort to provide an integrated learning experience for the students. Faculty members frequently value the presence of campus ministers who demonstrate an appreciation of the spiritual life and can articulate their Catholic heritage. In our consultations, we found that many leaders in the academic community welcome a word from the Church on matters of mutual concern.[6] Our hope in this letter is to build on this fund of good will and to heal any wounds which linger from past mistakes and misunderstandings. With respect for the freedom and autonomy of the academic community, we believe it is time to foster a renewed dialogue between the Church and higher education, to the benefit of society as a whole.

8.   Third, we affirm the development of ecumenical and interfaith relationships. There are, of course, problems in resolving longstanding differences, and at some colleges and universities dialogue and cooperation have been difficult to establish and maintain. However, on many campuses, the Catholic community and other religious groups who share a common vision of ministry and who are interested in ecumenical and interfaith cooperation have developed strong working relationships. This occurs especially with other Christian Churches, with whom we share a common commitment to Jesus Christ, and with the Jewish community, with whom we hold a common heritage and shared Scriptures. In some situations, Catholic campus ministers share an interfaith center and collaborate in some ministerial tasks. In other places, the Catholic community cooperates with other religious groups through regular meetings, joint study, and shared prayer. Mutual trust has grown as members of various religious traditions work together on common programs, such as projects to promote social justice. We commend this ecumenical and interfaith progress and give full support to greater and more creative efforts in this direction. Catholics who are deeply rooted in their tradition and who maintain a strong sense of identity with their religious heritage will be better prepared to carry out this mission. We appreciate the contributions and cooperative attitudes of most of the various religious communities on campus. The Catholic community

on campus might also seek to engage those who are concerned with human ethical values of our society but do not directly relate their concerns to a faith tradition. To those who demonstrate less tolerant attitudes, we extend an invitation to join in the dialogue. In this pastoral message, we address the Catholic campus community and discuss its particular challenges and opportunities. While we will not treat directly the ecumenical and interfaith dimensions of campus ministry today, we hope that the Catholic communities on individual campuses will be prompted by this letter to renewed dialogue and collaboration in serving the common good.

9. Finally, this third stage in the history of the Newman Movement has produced a remarkable diversity of legitimate styles and approaches to campus ministry, designed to match available resources with the unique situations at particular colleges and universities. These creative responses range from well-organized teams serving the needs of a large university parish to an individual ministering part time in a small community college. The styles include ministries that are primarily sacramental and those that rely mainly on the ministry of presence. Some campus ministers work on Catholic campuses where they can influence policy decisions, while others serve in public institutions where they have little or no access to the centers of power. In some situations priests are working full time, while in others the ministry is carried out almost entirely by members of religious orders and lay people. Ministers on residential campuses can offer many set programs for students, while those who serve on commuter campuses must be attentive to the creative possibilities demanded by such a fluid situation. Most serve on one campus, although some are responsible for several colleges and universities. While we cannot discuss in detail all styles of ministry, we will offer principles and strategies designed to encourage all those concerned with the Church on campus to make vigorous and creative applications to their own situations.

B. Current Challenges and Opportunities

10. We believe this is the opportune time to address a challenging word to the Church on campus. Catholics are attending colleges and universities in numbers that far exceed their percentage of the general population.[7] It is crucial that these emerging leaders of Church and society be exposed to the best of our Catholic tradition and encounter dedicated leaders who will share their journey of faith with them. Thus, the time is right to encourage campus ministers to renew their own spiritual lives and to facilitate the faith development of the Catholics on campus.

11.   Today, there is a growing interest among many Catholics in various ministries. On campus, there is a great reservoir of energy and talent that could be utilized in the service of the Church and the world. Therefore, the time is right to challenge faculty members, administrators, support staff, and students to contribute their time and gifts to the common effort to help the academic community achieve its goals and to build up the Church on campus.

12.   The academic world is in the midst of an important debate on how to improve the quality of higher education in our country.[8] Fundamental questions about the purpose, methods, and direction of higher education must be addressed, as colleges and universities continue to define their mission and to improve their performance. Therefore, the time is right to encourage Catholics on campus to participate in these local debates and, thus, to contribute their insights and values to this crucial national discussion.

II. CAMPUS MINISTRY AND THE RELATIONSHIP BETWEEN THE CHURCH AND HIGHER EDUCATION

A. HISTORY

13.   Campus ministry is an expression of the Church's special desire to be present to all who are involved in higher education. Throughout its history, the Church has been instrumental in cultivating the intellectual life. During the period of the Fathers, great centers of learning at Antioch and Alexandria instructed the faithful and promoted the integration of faith and culture. The Church contributed her resources to the task of forming medieval universities and founded many of them, including the great schools of Bologna, Paris, Oxford, and Cambridge. In the modern world, government increasingly has taken over the responsibility for higher education, with a resulting split between the Church and the university. This has occurred in our own country with the establishment of a massive system of public higher education that has its own autonomy. Shortly after 1900, it was evident that enrollments in this system were growing faster than those in the Catholic and Protestant colleges, which for so long had constituted higher education in the United States. From the perspective of faith, Christians often detected in public institutions a growing secularism that celebrated the autonomy of reason and left little room for consideration of religious questions or moral values. This situation intensified after World War I, and the Church responded not only by increasing her traditional commitment to higher education, but also by trying to protect Catholic students from the antireligious elements perceived on public campuses. During this

period, the Church and higher education experienced a good deal of mutual misunderstanding. Some people in the academic world feared that the Church would try to reassert, in more subtle ways, its control over higher education. On the other side, members of the Church, at times, regarded secular higher education as a threat to the Christian way of life. The time has come to move beyond these misunderstandings and to forge a new relationship between the Church and higher education that respects the unique character of each. We remain convinced that "cooperation between these two great institutions, Church and university, is indispensable to the health of society."[9]

B. THE CONTRIBUTION OF HIGHER EDUCATION

14. We respect the autonomy of the academic community and appreciate its great contributions to the common good. Higher education benefits the human family through its research, which expands our common pool of knowledge. By teaching people to think critically and to search for the truth, colleges and universities help to humanize our world. The collegiate experience provides individuals with attitudes and skills that can be used in productive work, harmonious living, and responsible citizenship. Since higher education in the United States has taken on public service as one of its tasks, society has received significant assistance in solving human and technical problems. The Second Vatican Council placed this contribution in a personal context when it said that people who apply themselves to philosophy, history, science, and the arts help "to elevate the human family to a more sublime understanding of truth, goodness, and beauty and to the formation of judgments which embody universal values."[10]

15. The Church, as well as society as a whole, benefits from the contributions of higher education. The members of the Church hold a common faith in Jesus Christ, a faith that seeks understanding. When the academic world produces new knowledge and encourages critical thinking, it assists Christians in the process of deepening and articulating their faith. When higher education fosters fidelity toward truth in scientific research and collaborative efforts to improve the quality of life in our world, it helps to prepare for the acceptance of the gospel message.[11]

16. There is no doubt that the world of higher education has its own problems that must be addressed and dehumanizing practices that must be challenged. Fidelity to the Gospel demands critical judgment, as well as affirmation. It is, however, vital that campus ministry maintains a fundamental appreciation of the contributions made by higher education to society and the Church.

C. THE CONTRIBUTION OF THE CHURCH

17.   The Church brings to the dialogue with higher education its general mission to preach the Gospel of Christ and to help the human family achieve its full destiny.[12] Thus, the Church seeks to help higher education attain its lofty goal of developing a culture in which human beings can realize their full potential.[13] In providing this assistance, the Church joins its voice with others in promoting the ideal of educating the whole person. From our perspective, this means keeping the dignity and worth of human beings in the center of our reflections on the purpose of higher education. Education is the process by which persons are "assisted in the harmonious development of their physical, moral, and intellectual endowments."[14] It aims at the formation of individuals who have a sense of ultimate purpose and are moving toward greater freedom, maturity, and integration. At the same time, genuine education nurtures a sense of responsibility for the common good and provides skills for active involvement in community life.

18.   We think that it is important to keep the problems of higher education in a larger societal and educational context. Thus, family life must be seen as central to the process of educating the whole person, since "the family is the first and fundamental school of social living."[15] Moreover, improvement in the quality of higher education is dependent on primary and secondary schools doing a better job of cultivating the intellect, passing on the cultural heritage, and fostering constructive values. If students are better prepared by a healthy family life and solid primary and secondary education, institutions of higher learning can attend to their primary purpose, "the passionate and disinterested search for the truth," which makes human beings free and helps them achieve their full humanity in accord with their dignity and worth.[16] The search for truth should also include the ability to handle ethical issues and to achieve a harmonious integration of intellect and will.

19.   The Church also brings to the dialogue its traditional understanding of wisdom. We believe that the faith community and the institutions of higher learning are involved in a common pursuit of the life of wisdom.[17] There are various interpretations of wisdom, but we agree with those who hold that its pursuit includes discovering the highest principles that integrate all knowledge; uncovering the deepest secrets that constitute human nature; and achieving a personal synthesis in which knowledge and love are ultimately united. For us, the mystery of human existence is fully revealed in Jesus Christ. He reminds us of our profound dignity and our immense potential. He provides us with perspective and teaches by example how love illumines knowledge. The wisdom that we learn from Christ includes the cross, which confounds

the wisdom of the world (1 Cor 1:18–24). From the perspective of the cross, we are called to challenge the limitations and contradictions of the world (1 Cor 3:18–23). At the same time, our wisdom tradition includes an understanding of God's mysterious plan to bring all things in the heavens and on earth into unity under the headship of Christ (Eph 1:9–10). The risen Lord has poured out his Spirit on all creation and so we are moved to celebrate truth, goodness, and beauty wherever they are to be found. Since no single community can monopolize the gift of wisdom, the Church joins with the university and others in the search for wisdom. But, when the quest for wisdom is forgotten or diminished, then the Church must keep the ideal alive for the good of society. When the so-called wisdom of the world is employed in support of injustice, the Church must proclaim the wisdom of the cross, which challenges all oppressive structures. In the Church, the practical wisdom enunciated by the Hebrew sages is celebrated; the traditional philosophical wisdom is remembered; and the integrating wisdom of faith is proclaimed. For Christians, this whole quest for wisdom finds its summation and final fulfillment in Jesus Christ, who is the wisdom of God (1 Cor 1:24). We are convinced that the Christian wisdom synthesis, merely sketched out here, is a valuable resource in the continuing dialogue between the Church and higher education.

20.   In a new relationship, the Church can work with higher education in improving the human community and establishing a culture that enables all human beings to reach their full potential. While admitting our failures in the past, we are concentrating on the future and a new era of cooperation. In the dialogue, we expect to learn and benefit from the work of higher education and will contribute our support, experience, and insights.

D. Campus Ministry Described and Defined

21.   Campus ministry is one of the important ways the Church exercises her mission in higher education. Its goals include promoting theological study and reflection on the religious nature of human beings "so that intellectual, moral, and spiritual growth can proceed together; sustaining a Christian community on campus, with the pastoral care and liturgical worship it requires; integration of its apostolic ministry with other ministries of the local community and the diocese; and helping the Christian community on campus to serve its members and others, including the many nonstudents who gravitate toward the university."[18] Campus ministry gathers the Catholics on campus for prayer, worship, and learning in order that they might bring the light of the Gospel to illumine the concerns and hopes of the academic community. All

the members of the Church on campus are called, according to their own gifts, to share in this ministry, guided by the professional campus ministers. "The work of campus ministry requires continual evaluation of traditional methods of ministry and also new approaches which are licitly and responsibly employed. These latter can be highly appropriate in the campus setting, where there exists an audience receptive to the kind of sound innovation which may in the future prove beneficial to the larger Catholic community."[19] Such creativity has produced great diversity in organization, style, and approach, as campus ministers strive to form a searching, believing, loving, worshipping Catholic presence on campus. With this diversity in mind, campus ministry can be defined as the public presence and service through which properly prepared baptized persons are empowered by the Spirit to use their talents and gifts on behalf of the Church in order to be sign and instrument of the kingdom in the academic world. The eye of faith discerns campus ministry where commitment to Christ and care for the academic world meet in purposeful activity to serve and realize the kingdom of God.

III. PERSONS WHO SERVE ON CAMPUS

A. THE BAPTIZED

22.   The Church carries out its pastoral mission to the academic world both through its communal life and through the Christian witness of its individual members. "The baptized by the regeneration and the anointing of the Holy Spirit are consecrated as a spiritual house and a holy priesthood" (cf. 1 Pt 2:4–5), in order that through all their works they may "proclaim the power of Him who has called them out of darkness into His marvelous light."[20] All the faithful on campus, by virtue of their baptism, share in the task of bringing the humanizing light of the Gospel to bear on the life of the academic community. They are called to live out Christian values while engaging in the teaching, learning, research, public service, and campus life that constitutes the academic world. They are united with other believers in this work but make their own unique contributions, according to their personal talents and specific circumstances. "As generous distributors of God's manifold grace, put your gifts at the service of one another" (1 Pt 4:10). The Second Vatican Council further specified this scriptural teaching: "From the reception of these charisms or gifts, including those which are less dramatic, there arise for each believer the right and duty to use them in the Church and in the world for the good of [humankind] and for the upbuilding of the Church."[21] Thus, all the baptized members of the academic community

have the opportunity and the obligation, according to their unique talents and situations, to join with others to help higher education reach its full potential.

23. The faithful are called not only to bring Christian witness to the academic world, but also to exercise their baptismal prerogatives by helping to build up the Church on campus. While many persons today generously contribute their time, talent, and experience to the faith community, Catholic faculty, staff, and administration have a unique opportunity and calling to lead and direct campus ministry programs, according to their gifts. These individuals are particularly needed on the many campuses throughout the country where no campus ministry programs presently exist. This contribution is enhanced when individuals take time to prepare themselves through prayer and study for this work. In section four of this letter, perspectives and strategies will be enunciated to guide the various aspects of campus ministry. We hope that students, including the large number of older students,[22] administrators, faculty members, and all who are concerned with higher education will be able to make creative applications to their own situations based on the conviction that the Spirit moves among all the people of God, prompting them, according to their own talents, to discern anew the signs of the times and to interpret them boldly in the light of the faith.[23]

B. PROFESSIONAL CAMPUS MINISTERS

24. Some members of the Church on campus are called to lead the faith community. Ideally, these men and women are professionally trained and exercise the kind of leadership that serves and empowers others. As officially appointed campus ministers, they are sent to form the faith community so that it can be a genuine sign and instrument of the kingdom. Their task is to identify, call forth, and coordinate the diverse gifts of the Spirit possessed by all the members of the faith community. Their challenge is to educate all the baptized to appreciate their own calls to service and to create a climate where initiative is encouraged and contributions are appreciated. One of the most important functions of campus ministers is to provide a vision and a sense of overall direction that will encourage and guide the other members to contribute to the well-being of the academic community and the Church on campus. If they understand their own family relationships in a faith perspective, they will be able to help others who are trying to improve the quality of their family lives. Setting up programs that embody this vision is a concrete way of encouraging others and of demonstrating what can be done with cooperative efforts. The goal of this style of leadership is to multiply the centers of activity and to unleash the creative power of

the Spirit so that the community of faith can be an authentic sign and instrument of the kingdom.

25. Some professional campus ministers exercise the universal priesthood based on baptism, and others are ordained priests or deacons through the sacrament of holy orders. It is a sign of hope that a growing number of lay people serve as leaders in the faith community on campus. We commend members of religious orders who continue to make important contributions by gathering and encouraging the faithful. It is of historical significance that women "who in the past have not always been allowed to take their proper role in the Church's ministry"[24] find greater opportunities on campus to exercise their leadership abilities. Deacons often possess special talents and important life experiences that enhance their leadership skills. We encourage the priests who help form the faith community in a great variety of ways. Their prayerful celebration of the Eucharist, which invites active participation and manifests the unity of the congregation, as well as their compassionate celebration of the sacrament of reconciliation are especially important. All those officially appointed to lead the Church on campus have a great responsibility to form vibrant communities of faith and an exciting challenge to bring forth the gifts of individual believers.

26. In order to meet these challenges, campus ministers often form teams which provide a broader base of leadership to the faith community. Individual members bring their unique personalities and gifts to the team and work cooperatively to set direction and carry out some programs. The team members are co-responsible for the well-being of the faith community and accountable in their own areas of activity and competency. At the same time, they have the support of their colleagues when needed. Praying together helps the men and women on the team to keep in mind the true source and goal of their mission and to experience a sense of solidarity. We encourage the formation of such team ministries, which serve as models of ministry and community for the rest of the Church.

27. There are certain general challenges faced by all campus ministers. To be effective, ministers must attend to their own spiritual development. Campus ministers who are serious about their prayer life and can speak openly about their relationship to God will be able to direct others. Ministers who have wrestled with the great questions of meaning, purpose, and identity can offer helpful guidance to other genuine searchers. Those who have appropriated the faith and mined the riches of the Catholic heritage will be in a better position to invite others to join the faith community. If they genuinely care about the weak and the oppressed, they will inspire others to work for social justice. Finally, campus ministers who have achieved an integration of faith and culture

will naturally serve as role models for students and faculty members who are trying to achieve a similar synthesis. In summation, the leaders of the faith community must be perceived as persons who know the struggles of life and who are working to develop themselves spiritually.

28.   Campus ministers are also called to empower the faith community and its individual members in the task of helping their colleges or universities to reach their full potential. Ministers who have a genuine respect for academic life and for institutions of higher education will see clearly the importance of this work and find creative ways to respond. A healthy self-confidence will enable them to relate openly with faculty members and administrators and to empathize with students who are struggling with their personal growth. By gaining the respect and confidence of the various members of the academic community, they will find many ways to get involved on campus and promote human values in the institution. Campus ministers with solid training and good credentials will have more opportunities to enter into the mainstream of academic life on campus. Today, it is clear that campus ministers must not remain on the margins of the academic community but must accept the call to bring the light of the Gospel to the very center of that world.

29.   To prepare for meeting all these challenges, we encourage campus ministers to take responsibility for their own personal and professional development. Clear contractual arrangements that include carefully defined expectations and procedures for accountability and evaluation help to set a proper framework for their personal enrichment. Membership in appropriate professional organizations, participation in activities on diocesan, regional, and national levels, involvement in support groups with other campus ministers, and regular interaction with a spiritual director can provide motivation and direction for improving their performance. If campus ministers are to remain flexible in response to the rapidly changing needs of the campus community, they need to study contemporary developments in Scripture and theology while deepening their knowledge of the Christian tradition. Attaining an advanced degree or achieving competency in a particular area not only contributes to professional development, but helps gain respect in the academic world. Today, skills in counseling and spiritual direction, as well as knowledge of family systems and life cycles, group dynamics, and adult education are especially valuable for leaders of the faith community. An understanding of the nature and dynamics of the academic world enables campus ministers to apply Christian teachings and values more effectively.

30.   In addition to these common challenges, campus ministers find that the unique situations of their particular campuses create their own concerns and opportunities. For example, campus ministers at community colleges must respond to the needs of students who live at home

and have jobs. They often need assistance in defining their roles and responsibilities in the home. Many students are married and are present on campus only for their classes. Some ministers have been able, in these situations, to form small faith communities around shared prayer or social action projects. At these two-year colleges, the ministry of presence is especially important, as is securing the support and active involvement of interested faculty members. These institutions are often open to the addition of religious courses into the curriculum. Skills in marriage and career counseling are especially valuable. It is important for these campus ministers to maintain close relationships with neighboring parishes because that is where many students will find their primary faith community.

31.   It is possible also to identify other particular challenges. Campus ministers on private denominational campuses must be especially attentive to the ecumenical dimension. Those who work primarily with minority students, including recently arrived immigrants, refugees, and international students, must be in touch with their cultural background and family experiences, as well as the unique challenges they face in the academic world. Large state schools produce logistical problems for campus ministers in handling so many students. On commuter campuses, making contact with students is difficult in itself. All of these particular challenges represent opportunities for creative ministry.

32.   Professional campus ministers are crucial to the work of the Church on campus. They bear the heavy responsibility of guiding the faith community and empowering others to assist in the task of helping higher education reach its full potential. The extent and intensity of these demands remind them that they must gather others to assist them. They should expect support and guidance from the diocesan director of campus ministry, who is the usual liaison with the bishop and the local diocese. The director can help facilitate their personal growth, call for a proper accountability, and possible diocesan-wide programming. As the diocesan bishop's representative, the director encourages the interaction among campus ministers in the diocese who serve on public, Catholic, and other private campuses. We recognize our responsibility as bishops to offer all campus ministers moral support, to provide financial assistance to the degree this is needed and possible, and to help them achieve the competency they need to be effective witnesses of the Gospel.

IV. ASPECTS OF CAMPUS MINISTRY

33.   After situating campus ministry in the relationship between the Church and higher education and discussing the persons who perform

this service, we now turn our attention to six aspects of campus ministry. These ministerial functions reflect the general mission of the Church on campus and the distinctive situation of higher education today. In her ministry, the faith community on campus must be faithful to the essential teachings of the Church and, at the same time, read the signs of the times and accordingly adapt the message of the Gospel to meet the needs of the academic community.[25]

A. FORMING THE FAITH COMMUNITY

1. Community and Alienation on Campus

34.   Campus ministry attempts to form faith communities in an academic environment that knows both a healthy sense of solidarity and a good deal of alienation. Ideally, colleges and universities gather teachers and students together into a community of shared values and common dedication to the pursuit of truth. In fact, on campuses there is a good deal of collaborative effort. Organizations abound, close friendships are formed, interest groups gather the like-minded. Many administrators, faculty members, and students move easily in this world and find that it satisfies their needs for companionship and involvement. Many Christians freely gather into communities of faith in which they share their strengths and gifts with others.

35.   On the other hand, lonely voices on campus cry out for intimacy, and mildly estranged individuals express a desire for more personal interaction. Students who leave home and come to large universities often feel lost in the vast impersonal world. The world of research and scholarship can seem cold and demeaning to graduate students. Commuter students who are on campus only briefly for classes do not have the opportunity to form close bonds with others. Some sense of alienation seems inevitable for international students who must cope with a new culture. Recently arrived immigrant and refugee students experience the isolation and loneliness of being separated from family and homeland. Older students worry about fitting in and being accepted and, at times, have the added complication of marital and family pressures. Even students in small private colleges can experience a lack of depth in their relationships and a consequent sense of estrangement. Complaints are also heard from faculty members about the superficiality of their relationships with close colleagues and the lack of opportunities for interaction with those in other departments. Some feel cut off from the centers of power, as important academic decisions are made without their input. The difficulty of gathering students for anything except social events and concerts is a continuing problem for student affairs leaders.

Administrators speak openly about the fragmentation of campus life and search for ways to overcome it. The voices of estrangement are many and varied. Campus ministers who listen well know that there is a genuine hunger for community in the academic world, as well as a strong sense of solidarity.

2. *The Importance of Christian Community*

36.   The call to form communities of faith flows both from the very nature of the Gospel itself and from the pastoral situation on campus. Christianity is ecclesial by its very nature. The communal character of salvation is already clear in the Hebrew Scriptures: "It has pleased God, however, to make [human beings] holy and save them not merely as individuals without any mutual bonds, but by making them into a single people, a people which acknowledges Him in truth and serves Him in holiness."[26] This truth was exemplified in the life of Jesus Christ who, led by the Spirit, gathered together a community of followers. The Twelve served as official witnesses of his saving mission and symbolic representation of the new people of God. Through his striking parables and miraculous signs he proclaimed the kingdom in which all human beings, animated by the Spirit, were to live in peace and harmony. The death and resurrection of Jesus brought a new outpouring of the Spirit which "makes the Church grow, perpetually renews Her and leads Her to perfect union with Her Spouse."[27] Under the influence of the Spirit, the Church remembers the prayer of Jesus that "all may be one, Father, as you are in me and I am in you, so that the world may believe" (Jn 17:21). All the baptized, empowered by the Spirit, share responsibility for forming the Church into a genuine community of worship and service. Guided by the Holy Spirit, the Church is called, with all of its limitations and sinfulness, to wend its way through history as the visible sign of the unity of the whole human family and as an instrument of reconciliation for all.[28]

37.   Today, the Church on campus is challenged to be a credible sign of unity and a living reminder of the essential interdependence and solidarity of all people. Thus, the faith community seeks to gather those who wish to serve others and to bring healing to those in the academic world who are restricted by artificial barriers and wounded by alienating practices. The Church gains credibility when the dream of community produces genuine commitment and intelligent effort. In the ideal community of faith, the Mystery that rules over our lives is named and worshipped. Dedication to Christ is fostered, and openness to all truth, goodness, and beauty is maintained. The life of the Spirit is nourished and discussed. Positive images of God, Christ, Mary, and the afterlife

warm the heart and structure the imagination. The common good is emphasized and personal development encouraged. Individuals experience true freedom and at the same time accept responsibility for the well-being of the group. Traditional wisdom is available and the best contemporary insights are valued. Prayerful liturgies enable us to praise God with full hearts and create a sense of belonging, as well as nourish people for a life of service. Members are known by name and newcomers are welcomed. Unity of faith is celebrated while legitimate pluralism is recognized. Individuals find both support and challenge and can share their joys and sorrows. The members hunger for justice and have the courage to fight the dehumanizing tendencies in the culture. The community knows the sorrows of life but remains a people of hope. In this ideal community of faith, the members are of one heart and mind (Acts 4:32) and receive the spirit of wisdom which brings them to full knowledge of Jesus Christ who is the head of the Church (Eph 1:17–23).

38. By working toward the dream of genuine community, campus ministry unleashes human potential and contributes to the common struggle against the forces of alienation. A Church serious about building community reminds others of the beauty and nobility of a life lived in harmony and peace. The baptized who experience acceptance, healing, and empowerment in the faith community are better prepared to bring an understanding ear, a reconciling touch, and an encouraging voice to alienated persons on campus.

3. The Challenge of Forming the Faith Community

39. When the dream of a genuine faith community is alive, then the search for effective strategies is intensified. Attitudes are crucial. Campus ministers whose personal outreach is warm and welcoming are likely to gain the active participation of others in the community. The ministry of presence in which leaders of the faith community make themselves available by being on campus regularly and getting involved in activities and events is a valuable way of making initial contact with potential members of the faith community and of enhancing existing relationships. Administrators, faculty members, and students who sense that they are valued as persons and that their talents and initiatives are appreciated, will find involvement more attractive.

40. On many campuses, Mass and communion services have proven to be powerful means of building community. Ministers who put a great deal of effort into preparing liturgies that are in accord with the Church's liturgical directives and are prayerful, coherent, and aesthetically pleasing, generally find an enthusiastic response. If they keep in mind the sensibilities of the academic community and strive for wide participation,

the broad use of legitimate liturgical options, and a flexible style, the inherent community-building power of the Eucharist is enhanced. There is a greater recognition today that stimulating homilies that apply the Gospel realistically and convey positive religious images are especially important in fostering genuine religious conversion and a sense of closeness to the worshipping community and the Church as a whole.[29] It is a sign of hope for the future that so many collegians are gaining a deeper appreciation of the power of the Eucharist to raise the mind and heart to God and to serve as "a sacrament of love, a sign of unity, a bond of charity."[30]

41.   In many sacramentally oriented campus ministries, the adult catechumenate process has become an especially valuable means of incorporating new members into the Catholic Church and strengthening the faith of those who are already members. As a result, the Catholic faith community becomes stronger, more attractive, and inviting. The presence of adults who have freely chosen to join the Church moves some members to think more deeply about their own relationships to the Church. Those who serve as sponsors often gain a new appreciation of their faith and a renewed sense of the Church as a community of committed believers. A community will attract newcomers as more and more of its members demonstrate enthusiasm for the faith and an attractive style of Christian living.

42.   On other campuses, different forms of community building predominate. For example, campus ministers at some commuter colleges form community through Bible study programs. Through personal contact, they gather together faculty members and students for shared reading and discussion of the Scriptures. This leads into group prayer and joint projects to serve others. Such programs reveal the power of the Scriptures to call individuals out of their isolation and to give them a sense of solidarity as they struggle to live out the Christian life in the academic world.

43.   The experience of Christian community on campus is important to the life of the whole Church. Students who have such a positive experience and are taught their responsibilities to the larger Church will continue to be a very valuable resource for family, parish, and diocesan life when they leave school. Campus ministers can prepare for this by maintaining good ties with local parishes and giving students the opportunity to be of service there.

44.   Building up the community of faith on campus is the responsibility of all baptized persons. The desire to serve and the hunger for community must be tapped. Individuals who are personally invited to join in this task and given freedom and encouragement to use their gifts and talents for the benefit of the community are more likely to respond. It is the

duty of leaders to provide vision and encourage others to accept their responsibilities. The task of forming Christian communities on campus encounters great difficulties but also brings deep satisfaction. This crucial aspect of campus ministry is worthy of vigorous and creative efforts so that the Catholic community can be an authentic sign and instrument of the kingdom on campus.

B. APPROPRIATING THE FAITH

1. The Challenges to Faith on Campus

45.   Campus ministry has the task of enabling Catholics to achieve a more adult appropriation of their faith so that they can live in greater communion with God and the Church, give more effective witness to the Gospel, and face the challenges to belief that exist in the academic world. In the classroom, students learn to question traditional assumptions and to tolerate diverse opinions on important questions that cause some to doubt their religious beliefs. Most students eventually encounter the modern critics of religion who charge that belief is either infantile or dehumanizing. In some classes, the scientific method that has advanced human learning so effectively is presented as a total worldview, which supplants religion and renders obsolete other approaches to truth. Some professors give the impression that maturation involves rejection of religious beliefs. In these and other ways, the academic world challenges the traditional belief systems of many students.

46.   Campus life tends to reinforce these intellectual challenges. Catholic students, at times, find their faith shaken by encountering peers who profess widely divergent worldviews and life styles. Today, a significant number of Catholics are attracted away from their religious heritage by fundamentalist groups that employ aggressive proselytizing tactics and promise clear answers and instant security in the midst of a frightening and complex world. When students learn more about the harsh realities of life and the monstrous evils that have been part of human history, they are, at times, forced to question their belief in a God who seems callous in allowing such human suffering. Finally, the whirl of campus life, with its exhilarating freedom and the pressure of making good grades, can so dominate the attention of students that they drift away from their faith without much real thought.

47.   Many Catholics on campus, including faculty members, are unprepared to deal with intellectual challenges to the faith. They are unable to explain their belief to interested friends or to defend it against attacks by hostile critics. Their understanding of the faith has not kept pace with their knowledge in other areas. The legitimate pluralism of theology

and spirituality in the Church confuses them. They have not achieved an adult appropriation of their religion that would enable them to speak about it not only with conviction but also with intelligence. At times, this produces frustration and anger over the inadequacy of their religious training.

48.   These problems are intensified by the general religious illiteracy in our culture. Public education is not committed to passing on the religious heritage. Many good people do not recognize the importance of religious knowledge for a well-rounded education. Most colleges and universities still do not have departments or programs of religious studies, nor do they provide adequate opportunities to explore the religious dimension of various disciplines in the curriculum. In the academic world, there are still those who think that teaching about religion necessarily involves proselytizing and that it cannot be done in an academically sound way. This attitude compounds the problems of campus ministers who seek to promote a more mature appropriation of the faith among Catholics.

49.   On the positive side, the challenges on campus prompt some Catholics to explore and deepen their belief. Doubts, which are frequently a part of faith development, at times lead to further study and renewed convictions. The academic world provides intellectual stimulation and helpful resources for those who want to explore their religious tradition. There is a growing interest in religious studies and an increase in programs and courses around the country. Some public institutions have excellent departments or programs in religious studies that demonstrate that this can be done legally and according to proper academic standards. Today, within the academic community a few voices are heard insisting that a well-educated person should have a knowledge of religion. At some institutions, campus ministry has produced excellent programs in theological studies that supplement the offerings in the curriculum through a wide variety of credit and noncredit courses, seminars, and lectures. The faculty members and students who have achieved a more mature appropriation of their faith provide important witness on campus and are a sign of hope in the struggle against religious illiteracy.

2. Principles for Appropriating the Faith

50.   By its very nature, Christianity calls us to an ever-deeper understanding and appreciation of our faith. Baptism initiates us into a lifelong process in which we are gradually formed anew in the image of our Creator and thus grow in knowledge (Col 3:10). The Scriptures remind us that this process means moving beyond childish ways to more mature approaches: "Let us, then, be children no longer, tossed here and there, carried about by every wind of doctrine that originates in human trickery and skill in proposing error. Rather, let us profess the truth in love

and grow to the full maturity of Christ the head" (Eph 4:14–16). The Scriptures also call us to move beyond illusion to a deeper way of thinking and relating to God: "You must lay aside your former way of life and the old self which deteriorates through illusion and desire, and acquire a fresh, spiritual way of thinking" (Eph 4:22–23). Members of the faith community who achieve a more mature grasp of their Christian faith are in a better position to understand themselves and their world. Those who continue their theological education are better able to reflect on their experiences in the light of the Gospel. By assimilating the meanings and values in the Christian tradition, believers are better equipped to affirm the positive meanings and values in the culture and to resist those who are opposed to the Gospel. Individuals who are well grounded in their own Catholic heritage are better prepared to enter into ecumenical and interfaith dialogue and cooperation. The Second Vatican Council reminded us that Christians have the task of achieving "a public, persistent, and universal presence in the whole enterprise of advancing higher culture."[31] The Council called upon Christians to "shoulder society's heavier burdens and to witness the faith to the world."[32] Those best qualified for this great work are the believers who have understood the implications of their faith and are able to articulate their deepest beliefs. The Scriptures offer us this advice: "Should anyone ask you the reason for this hope of yours, be ever ready to reply, but speak gently and respectfully" (1 Pt 3:15–16). To respond credibly, intelligently, and sensitively to honest inquiry requires careful and systematic preparation. All the members of the community of faith have a right to the kind of theological education that prepares them to meet this responsibility.[33] When we consider the demands of the academic world, it is clear that the Church on campus has a special responsibility to enable all of its members to appropriate the faith more deeply in order to give effective witness to the academic community.

51.   The importance of achieving an intelligent appropriation of the faith can also be established by examining the nature and purpose of education. As we have noted elsewhere, "a truly liberating and elevating education is incomplete without the study of theology or religion."[34] We must continue to encourage the study of religion in our society as a whole because, as Cardinal Newman insisted, religious truth has an inherent value and is "not only a portion but a condition of general knowledge."[35] Educated persons should know something of the history, teachings, and practices of the various world religions and be especially versed in the Judeo-Christian tradition, which shaped Western civilization in general and our own culture in particular. Furthermore, they should be aware of the religious aspects of other disciplines, such as literature, history, and art, as well as the religious dimension of our contemporary culture.[36]

52.   Traditionally, theology has been known to the Church as the "Queen of the Sciences." Today, we must emphasize its continuing power to keep alive the great questions of meaning, purpose, and identity and to provide a coherent vision of life, which serves as a framework and unifying principle for all learning. Theological study helps to produce the kind of intellect described by Cardinal Newman "which cannot be partial, cannot be exclusive, cannot be impetuous, cannot be at a loss, cannot but be patient, collected, and majestically calm, because it discerns the end in every delay; because it ever knows where it stands, and how its path lies from one point to another."[37] The study of theology not only helps us gain this kind of perspective, but also helps us to understand in greater depth Jesus Christ who reveals to us the secrets of the Father. In a well-rounded Christian education, the teachings of the Church are presented with fidelity to the magisterium and with the contemporary situation in mind. This kind of solid theological training enables the members of the faith community to achieve a genuine synthesis of their rich religious heritage and the best in the contemporary culture.

53.   A Christian faith that fails to seek a more mature understanding is not faithful to its own inner dynamism. A culture that is unaware of its religious roots and substance is impoverished and weakened. Educated Christians who have not grown beyond an adolescent level of faith development are limited in their ability to achieve personal integration and to make a contribution to society. These dangers remind campus ministry to maintain its dedication to forming the best possible learning community. The goal is that all of the members of the community achieve a deep understanding of their faith so that they are better prepared to witness to the kingdom of truth in the world.

3. Strategies for Appropriating the Faith

54.   In order to move toward these goals, it is vital that campus ministry creates a climate in which theological learning is respected. Campus ministers help to produce this climate by reminding all the members that they need an adult appropriation of the faith that matches their learning in other areas, in order to function as effective Christians in the world. This message is strengthened if the campus ministers are perceived as being serious about continuing their own theological education. The presence of faculty members and students who are already finding enlightenment and satisfaction in theological studies is a powerful motivation for others. A tradition of pursuing theological learning must be established in which all the members sense their responsibility to achieve a more mature understanding of their faith.

55. If the faith community shares this broad appreciation of the importance of religious studies, then individual programs are more likely to be successful. Program planners should be aware of the courses on campus that deal with religious matters, as well as the current needs and interests of faculty and students. For example, the existence on campus of an increasing number of fundamentalist groups has intensified the need for scripture courses that combine the historical-critical method with opportunities for personal application and shared prayer. Such courses tap the current interest in relating the Scriptures to everyday life and prepare members of the faith community to deal with the aggressive recruiting methods employed by some fundamentalist groups. In general, campus ministry should supplement the religious offerings in the curriculum and provide a wide variety of opportunities for Catholics to study and appropriate their religious heritage and to reflect critically on their experiences in the light of the Gospel.

56. Effective strategies must deal realistically with the situations of the targeted audiences. Theological studies can be made more attractive for students by arranging credit for courses offered by the campus ministry program. For example, through a theologian-in-residence program, students on a state university campus could gain academic credit from a nearby Catholic college for theology courses taught at the campus ministry center on the state campus. Programs for faculty members and administrators must respect their vast experience while, at the same time, taking into account their general lack of systematic theological training.

57. Campus ministry has the responsibility not only to provide theological education for Catholics, but also to work with others to improve the response of higher education to the problem of religious illiteracy in our culture. The key to making progress in this area is to overcome the unfortunate assumption that the study of religion cannot be a genuine academic discipline. The academic community must be shown that religion is worthy of careful and systematic study because it is central to human existence and is an important wellspring of our culture. Professors who deal with religious questions in their courses can help to overcome this bias by teaching this material according to rigorous academic standards of objectivity and with obvious respect for opposing opinions. If the bias against religion as an academic subject can be overcome, then a variety of positive steps might be possible, such as establishing a religious studies program, organizing a lectureship devoted to religious questions, and founding an endowed chair for Catholic thought. If the climate on campus were more open, then campus ministers with advanced degrees might find opportunities to teach part time in appropriate departments or programs. Even if some of these larger initiatives are not possible, campus ministers still can provide a valuable service for students by

identifying the courses on campus in which the religious aspect is treated well and fairly.

58. In the faith community, it is understood that religious literacy is for the well-being of society and that theological learning is for the sake of a deepened faith. The goal is an adult appropriation of the faith that fosters personal commitment to Christ and encourages intelligent witness in the world on behalf of the Gospel.

C. FORMING THE CHRISTIAN CONSCIENCE

1. Moral Relativism on Campus

59. The Church on campus must facilitate the formation of a Christian conscience in its members so that they can make decisions based on gospel values and, thereby, resist moral relativism. Many questions of personal values and ethics inevitably arise for individuals in the academic community. Students are concerned with the moral dimension of such matters as relating to family members, abortion, sexual conduct, drinking and drugs, forming friendships, honesty in their studies, and pursuing a career. At times, faculty members experience a conflict of values as they try to balance their research and teaching and attempt to remain objective in the classroom while expressing their personal opinions. Their integrity can be tested as they fight against grade inflation and struggle to maintain academic freedom while accepting external funding for research. Individual courses often produce particular ethical and value questions. This occurs in obvious ways in philosophy, literature, and the life sciences and in more subtle ways in the physical sciences and technology courses. For example, a computer course may be based on assumptions about human nature that need to be discussed. Ethical questions also arise in relation to institutional policies and practices, such as whether a particular college or university is demonstrating a proper respect and care for the athletes it recruits and utilizes.

60. As members of the academic community deal with these questions, they unavoidably come under the influence of the moral climate that dominates their particular college or university. The eyes of faith discern, in the academic world as a whole, the predictable mixture of grace and sin that characterizes all institutions. On the one hand, the climate is shaped by high idealism, dedicated service, a long tradition of civil discourse, great tolerance for opposing views, sensitive care for individuals, hard work, and a deep love for freedom. Examples of personal virtue are evident in students who resist intense peer pressure and maintain their high moral standards; in faculty members who make financial sacrifices to stay in the academic world and who carry on their

teaching and research with responsibility and integrity; in administrators who consistently speak the truth and treat all members of the academic community humanely. Organizations and groups often help raise the moral tone of the campus by being involved in charitable activities and espousing high ideals. In some fields, such as business, medicine, law, and the life sciences, more courses are being offered that deal with ethical questions. Periodically, a wave of idealism sweeps our campuses which reminds us of the great potential for goodness in the academic community.

61.   On the other hand, Christians recognize in the academic world a strong strain of moral relativism that tends to reduce genuine freedom to license and an open-minded tolerance to mindlessness. Rational discourse about ethical questions degenerates into nothing more than sharing personal feelings. Sin is reduced to neurosis or blamed on societal pressures. The project of forming a healthy conscience is neglected in favor of a selfish individualism. In this climate, some persons assume that it is impossible or useless to make judgments about whether particular actions are right or wrong, whether some values are better than others, and whether certain patterns of behavior are constructive or destructive.

62.   If this philosophy predominates on campus, Catholics are hard pressed to maintain their values and principles. They find it harder to mount an effective critique of institutional practices that violate the high ideals of higher education and fail to respect the dignity of human beings. Young adults who are moving through various stages of moral development are often confused by mixed messages and conflicting philosophies. Students must contend with peer pressures to enter into the drug scene, to cheat on exams, to engage in promiscuous sexual activity, to have abortions, and, in general, to adopt a hedonistic life style. Some older students find that their commitments to spouses and families are called into question. Faculty members and administrators, at times, experience subtle pressures to go along with morally questionable institutional policies and practices.

2. Conscience in a Catholic Perspective

63.   In this situation, campus ministry has the crucial task of assisting in the formation of Catholic consciences so that individuals who will continue to face very complex ethical issues throughout their lives are prepared to make good moral judgments according to gospel values. The Scriptures remind us: "Do not conform yourself to this age but be transformed by the renewal of your mind so that you may judge what is God's will, what is good, pleasing and perfect" (Rom 12:2). Conscience formation involves just such a transforming renewal of mind in accord

with the will of God.[38] For, conscience is that "most secret core and sanctuary of a person where one is close with God."[39] There we hear the voice of God echoing in the depths of our being and calling us to heed the law written on our hearts. As Cardinal Newman wrote in the last century: "Conscience does not repose on itself, but vaguely reaches forward to something beyond itself and dimly discerns a sanction higher than self for its decisions, as is evidenced in that keen sense of obligation and responsibility which informs them."[40] "Conscience, then, though it is inviolable, is not a law unto itself."[41] It is rather through our conscience that we detect a call from God, summoning us to live the good and avoid evil. It is in response to this call, heard in the secret recesses of our hearts, that we make the judgments of conscience required by the concrete circumstances of our daily lives. This requires an informed conscience, one nourished in prayer, enlightened by study, structured by the Gospel, and guided by the teachings of the Church. Self-deception is all too easy; blindness and illusion can easily mislead us. "Beloved, do not trust every spirit, but put the spirits to a test to see if they belong to God" (1 Jn 4:1). Thus, we need the community of faith to challenge our illusions and to call us to greater self-honesty.

64. In emphasizing the objective call from God, mediated through the Church, we do not want to lose sight of the fact that the divine summons must be answered freely and intelligently. "Morality, then, is not simply something imposed on us from without, but is ingrained in our being; it is the way we accept our humanity as restored to us in Christ."[42] Thus, all human beings are bound to follow their conscience faithfully in order that they may set the course of their lives directly toward God.[43] We are freely responsible for ourselves and cannot shift that burden to anyone else. We come to the full measure of freedom by putting on the mind of Christ. When Christ freed us, he meant us to remain free (Gal 5:1). By preaching Christ and his message of freedom, the community of faith seeks to inform the consciences of all of its members. The Christian who possesses a conscience structured by the Gospel of Christ and who is guided by the continuing presence of Christ's spirit in the Church is better prepared to deal with the rapidly changing complexities of the world today. When genuine virtue is acquired, then good actions flow more spontaneously and new strength is found to live according to one's ideals. Individuals whose conscience has been tutored by the Gospel understand that their task is not only to resist evil but to help transform the world.

65. This portrayal of the informed Christian conscience stands in stark contrast to moral relativism. If morality is based on the call of God, then it cannot be totally arbitrary. Moral relativism betrays the essential structure of human persons who are ultimately dependent on a God who

calls all of us to account. A conscience that remembers its source and is nourished and supported by the community of faith is the best resource for dealing with the complex questions of personal values and ethics.

3. Methods of Conscience Formation

66.   Campus ministry is called to bring the Gospel of Christ to bear on the moral problems faced by members of the academic community. This can be done by personal encounters such as spiritual direction and counseling, as well as through homilies, classes, and seminars. When campus ministers address these questions, it is vital that they are perceived as being in touch with the texture and complexities of the moral problems generated by campus life. They also must have a working knowledge of the wisdom found in the Catholic tradition on particular moral questions. A good way for campus ministers to multiply their effectiveness is by facilitating peer ministry programs in which individuals who have successfully dealt with particular moral problems can help others in similar situations. For example, a senior athlete who managed to keep a healthy perspective on sports and maintain good grades could be prepared to speak with other athletes struggling to keep their values intact in highly pressurized situations. Students who have freed themselves from the drug scene could help others interested in breaking their drug habits. For older students struggling to keep their marriages together, conversations with faculty members who kept their commitments in similar circumstances could be mutually beneficial in enriching their married lives. In all such peer ministry approaches, it is important that those serving others are well prepared through a proper grounding in gospel ideals and church teachings on these moral questions. Engaging members of the faith community in such peer ministry programs is a valuable way of extending the effort to form Christian consciences.

67.   Courses or seminars provide a more structured approach to the formation of conscience. For example, undergraduate students can be gathered for a seminar on the question of premarital sex, contraception, and abortion. An open atmosphere is needed so that the students can speak freely about the prevailing attitudes and peer pressures on campus, as well as about their own outlooks and modes of decision making. A skillful leader can use the discussion as a basis for bringing out the Christian teaching that insists that sexuality is best understood in terms of personal relationships and that intercourse is a sign of the total commitment associated with marriage. In dealing with this and all areas of personal morality, the Catholic tradition must be presented as containing a wisdom that illuminates the mystery of human existence

and encourages behavior that is in the best interest of the individual and society.

68.   A good deal of conscience formation must be done on an individual basis. Counseling, spiritual direction, and the celebration of the sacrament of reconciliation provide excellent opportunities to apply Christian teachings to an individual's precise situation and current stage of moral development. Through these means, persons can gradually discover the illusions and destructive patterns that impede the development of a conscience fully attuned to the Gospel. Such settings also provide the occasion to proclaim the great mercy of our God, who deals patiently with our weaknesses and guides us gradually to full growth in Christ.

69.   If campus ministry hopes to deal effectively with questions of personal values and ethics, it must be concerned with the general moral climate on campus. When individuals maintain high moral standards despite pressures, they make an important personal contribution to the moral tone of the academic community. Since colleges and universities have the task of fostering critical thinking and transmitting our cultural heritage, they should include questions of values and ethics in this general mission. Members of the faith community who understand the importance of the moral dimension of life are called to join with others in promoting a more extensive and informed discussion of ethical issues on campus. This can be done in a great variety of ways, such as facilitating an appreciation of the need for courses on ethics in each department and program, encouraging professors to treat the questions of ethics and values that arise in their courses, and sponsoring lectures and seminars on particular moral questions. It is especially helpful to get the whole academic community involved in concentrated discussions. For example, campus ministers could join with other interested groups in sponsoring a "Values and Ethics Week" on campus, designed to deal directly with moral issues. During this week, all professors are encouraged to spend class time discussing the ethical implications of their courses. Informal discussions and structured seminars are arranged throughout the week. In order to give the whole program momentum and status, major speakers are brought in to address current ethical concerns. The important element in these strategies is to move the academic community to carry on its proper task of promoting critical thinking in the area of values and ethics.

D. EDUCATING FOR JUSTICE

1. *The Search for Justice on Campus*

70.   Campus ministry is called to make the struggle for social justice an integral part of its mission. The academic world generates questions not

only of personal morality but also of social justice, which includes issues of peace and war, as well as reverence for life in all phases of its development. Some questions arise as colleges and universities determine their internal policies and practices. How, for instance, should they balance their concern for quality education with a policy of open access that gives disadvantaged students the opportunity for higher education?[44] Issues also emerge as higher education interacts with other institutions. A prime example is whether universities can maintain their integrity, freedom, and a balanced research program while accepting massive funding from the Department of Defense for research on weapons systems. Periodically, a social justice issue captures the imagination of a significant number of students on campus, producing demonstrations and an appeal for direct action. A more sustained commitment to particular justice issues is demonstrated by some individuals, such as those who remain active in the peace movement over a long period of time and those who maintain the effort to gain legal protection for unborn human life. Such persons of conscience often encounter apathy, misunderstanding, and rejection and therefore deserve the special support and encouragement of the Church.

71. The academic community could generate intense debate over all these issues. In general terms, some want the university to remain detached from social issues, while others look for more active involvement to achieve a more just society. Most agree that higher education makes a valuable contribution by providing a forum for discussing the great questions of the day in a civil and reasoned fashion so that constructive solutions can be worked out.

72. Finally, it must be admitted that there is a great deal of apathy in evidence on campus today. Many are caught up in their own concerns and have little if any interest in social matters. Others who have been actively involved are now weary of the battles and have retreated into less demanding activities. Most students do not even think in terms of altering unjust structures through political action or social involvement. In general, alongside striking examples of personal commitment to justice, we sense a strong current of individualism that undercuts concern for the common good and eclipses the urgency of social concerns.

2. Principles of Catholic Social Teaching

73. Campus ministry is called to be a consistent and vigorous advocate for justice, peace, and the reverence for all life. All the baptized should understand that "action on behalf of justice is a significant criterion of the church's fidelity to its missions. It is not optional, nor is it the work of only a few in the Church. It is something to which all Christians are called according to their vocations, talents, and situations in life."[45] With

this in mind, campus ministers have the responsibility of keeping alive the vision of the Church on campus as a genuine servant community that is dedicated to the works of justice, peace, and reverence for life, in all stages of its development.

74.   As we noted in our pastoral letter on peace, "at the center of all Catholic social teaching are the transcendence of God and the dignity of the human person. The human person is the clearest reflection of God's presence in the world; all of the church's work in pursuit of both justice and peace is designed to protect and promote the dignity of every person. For each person not only reflects God but is the expression of God's creative work and the meaning of Christ's redemptive ministry."[46] In our day, the sanctity of the life of the unborn calls everyone to protect vigorously the life of the most defenseless among us. When we reflect further upon Christ's redemptive ministry, we see that he demonstrated a special care for the poor and the outcasts of his society. He came "to bring glad tidings to the poor, to proclaim liberty to the captives" (Lk 4:18). In identifying himself with suffering persons, he provided us with the strongest motivation to work for justice for all (Mt 25:31–46). In word and deed, Jesus taught us the essential unity between love of God and love of neighbor. His followers understood that if you claim to love God and hate your neighbor, you are a liar (1 Jn 4:20). The Gospel he proclaimed and the Spirit he sent were to transform and renew all of human existence, the social and institutional dimensions, as well as the personal.[47] This analysis suggests a rationale for the commitment to justice, a rationale that should be known and understood by all members of the Church.

75.   In the struggle for justice, we need Christians who understand that "knowledge of economics and politics will not in itself bring about justice, unless it is activated by human and religious ideals. However, religious ideals without the necessary secular expertise will not provide the kind of leadership needed to influence our complex society."[48] The faith community on campus, which includes individuals with significant academic achievements, is especially well equipped to achieve the integration of an informed faith with knowledge and skill in the social arena. To accomplish this, there must be great emphasis on "teaching and learning the tradition of Catholic social thought, the creation of an environment for learning that reflects a commitment to justice, and an openness on the part of all Catholics to change personal attitudes and behavior."[49] We call special attention to the coherent body of Catholic social thought developed during the past century in papal encyclicals and reflected in our pastoral letters.[50] It is especially important for Catholics on campus to assimilate these teachings and to use them in their work for justice.

76.   As the faith community carries on this educational task, it must remember that the goal is not learning alone, but constructive action to eradicate injustice and to transform society. Christians must learn how to empower individuals and groups to take charge of their own lives and to shape their own destinies. The sin that infects the social order must be not merely analyzed, but attacked. Unjust structures and institutions must be changed, as must policies and laws that fail to respect human life. To be a credible partner in this task, the Church on campus should remember that "any group which ventures to speak to others about justice should itself be just, and should be seen as such. It must therefore submit its own policies, programs, and manner of life to continuing review."[51]

3. Working for Justice

77.   Considering the apathy on campus, the faith community has the vital task of raising consciousness on social issues and providing motivation for study and action. Leaders in the faith community who are already actively committed to the struggle for justice are a valuable resource in this effort. Drawing on their own experience, they can try to recruit others to work on specific justice issues. The very presence in the faith community of a core group dedicated to justice serves as an example and invitation to others to contribute their own talents and gifts to create a more humane society. Since apathy and excessive individualism are such pervasive problems, it is important for all those who are concerned about social justice to sustain their efforts even in the midst of limited successes.

78.   Education for justice can be carried out in a variety of ways, ranging from scripture studies and liturgies with a justice orientation to seminars and guided readings on a particular justice issue. Education for justice is enhanced by including an action component. For example, a seminar on hunger that raises consciousness on the issue should include suggested actions, such as joining an appropriate organization, writing congresspersons, or helping out in a local food distribution center. Given the gravity of the nuclear threat, it is especially important to study the issue of peace and war. Such studies should include a discussion of ways to implement the summons to peacemaking contained in our pastoral letter *The Challenge of Peace: God's Promise and Our Response.*

79.   Since the struggle for social justice demands involvement and not simply objective analysis, the Church on campus should provide ample opportunities for all of its members to work directly in programs and projects designed to create a more just social order in which peace and reverence for life are possible. Students who are involved in service

projects, such as visiting nursing homes, tutoring disadvantaged children, or helping out during vacations in impoverished areas of the country, often grow in appreciation of the people they serve, as well as discover more about the complexity of institutional problems. Systematic reflection on such experiences in the light of the Gospel and the social teachings of the Church enhances their learning and prepares them to be lifelong seekers after justice.

80.   Campus ministry has the responsibility to work with others to enable higher education to live up to its commitments and ideals in the area of social justice. Individuals have many opportunities to speak on behalf of those who are powerless. For instance, administrators and faculty members who are helping to set admissions policies or who are involved in hiring decisions can raise up the concerns of the disadvantaged and underrepresented. Students in various organizations can be vigilant so that the rights and sensibilities of international and minority students are respected. Individuals and groups who are attuned to the social dimension of the Gospel can raise ethical questions about institutional policies.

81.   Periodically, issues arise that call for a more public response by the Church on campus. Campus ministers, for instance, may be asked to be advocates for a group of students who are seeking redress of legitimate grievances or to provide leadership on a particular issue, such as combating the problems of racism and sexism. These are important opportunities, and campus ministers should respond by drawing on the social teaching of the Church and giving public witness to the Church's concern for justice and peace.

82.   Finally, the faith community can touch the conscience of the academic world by sponsoring programs on campus designed to raise consciousness and to promote justice and peace. For example, the Church could organize a day of fasting on campus, with the meal money saved going to help feed hungry people. This is a means of alerting individuals to the magnitude of the problem, of offering concrete help to the hungry, and of witnessing to the social dimension of the Gospel.

E. Facilitating Personal Development

1. Self-fulfillment in the Academic World

83.   Campus ministry has the task of promoting the full personal development of the members of the academic community in a setting that is filled with rich, if often neglected, resources for self-fulfillment. Colleges and universities provide marvelous opportunities for healthy

personal growth. Classes, lectures, and seminars provide intellectual stimulation. Cultural and social events broaden horizons and facilitate emotional growth. The greatest catalyst for development comes from interaction with the concerned people who make up the academic community. There are campus ministers who can provide guidance for the spiritual quest; administrators who possess broad visions and sensitive hearts; faculty members who are generous in sharing the results of their scholarship; international students who bring the richness of different cultures; and peers who are willing to share friendship and the common struggle for greater maturity. With all of these resources, many individuals find the academic world to be an ideal setting for establishing their identities, forming relationships, developing their talents, preparing for leadership, discerning their vocations, and charting the direction of their lives.

84.   On the other hand, this vast potential for growth is often ignored or impeded. Some students think of college only in terms of opening the door to a good job and a secure future. They attend classes, gain credits, and manage to graduate. Learning to think critically and achieving a well-rounded personality through involvement on campus are not part of their program. For these students, the call to self-fulfillment either falls on deaf ears or is interpreted exclusively in terms of a lucrative career and material success. The great potential of higher education to promote personal development can also lie dormant because of the policies and practices of colleges and universities themselves. The traditional task of producing well-rounded individuals who are prepared to serve the common good can recede into the background, as policy decisions are made on the basis of declining enrollments and financial pressures. Recently, voices from within the academic community have been raised, claiming that higher education has not remained faithful to its traditional goals and is not living up to its potential. Some say this is because students are not involved enough in the whole learning process.[52] One report claims that administrators and faculty have lost their nerve in the face of cultural trends and student pressures. It charges that leaders, by failing to insist on the systematic study of the humanities, have effectively deprived students of the cultural heritage that is needed for a well-rounded education.[53] Others decry the lack of a coherent curriculum and call for diverse learning experiences that foster critical thinking and help produce integrated persons who can live responsibly and joyfully as individuals and democratic citizens.[54] Among the critics, there is general agreement that reform is needed so that colleges and universities can achieve their proper goal of facilitating the full personal development of students.

2. Christian Perspectives on Self-fulfillment

85.   The Church has the task of distinguishing and evaluating the many voices of our age.[55] Campus ministry must be attuned to the voices of reform in the academic community and be prepared to function as the friend of genuine personal development and as an ally in the quest for healthy self-fulfillment. Our Scriptures remind us that the Spirit calls us to put aside childish ways and to live with greater maturity (1 Cor 14:20). For us Christians, Jesus Christ is the perfectly fulfilled human being.[56] In him, we see the depth of our potential and sublime character of our call. "He blazed a trail, and if we follow it, life and death are made holy and take on a new meaning."[57] By following this path of truth and love, we can grow to full maturity in Christ (Eph 4:15). The Spirit of Jesus, poured out through his death and resurrection, energizes us for the task of developing our potential. The same Spirit enables us to recognize and overcome the selfishness in our hearts and the contradictions in the culture that distort the quest for healthy self-fulfillment. When individuals pursue personal development within the community of faith, they are constantly challenged to use their talents in the service of others and to stay open to the Spirit, who accomplishes surprising things in us (Jn 3:8).

86.   The Second Vatican Council has given contemporary expression to these biblical insights.[58] Human dignity demands that persons act according to intelligent decisions that are motivated from within. We should pursue our goals in a free choice of what is good and find apt means to achieve these laudable goals. The Christian vision of human existence safeguards the ideal of full human development by rooting it in the sacredness of the person. All persons are worthy of respect and dignity and are called to perfection because they are "a living image of God"[59] and possess a "godlike seed" that has been sown in them.[60] This intrinsic relationship with God, far from limiting the drive for personal development, frees human beings to pursue their fulfillment and happiness with confidence.[61] Furthermore, life in community teaches us that personal freedom acquires new strength when it consents to the requirements of social life, takes on the demands of human partnership, and commits itself to the service of the human family.[62]

87.   These principles remind us that Christians must proclaim an ideal of self-fulfillment that is solidly rooted in the sacredness of persons, is placed in the service of the common good, and stays open to the God who is the source of all growth.

88.   When campus ministry brings the light of the Gospel to the educational process, the search for personal development leads to a Christian humanism that fuses the positive values and meanings in the culture with

the light of faith.[63] Genuine Christian humanists know that the heart is restless until it rests in God and that all persons are unsolved puzzles to themselves, always awaiting the full revelation of God.[64] Thus, for them, personal development is perceived as a lifelong adventure, completed only in the final fulfilling union with the Lord. Christian humanists know that history and all cultures are a mysterious mix of grace and sin[65] and that where sin exists, there grace more abounds (Rom 5:20). Thus, while rejecting the sinful elements in the culture, they are able to assimilate the grace-inspired meanings and values in the world into a comprehensive and organic framework, built on faith in Jesus Christ. As individuals pursue their personal development, the ideal of Christian humanism lights the path and sets the direction.

3. Achieving Personal Development in a Christian Context

89. Campus ministry can facilitate personal development through vibrant sacramental life, courses, seminars, and retreats that enable Catholics on campus to integrate their collegiate experience with their Christian faith. Through pastoral counseling and spiritual direction, campus ministers can encourage individuals to make use of the resources on campus and guide them on the path toward a Christian humanism. This important work is enhanced when the ministers are perceived as persons of prayer who are serious about their own personal growth.

90. It is helpful to multiply these efforts by bringing together, in a personal encounter, those who share the journey toward Christian maturity. A program that enables an individual faculty member to meet on a regular basis outside the classroom with a particular student for friendly conversation and serious discussion provides great opportunities for the kind of exchange that is mutually enriching. Faculty members who are inspired by gospel ideals and undergo training for this kind of program are in an excellent position to be role models for students and, perhaps, spiritual mentors. Students, in turn, bring to the relationship their distinctive experience and challenging questions, which can be a catalyst for mutual growth. A great variety of such programs is possible. The key is to increase the opportunities for more personal contact between members of the faith community so that they can assist one another in the quest for a genuine Christian humanism.

91. Since there is a temptation to reduce self-fulfillment to a selfish individualism, campus ministry provides a valuable service by keeping alive the ideal of Christian humanism, which recognizes that personal growth must be open to the transcendent and in service to the common good. Through prayer groups and liturgical celebrations that link life and worship, in lectures and seminars that relate current questions

and the Christian tradition, by service projects and actions for justice that put personal gifts at the service of others, the community of faith publicly manifests the Christian ideal of self-fulfillment. The sacrament of reconciliation is a powerful means for personal development since it enables individuals to confront the sins and destructive patterns that inhibit their progress and to hear again the compassionate summons to grow into greater maturity in Christ. Communal penance services that encourage an examination of the distinctive challenges and opportunities for personal development presented by campus life are especially effective in making the ideal of Christian humanism more concrete.

92. Inspired by this ideal, individual members of the faith community have the responsibility to assist their colleges or universities in the task of educating whole persons for lifelong growth and responsible citizenship. This is done in obvious ways by students who study hard and take advantage of cultural opportunities on campus and by faculty members who teach well and take a personal interest in students. In addition, there is the challenge of establishing institutional policies and practices that better facilitate these goals. Today, there is a general consensus that undergraduate education must be improved by various means, such as setting higher standards for classroom work, establishing a more coherent curriculum, and improving teacher performance through better preparation and proper incentives.[66] As the precise shape of the reforms is debated on particular campuses, it is vital that the voices of Christian humanists be joined with others of good will, on behalf of reform, which makes possible the education of the whole person. Trustees, administrators, and deans, as well as faculty members and students who serve on appropriate committees can promote policies that clearly place the well-being of students in the center of the academic enterprise. The opportunities are many and varied for members of the faith community to work with others in an effort to improve the quality of higher education so that a healthy personal development is facilitated. What is needed is the conviction that this is an essential aspect of bringing Christian witness to the campus.

F. Developing Leaders for the Future

1. Potential Leaders on Campus

93. Campus ministry has the great opportunity to tap the immense pool of talent in our colleges and universities and to help form future leaders for society and the Church. Large numbers of intelligent and ambitious young people are on campuses, gaining the knowledge and skills needed to launch them into eventual positions of leadership in the

world. Many of the older students at our colleges and universities are acquiring new knowledge and skills that will enhance their opportunities to influence their world for the good. The intense course of studies pursued by graduate students equips them with specialized knowledge that can be used for the common good. When international students, trained on our campuses, return to their own countries, they carry with them knowledge and skills that can be extremely valuable in promoting progress in their own societies. While not all of the students on campuses today will assume prominent leadership positions, everyone will have opportunities to provide some leadership in their various communities.

94.   The large numbers of Catholics attending colleges and universities are potential leaders not only of society, but of the Church as well. Parishes require women and men who, in actively proclaiming the Gospel, combine commitment and good will with knowledge and skills. The Catholic community is in great need of more priests who will dedicate themselves to serving the needs of others. The religious orders are looking for new members who will live a life of dedicated service. In searching for this kind of church leadership for the future, we naturally turn to our colleges and universities, where so many of our talented young people are being educated.

95.   The search for church leaders on campus should also extend to Catholic administrators and faculty. The local Church should make every effort to train individuals to carry out campus ministry on campuses where there are no professional campus ministry personnel. These men and women who are blessed with extensive education perform an important Christian service in the academic world and constitute an immense resource for church leadership. Not all of these individuals have the time or calling to assume leadership positions within the faith community. However, as a whole, they constitute a valuable pool of leadership talent that could be better utilized for the benefit of the Church.

2. Leadership in the Christian Perspective

96.   From the perspective of faith, the Scriptures present a distinctive understanding of leadership. Jesus told his followers, "You are the light of the world . . .your light must shine before all so that they may see goodness in your acts and give praise to your heavenly father" (Mt 5:14–19). This suggests that all the disciples of Jesus carry the responsibility of offering personal witness in order to make a difference in the world and of using their influence to bring others to a greater appreciation of the goodness of God. This kind of leadership is to be carried out according to one's own unique talents. As the Apostle Paul indicated: "Just as each

of us has one body with many members, and not all the members have the same function, so too we, though many, are one body in Christ and individually members one of another. We have gifts that differ according to the favor bestowed on each of us" (Rom 12:4–6). Paul also reminds us of the deep purpose involved in such gifts when he says, "To each person the manifestation of the Spirit is given for the common good" (1 Cor 12:7). In the Christian community, genuine leadership is based not on coercive power or high status, but on loving service that leads to the empowerment of others (Mk 10:42–45). Thus, the clear teaching of Scripture is that gifts and talents are not given simply for personal advantage; they are to be used generously for the benefit of others and for the good of society and the Church.

97.   The Second Vatican Council recognized the great opportunities for this kind of Christian leadership and called on all adult Christians to prepare themselves for this task. "Indeed, everyone should painstakingly ready himself [or herself] personally for the apostolate, especially as an adult. For the advance of age brings with it better self-knowledge, thus enabling each person to evaluate more accurately the talents with which God has enriched [each] soul and to exercise more effectively those charismatic gifts which the Holy Spirit has bestowed on [all] for the good of [others]."[67] Thus, from the perspective of faith, it is clear that effective leadership in the contemporary world is connected both with a sense of loving service and with a more mature development in self-knowledge.

98.   The nature of Christian leadership can also be understood from the viewpoint of the vocation we all receive from God. Through baptism, "all the faithful of Christ of whatever rank or status are called to the fullness of the Christian life and to the perfection of charity. By this holiness a more human way of life is promoted even in this earthly society."[68] This baptismal vocation gives to every Christian the special task "to illumine and organize" temporal affairs of every sort "in such a way that they may start out, develop, and persist according to Christ's mind."[69] Individuals may choose to live out this general vocation as single persons, as members of the clergy or religious orders, or as married couples. In all of these states of life, there are opportunities large and small for exercising a leadership that is based on service and helps to humanize our world.

3. Strategies for Forming Christian Leaders

99.   Campus ministers can facilitate the development of Christian leaders by encouraging members of the faith community to identify their gifts and to use them for the common good. Individuals must be helped

to overcome their fears and to gain confidence in their abilities. They need proper training and opportunities to improve their leadership skills. For example, retreats for liturgical ministers can help them sense the importance of their roles at Mass and enable them to perform these roles prayerfully and competently. A leadership training session for officers in Catholic student organizations, at the beginning of the academic year, can give them added confidence and practical skills. Campus ministers who work with student organizers of a social justice project can provide them with Christian principles and practical advice that will enhance their effectiveness as current and future leaders.

100. In addition to developing leaders within the faith community, campus ministers should also encourage students to exercise their influence in other groups and activities. It helps to remind them that involvement in the life of their college or university is a significant factor in getting more out of the collegiate experience and that all Catholics on campus have the responsibility to work for the betterment of the academic community.

101. The development of leaders involves helping students to discern their vocations in life and to prepare for them. Most young people on campus today need guidance in preparing for marriage and family life. The preparation should include programs that encompass the following elements: the sacrament of marriage as an interpersonal relationship; the identity and mission of the family; the role of human sexuality and intimacy; conjugal love as union and as sharing in the creative power of God; responsible parenthood; and the couple's responsibilities to the larger community.[70] A significant number of collegians seriously consider vocations to the priesthood or religious life.[71] Campus ministers are in an excellent position to promote these vocations. A program in which campus ministers gather interested students together regularly for discussions and prayer is a valuable way of helping them discern the promptings of the Spirit. Students moving in the direction of the single life often need personal assistance in order to deal with societal pressures and cultural stereotypes.

102. In order to get more faculty members and administrators to exercise leadership in the faith community, campus ministers need to establish personal contact with them, offer them opportunities that fit their particular expertise, and provide them with training, if necessary. For example, counselors on campus could run marriage preparation and enrichment programs for the faith community, after studying the Church's teachings on marriage. It would also be helpful to gather the Catholic faculty and administrators together, on occasion, to give them a sense of group identity and to encourage their active participation in the Church on campus. This could be done through a retreat in which they explore ways of integrating their faith with their professional concerns.

The more this integration takes place, the better role models they will be for students, who are the emerging leaders of society and the Church.

EPILOGUE

103. In this pastoral letter, we have placed campus ministry in its historical and cultural context and have examined it from the viewpoint of the persons who carry it out, as well as the tasks they perform. We are convinced that this ministry is vitally important for the future of Church and society. As bishops, we recognize our responsibility to "see to it that at colleges and universities which are not Catholic there are Catholic residences and centers where priests, religious, and [lay persons] who have been judiciously chosen and trained can serve as on-campus sources of spiritual and intellectual assistance to young college people."[72]

104. The revised *Code of Canon Law* has reinforced this responsibility by reminding us that the diocesan bishop is to be zealous in his pastoral care of students, even by the creation of a special parish, or at least by appointing priests with a stable assignment to this care.[73] We know it is important to find dedicated persons for this ministry who have a solid faith, a love for the academic world, and the ability to relate well to both inquiring students and an educated faculty. They need proper training, which includes personal development, practical experience, and theological study. Advanced degrees are helpful in order to gain credibility in the academic world. We are committed to providing the best professional campus ministers possible and intend to hold them accountable for dedicated and creative service to the academic community. Our responsibilities extend to ensuring that within each diocese adequate funding is available for campus ministry and that there is an overall plan for allocating resources.

105. Our hope is that this pastoral letter will mark the beginning of a new phase in the history of Catholic campus ministry in the United States. In our vision of the new era, campus ministry will succeed more than ever before in forming the faithful into vibrant communities of faith and in empowering them to bring the light of the Gospel to the academic world. Campus ministry will be better understood and supported by the Church as a whole and will therefore be strengthened to make its voice heard in the center of campus life. The spiritual life of the Church on campus will be renewed so that it can be a more potent force, enabling the academic community to live up to its own ideals. The faith community will be more in touch with its Catholic roots so that it can confidently enter into deeper dialogue and more productive relationships with other religious groups on campus. A contemporary

Christian humanism will flourish, which will demonstrate to all the value of an adult faith that has integrated the best insights of the culture. The Church on campus will be seen more clearly as a genuine servant community, dedicated to social justice, and therefore will be a more effective sign and instrument of the kingdom of peace and justice in the world. In the new era, the Church and higher education will find more productive ways of working together for the well-being of the whole human family. In our vision, campus ministry, empowered by the Spirit, faces a future bright with promise.

NOTES

1. "Catholic Higher Education and the Pastoral Mission of the Church," in *Pastoral Letters of the United States Catholic Bishops*, 4 vols., ed. Hugh J. Nolan (Washington, D.C.: USCC Office of Publishing and Promotion Services, 1983–84), vol. 4, 1975–1983, no. 64, footnote 32. (Hereafter all pastoral letters will be cited from the Nolan text.)

2. Ibid.

3. There are over 3,300 institutions of higher learning in the United States. The 1985 fall enrollment was 12,247,000 of which approximately 9.6 million attend public colleges and universities and 2.7 million attend private institutions. In the total student population, 43% are 25 or older and 45% attend part time. In recent times Catholics have constituted around 39% of the freshman class. For these statistics, see *Chronicle of Higher Education*, September 4, 1985.

4. "Catholic Higher Education," nos. 45–46.

5. See John Whitney Evans, *The Newman Movement* (Notre Dame: University of Notre Dame Press, 1980).

6. Among the many consultations with administrators, faculty, students, selected experts, and others, we found especially helpful the close to three hundred responses received from presidents and elected faculty leaders representing institutions of higher education from all fifty states who informed us of their hopes and concerns.

7. In both 1983 and 1984, 39.3% of college freshmen were Roman Catholic. See Alexander W. Astin, *The American Freshman National Norms for Fall 1983* (and *1984*), published by the American Council on Education and the University of California at Los Angeles. Catholics constitute about 25% of the general population in the United States.

8. Cf. "Involvement in Learning: Realizing the Potential of American Education" (National Institute of Education, 1984); William J. Bennett, "To Reclaim a Legacy" (National Endowment for the Humanities, 1984); "Integrity in the College Curriculum: A Report to the Academic Community" (Associa-

tion of American Colleges, 1985); and "Higher Education and the American Resurgence" (Carnegie Foundation for the Advancement of Teaching, 1985).

9. "To Teach as Jesus Did: A Pastoral Message on Catholic Education," in *Pastoral Letters*, vol. 3, 1962–1974, no. 63.

10. "Pastoral Constitution on the Church in the Modern World," in *The Documents of Vatican II*, ed. Walter M. Abbott, SJ (New York: American Press, 1966), no. 57. (Hereafter all documents from Vatican II will be cited from the Abbott text.)

11. Ibid.

12. Ibid., no. 92.

13. "The Church of the University," *The Pope Speaks*, vol. 27, no. 3 (Fall 1982), p. 252.

14. "Declaration on Christian Education," in *Documents of Vatican II*, no. 1.

15. John Paul II, *On the Family* (Washington, D.C.: USCC Office of Publishing and Promotion Services, 1982), no. 37.

16. "The Church of the University," p. 250.

17. Ibid., p. 252.

18. "To Teach as Jesus Did," no. 67.

19. Ibid., no. 69.

20. "Dogmatic Constitution on the Church," in *Documents of Vatican II*, no. 10.

21. "Decree on the Apostolate of the Laity," in *Documents of Vatican II*, no. 3.

22. Over two-fifths of the current student population are 25 years of age or older. See footnote 3.

23. "Called and Gifted: The American Catholic Laity," in *Pastoral Letters*, vol. 4, 1975–1983, no. 19.

24. Ibid., no. 27.

25. "The Church in the Modern World," no. 44.

26. "Dogmatic Constitution on the Church," no. 9.

27. Ibid., no. 4.

28. Ibid., no. 48.

29. Fee et al., *Young Catholics* (New York: William H. Sadlier, Inc., 1980), pp. 154–55.

30. "Constitution on the Sacred Liturgy," in *Documents of Vatican II*, no. 47.

31. "Declaration on Christian Education," no. 10.

32. Ibid.

33. Ibid., no. 2.

34. "Catholic Higher Education," no. 22. In this regard, it is important to distinguish theology, which involves a faith perspective and commitment, from religious studies, which can proceed in a more neutral fashion.

35. John Henry Cardinal Newman, *The Idea of a University* (Garden City, N.Y.: Image Books, 1959), p. 103.

36. "Catholic Higher Education," no. 22.

37. Newman, *The Idea of a University*, p. 159.

38. "The Church in the Modern World," no. 16.

39. Ibid.

40. Cited in "The Church in Our Day," in *Pastoral Letters*, vol. 3, 1962–1974, no. 205.

41. Ibid., no. 206.

42. "To Live in Christ Jesus," in *Pastoral Letters*, vol. 4, 1975–1983, no. 22.

43. "Declaration on Religious Freedom," in *Documents of Vatican II*, no. 3.

44. See the report by the Southern Regional Education Board's Commission for Educational Quality, "Access to Quality Undergraduate Education," *Chronicle of Higher Education*, July 3, 1985, p. 9ff.

45. United States Catholic Conference, *Sharing the Light of Faith: National Catechetical Directory for Catholics of the United States* (Washington, D.C.: USCC Office of Publishing and Promotion Services, 1979), no. 160.

46. "The Challenge of Peace: God's Promise and Our Response," in *Pastoral Letters*, vol. 4, 1975–1983, no. 15.

47. "The Church in the Modern World," no. 26.

48. "Catholic Higher Education," no. 39.

49. "To Do the Work of Justice," in *Pastoral Letters*, vol. 4, 1975–1983, no. 8.

50. For important papal documents, see David J. O'Brien and Thomas A. Shannon, eds., *Renewing the Earth: Catholic Documents of Peace, Justice, and Liberation* (Garden City, N.Y.: Doubleday, 1977). Among our more recent pastoral letters and statements on social justice and peace we call attention to: "The Challenge of Peace: God's Promise and Our Response"; "Brothers and Sisters to Us"; "To Do the Work of Justice"; and our forthcoming pastoral letter on the economy. Finally we note the valuable insights in the pastoral letter *What We Have Seen and Heard: A Pastoral Letter on Evangelization from the Black Bishops of the United States* (Cincinnati: St. Anthony Messenger Press, 1984).

51. *Sharing the Light of Faith*, no. 160.

52. See "Involvement in Learning."

53. See Bennett, "To Reclaim a Legacy."

54. See "Integrity in the College Curriculum."

55. "The Church in the Modern World.", no. 44.

56. Ibid., no. 22.

57. Ibid.

58. Ibid., no. 17.

59. "Pastoral Letter on Marxist Communism," in *Pastoral Letters*, vol. 4, 1975–1983, no. 14.

60. "The Church in the Modern World," no. 3.

61. Ibid., no. 21.

62. Ibid., no. 31.

63. This term, *Christian humanism*, has been used in the Church to suggest the ideal of integrating positive cultural values and meanings in a faith perspective. For a recent usage of this term, see "Catholic Higher Education," no. 19.

64. "The Church in the Modern World," no. 21.

65. Ibid.

66. We recall the four reports cited in note 8.

67. "Decree on the Laity," no. 30.

68. "Dogmatic Constitution on the Church," no. 40.

69. Ibid., no. 9.

70. John Paul II, *On the Family*, no. 66.

71. Fee et al., *Young Catholics*, pp. 154–55.

72. "Declaration on Christian Education," no. 10.

73. *Code of Canon Law*, (Washington, D.C.: Canon Law Society of America, 1983), nos. 813–814.

Synthesis of Responses Received from U.S. Catholic College and University Presidents to the Pontifical Document On Catholic Universities

Prepared by Alice Gallin, O.S.U.,
Association of Catholic Colleges and Universities
for Transmission to the
Congregation for Catholic Education
February 11, 1986

CONTEXT

A. AMERICAN HIGHER EDUCATION

In order to appreciate the responses from the presidents of Catholic colleges and universities to the *Schema*, it will be helpful to review the actual situation of American higher education of which Catholic higher education is an important part. There are over 3000 colleges and universities in the United States; this includes about 1600 "independent" institutions; the rest are public institutions, i.e., tax-supported. There is no national Ministry of Education, nor are there nationally sponsored institutions—except for the military. The early colleges in the USA were church-related and, therefore, private or, as they are currently called, independent; only in the late nineteenth century did we begin to have "public" colleges, located primarily in the rural areas whereas the independent ones had tended to be in or near large cities. Today there are approximately 580 state colleges and universities and 1,221 community or two-year colleges.

American higher education is currently serving twelve million students. Of the 1600 independent institutions, some 800 are now

---

From the files of the Association of Catholic Colleges and Universities

considered to be church-affiliated; of that number the 235 Catholic colleges/universities are clearly the largest single group.

What unites all these very different institutions—public and independent—is that they are all degree-granting institutions monitored not by government but by regional accrediting agencies and by specialized professional groups—e.g., engineers, medical schools, nursing, teaching. Unless an institution is fully "accredited" it has little status in the public arena, and it is not normally eligible for funding by government or private agencies. In our typical "American" way (cf. Tocqueville), we form ourselves into such voluntary associations and we then abide by the decisions of our elected officials. Hence, curricula, faculty rights, student life, and financial management are all reviewed periodically by an accrediting team. One of the team's major criteria is how well the institution fulfills its own stated purposes and objectives. As a result, the process of evaluation by an accrediting agency is regarded as an appropriate way to guard the quality of education because it is done in accordance with the accepted American principle of academic freedom.

Higher Education has also organized itself on the national level into associations (e.g., American Council on Education, National Association of Independent Colleges and Universities, National Association of State Universities and Land-Grant Colleges; Association of American Universities, as well as the Association of Catholic Colleges and Universities). Within each of these associations, there is a legal board of directors which directs the services offered by the association to the members and speaks on their behalf to government officials and the general public. Each month the heads of these associations located in Washington meet and discuss common concerns. In this way Catholic colleges and universities are part of a far wider educational community.

B. CATHOLIC HIGHER EDUCATION IN THE USA

1. Students

There are 235 Catholic colleges and universities in the United States, enrolling nearly 600,000 students. These institutions range in size from under 100 students to over 20,000. They are primarily undergraduate institutions, enrolling students for their first degree beyond the high school diploma; however, many of these baccalaureate students are men and women over twenty-five years of age. Four-fifths of our 600,000 students are undergraduates. Fifty-seven percent are women. Approximately half of our institutions grant some graduate degrees; about ten are considered full-research universities.

Catholic colleges and universities attract students and faculty from diverse backgrounds and cultures. Approximately sixteen percent of our students are members of various U.S. minority ethnic groups such as Blacks, Hispanics, American Indians and Asians. On our campuses, the number of students who identify as Catholics ranges from ten percent of the student body to ninety-five percent. The same diversity would likely be found in the composition of our faculties.

2. Finances

With few exceptions, Catholic colleges and universities in the United States receive little or no operating revenues from the hierarchy of the Roman Catholic Church. Only fourteen of the 235 enjoy regular financial support (of varying amounts) from their dioceses; only one, The Catholic University of America, is the beneficiary of an annual nation-wide collection. Their financial support thus comes largely from the same sources which support other, non-Catholic independent institutions: seventy percent comes from the tuition and fees paid by students, ten percent from government institutional grants and other appropriations, nine percent from private gifts (including whatever monies or services are given by the sponsoring religious body), less than three percent from endowment income, and roughly five percent from other sources. It is crucial to note the extremely heavy reliance on tuition and fees at Catholic colleges and universities, and to note also that over seventy percent of our students benefit from federal and state financial aid programs which assist them in paying that tuition as well as other expenses.

These programs provide qualified (i.e., middle- to low-income) students with grants and loans to attend the accredited college of their choice. In order to enroll students with such aid, Catholic institutions therefore must meet the standards for accreditation by regional accrediting agencies recognized by civil authorities. Without such student aid, thousands of potential students would be unable to use the grants to which they are entitled as citizens at a Catholic college/university. We would thus be depriving the students of what is rightfully theirs—the opportunity to study at a Catholic college/university. Few, if any, of the 235 Catholic college and universities in the United States could long survive in such circumstances. The aid received directly and indirectly by our Catholic colleges and universities from state and federal grants exceeds one-half billion dollars ($500,000,000) per year.

3. Legal Status (Governance)

The religious communities of men and women that founded our colleges and universities struggled long and hard to secure state charters and to achieve full accreditation by the regional accrediting offices that in our country take the place of a National Ministry of Education. Such accreditation, as well as the federal and state funding that accompanies it, requires that institutions respect academic freedom and that the curriculum not be used for proselytizing on behalf of any religion. The courts in the United States have been meticulous in their decisions regarding the necessary separation of church and state; questions of federal and state aid have depended on proof that the particular institution in question is not "sectarian" in the legal sense of that term.

The present reality of government funding to students attending Catholic colleges/universities and the eligibility of our institutions for direct grants for research or construction is a very complex issue, one which needs to be understood by those who think we exaggerate the problems that would result from the imposition of external ecclesiastical control.

In the United States there has never been a general ruling of the Supreme Court holding that all church-related colleges are eligible for public funds. On the other hand two important legal decisions (*Tilton* and *Roemer*[1]) have decided that the eight specific church-related colleges involved in those cases were eligible for public aid. The determination that they were eligible was based on the Supreme Court's analysis of how the institutions operated, specifically that:

1. They did not discriminate on religious grounds in student admissions and faculty hiring;
2. They did not compel attendance at religious exercises;
3. While they required students to take courses in theology, those courses were taught as academic disciplines and not to indoctrinate students in the beliefs of the sponsoring faith;
4. No aspect of their curriculum was used to indoctrinate students in the beliefs of the sponsoring faith;
5. They subscribed to generally accepted standards of academic freedom.

These were the grounds for the Court's decision that the specific eight colleges involved were eligible for public funds. Therefore, it is virtually certain that such aid would be withdrawn if these practices were altered.

In some of the cases involving Catholic elementary and secondary schools, moreover, it has been clear that "being controled by churches" or "having as purpose the teaching, propagation and promotion of a particular religious faith" are reasons for disallowing any form of aid to schools. There are many persons and organizations in American society that would welcome an opportunity to halt funds to our

Catholic colleges and universities; hence it is extremely important that the *Schema* not use any language to describe our relationship with the Church which could be incriminating. The responses from our presidents to the "Norms" section of the draft show great sensitivity on this point, and, understandably so, when one realizes that we are speaking of a potential loss of one half billion dollars ($500,000,000) a year, a loss which would certainly close many institutions and jeopardize the continuance of the rest.

One quotation from the *Roemer* case is particularly relevant. The Archbishop of Baltimore was *ex-officio* a member of the Board of Trustees of Mount Saint Mary's College, one of the defendant institutions, but the Court found that he had not "intruded into or dominated" the deliberations of the Board:

> Despite their formal affiliation with the Roman Catholic Church, the colleges are "characterized by a high degree of institutional autonomy." None of the four receives funds from, or makes reports to, the Catholic Church. The Church is represented on their governing boards, but as with Mount Saint Mary's, "no instance of Church considerations into college decisions was shown."

It is clear that the favorable decisions regarding public aid to Catholic colleges or universities are founded on a perception by the court that the Church does not control them. We enjoy, on the other hand, complete freedom of religion, and each institution's Board of Trustees is free to determine policies regarding faculty, curricula, student life, relations with the civic community, etc., as long as they do not violate other laws or accrediting agencies' standards. In our Catholic colleges/universities today the Board is composed of both members of the sponsoring religious community and lay members, generally those men and women who are prominent in civic, educational, and business circles. They are both Catholic and non-Catholic but all are deeply committed to the Catholic mission of the institution.

The Board of Trustees holds legal authority from the state over all operations of the institution, and in turn, has full fiscal and legal responsibility for it. This is a form of governance peculiarly American, but it is absolutely essential to the existence of independent higher education here.

CRITIQUE

This understanding of the system of Catholic higher education in the United States is the necessary context for reading the responses to the proposed *Schema* on Catholic universities. The ACCU distributed the draft to 235 Catholic colleges and universities in July 1985 and provided a response form that would give us the opportunity of receiving suggested re-wordings as well as general responses. Each section of the draft had a separate page for a response. The responses of 79 of the 235 institutions have been collated by means of a word processor, and we are thus able to view them section by section. A summary of these is attached for use by the drafting committee (Appendix A). In addition we received responses in letter form from 31 other institutions. Thus, responses from 110 were included in compiling this synthesis. It is my understanding that additional institutions have responded directly to the Congregation.

You will understand from the above description of our situation in the United States why most of those responding would find it more advantageous to the work of the Church in American Higher Education if this kind of juridical document were not issued at all. They are satisfied with the description of a Catholic university given in the 1972 document issued under the auspices of the International Federation of Catholic Universities.[2] In addition to that, the description of the relationship between the Church and Catholic colleges and universities in the United States given in the NCEA College and University Department statement of 1976[3] and included, by reference, in the American bishops' pastoral of 1980 (*Catholic Higher Education and the Pastoral Mission of the Church*[4]) is satisfactory. The bishops' pastoral is well-accepted on our campuses because it is sensitive to American law and history. Given these documents and the accumulated literature of the past decade on the identity and purpose of Catholic colleges and universities (a topic frequently addressed in ACCU publications), the majority of our presidents do not understand why the Holy See considers it "opportune" to issue another statement on the subject. They would say "*non placet.*" to the proposed *Schema* in its present form.

Many do however express satisfaction at the objective of the document—that is, to give strong support to the ministry exercised by Catholic religious and laity in the field of Catholic higher education around the world. If this could be highlighted in the text they would be grateful.

Because our institutions in the United States are so diverse in size, history, and circumstances, a meaningful synthesis of the complex responses is very difficult. I shall try to focus on the areas of general agreement, and then to detail the problems which emerged as the respondents thoughtfully and critically read the text.

I shall follow the divisions in the document: PROEMIUM and NORMS. I do this to keep my report of the responses more accurate, but at times ideas are grouped together, so that the exact order of Articles is not always observed. For a line-by-line critique one should consult Appendix A.

PROEMIUM

There is strong support for the emphasis given to cultural pluralism and the recognition of a Catholic tradition of university education as a means of contributing to the total development of the human person. The strong and fruitful Roman Catholic tradition that linked the love of learning and the desire for God should be further developed. Such persons as Benedict, Albert the Great, Thomas Aquinas, Robert Bellarmine, and John Cardinal Newman should be cited as a way of establishing the context. This should be done honestly and modestly, not in a triumphalist tone. Perhaps scholars from other lands and cultures could also be added.

In this section there could be more emphasis on the nature of a *university* as a place where the truth is sought through rigorous study and disciplined dialogue, where the frontiers of knowledge are expanded, and a new generation of students becomes excited about learning. The present document presents the university as a kind of seminary, a place for "formation," a comfortable home where "the truth" already exists. Hence, the relationship between science and faith is presented as a "problem" rather than as a dynamic interaction which helps to move the human race forward. Unless an appreciation of and confidence in the institution of the university as such (not just as Catholic) is established in the beginning of the document, the later sections which deal with Catholicity will have nothing to build on.

Because the contexts for higher education vary so widely in different cultures and nations, the document should avoid general statements such as, " . . . the ecclesial community wants her universities to be more effective and more numerous . . . " How is it known what the "ecclesial community" wants? How is it defined? In the United States the Catholic community is not interested in *more* Catholic colleges and universities since it is already very difficult to support 235 of them. Elsewhere— perhaps Africa—the local Catholic community *may* want more.

Sections 28, 29, 30, 31 meet with a great deal of approval. Here the emphasis is on creating an environment within which men and women will be drawn, in freedom, to participate in a life-long dialogue between faith and culture. The university can be, indeed, the place where the church and the culture interact, and the sections that support that idea are good. Many see the university as the "mediator" of Church and culture. But, precisely because both sides of the dialogue— university/culture–encompass vast diversities, there can be no one set of governing principles for the relationship between them. This the document recognizes in articles 46–48, but contradicts in Article 49. Most of the respondents are deeply involved in the effort to manifest their "Catholic character" and desire to give witness to the world around them of the faith that has inspired their ministry in the universities. They aim to do this in three ways: research, teaching, and service, and they recount in their responses just how they seek to accomplish the task. Orientation of trustees and faculty to the Catholic tradition and mission of the institution is essential, and they have programs and retreats for that purpose. Attention to the bishops' pastorals concerning the needs of our times is mentioned in many of the reports as one of the ways the university serves the church. The public clarity of their central mission—the full development of persons through education—is, perhaps, the best way of manifesting their Catholic character, and this is a priority for many of our presidents. For just as the Gospel focuses on the human person, so too the Catholic college/university makes the good of the person its central concern.[5]

Many respondents comment on the faulty and ambiguous ecclesiology in the *Proemium.* This may be due, in part, to the problem of translation, but it could be a more basic problem than that. The word "church" is used with and without capitalization—does this signify a different meaning? When one reads "ecclesial community" it is unclear if that is different from "the church." Whenever the document takes on a regulatory tone, "the church" is understood to mean the hierarchy. There are many examples pointed out by the presidents of the colleges in which the usage of "church" rather than "Church" alters the meaning of the text. The best example is probably when it speaks of the "church" as founding the universities and later refers to the "ecclesial community" and "her" universities, yet in the United States Catholic colleges and universities were founded almost exclusively by religious communities who sought charters from the state. They were not founded by the hierarchy—with a few exceptions—and were not funded by them or chartered by them. The "ecclesial community's" involvement comes through the sponsoring congregations and orders and through parents of students, millions of alumnae/i and friends who support the institutions. The respondents are dismayed at the lack of recognition of the role of the sponsoring religious community. (The comes up again under the *Norms.*) All of Section V suffers from this ambiguous ecclesiology.

The whole of the *Proemium* needs to be rewritten in such a way that the "universality" of the institution referred to as "a Catholic university" is tempered by recognition of the remarkable diversity among the institutions and the cultures in which they exist. Almost every statement made about "Catholic universities" should say "some" or "a few" or "in some countries" etc.; otherwise the statements are false. In section III this is especially true: the economic and cultural circumstances are so different from Indonesia to Rome to Washington that the political stance of the universities *vis-à-vis* the state must vary. Where the state is hostile to the existence of Catholic universities, a particular political action or public statement on the part of the Church may be needed to demonstrate the right of a Catholic university to exist. In other countries, e.g., the United States, the state is not hostile to Catholic universities and it would be detrimental to the mission of these universities if the Church were to assume an adversarial position *vis-à-vis* the state on their behalf. The respondents are quite clear in their confidence in the present relationship between the universities and the various states as well as the federal government, and they resist any suggestion in the Vatican document that this present relationship should be changed.

The recognition of pluralism (*Schema*, Article III, #10) as reason for "appropriate space and freedom" for the Catholic university is applauded; at the same time it is pointed out that this also requires respect for the space and freedom desired by others and for a proper accountability back to the pluralistic society for the way in which the mission of the university is carried out. It is the state and not the Church which charters our universities, and the respondents see no reason to seek a change because the state leaves the universities free to carry out their mission and even assists them with funds as long as academic standards are met and academic freedom respected.

The safeguarding of the "Catholic" character of the university is the responsibility of the duly elected board of trustees, and we have never before asserted that it is "equally the special task" of the pastors of the Church. This shift of responsibility has nothing to recommend it. Rather, the respondents suggest that the document should urge the bishops (who are probably meant by "pastors" here) to continue to support, encourage, and assist the colleges and universities in carrying out what is ultimately the trustees' responsibility. It is an accepted axiom that power and responsibility must go together; therefore, this responsibility of the trustees for the Catholic character of the institution must reside in each board of trustees which alone has the legal power to act.

The respondents who commented on the articles dealing with non-Catholics are unanimous in rejecting the way that persons of other faiths are dealt with in this document. Our institutions are committed to an ecumenical spirit, one which has permeated their campuses at least since Vatican II, and they find it embarrassing to have references such as that in the *Proemium*, Section V, Article 26, because they have found that many of our Christian (non-Catholic) sisters and brothers have a profound prayer life, a deep knowledge of scripture, and a commitment to the Gospel as strong as our best Catholics do. The criterion for accepting them into faculties should be their commitment to the goals of the university, not their personal membership in a church. We are strengthened in our faith through their presence, and we hope they are equally assisted by ours.

This true partnership with non-Catholics is regarded by our presidents as an essential dimension of the "Catholic character" of the university. Section V should be retitled since what the document actually describes in this section is the "Catholic character," and the use of that phrase would have less theological problems than the title "ecclesial function."

NORMS

As we move into this section, the document receives far less praise. The respondents recognize that the Holy See is attempting to deal with the situations of Catholic universities around the world, but they respectfully suggest that it cannot be done in this way. Article 51 of the *Proemium* states that "the same laws apply to them (Catholic universities) as apply to every university." In the United States that means that the university must protect academic freedom and judicial due process for faculty, have nondiscriminatory policies toward students and faculty, and recognize the legal autonomy and responsibilities of boards of trustees. A college or university cannot relinquish such basic characteristics without losing its status in American civil and constitutional law.

The characteristics of a Catholic university cited in Article 1, Section 2 seem adequate. Further statements simply confuse the issue since in different cultural situations there are varying possibilities of being overtly "Catholic," and the important thing is the internal commitment to the values of the tradition and the external witness in terms of achievement and service. The document assumes that institutions which have legally approved statutes dating back many years can easily rewrite them and get new state approval; this is not the case and would arouse considerable opposition. The respondents have no problem with the fact that only The Catholic University of America bears the title "Catholic"; no other college or university is seeking to use the title. Article 8 would be a recommendation that could not be implemented legally, except as a kind of advisory group. We already have such a structure in the Bishops' and Presidents' Committee begun in 1974, and the respondents are grateful for this channel of communication. This Committee has six bishops and six presidents and meets annually or more often if needed.

Article 9 is simply unenforceable; how does the bishop now see that the individuals in his diocese "observe the principles of Catholic doctrine?" What does this concept include? Exclude? Who decides? Everything in the *Norms* that creates this kind of impossible responsibility on the part of the bishop only tends to weaken his real moral authority because the norm is known to be unenforceable.

The attempt to identify different types or categories of Catholic universities (*Norms*, Chapter III) proves to be highly unsatisfactory. Catholic colleges/universities in the USA cannot be put in any of the stated categories, and yet they constitute the most numerous segment of Catholic higher education in the world. A close reading of the text indicates four ways of being Catholic: a) erected or approved by the Holy See (only The Catholic University of America would qualify); b) approved by Episcopal Conferences (none of ours); c) "depend on" (meaning legally? financially? governmentally?) or "are administered by a religious family or some other canonical entity" (this used to be true but is no longer so for most colleges and universities in the USA); or d) "those who by reason of a common decision by those concerned" (this would pertain) but "*on condition that* these universities have a *juridical* connection with the diocesan Ordinaries concerned" (this would not apply). If the document allows only these four ways of being "Catholic" then only a few of our 235 will still be "Catholic." I am sure that is not the intent. We are *de facto* recognized by our bishops and the ecclesial and civil communities as Catholic—and have been for a century—but have no juridical links with the Ordinaries. The statement in the *Norms*, Chapter I, Article 1, #1, seems sufficient as an assertion of Catholic identity.

As you can see from the individual comments attached, our presidents are very sensitive on the issue of being "Catholic." They consider their institutions to be such and have a long and enviable record of serving the church and their local communities. In the process of giving an excellent education, they have found ways of meeting social needs, of preparing millions of Catholic lay men and women for their lives in parish and city, and of educating leaders for the clerical ranks and religious communities as well as in business and political life. How then could their colleges no longer be considered "Catholic" at the discretion of a local bishop? They suggest that any determination of such a serious nature be made only after a careful juridical process involving the authorities of the colleges/universities and the sponsoring religious community. Consequently, Chapter III, Article 9, Section 3 presents serious problems.

Norms, Chapter IV, Article 26 is, of course, self-contradictory. There is no way *within* the statutes of our universities that teachers or administrators who lack something as vague as "doctrinal integrity and uprightness of life" could be dismissed. This could easily lead to an atmosphere of mistrust and suspicion, totally alien to the kind of Christian community desired.

The real crux of the document is perceived by many to be the assertion of a power on the part of the bishop to control theologians (*Norms*, Chapter IV, Article 31) and to assure "orthodoxy" in their teaching. At stake here is the relationship of faculty members teaching theology in a Catholic college/university in the United States to the faculties of other disciplines and to the administration and trustees (who are themselves committed to a Catholic character for the institution and are not state officials as in Europe and elsewhere). What is proposed here is contrary to the American values of both academic freedom and due process, both of which are written into most university statutes and protected by civil and constitutional law.

The American bishops have been at pains to distinguish their role as teachers protecting the Magisterium for the sake of the public order of the church from the role of the theologians whose task it is to explore new insights and push beyond present understandings of the faith. The university is the home of the theologian, not the bishop, and the bishop must respect that fact. The same freedom must be given to theologians as to the faculty in all other disciplines, and while, on occasion, it is the duty of a bishop to declare that a particular teaching of an individual theologian contradicts the teaching of the church, he ought to respect the university's need to be a place of free inquiry. This is the general position taken by our presidents. As seen above, it harmonizes with the rulings in the *Tilton* and *Roemer* cases.

Chapter V, Article 31, is already a part of the code of canon law and to repeat it here by itself could give rise to a false understanding. One must read a particular canon within the context of the whole code, its history, and its nature as canon law—a very different concept of law from American civil/constitutional law. In the areas of the teaching of theology/religious studies there are some suggestions for proposing a national or regional consultative board of bishops and theologians/canon lawyers to help advise presidents of universities when disputes arise concerning the parameters of Catholic theological teaching.

Given the large numbers of students from other faiths now in our classrooms, university theology courses are generally not seen as catechetics, nor could academic credit be given for such courses if they were taught in a proselytizing way. Our universities respect religious pluralism and seek to explore the meaning of religious experience for a total society and within diverse cultural groups; this seems to be overlooked in the document. The respondents are clear that they want excellent teachers of Roman Catholic theology on their faculties, and such faculty members are expected to present the "teaching of the church" clearly and to distinguish it from theological speculation. It would indeed be unfortunate if Roman regulation were to force our best theologians to seek employment in secular rather than Catholic universities to avoid harassment. This fear is expressed by many respondents.

While ninety-nine percent of the Catholic colleges and universities have Catholic presidents, it would be unfortunate to state that it must always be so. There are many of our Christian colleagues who bring deep gospel values with them to our campuses, and if one of them were willing to undertake the duties of president it would be discriminatory to rule him/her out from the outset. If the person is not in harmony with the mission and goals of the university the fact that he/she is Catholic is no help; the converse could be true of the non-Catholic. These things are better left to the wisdom and prudence of the board of trustees which selects the president.

In conclusion, the presidents who responded to the consultation expressed widespread apprehension about the document in its present form. Their comments can be summarized as follows:

1. They would prefer a document that is positive about the ministry to be exercised in and through Catholic institutions of higher learning. They suggest not dividing it into *Proeminum* and *Norms* but unifying it as one Apostolic letter urging those in university work to be true to their undertaking. Relations between the universities and the bishops should be decided upon country by country since in the history of each region, relationships have already been formed and cultural differences are understood.

2. The authors should develop a consistent ecclesiology and then use the appropriate terms, clearly defined, to express the relationship envisioned between the Church and the university.

3. The authors should develop more fully the idea of cultural pluralism and work out its implications in the practical order. At present the *Norms* contradict the understanding of cultural pluralism.

4. The authors should scrutinize carefully all references to persons of other religious faiths so as to be true to the ecumenical spirit inherent in the notion of an authentic Christianity.

5. The authors should utilize more fully the understanding of the relationship between the church and the world as expressed in *Gaudium et Spes*, explaining how that particular document of Vatican II influences one's understanding of the role of the university as mediator of culture.

6. The authors should find some terminology which will include equally "colleges" and "universities" since both are degree-granting institutions in the United States. Some universities are more research-oriented than others—but all accept a threefold mission of teaching,

research, and service. "Higher Education" or "Catholic colleges and universities" could be used. A footnote does not solve the problem.

7. It is extremely important that the English text be correct in its use of words and phrases. Of particular note is the difficulty encountered by our readers in the use of "sexist" or "noninclusive" language, i.e., using "man" as a generic term. Current usage here is "person" or "men and women," and should be followed in the English text of any document.

There are many specific suggestions for use in revising the text given in the Appendix. It is our hope that the final document will be pastoral in tone rather than juridical, and that the rich diversity that exists among Catholic universities will be appreciated and strengthened.

NOTES

1. *Tilton* v. *Richardson*, 430 U.S. 672 (1971); *Roemer* v. *Board of Public Works*, 426 U.S. 736 (1976).

2. "The Catholic University in the Modern World," *College Newsletter*, XXXV, 3 (March 1973), NCEA College and University Department, Washington, D.C.

3. "Relations of American Catholic Colleges and Universities with the Church," *Occasional Papers on Catholic Higher Education*, 11, 1 (April 1976), NCEA College and University Department, Washington, D.C.

4. *Catholic Higher Education and the Pastoral Mission of the Church*, United States Catholic Conference, November 13, 1980, Washington, D.C.

5. Cf. William J. Sullivan, S.J. "The Catholic University and the Gospel Vision," paper delivered at the IFCU General Assembly in August 1985, Santo Domingo.

Response of the Board of Directors of the Association of Catholic Colleges and Universities on "Proposed Schema for a Pontifical Document on Catholic Universities"

February 14, 1986

His Eminence William Cardinal Baum Prefect of Sacred Congregation for Catholic Education

Attention: Cardinal Baum

The responses to the consultation initiated by the Sacred Congregation on Catholic Education which have been received by the Executive Director of the ACCU from our member colleges and universities have already been submitted to your office. We hope that the historical background and the current legal and financial status of our institutions presented in that synthesis will be helpful in your assessment of the responses.

The Board of Directors of ACCU, elected by the member institutions, would like to assist the process of consultation further by submitting its own evaluation of the document based not only on the comments contained in the synthesis but also on their own experiences.

The role played by the 235 Catholic colleges/universities in the United States in the life of the Church and of the broader society is a significant one. The day-to-day administration of our own Catholic colleges or universities, with its attention to faculty matters, alumnae/i concerns, government relations, fund raising and budget balancing, and interaction with the other 3,000 colleges and universities in the country gives the members of this Association special competence in developing a critique of the *Schema*. They see the issues from a practical as well as theoretical point of view.

Before commenting on specific articles of the document and for the sake of clarity, our Association must state that in its present form the *Schema* (*Proemium* and *Norms*) communicates a juridical tone that is inappropriate to the relationship of the Church with the university. We respectfully request that an entirely different approach be taken by the Holy See in communicating its desire to promote and strengthen Catholic higher education throughout the world.

We do understand from our colleagues in other countries that some of them would find a strong and overt "ecclesial" link supportive of their stance *vis-à-vis* a hostile government. However, a universal statement of Church affiliation and control which might help such institutions would be disastrous for the colleges and universities of our country and many others.

Freedom of religion and of association, guaranteed by the United States Constitution, has meant freedom to fund, support and govern our own colleges and universities. Our charters have been granted by the several states empowering us to confer degrees for various professions as well as for the usual academic degrees. The accreditation of our institutions is done by independent accrediting agencies, organized on a regional and/or professional basis and directed not by government but by the academic community itself. The very life of our colleges and universities, therefore, is one of academic freedom and self-regulation by the academic community. Within this structure, our 235 Catholic institutions of higher learning have flourished and, in our opinion, any attempt to subvert this independence would result in the diminishment of their influence on the total higher education community and, ultimately, in their being excluded from that community of teachers and scholars. It has been a long struggle to convince our colleagues in other institutions that we are free in our search for truth, that we do believe in the ultimate harmony of the knowledge that comes from faith with the knowledge that comes from the various disciplines of learning, and that we do not use our educational opportunity to promote uncritical conversion to the Roman Catholic Church.

We recognize that such is not the situation in other parts of the world, and we do not seek to impose our values and our situation on others. Nevertheless, it must be recognized that there is no country in the world that has such a strong cohort of Catholic colleges and universities as does the United States. Here they are visible not only individually but collectively, entering into national dialogue with other higher education associations, government offices, and the National Conference of Catholic Bishops. Since 1974 ACCU has enjoyed the opportunity for an on-going relationship with the NCCB by means of the Bishops' and Presidents' Committee. This Committee is composed of six Catholic college presidents and six bishops, selected by their respective constituencies to meet annually or more often as need arises. The conversations which are carried on in that Committee have done much to develop a genuine cordiality among the members and also to promote dialogue on the local ecclesial level between college presidents and diocesan bishops.

The moral support which the bishops of our country have given to our Catholic colleges/universities has increased during the past ten years as they have become better informed about our concerns. You will remember that in November of 1982 the Vice-Chairman of NCCB accompanied the delegation from ACCU that visited with Pope John Paul II concerning the revisions being made in the Code of Canon Law. The Bishops' and Presidents' Committee has continued to assist us in our analysis of this proposed *Schema*. Such harmony between ecclesial authorities and university authorities is one of our major goals, and we would argue that our method of seeking it is proving successful whereas the juridical links proposed in the document would make us seem to be adversaries. We are confident that such is not your desire.

The basic intent of the *Schema* is not clear, but we assume that it is to strengthen and promote the life and mission of Catholic colleges and universities. To do this, we suggest, requires a recognition of two basic realities: a) that the university is a place for an intellectual journey toward truth and not a place where one receives "the truth" already known and packaged; and 2) that at the end of the twentieth century we have a new understanding of and respect for genuine cultural pluralism and its impact on the ministry of education.

Our Roman Catholic tradition is rich in its articulation of both these realities. From the early "schola" through the medieval universities of Paris and Bologna to the insights of John Henry Newman, the Church has commended the use of the intellect in the search to know all that can be known of human experience and cosmological wonders. Even while making practical mistakes of judgment—as in the case of Galileo—the Church has never ceased to proclaim with Thomas Aquinas that reason and faith are complementary not contradictory gifts to the human person. Unfortunately, the draft document which we have before us today says little of this tradition. In fact, it sets up a confrontation between "science" and faith and communicates a distrustful attitude toward exploration and creativity in research and teaching. We would recommend that the more positive approach of our tradition to the link between the love of learning and the desire for God be the basic orientation of any statement to be made on universities.

The second reality—cultural pluralism—has been strongly under-lined in the writings of modern pontiffs as well as in the works of major theologians. The interaction of faith and cultures is the focus of the section on culture in *Guadium et Spes* and has been repeatedly cited by the present Pope as well as by John XXIII, and Paul VI. Indeed, the establishment of a Pontifical Council for Culture by John Paul II emphasized the significance of the study of multiple cultures and the need for sensitivity in the "inculturation" process whereby the Church seeks to bring the Gospel to new cultures. The university is, *par excellence*, the place where the mediation needed between culture and faith takes place. The work of Catholic scholars is most profound when it takes place on the margins of accepted thought, exploring new horizons and posing new questions. Such a task requires the greatest freedom from *a priori* judgments. It requires enormous trust on the part of governing authorities— whether they be of the academic, state, or Church communities. On this point—cultural pluralism—we recommend further explication of this reality in the document itself, and a consistency between *Norms* and *Proemium* if such a format must be retained. The present draft in its *Proemium* (#10, 11, 35, 46) speaks intelligently and positively of cultural pluralism and points out that because of it no law can apply universally, but then in the *Norms* (#48) it presents laws intended for *all* Catholic universities no matter their cultural context.

The task which you have undertaken is a difficult one. We would urge you to read carefully and reflect deeply on the objections contained in the responses from our presidents which have been presented to you by our office. In addition, more particular observations submitted by various scholarly organizations such as The Canon Law Society of America and The Catholic Theological Society of America deal directly with the content of specific articles. As officials of the ACCU we consider our expertise to be more generic than that of the scholarly organizations and have consequently limited our comments to the broad principles involved.

To summarize the main problems which we perceive in the present draft:

1. Lack of a positive explication of the role of the university as such; without this, the development of a notion of "Catholic" university is impossible and what is said lacks credibility.

2. The absence of understanding of and appreciation for the role played by the various communities of religious women and men in the founding of and support for our colleges/universities. The rights of such sponsoring religious bodies must be adequately recognized and are so recognized by the American bishops, but are not explicated in this *Schema*.

3. In the section which delineates the various ways in which universities may be "Catholic" (*Norms*, chapter III) there is no

category which describes our institutions. In each case there seems to be the assumption of a juridical tie with either the Holy See or the local Ordinary. Most of our colleges and universities have had no such link; they were established by communities of religious men or women who secured charters from the several states empowering them to confer degrees. They have seen, and still see, their Catholic character and mission as residing in their commitment to establish and assure a Christian presence in the university world. The ideal they cherish is to be a " . . . place where Catholicism is vitally present and operative" (IFCU document of 1972). Over the years our Catholic colleges and universities have been recognized *de facto* as Catholic by the bishops and the Catholic community in our country. The statements made in the *Norms* (articles 1 and 2) about the nature of a Catholic university are acceptable, but the articles that follow are not. To promulgate such categories would be to undermine the good relationships now existing between Church authorities and universities. It would be a big step backward.

In our opinion, the relationship between Catholic colleges and universities in the United States is one based on history, custom, and three recent documents that have served to enunciate that relationship: 1972, 1976, 1980.* A reaffirmation of these statements, with amendments as needed, would serve our need to have our "mission" confirmed and strengthened. Perhaps the Congregation might wish to reread and study these documents so that a new document would be consonant with what has already been stated publicly. Otherwise, confusion may well result.

We trust that the observations we have made will be useful to the Congregation in its important work. If there are questions on its part, we shall be glad to attempt clarification of our views. The future of Catholic higher education will benefit from honest and open collaboration between the academic community and the Congregation and we, on our part, have attempted to facilitate such a spirit by supporting the wide consultation initiated by the Congregation. We hope that the members of the Congregation will receive our comments in the same spirit.

NOTES

*1972 - "The Catholic University in the Modern World,"' *College Newsletter*, XXXV, 3 (March, 1973), NCEA College and University Department, Washington, D.C.

1976 - "Relations of American Catholic Colleges and Universities with the Church," *Occasional Papers on Catholic Higher Education*, 11, 1 (April, 1976), NCEA College and University Department, Washington, D.C.

1980 - *Catholic Higher Education and the Pastoral Mission of the Church*, United States Catholic Conference, November 13, 1980, Washington, D.C.

Statement of Presidents of Leading Catholic Universities of North America on the Schema for a Proposed Document on the Catholic University

(Drafted after the meeting of September 30, 1985 and published in June 1986)

1. Presidents of fourteen (14) leading Catholic universities of North America (listed below) are sympathetic to the fundamental purpose of the proposed pontifical document on Catholic universities. We understand this purpose to be the clarification of the distinctively Catholic character of our institutions. Surely, if the Catholic university is to fulfill its mission, then its sense of Catholic identity must be clear and confident.

2. We also recognize and share the concern reflected in the Schema that authentic Catholic doctrine be communicated in compelling fashion, and not be confused with speculative opinions.

3. Finally, we fully support the important mission assigned by the Schema to the Catholic university: to be a place of dialogue between religious faith, on the one hand, and science (reason) and culture, on the other, as well as a promoter of values (Proemium, IV).

4. Unfortunately, we believe that the Schema, if published in its present form, would not promote these important objectives. In fact, the publication of this Schema would, in our judgment, actually cripple the present efforts of our North American universities to fulfill the mission the Schema describes.

5. Secularistic critics of Catholic education would find that their most searing critiques of Catholic universities had been confirmed by the Vatican itself. For if the relationship of these universities to the Church, as defined in this Schema, must necessarily involve control by the Church,

From the files of the Association of Catholic Colleges and Universities

then Catholic universities cannot respect academic freedom, and cannot enjoy true institutional autonomy. Any contractual obligations entered into by such institutions would be subject to the approval or disapproval of Church authorities outside of the university. This, at least, would be the view of most of the academic communities in North America and a good part of our general public.

6.   Our critics would charge that such direct ecclesiastical control means that our institutions are not universities at all but places of narrow sectarian indoctrination; hence they have no right to claim public monies to support what would be described as their proselytizing mission. If such a view prevailed in our courts, then decades of sacrifice by generations of faculty, students, and benefactors of Catholic universities in North America would have been squandered.

7.   There are any number of specific points in the Schema that need revision. We want to emphasize, however, that the single most important problem in the present document is this recurring insistence that any authentic Catholic university must be under the jurisdictional control of ecclesiastical authorities. In Chapter 3 of the norms, four different categories of Catholic university are identified, but all of them contain the notion of ecclesiastical control. For this reason none of them fits the actual situation of the vast majority of Catholic universities in North America. We believe that another category of Catholic university must be recognized.

8.   Ordinarily, our universities are not canonically erected but are chartered by the state; they are governed not by the local ordinary but by an independent board of trustees, which is generally composed of a majority of lay people and often includes at least some non-Catholics.

9.   Nonetheless, we believe our institutions are authentically Catholic universities. They are Catholic not only in their original tradition but in their continuing inspiration. Although not under direct Church control, they provide a broad range of opportunities for Church influence.

10.   The pastoral efficacy of this influence is unquestioned. One thinks, for example, of the important role Catholic universities in North America have played in the discussion of the recent pastoral letters of the Catholic bishops of the United States. One thinks also of the lively sense of faith reflected in the well-attended student liturgies that take place in our university churches. The success of these efforts and others, however, depends on the recognition of the Catholic university's special character as a university.

11.   The Catholic university is a Church-related academic community. It relates to the mission of the Church, but not as a seminary, nor a parish nor a diocese nor as anything but a university. It is important to

affirm the Catholic identity of our universities, but it is also important that they be authentic universities.

12. If our universities accepted as part of their self-definition the relationship between the Church and the university described in the Schema, then the credibility that they have earned over many years would be quickly eroded. Furthermore, many of the juridical provisions in the present draft, which subject the structures and processes of Catholic universities to external Church control, would expose our institutions to damaging litigation concerning contractual obligations and possible claims of discrimination in personnel matters. In the light of the principle of ascending liability, the affirmation of a juridical link between the universities and the hierarchy of the Church could make our bishops vulnerable to such litigation as well.

13. One of the most important values to be protected in an authentic university is academic freedom. If theology is to be granted the same academic integrity of other disciplines, theologians also must enjoy authentic academic freedom. We realize that in the case of theology, a special problem exists, since the orthodoxy of Catholic doctrine is also an important value to be preserved. The tension between a theologian's academic freedom and the legitimate pastoral concern for doctrinal orthodoxy certainly deserves particular attention. In our judgment, however, the approach taken in the Schema to this complex issue does not respect this tension. If the university is to be a place of dialogue between faith on the one hand and reason and culture on the other, then the academic freedom of the theologian must be recognized and respected. Otherwise Catholic theology would not enjoy the academic respect of other disciplines.

14. How should the Church then exercise its responsibility to protect doctrinal orthodoxy? As is the case in other academic disciplines, erroneous theological opinions are often corrected by the self-criticism of the scholarly theological community. It also may be necessary, on occasion, for Church authorities to make a forthright statement that a particular theological position is inconsistent with authentic Church teaching.

15. Episcopal affirmations of Catholic doctrine will be recognized to be the legitimate exercise of the right of any community of faith to define the content of its own belief. This kind of episcopal statement could not fairly be interpreted as a violation of academic freedom. No attempt would be made to interfere with the autonomy of the academic community, since no authority external to the university would attempt to impose sanctions on a faculty member because of the intellectual opinions he or she might hold. In fact, the tension between the concern of Church authority for doctrinal orthodoxy and the academic freedom

of the theologian can be a creative tension, if the distinctive yet complementary roles of bishops and theologians are properly understood and respected.

16.   Because we are personally and collectively committed to the important mission of the Catholic university, we are all the more concerned that the good intentions of the proposed document not be subverted by provisions that do not take into sufficient account the pluralism of cultures and political systems in which Catholic universities exist around the world. Furthermore, in the case of the Catholic universities of North America, the present Schema ignores the pluralism that exists within our institutions, where many non-Catholics work side by side with Catholics and where the methodologies of different academic disciplines demand their own proper respect.

17.   With particular reference to the institutional autonomy of the university and the academic freedom of the theologian, we believe that the formulations of the 1972 document on "The Catholic University in the Modern World" were far more successful in addressing these important issues than the present Schema. In the continuing discussion and revision of this Schema, we trust that the 1972 document and the experience from which it emerged will be given careful attention. Failure to do so, we fear, can result in serious, if not fatal, damage to the very institution the pontifical document seeks to promote: the Catholic university of today.

Rev. William Byron, SJ, President
Catholic University of America, D.C.

Rev. Norman Choate, CR, President
University of St. Jerome's College, Canada

Rev. John Driscoll, OSA, President
Villanova University, PA

Brother Raymond L. Fitz, SM, President
University of Dayton, OH

Rev. Thomas Fitzgerald, SJ, President
St. Louis University, MO

Dr. Author E. Hughes, President
University of San Diego, CA

Rev. Timothy Healy, SJ, President
Georgetown University, D.C.

Rev. Theodore M. Hesburgh, CSC, President
University of Notre Dame, IN

Rev. Robert A. Mitchell, SJ, President
University of Detroit, MI

Rev. J. Donald Monan, SJ, President
Boston College, MA

Rev. Joseph O'Hare, SJ, President
Fordham University, NY

Rev. John P. Raynor, SJ, President
Marquette University, WI

Rev. William J. Rewak, SJ, President
University of Santa Clara, CA

Rev. John T. Richardson, CM, President
DePaul University, IL

*M. Jean-Guy Paquet, Recteur
Laval University, Quebec, Canada

---

* [Did not attend meeting but signed document]

Address, Pope John Paul II to Leaders of Catholic Higher Education

Xavier University of Louisiana
September 12, 1987

Dear Friends; Dear Leaders in Catholic Higher Education:

At the end of this day dedicated to the prayerful celebration of Catholic education in the United States, I greet you, and all those whom you represent, with esteem and with affection in our Lord Jesus Christ. I thank the Association of Catholic Colleges and Universities for having arranged this meeting. I express my gratitude to Dr. Norman Francis and to all at Xavier University for their hospitality at this institution, which, in so many ways, serves the cause of Catholic higher education.

> I will bless the Lord at all times; his praise shall be ever in my mouth.
> Glorify the Lord with me, let us together extol his name (Ps 34:2,4).

Yes, let us join in thanking God for the many good things that he, the Father of Wisdom, has accomplished through Catholic colleges and universities. In doing so, let us be thankful for the special strengths of your schools—for their Catholic identity, for their service of truth, and for their role in helping to make the Church's presence felt in the world of culture and science. And let us be thankful above all for the men and women committed to this mission, those of the past and those of today, who have made and are making Catholic higher education the great reality that it is.

The United States is unique in its network of more than two hundred and thirty-five colleges and universities which identify themselves as Catholic. The number and diversity of your institutions are in fact without parallel; they exercise an influence not only within the United States but also throughout the universal Church, and they bear a responsibility for her good.

Two years from now you will celebrate the two hundredth anniversary of the founding by John Carroll of Georgetown University, the first Catholic university in the United States. After Georgetown, through the leadership of religious congregations and farseeing bishops, and with the generous support of the Catholic people, other colleges and universities have been established in different parts of this vast country. For two centuries these institutions have contributed much to the emergence of a Catholic laity, which today is intimately and extensively involved in industry, government, the professions, arts, and all forms of public and private endeavor—all those activities that constitute the characteristic dynamism and vitality of this land.

Amidst changing circumstances, Catholic universities and colleges are challenged to retain a lively sense of their Catholic identity and to fulfill their specific responsibilities to the Church and to society. It is precisely in doing so that they make their distinctive contribution to the wider field of higher education.

The Catholic identity of your institutions is a complex and vitally important matter. This identity depends upon the explicit profession of Catholicity on the part of the university as an institution, and also upon the personal conviction and sense of mission on the part of its professors and administrators.

During my pastoral visit to this country in 1979, I spoke of various elements that contribute to the mission of Catholic higher education. It is useful once again to stress the importance of research into questions vital for the Church and society—a research carried out "with a just sense of history, together with the concern to show the full meaning of the human person regenerated in Christ"; to emphasize the need for educating men and women of outstanding knowledge who, "having made a personal synthesis between faith and culture, will be both capable and willing to assume tasks in the service of the community and of society in general, and to bear witness to their faith before the world"; and finally, to pursue the establishment of a living community of faith, "where sincere commitment to scientific research and study goes together with a deep commitment to authentic Christian living" (Address at The Catholic University of America, Washington, D.C., October 7, 1979, no. 3).

To appreciate fully the value of your heritage, we need to recall the origins of Catholic university life. The university as we know it began in close association with the Church. This was no accident. Faith and love of learning have a close relationship. For the Fathers of the Church and the thinkers and academics of the Middle Ages, the search for truth was associated with the search for God. According to Catholic teaching—as expressed also in the First Vatican Council—the mind is capable not only of searching for the truth but also of grasping it, however imperfectly.

Religious faith itself calls for intellectual inquiry, and the confidence that there can be no contradiction between faith and reason is a distinctive feature of the Catholic humanistic tradition, as it existed in the past and as it exists in our own day.

Catholic higher education is called to exercise, through the grace of God, an extraordinary "share in the work of truth" (3 Jn 8). The Catholic university is dedicated to the service of the truth, as is every university. In its research and teaching, however, it proceeds from the vision and perspective of faith and is thus enriched in a specific way.

From this point of view one sees that there is an intimate relationship between the Catholic university and the teaching office of the Church. The bishops of the Church, as *Doctores et Magistri Fidei*, should be seen not as external agents but as participants in the life of the Catholic university in its privileged role as protagonist in the encounter between faith and science and between revealed truth and culture.

Modern culture reflects many tensions and contradictions. We live in an age of great technological triumphs but also of great human anxieties. Too often, today, the individual's vision of reality is fragmented. At times experience is mediated by forces over which people have no control; sometimes there is not even an awareness of these forces. The temptation grows to relativize moral principles and to privilege process over truth. This has grave consequences for the moral life as well as for the intellectual life of individuals and of society. The Catholic university must address all these issues from the perspective of faith and out of its rich heritage.

Modern culture is marked by a pluralism of attitudes, points of view, and insights. This situation rightly requires mutual understanding; it means that society and groups within society must respect those who have a different outlook from their own. But pluralism does not exist for its own sake; it is directed to the fullness of truth. In the academic context, the respect for persons which pluralism rightly envisions does not justify the view that ultimate questions about human life and destiny have no final answers or that all beliefs are of equal value, provided that none is asserted as absolutely true and normative. Truth is not served in this way.

It is true of course that the culture of every age contains certain ambiguities which reflect the inner tensions of the human heart, the struggle between good and evil. Hence the Gospel, in its continuing encounter with culture, must always challenge the accomplishments and assumptions of the age (cf. Rom 12:2). Since, in our day, the implications of this ambiguity are often so destructive to the community, so hostile to human dignity, it is crucial that the Gospel should purify culture, uplift it, and orient it to the service of what is authentically human. Humanity's very survival may depend on it. And here, as leaders in Catholic education in the United States, you have an extremely important contribution to make.

Today there exists an increasingly evident need for philosophical reflection concerning the truth about the human person. A metaphysical approach is needed as an antidote to intellectual and moral relativism. But what is required even more is fidelity to the word of God, to ensure that human progress takes into account the entire revealed truth of the eternal act of love in which the universe and especially the human person acquire ultimate meaning. The more one seeks to unravel the mystery of the human person, the more open one becomes to the mystery of transcendence. The more deeply one penetrates the divine mystery, the more one discovers the true greatness and dignity of human beings.

In your institutions, which are privileged settings for the encounter between faith and culture, theological science has a special role and deserves a prominent place in the curriculum of studies and in the allocation of research resources. But theology, as the Church understands it, is much more than an academic discipline. Its data are the data of God's Revelation entrusted to the Church. The deeper understanding of the mystery of Christ, the understanding which theological reflection seeks, is ultimately a gift of the Holy Spirit given for the common good of the whole Church. Theology is truly a search to understand ever more clearly the heritage of faith preserved, transmitted, and made explicit by the Church's teaching office. And theological instruction serves the community of faith by helping new generations to understand and to integrate into their lives the truth of God, which is so vital to the fundamental issues of the modern world.

Theology is at the service of the whole ecclesial community. The work of theology involves an interaction among the various members of the community of faith. The bishops, united with the pope, have the mission of authentically teaching the message of Christ; as pastors, they are called to sustain the unity in faith and Christian living of the entire People of God. In this they need the assistance of Catholic theologians, who perform an inestimable service to the Church. But theologians also need the charism entrusted by Christ to the bishops and, in the first place, to the bishop of Rome. The fruits of their work, in order to enrich the life-stream of the ecclesial community, must ultimately be tested and validated by the Magisterium. In effect, therefore, the ecclesial context of Catholic theology gives it a special character and value, even when theology exists in an academic setting.

Here, the words of Saint Paul concerning the spiritual gifts should be a source of light and harmony for us all:

> There are different gifts but the same Spirit; there are different ministries but the same Lord; there are different works but the same God who accomplishes all of them in everyone. To each person the manifestation of the Spirit is given for the common good (1 Cor 12:4–7).

In the different offices and functions in the Church, it is not some power and dominion that is being divided up, but rather the same service of the Body of Christ that is shared according to the vocation of each. It is a question of unity in the work of service. In this spirit I wish to express cordial support for the humble, generous and patient work of theological research and education being carried out in your universities and colleges in accordance with the Church's mission to proclaim and teach the saving wisdom of God (cf. 1 Cor 1:21).

My own university experience impels me to mention another related matter of supreme importance in the Catholic college and university, namely, the religious and moral education of students and their pastoral care. I am confident that you too take this special service very seriously, and that you count it among your most pressing and most satisfying responsibilities. One cannot meet with college and university students anywhere in the world without hearing their questions and sensing their anxieties. In their hearts your students have many questions about faith, religious practice and holiness of life. Each one arrives on your campuses with a family background, a personal history, and an acquired culture. They all want to be accepted, loved and supported by a Christian educational community which shows friendship and authentic spiritual commitment.

It is your privilege to serve your students in faith and love; to help them deepen their friendship with Christ; to make available to them the opportunity for prayer and liturgical celebration, including the possibility to know the forgiveness and love of Jesus Christ in the sacraments of penance and the eucharist. You are able, as Catholic educators, to introduce your students to a powerful experience of community and to a very serious involvement in social concerns that will enlarge their horizons, challenge their life styles, and offer them authentic human fulfillment.

University students, for example, are in a splendid position to take to heart the Gospel invitation to go out of themselves, to reject introversion, and to concentrate on the needs of others. Students with the opportunities of higher education can readily grasp the relevance for today of Christ's parable of the rich man and Lazarus (cf. Lk 16:19ff.), with all of its consequences for humanity. What is at stake is not only the rectitude of individual human hearts but also the whole social order as it touches the spheres of economics, politics, and human rights and relations.

Here in the Catholic university centers of the nation, vivified by the inspiration of the Gospel, must be drawn up the blueprints for the reform of attitudes and structures that will influence the whole dynamic of peace and justice in the world, as it affects East and West, North and

South. It is not enough to offer to the disadvantaged of the world crumbs of freedom, crumbs of truth, and crumbs of bread. The Gospel calls for much more. The parable of the rich man and the poor man is directed to the conscience of humanity, and, today in particular, to the conscience of America. But that conscience often passes through the halls of academe, through nights of study and hours of prayer, finally to reach and embrace the whole prophetic message of the Gospel. "Keep your attention closely fixed on it," we are told in the Second Letter of Peter, "as you would on a lamp shining in a dark place until the first streaks of dawn appear and the morning star rises in your hearts" (2 Pt 1:19).

Dear brothers and sisters: as leaders in Catholic university and college education, you have inherited a tradition of service and academic excellence, the cumulative effort of so many who have worked so hard and sacrificed so much for Catholic education in this country. Now there lies before you the wide horizon of the third century of the nation's constitutional existence, and the third century of Catholic institutions of higher learning serving the people of this land. The challenges that confront you are just as testing as those your forefathers faced in establishing the network of institutions over which you now preside. Undoubtedly, the greatest challenge is, and will remain, that of preserving and strengthening the Catholic character of your colleges and universities—that institutional commitment to the word of God as proclaimed by the Catholic Church. This commitment is both an expression of spiritual consistency and a specific contribution to the cultural dialogue proper to American life. As you strive to make the presence of the Church in the world of modern culture more luminous, may you listen once again to Christ's prayer to his Father for his disciples: "Consecrate them by means of truth—'Your word is truth'" (Jn 17:17).

May the Holy Spirit, the Counsellor and Spirit of Truth, who has enlivened and enlightened the Church of Christ from the beginning, give you great confidence in the Father's word, and sustain you in the service that you render to the truth through Catholic higher education in the United States of America.[1]

NOTE

1. In conclusion, the Holy Father offered the following impromptu remarks.

I am grateful for your presence this evening. Through your presence I could be present also, not only among you but also in more than 200 academic institutions, universities and colleges, in the United States—Catholic institutions for the culture of Catholic higher education. I could be present among all of the teachers—the academic teachers, all the professors, and among all of the students.

I should be very grateful if you can transmit my affection to all of them.

We are working together. You, you are aware of having a special participation in the prophetic mission of the Church—more, of Christ Himself. The Church participates in the prophetic mission of Jesus Christ. And the teaching of the Church and all kinds of institutions who serve the teaching of the Church belong to this large concept, large reality of the participation of the prophetic mission of the Church.

It is now clearer, perhaps, as before in the light of the Second Vatican Council, especially in the light of *Luman Gentium*. It is clear how the whole community of scholars, of teachers—of academic teachers, in the Church, in the Catholic universities, in the Catholic colleges, how all of them are having this special mission and this profound responsibility in the name of Jesus Christ who is our supreme teacher. In the name of Jesus Christ who is our supreme and unique teacher. Who is not only teacher; who is the truth; who is the way; who is the life. In His name, I express my gratitude to all of you for this meeting and for all of your activities.

And now I wish you a good night, good night and good sleep. Thank you very much.

Summary of Responses to the 1985 Draft Schema On the Catholic University

February 1, 1988

INTRODUCTION

On April 15, 1985, a draft schema for a Pontifical Document on Catholic Universities was sent to 610 Catholic universities and other institutions of higher education, 10 associations of Catholic universities, 40 episcopal conferences, 200 local ordinaries who have a Catholic institution of higher education within their diocese, and 24 religious congregations and secular institutes engaged in the higher education apostolate. At the same time, the draft schema was sent to 17 pontifical universities and faculties in Rome, and 27 dicasteries within the Roman Curia.

In May of 1987, taking advantage of an International Meeting of Laity held in preparation for the Synod of Bishops and, in October, the presence of observers at the Synod itself, the draft schema was distributed to approximately 200 lay people, many of them parents of university students; some were themselves students in a Catholic university.

All were asked to examine the draft and offer suggestions "in full freedom and frankness."

The response to this request went beyond expectations: in number, and also in depth and quality. 344 letters and documents have been received by the Congregation for Catholic Education, representing the responses of more than 540 individuals and groups. As might be expected, these responses vary greatly in their perspective and, in many cases, in their recommendations. They range in length from less than one page to a booklet of more than 300 pages.

The Congregation for Catholic Education wishes to express its deep gratitude to all those who have studied the proposed document and have

---

From the files of the Association of Catholic Colleges and Universities, printed in *Origins* 17, No. 41 (March 24, 1988): 268–270.

responded to its request to offer suggestions. Whatever their length or recommendations, each response shows a genuine appreciation of the Catholic university and a serious study of the draft schema. The positive comments have confirmed the work that had already been done; the criticisms and proposed changes have helped to clarify the problems and provided a rich source of material for the eventual writing of a final document.

Please keep in mind that the summary on the following pages concentrates on general themes and makes only passing mention of the suggestions which note elements which may be missing from the draft or propose new wordings and even entire new paragraphs for the draft. Although they are not given in detail here, these important and valuable suggestions have been studied carefully and will be incorporated as far as possible when the draft schema is revised.

PART 1. NUMERICAL SUMMARY AND OVERALL ASSESSMENT

1. RESPONSES RECEIVED[1]

1.1. It is difficult to determine the exact number of *Catholic institutions of higher education* which responded to the request. Individual responses were received from 129 institutions, and 110 United States institutions responded through a survey. Approximately 90 other Catholic institutions of higher education responded through an association, a religious congregation, or their local ordinary. In some cases these latter groups forwarded the university responses intact; in other cases the responses were summarized and integrated into an overall response; in still other cases they were referred to only indirectly. A few universities responded *both* individually *and* through an association. Thus, directly or indirectly, at least 325 of the approximately 650 Catholic universities and other institutions of higher education responded to the request received from the Congregation for Catholic Education. 277 of these can be identified individually or nationally:

1.1.1. *Asia and Oceania:* 63 responses.

Australia — 2	Korea — 1
Bangladesh — 1	Lebanon — 1
India — 22	The Philippines — 8
Indonesia — 12	Sri Lanka — 1
Israel — 1	Taiwan — 1
Japan — 12	Timor — 1

1.1.2. *Europe:* 22 responses.

Belgium — 3	The Netherlands — 1
France — 5	Poland — 1
Germany — 1	Portugal — 1
Great Britain — 2	Spain — 4
Ireland — 1	Switzerland — 1
Italy — 2	

1.1.3. *Latin America:* 47 responses.

Argentina — 8	Ecuador — 1
Brazil — 14	El Salvador — 1
Chile — 2	Mexico — 11
Colombia — 6	Paraguay — 1
The Dominican Republic — 1	Peru — 2

1.1.4. *North America:* 145 responses.

Canada — 16	The United States — 129

1.2. Ten responses were received from national and international *university associations;* of these, five simply transmit the responses from their member institutions (either individually or in summary form), two are actually responses from a single individual, and three are responses from the executive board of the association (The International Federation of Catholic Universities, and the national associations of India and the U.S.A.). An additional ten responses were received from *other organizations:* two from more specialized university associations, two from Catholic Education Departments and six from associations of Catholic scholars in the United States.

1.3. 22 responses were received from episcopal conferences (Africa 1, Asia 5, Europe 8, Latin America 6, North America 2). Four of these are the responses of a single individual (a staff member responsible for relations with Catholic universities); four are brief letters of acceptance and support. The other fourteen are more detailed and indicate thorough study of the document, often in conjunction with a committee of university representatives.

1.4. While many bishops responded through an episcopal conference (the bishops of the United States, in particular, responded to a survey whose results were forwarded to the Congregation by their episcopal conference), responses were also received directly from 63 *individual bishops* (Asia 8, Europe 14, Latin America 22, North America 19). Of these, ten are actually university responses forwarded by the bishop, while 31 are rather brief statements which support the document and its purposes and offer a few suggestions. The other 22 responses contain more detailed comments.

1.5.   Responses were received from 22 *religious congregations.* Three offer no comments because they are not involved in the university apostolate; seven referred the draft schema to their individual universities and those responses are indicated in the institutional responses below. Twelve gave a general response on behalf of the religious congregation.

1.6.   Seven responses were received from the *pontifical universities and faculties in Rome,* and nineteen from the *dicasteries* within the Roman Curia.

1.7.   The responses from laity are still arriving in the Congregation; so far twenty have been received (Belgium, England, France (3), Germany (2), India, Ireland, Italy (4), Poland (2), Portugal, Switzerland, U.S.A. (3)).

1.8.   An additional 40 letters were sent by interested individuals, nearly all of them commenting on the purposes of the schema rather than on its contents. 35 of these letters are from North America (32 from the United States and three from Canada).

2. Overall Assessment of the Draft Schema[2]

2.1. *Acceptance by Catholic Universities and*
Other Institutions of Higher Education, and by
National and International University Associations

It is possible to assess the degree of acceptance of 266 institutions; the others are incorporated into the summary response of an association.

2.1.1. The response indicates basic agreement with the present draft schema and offers few or no suggestions:

> *32 responses*— 12.0%.
> Asia and Oceania — 16 (Australia, India (5), Israel, Korea, The Philippines (7), Timor).
> Europe — 2 (Italy, Ireland).
> Latin America — 10 (Argentina, Brazil (6), Colombia (2), El Salvador).
> North America — 4 (U.S.A. (4)).

2.1.2. The response accepts the present draft, and offers suggestions to improve the style or to clarify points ambiguously expressed. These is an occasional suggestion for a more substantive change:

> *53 responses*— 19.9%.
> Asia and Oceania — 9 (Bangladesh, India (5), Indonesia, The Philippines, Sri Lanka).
> Europe — 8 (France (2), Germany, Italy, Portugal, Spain (3)).
> Latin America — 18 (Argentina (5), Brazil (3), Colombia, Ecuador, Mexico (6), Paraguay, Peru).
> North America — 18 (U.S.A. (18)).

2.1.3. The response is ambiguous:

— Basic agreement, with suggestions for improved expression, style, etc., *because the document only applies to Catholic universities canonically established.* (Some assume that this is the only possible Catholic university; others explicitly say that there are Catholic universities to which the draft schema does not apply. These same assumptions seem to be implicit in some other responses from the educational institutions.):

  9 responses — 3.5%.
  Asia and Oceania — 1 (India).
  Europe — 2 (Poland, Spain).
  Latin America — 6 (Argentina, Chile, The Dominican Republic, Mexico (2), Peru).

— Basic agreement, with few and minor suggestions, *because the document does not apply to us:*

  11 responses — 3.8%.
  Asia and Oceania — 10 (India (10).
  Europe — 1 (Great Britain).

2.1.4. The response is more critical of the present text, and offers major substantive suggestions for revision:

  126 responses — 47.4%.
  Asia and Oceania — 25 (India, Indonesia (11), Japan (12), Taiwan).
  Europe — 6 (Belgium (2), France, Great Britain, The Netherlands, Switzerland).
  Latin America — 10 (Brazil (5), Chile, Colombia (3), Mexico).
  North America — 85 (Canada (13), U.S.A. (72)).

  (Also the Executive Council of the International Federation of Catholic Universities and the Executive Councils of the national associations of India and the United States.)

2.1.5. The response urges that no document be published, or asks that the document to be published should be pastoral rather than juridical (i.e., an exhortation, without any norms):

  36 responses — 13.5%.
  Asia and Oceania — 3 (Australia, India, Lebanon).
  Europe — 3 (Belgium, France (2)).
  Latin America — 3 (Argentina, Mexico (2)).
  North America — 27 (Canada (3), U.S.A. (24)).

2.2. Acceptance by Episcopal Conferences

Nearly all of the episcopal conferences expressed agreement with the need for a document such as the draft schema and stressed its potential importance for the Catholic universities and for the Church, but nearly all had suggestions to offer.

2.2.1. The response accepts the present draft, and offers suggestions to improve the style or to clarify points ambiguously expressed:

> *9 responses*(40.9%) — Australia, Bangladesh, Belgium, Germany, India, Korea, Paraguay, Thailand, Zaire.

2.2.2. The response contains some substantive suggestions, but expresses basic agreement with the overall contents of the present text:

> *3 responses*(13.6%) — Argentina, The Dominican Republic, Poland.

2.2.3. The response is more critical of the present text, and offers major substantive suggestions for revision:

> *10 responses* (45.5%) — Canada, Chile, Colombia, England and Wales, Ireland, Italy, Mexico, The Netherlands, Switzerland, The United States.

2.3 Acceptance by Individual Bishops

Like the episcopal conferences, the individual bishops are in favor of having a document on the Catholic university, and support the general themes in the present draft schema.

Seven bishops forward a university response without any comments of their own on the present draft. Of the remaining 56 responses from individual bishops:

2.3.1. The response accepts the present draft, and offers suggestions to improve the style or to clarify points ambiguously expressed:

> *16 responses* — 28.6%.
> Asia and Oceania — 3 (India (2), Taiwan).
> Europe — 4 (England, France, Italy (2)).
> Latin America — 4 (Argentina, Bolivia, Brazil, Colombia).
> North America — 5 (Canada, U.S.A. (4)).

2.3.2. The response is ambiguous, because it assumes that the document only applies to canonically established Catholic universities:

> *2 responses* — 3.6%.
> Europe — 2 (England, Opus Dei).

2.3.3. the response contains some substantive suggestions but expresses basic agreement with the overall contents of the present text:

> *21 responses* — 37.5%.
> Europe — 6 (Austria, Italy (2), Portugal, Spain (2)).
> Latin America — 12 (Argentina (4), Brazil, Chile (2), Colombia (2), Mexico, Paraguay, Puerto Rico).
> North America — 3 (U.S.A. (3)).

2.3.4. The response is more critical of the present text, and offers major substantive suggestions for revision:

> *17 responses* — 30.4%.
> Asia and Oceania — 2 (Lebanon, The Philippines).
> Europe — 2 (France, Germany).
> Latin America — 2 (Mexico, Peru).
> North America — 11 (Canada (3), U.S.A. (8)).

2.4. *Acceptance by Religious Congregations*

As already indicated, only twelve of the religious congregations sent an overall response from the Congregation as such. Of these, five (41.7%) accept the present draft and offer only minor suggestions, while seven (58.3%) are more critical and offer more substantive suggestions for revision.

2.5. *Acceptance by Lay People*

Four of the twenty lay people who responded speak about what a Catholic university should be, but do not comment specifically on the present draft. Of the remaining sixteen, twelve (75%) accept the draft in its present form with only minor suggestions; four (25%) are critical of some parts of the draft and have more substantive suggestions.

2.6. The responses from the pontifical universities and faculties in Rome and from the dicasteries within the Roman Curia suggest topics that could be added to the draft and improvements in style. With the exception of one rector who is quite critical of it, these responses speak of the need for a document but do not attempt to evaluate the present draft schema.

3. AN OVERVIEW OF THE RESPONSES

3.1. *Catholic Universities and other Institutions of Higher Education*

As a general norm (but with important exceptions), larger and more complex institutions are more critical of the draft, while smaller institutions are more accepting. As a general tendency (again with important exceptions), institutions in Asia (except The Philippines), North America, Northern Europe (Belgium, France, Germany, Great Britain, Holland, Switzerland), and some countries in Latin America, are more accepting. A response from an institution that is not canonically established is, in most cases, more critical than a response from an institution that has been so established—especially when the latter assumes that *all* Catholic universities are canonically established, or that the draft only applies to such universities.

3.2. Episcopal Conferences and Individual Bishops[3]

While nearly all speak quite positively about the need for a document on the Catholic university, both episcopal conferences and individual bishops tend to follow the geographical pattern of the universities in their evaluation of the present draft schema. Some responses from both episcopal conferences and individual bishops point to concrete difficulties which would arise if the schema were to become final in its present form—as do the responses from institutions in the same countries.

The one exception to this general pattern is the set of responses from individual bishops in the United States: seven bishops write ̇in strong support of the proposed Norms, contrary to the response received from the episcopal conference, some responses received from other bishops, and the majority of the responses received from the institutions of higher education in that country. Some quotations included in the survey forwarded by the episcopal conference suggest that other U.S. bishops also support the proposed Norms.

3.3. Religious Congregations

The responses of religious congregations are consistent with those of the others in the sense that a response from a congregation responsible for many institutions in North America and Asia tends to be more critical, while one from a congregation whose institutions are primarily in Europe and Latin America tends to be more accepting.

3.4. Lay People

Nearly all of the twenty responses received so far from the lay people say that they are not able to comment in detail about the draft schema. At the same time, a constant theme in these responses is an expression of great concern for Catholic universities; the lay people want these institutions to be excellent as universities, but at the same time they want them to be truly "Catholic": in fidelity to the Church, in care for the intellectual and pastoral formation of the students, and as a visible and effective presence of the Church in the university world.

3.5. Other Responses

As already noted, responses from the more specialized associations and from individuals come primarily from the United States and Canada, four of the six U.S. professional associations are critical of the present draft schema, while the other two support it strongly. Of the 35 letters received from individuals in those two countries, 13 from the U.S. and three from Canada are strongly critical of the present draft, while 16 letters from the U.S. support it and express explicit disagreement with the responses sent from the majority of the Catholic institutions of higher learning in that country.

PART II. CONTENTS OF THE RESPONSES

4. INTRODUCTION

The sections that follow summarize the comments and suggestions contained in all the responses: from institutions of higher education and university associations, from episcopal conferences and individual bishops, from religious congregations, Roman institutions, invited laity and interested individuals. A concluding section concentrates on some of the more specific concerns of episcopal conferences and individual bishops.

Since the primary purpose of this summary is to assist in a revision of the present draft schema, it will give greater emphasis to the difficulties pointed out in the responses and the suggestions for substantial change that are offered. Expressions of praise or approval are summarized rather briefly; points about which there is general agreement are not always noted explicitly. Suggestions for changes in style, grammar, and expression are not included unless these are a part of more substantive suggestions. (These points of general agreement and stylistic suggestions have not been ignored; they will be important source material when the draft schema is revised.)

REACTIONS TO THE DRAFT SCHEMA AS A WHOLE

5.1. General Reactions

5.1.1. Many responses indicate that there is need for a document such as the draft schema, and most indicate that they are in agreement with its general purpose: to clarify the distinctively Catholic character of the institutions, and to ensure that authentic Catholic doctrine is communicated in these institutions. A few responses, while praising the draft, suggest that it is not strong enough in insisting on adherence to the doctrines of the Catholic faith; they suggest that appropriate means for enforcing the Norms be made a part of the final document.

5.1.2. A few responses in each group (institutions of higher education, bishops, religious congregations) accept and praise the document and urge its publication in its present form. "The Congregation for Catholic

Education is to be commended for a document which is positive in tone and contemporary in language and speaks with clarity and openness to the academic world" (Philippines). Most of the responses accept the themes and praise at least some parts of the draft, even though the response may include suggestions for substantial changes in its contents. Even those few responses from the educational institutions which are negative (i.e., they would prefer no document at all) at least include a note of gratitude for the interest in Catholic universities being shown by the Church. "Il a paru excellent a tous de manifester l'intérêt de l'Eglise toute entière pour les Universités Catholiques" (France).

5.1.3. Responses from both the institutions and from bishops noted that the study of the schema gave them an opportunity to reflect on the mission of the Catholic university today. It also provided an opportunity for dialogue, within the institutions and between institutions and bishops, about this mission.

5.2. Some Examples of Areas in Which the Responses Express General Agreement with the Draft Schema

5.2.1. If a university wishes to call itself Catholic, then there ought to be a relationship between the Church and the institution, at least in what has to do with Catholic doctrine.

5.2.2. The draft schema responds to a need for greater development of the identity of a Catholic university. "Such a document will contribute greatly to the proper organization and administration of Catholic universities or institutes that are inspired by the Catholic ethos" (Ireland). "Se piensa que [el documento] puede contribuir a proteger la identidad católica de las Universidades" (Chile).

5.2.3. The document rightly emphasizes the role of the university as an instrument of dialogue between faith and culture and as a place of formation in values. Some responses would like the emphasis on value education to be even greater and perhaps even be the central theme of the document.

5.3. Suggestions of a General Nature, Grouped into Thematic Areas

5.3.1. The document should include a description of the university as a university.

While the document is correct in its focus on the Catholic nature of the institution, it is only through a proper understanding of the nature of a university that the distinctive nature of a *Catholic* university can be determined. (The responses are detailed; the following points are only an outline of the many suggestions.)

a.   A university has its own identify and nature, and therefore a basic autonomy, as a human institution. It can be used by the Church (and by others) to help in achieving other ends, but this use must not destroy its own essence as a university. (It is not, for instance, a parish or catechetical center; it is not a social institute.)

b.   An essential role of the university is education through critical thinking. In this it differs, at least in part, from a seminary or ecclesiastical faculty, where the primary emphasis is on formation for service in the Church. Therefore a document on the Catholic university describes an institution quite different from that of *Sapientia Christiana*; to begin with the concept of an ecclesiastical university and then try to make those changes necessary to fit the case of the Catholic university is to assume a parity that does not exist and is to run the risk of distortion. "Universities are where differing ideas on the whole of human endeavors are afforded the opportunity of interplay, of cross-pollination. . . . The schema needs to recognize more positively the requirements of a true university as a privileged place for civilized discourse and the presentation of divergent views" (U.S.A.). "Las universidades eclesiáticas son propias de la Iglesia. . . . Las universidades católicas son en cambio centros de educación superior que. . . cultivan muy variadas ciencias profanas en sus diversos centros de estudios civiles. Son así medios con los que la Iglesia realiza una presencia pública, constanta y universal. . . ." (Spain).

c.   Though they can lead to abuses, academic freedom and tenure are recognized today as integral to this "critical thinking": as necessary for the pursuit of truth and for freedom of research. "In their academic work, faculty are not just permitted to follow their minds wherever the pursuit of truth leads them—it is demanded of them" (U.S.A.). "The advances in the culture we all enjoy are results of free enquiry. Confidence in the ability of the human mind to distinguish the true from the false, the valid from the invalid, and the real from the sham is at the root of the philosophies both of Augustine and of Aquinas. Interference in free enquiry and free expression on the part of university administrators or hierarchy would be counterproductive to the church's interests in the long run" (Canada).

d.   The document correctly stresses the Church's right to establish universities, but it does not sufficiently indicate that these institutions grant civil degrees and therefore are also subject to civil charters, accrediting agencies, professional associations, and public legislation. To take one example, the regulations for the hiring and dismissal of teachers are often a matter of civil law.

e.   A university is primarily concerned with "secular" knowledge: physical and social sciences, humanities, and the various professions. While the schema recognized this in its initial definition, both the

Proemium and the Norms seem to concentrate primarily on theology and theologians, ignoring most of what takes place in a university.

f.   The purposes of a university are traditionally defined to be "research, teaching,[4] and community service." (The third item is missing from some parts of the draft schema.) In addition to the search for the communication of truth, it must serve both society and the Church according to its nature as a university. Its role is not simply to be a witness to the faith, and its role of "evangelization" needs to be carefully defined. "Education is in itself a service of the Church and not just a means of evangelization or catechesis" (India).

5.3.2. *The role of a Catholic university, as Catholic, needs to be defined more completely.*

The responses agree with and praise much of the description in the draft schema of the Catholic university's role, especially the description of the service that the Catholic university offers to the Church. They suggest, however, that other elements need to be added to this description.

a.   The most important characteristic of the Catholic university is that it be excellent as a university. Quality and excellence in its ongoing search for truth, in its teaching, and in its community service is the best way that it can serve the Church. Within this identity as a university, it establishes its distinctive role as a Catholic university by infusing Christ, the gospel, theological thought, and Catholic teaching into its search for truth, the education of its students, and its service of the community.

b.   The 1972 document on "The Catholic University in the Modern World" (approved by the Congregation for Catholic Education in 1973[5]) is a more nuanced and thorough description of a Catholic university. It should be used more extensively as the basis for a pontifical document. In the present draft, it is sometimes quoted out of context. (Responses also suggest greater and more effective use of the documents of Vatican II, and refer to the 1985 document on freedom within the university of the International Federation of Catholic Universities and the pastoral letters of the bishops of the United States, Colombia, Brazil, and Paraguay that speak about the Catholic university. Responses from English-speaking countries suggest that good use could be made of *The Idea of a University* by Cardinal John Henry Newman.)

c.   It is as an academic institution that the Catholic university can be of positive help to the Church in its dialogue with culture, and in making theology (and the Catholic faith in general) relevant in today's world. "Rather than 'preaching the gospel' the Catholic university is responsible for unfolding the meaning of the gospel for our contemporary world. In order to do this, the Catholic university must be committed to developing a theological tradition from the gospel teaching that is on the same intellectual level as the contemporary development of all the other academic disciplines" (U.S.A.). But the dialogue with culture is not one-sided, and the Catholic university can help the Church by assisting it to learn from culture.

— Several responses objected to the statement that the Catholic university is "a part of" the Church (and the implications of this that appear throughout the draft schema). It has its own identity distinct from (though not independent of) the Church.

— Because of the critical and prophetic role of a university, a Catholic university cannot simply be an instrument for the "transmission" of Catholic doctrine, or even of the message of Christ. "Devese comprender o serviço que a universidade Católica presta á Igreja não como simples defesa apologética, mas como função crítica que procura também denunciar e corrigir erros e defeitos e principalmente, abrir novos horizontes para a ação da Igreja e sua presença no mundo" (Brazil).

— The Catholic university is indeed a privileged place for dialogue between theology and other branches of knowledge, but it must be a true dialogue in which each side is open to and learns from the other. (The draft schema suggests an influence of theology on other branches of knowledge, but does not speak of an influence in the other direction.)

d.   The Catholic university must show that the Christian vision of the world is compatible with authentic scientific research: that a knowledge of God and Christian revelation can clarify the discoveries of science. This should include a recognition of the autonomy and the contributions of science. "Un dogmatisme excessif, une exclusive rigoureuse à l'égard des personnes iraient contre ce but. L'esprit d'écoute et d'accueil peut faciliter au contraire la perception de cette finalité" (France).

e.   The draft schema seems to identify the Catholic nature of the university too closely with fidelity to Catholic doctrine in teaching and research. Responses say that, while fidelity is necessary, this view of the Catholic university is too narrow. (1) the greater part of the teaching and research in a Catholic university has little direct relationship to Catholic doctrine. (2) While adherence to Catholic doctrine cannot be ignored, it is a spirit present throughout the whole university that really makes it Catholic: the way in which the various disciplines are taught and research is carried on, a communication of values along with the search for truth, the treatment of individuals and the human dignity that is fostered by this treatment, the pastoral care of students, teachers, and auxiliary staff personnel,[6] the creation of a community within the university. In this sense, the *entire* activity of the university is related to faith life and to the formation of mature human beings as children of God.

f.   The tension between academic freedom and fidelity to Catholic doctrine, especially in (but not limited to) the area of theological teaching and research, is not sufficiently recognized. The present draft seems to be too one-sided on this question and to stress authority and fidelity at the expense of legitimate freedom. Responses recognize the complexity of this problem and the reality of the tension, but they point out that theologians have been encouraged by the Second Vatican Council to confront the major issues that face contemporary society, that there is no more appropriate forum for this than the Catholic university, and therefore that sufficient freedom must be given to these theologians to explore various approaches. While they must respect the prerogatives of the hierarchy, theologians in a university setting require trust and support from the broader Church if their efforts are to bear fruit. "The schema would reduce theology in the university to an instrument of the Magisterium rather than a separate but related form of service of the Church. . . . If the university is to be a place of dialogue between faith on the one hand and reason and culture on the other, then the academic freedom of the theologian must be recognized and respected. Otherwise Catholic theology would not enjoy the academic respect of other disciplines" (U.S.A.).

g.   Responsibility for defining and maintaining its Catholic nature must lie primarily *within* the university. The schema, therefore, should respect the rights and the responsibilities of internal governance (rector/president, statutes, boards of trustees, in some cases a religious congregation), and place the primary responsibility there. Other Church authorities, such as the local ordinary, exercise "vigilance." "The document should urge the bishops to continue to support, encourage, and assist the universities in carrying out what is ultimately the trustees' responsibility" (U.S.A.).

— The exact relationship between the Catholic university and Church authorities (local ordinary, episcopal conference, or Holy See) is often the result of historical and cultural circumstances. The document, both in Proemium and in Norms, has to be carefully nuanced in describing this relationship, depending on the nature of the Catholic university itself and the country in which the university is located.

— Responses from both institutions and from bishops suggest that the relationship between the Catholic university and Church authorities (including its bishops, episcopal conferences and the Holy See) should be primarily pastoral rather than juridical; they insist that ongoing dialogue is necessary in order to promote greater understanding on both sides.

— A few respondents say that bishops do not give sufficient priority to Catholic universities; they ask that the document give greater stress to the need for support from the bishops, and from the Catholic community in general.

h. Some responses insist that theology (and also philosophy) courses must be a part of the *required* curriculum in a Catholic university.

i. A Catholic university, like any university, is engaged in research in a wide variety of areas. As Catholic, it will give a certain priority to research in areas and issues vital to the Church: theological and philosophical issues; poverty and social justice and ways to achieve a social transformation; issues of peace and international relations; bioethical issues.

j. The Catholic university, in contrast to a present trend in university education, should stress a liberal education for the total formation of the human person. Professional training in a Catholic institution needs to include this humanistic element which will aid in total formation.

k. Other roles of the Catholic university should be mentioned in the document: e.g., service of the needs of the Catholic community in the region where the university is located; formation of a Catholic laity able to have a positive influence on society; formation of teachers for Catholic primary and secondary schools.

5.3.3. *The wide variety of Catholic universities, and Catholic institutions of higher learning that are not universities, needs to be recognized more explicitly both in the Proemium and in the Norms.*

a. Some recognition should be given to the fact that different types of institutions have different specific roles. The liberal arts college, for instance, is concerned with teaching (and integral formation of the student) more than with research. The professional institution is ordered toward specific training for a profession, though it must not ignore human formation. Not all institutions are engaged in the dialogue between faith and culture in the same way.

b. Most Catholic universities (and other institutions of higher learning) outside of Europe have been founded by religious congregations of men and women, with the approval (often informal) of the local ordinary. This should be recognized, and these Congregations should be encouraged to renew their dedication to this important apostolate.

c. Some concrete goals of a Catholic university may depend (or have depended in the past) on historical and cultural circumstances. In India, and other countries of the Near East and East Asia, the Catholic university has been an instrument for pre-evangelization, helping to spread the knowledge of, and win acceptance for, the Church. In Latin America, it is an important instrument for social development. In the United States, it had played an effective role in bringing an immigrant population out of poverty into the mainstream of the life of the country.

5.3.4. Expressions used should not assume that all, or nearly all, teachers (or students) are Catholics. The ecumenical role of the Catholic university needs greater stress.

a.   In many Catholic universities today (nearly all in some countries), many of the teachers and a significant proportion of students are not members of the Catholic Church. This may be the result of geographical location, or it may be a deliberate choice: in order to serve the people of the region more adequately, in order to improve academic quality (because it is impossible to find sufficient numbers of qualified Catholic professors), in order to promote ecumenical dialogue, or to enable the Catholic university to be a part of the "mainstream" of university education. Whatever the reason, the presence of members of other faiths, both as teachers and as students, is seen as positive by many of those who responded, and they suggested that both the tone and the content of the present draft be changed to reflect this positive reality.

b.   While those who belong to other churches or espouse other faiths (and also those with no faith) are expected to respect the Catholic nature of the university, the university (and also the Catholic Church) can learn from these people through honest dialogue.

c.   The Catholic university should provide those who are not members of the Catholic Church with opportunities to learn about the Catholic faith, but it should also provide opportunities for them to grow in their own faith and religious commitment. Religious liberty must be respected, and any suggestion of indoctrination must be avoided. (This same attitude, according to some responses, should also be extended to non-practicing Catholics.)

d.   Without losing sight of the Catholic identity of the university, the document should put greater stress on inter-religious dialogue and ecumenism, and the special opportunity the Catholic university has in this area. it should also recognize the important role of the university in dialogue with non-Christians.

e.   The distinct role of the Catholic university in a country in which Catholics (and Christians) are a small minority (e.g., India, Japan, Indonesia, Lebanon, Thailand, China, Korea) needs to be specifically recognized in the document.

5.3.5. The nature of the Church, and the relation between the Church and the Catholic university, needs to be developed more carefully.

a.   It is not clear when a reference to "Church" is actually to the hierarchy and when it is meant to refer to the entire People of God. It is not always clear whether "Christian" is used as a synonym for "Catholic" or whether it refers also to members of other Christian churches.

b.   The Christian faith and the Gospel message, Christian principles, and the Christian tradition should receive greater stress. There should be more reference to Christ, and quotations from Scripture should be used. The constant repetition of "Catholic doctrine" can be distorting (and in a few instances the expression is inappropriate). Faith is not simply acceptance of a set of beliefs; it must include a life of charity. "The Magisterium has to be presented in relation to the Word of God and tradition, in the service of the truth" (Brazil).

c.   The present draft gives the impression that the Church is already in possession of the truth in its entirety which it simply *presents* in the dialogue and to the research. The Church is pictured as a static and perfect entity not influenced by outside forces.

d.   The document should recognize that other Christian churches, as well as non-Christian religions, also have values and a tradition. As an example, claims should not be made for the Catholic Church which are actually a part of the Judeo-Christian religion. In particular, the Catholic university shares many characteristics with other Christian universities.

e.   Though fidelity is necessary, the way in which this fidelity to the Magisterium is expressed (and enforced) needs a more careful and nuanced development. Some object to a document which seems to suggest that the Church should "control" the Catholic university.

5.4. Suggestions for Topics That Are Missing and Should Be Included in the Document

5.4.1. Part of the role of a Catholic university is the promotion of Christian principles. For a Catholic university, therefore, the search for and communication of truth is not enough; structures need to be set up which will communicate values and encourage Christian behavior.

5.4.2. The document should consider the problem of relations between the Catholic university and secular authorities of the state or religion.

5.4.3. The document should include a discussion of the need for a Catholic university to be engaged in an ongoing dialogue with government, private, and other Catholic universities; it should speak about the need for teachers to be actively involved in various professional associations at the international level.

5.4.4. Many responses insist that financial stability of a Catholic university is a necessity for survival; they suggest that the document mention the duty of governments, and also of Catholic groups and individual Catholics, to provide financial support to private university education.

5.4.5. A few responses ask that the document mention the need to form competent teachers, both for research and for teaching.

5.4.6. Responses from those institutions which are not universities ask that the final document use a more inclusive terminology ("Institutions of Higher Learning"?) which will refer to all institutions. They are not satisfied with a footnote reference.

5.4.7. Sections dealing with Catholics in non-Catholic universities, whether teachers or students, should either be omitted or put in an appendix.

5.5. Reactions and Suggestions, Frequently Expressed, Which Concern Tone and Style Rather Than Specific Content

5.5.1. The document should be more positive, more encouraging, more inspiring. Greater use should be made of the documents and the spirit of the Second Vatican Council.

5.5.2. The tone should be less triumphalistic, less authoritarian, less preoccupied with control, less limited to the hierarchical Church. The principles of collegiality and subsidiarity so characteristic of the documents of Vatican II seem to be absent. "Ne se situe pas dans une problématique dichotomique où l'Eglise serait porteuse de valeurs et le monde serait sans valeur et où l'Eglise devrait ainsi illuminer le monde de ses valeurs. . . . Se situe davantage dans un processus dialectique où l'Eglise est le lieu de *reconnaissance* d'une présence de l'Esprit *dans le monde*" (Belgium). "The emphasis and tone give the impression that canonical links are more important than a Catholic education which comes from a dynamism, a spirit, an inspiration which animates staff, students, curriculum, research, and the institution itself (IFCU).

5.5.3. There is a dualism in the present draft: Church vs. society, university vs. hierarchy, sacred vs. secular, ecclesial vs. civil society. "The Church should see itself more in terms of the salt, the leaven, the light for the world. The university is a missionary presence of the Church in the world" (Taiwan).

5.5.4. The present draft is Western in tone; it does not take the Third World or non-Christian countries into account.

5.5.5. The mutual character of the relationship between the Catholic university and the Church needs to be developed in a more balanced way. "There are rights and duties, services and enrichments, and also specific contributions on both sides" (Belgium).

5.6. Some More Specific Situations

5.6.1. Some European universities such as those in The Netherlands and Switzerland note that they are simultaneously government and Catholic: juridically, they are government institutions; in inspiration they are Catholic. Church "control" of these institutions is therefore not possible. "The Catholic nature comes from a common desire, and not from a juridical statute" (The Netherlands).

5.6.2. In countries whose universities follow the English pattern (England itself, and also Canada, Australia, and India), university colleges are, with rare exceptions, not independent: they are incorporated into a government university which determines the curriculum and most other aspects of university life, provides financial support, and grants the degrees. In structure, curriculum, and training, the Catholic institutions in these countries are similar to any other government college; their Catholic nature must be established through other means. In its present form, the schema could not be applied in these countries. "University colleges are affiliated to Province universities, and interference in them would be seen as interference in the Province university itself" (Canada).

5.6.3. The special situation of Catholic universities in non-Christian countries (such as India, Lebanon, Japan, and Indonesia), where most students and teachers are not members of the Catholic faith, has already been referred to. Many parts of both the Proemium and the Norms seem to assume that all, or nearly all, teachers and students are Catholics, and no mention is made of the special role of Catholic universities in these countries. "The Schema presupposes the conditions of Catholic or Christian countries. Non-Christian teachers and students are often treated as a marginal entity" (Japan).

5.6.4. In Mexico, where Catholic institutions are forbidden by law but are unofficially tolerated, responses speak of a "university of Christian inspiration" as distinct from a Catholic university which has been canonically established.[7] An open and official relationship with the Church is not possible. "The document as it stands could not be applied in Mexico" (Mexico).

5.7. The United States

5.7.1. Nearly all Catholic institutions of higher education were founded by religious congregations. Only a few have been canonically established; most received informal approval from the local ordinary and formal approval (a charter) from the civil government. Civil law requires that ultimate authority in a university be in the hands of a board of trustees but membership on these boards consisted entirely of members of the religious congregation.

5.7.2. About 25 years ago, with the knowledge and approval of Church authorities (major superiors of the religious congregations and local ordinaries in the United States), many of these Catholic institutions began to take on a new form. In order to improve teaching and research, academically qualified teachers were hired whether Catholic or not, though "preference" was still given to Catholics. The institutions endorsed the principles of academic freedom and tenure for teachers, thus winning both accreditation and acceptance from other universities. The boards of trustees were expanded to include a majority of lay people—not necessarily Catholics but men and women sympathetic to the purposes of the institution. These and similar changes were made for educational, political, and financial reasons: a reputation for the free and unhampered search for truth; acceptance of Catholics into the intellectual life of the country, which would make dialogue possible in a pluralist culture and create the possibility of having an influence on American life; eligibility for greater financial support (both government and private) which would help the institutions to survive and grow. Though means were taken to ensure the continued Catholic nature of the institution, "control" is no longer in the hands of the religious congregation.

5.7.3. In responding to the draft schema, most institutions of higher education in the United States, along with most of the bishops in that country and four of the professional associations, suggest that the good made possible by this form of Catholic university outweighs the risks and difficulties inherent in a university which is "Catholic" but not under the juridical control of Church authorities. The responses from these educational institutions and from the episcopal conference are, therefore, very critical of the present draft schema: neither the Proemium nor the Norms reflect the diversity among Catholic universities; some of the proposed norms, as well as violating civil law (cf. 6.2.2. below), threaten the present status of the institutions.

a.   No external authority may interfere in the internal operations of the university; the religious congregation and the local ordinary (or episcopal conference) are, of course, free to deal with individuals in the university.

b.   Generally accepted standards of academic freedom and tenure for all professors must be respected and upheld as at any other university in the United States.

c.   These institutions may not discriminate on religious grounds in student admissions and hiring of teachers.

5.7.4. Not all Catholic institutions of higher education in the United States have followed the path just described. Some institutions maintain that such a change in priorities can mean losing the Catholic identity of the institution, endangering orthodoxy and fidelity to the Church. Though not canonically established, and though they must obey civil law, these institutions continue to follow the more traditional pattern. Boards of trustees continue to be made up of members of a religious congregation or carefully chosen lay Catholics; both teachers and students are nearly all members of the Catholic faith. These institutions, along with two of the professional associations and some of the United States bishops (cf. 2.2.3.), approve the substance of the schema in its present form and insist that it is needed in order to preserve Catholic values and teach Catholic doctrine in the Catholic university.

6. REACTIONS THAT REFER MORE
SPECIFICALLY TO THE PROEMIUM

6.1. *General Reactions and Areas of General Agreement*

6.1.1. The *themes* developed in the Proemium received nearly universal praise and acceptance: the importance of education, the need for a mature and serious understanding of the Catholic faith, the university as a place of dialogue between faith and culture, the emphasis on cultural pluralism and on the full development of the human person, the need for guidance by the Magisterium and for a closer relationship with the local ordinary. The responses suggest many ways in which the *treatment* of these themes could be improved for greater clarity or a more logical development.

6.1.2. Some would like the present Proemium (with a change of name) to be expanded and to become the major part of the proposed document. A few responses suggest that it be reduced to a brief introduction, and that the major emphasis be given to the Norms.

6.2. *Suggestions for Changes*

6.2.1. Restructure the Proemium in a more logical order that gives a theological foundation, avoids repetitions, and makes it more concrete and more applicable to today. (Several of the responses contain suggestions for a new outline, and nearly all of them include suggestions for revised paragraphs and even entire sections.)

6.2.2. The Proemium should begin with the teaching mission of the Church, and develop the relationship between the Church and the university in a way that shows how each has benefited from the other.

6.2.3 Revise the historical section to include more recent history, to recognize the contributions of others to the development of the university (as well as to recognize that the involvement of the Church in this development was limited to the West), and to admit the tensions that have sometimes developed between the Church and the university world. Include the contributions of religious congregations to the development and growth of the Catholic university and, in more recent history, the increasing role of lay people. Give greater development to a love of learning joined to the desire for God that has characterized Catholic thought through the centuries (and mention persons such as

Benedict, Albert the Great, Thomas Aquinas, Robert Bellarmine, and John Henry Newman).

6.2.4. Give greater recognition to the diversity of cultures and regional circumstances, as well as to the diversity of Catholic universities in the world. The "positive and negative factors," to take one example, need to be qualified and reflect this diversity.

6.2.5. Reduce the number of quotations (or put them into footnotes). Include quotations from Scripture, Vatican II (*especially Gaudium et Spes*), and make a better choice of the encyclicals and the discourses of recent popes.

6.2.6. Too little recognition is given to the autonomy of the various secular sciences. The draft Proemium sets up a confrontation between science and faith and communicates a distrustful attitude toward exploration and creativity in research and teaching.

6.2.7. Many terms used need greater clarification ("culture" or "various cultures"?; "science" or "human knowledge"?; "evangelization"; "the ecclesial community"; "faith becomes culture"). Others are open to misunderstanding ("integral truth"; "unicity of truth"; "faith confronts knowledge").

6.2.8. The Proemium should include all of the basic characteristics of the Catholic university that the second part (the Norms) will speak about.

6.2.9. The reasons given for the present schema are inadequate. For some, the timing is inappropriate: in addition to the pressures of today (from civil law, from financial difficulties), more time is needed to assess the effects of the new Code of Canon Law (difficulties, doubts, lacunae, etc.) before promulgating more laws.

7. Reactions That Refer More Specifically to the Norms

7.1. General Reactions and Areas of General Agreement

7.1.1. The Norms, in general, receive more criticism—both from those who want them strengthened and from those who ask that they be drastically revised and perhaps reduced to a few basic principles.

7.1.2. Most responses agree with the insistence that teaching in a Catholic university be in accordance with Catholic doctrine and they agree that there should be adequate means to ensure this.

7.1.3. As already noted, a few responses suggest that the document is not strong enough in insisting on adherence to Catholic doctrine, and that appropriate means for enforcing the Norms be made a part of the final document.

7.2. Suggestions for Changes

7.2.1. The Norms do not take account of the fact that not all Catholic universities are canonically established. No distinction is made between a juridical relationship with the Church and a relationship which is one of "influence" rather than "control."

7.2.2. Responses from Asia, Latin America, North America, and Northern Europe point out that some proposed norms would violate civil law in their countries. Statutes must receive the approval of the civil government and nothing can be introduced into them which would be contrary to civil law or would endanger the nature of the university. (Thus statements about the Catholic nature may have to be put into documents other than the statutes.) Dismissal of teachers is subject to civil law, and requirements of orthodoxy which would restrict legitimate freedom are not permitted. In any disciplinary action, whether of the individual or the institution, due process must be respected.

7.2.3. Some norms are clear regulations while others are exhortations. A certain consistency is needed.

7.2.4. To simply quote canon law in the Norms could give rise to a false understanding. One must read a particular canon within the context of the whole code. Therefore, if canons are quoted at all, they must be given a context in which they can be understood properly.

7.2.5. In addition to difficulties of a more general nature already mentioned, many respondents in several different parts of the world commented on certain specific norms:

— §21 (a report to the Congregation for Catholic Education every five years): if it is truly needed (and many question this), then it is necessary to indicate precisely what kind of information is desired, and how it differs from information already given to professional associations, accrediting agencies, civil governments, and episcopal conferences.

— §25 (the rector must always be a Catholic): the title ("rector") is not universally used; more importantly, responses indicate that stating this as a universal requirement may be contrary to civil law; in any case, while it is highly desirable, there may be occasions when someone other than a Catholic would be the person most suitable and the Norm should allow for exceptions.

— §32 (awarding of the Doctorate *Honoris Causa*): The Norm seems to be solving a particular problem with a universal rule. Many responses suggested that this Norm be dropped, or at least explained and moved to a more logical place within the document.

— §39.2 (the Congregation for Catholic Education "presides over" the planning of Catholic universities): responses suggested that the

Congregation could coordinate this activity, but the actual planning could be done more effectively on the local and regional levels.

— §44–49 (on Catholics in non-Catholic universities): all need radical revision, and should probably be the basis of a separate document.

7.3. Other Reactions

7.3.1. Some responses from Australia, Canada, and the United States note that the present Norms could eliminate financial assistance from governments and from private sources: to the university, and also to the students. This would contradict the last Norm, which urges that the Catholic institutions be more open to students of limited financial means.

7.3.2. The document seeks to address the identity of, and issue Norms about, institutions which are already in existence, some for hundreds of years. It must make certain that the end-product of the consultation provides sufficient flexibility to accommodate the identity and rights of the Church's institutions as the Church has already established and promoted them.

7.3.3. The relation between the Catholic university and the Church is put on a merely juridical basis. A relationship which is pastoral, fraternal, and mutually helpful is more important.

7.3.4. A few responses suggested that the "competent ecclesiastical authority" should be specified in the Norms.

7.3.5. A Few responses suggested that the permission to use the word "Catholic" and especially "pontifical" in the title of the Catholic university should be based on clearly developed criteria that would include excellence as an academic institution; they further suggest that these universities should be evaluated at regular intervals.

7.4. A large number of responses, including some in basic agreement with the present draft, suggest that the document, especially in its Norms, should be limited to general principles (and some suggested that these should be "guidelines" rather than "Norms"); more specific determinations and details should be left for regional groups, e.g., to episcopal conferences. These would then be approved by the Holy See.

7.4.1. Diversity among Catholic universities because of history, foundation (and the purposes of the foundation), cultural differences, the role of religious congregations, and the need to respect civil law, all make a single detailed description of the Catholic university and its purposes, as well as detailed norms valid for all, impossible.

7.4.2. Many of the responses from Latin America suggest the need to learn from the Latin American experience, as expressed in the documents of Medellin and Puebla. Responses from Latin America and India suggest the need for greater attention to social justice, poverty, and developmental issues. General principles in these areas which have universal application could be added to the draft, but these are additional examples of topics that could be covered more adequately in supplementary regional documents.

8. SPECIFIC CONCERNS EXPRESSED IN RESPONSES FROM BISHOPS

Most of the comments and suggestions contained in responses from episcopal conferences and from individual bishops are included in the summary given on previous pages. This last section highlights specific concerns mentioned by these bishops as they view the Catholic university from their perspective as Pastors in the Church.

8.1. Every response from an episcopal conference or individual bishop notes the importance of the proposed document. They recognize the potential of the Catholic university as an instrument which offers a Christian formation for future leaders in the world, and which brings the Church into dialogue with culture in the intellectual world of higher education. They are conscious of a need to define the Catholic nature of these universities more explicitly and more carefully so that their role of service to the Church can be more effective. While some responses are quite critical of the present draft, the suggestions are intended to help strengthen the document, so that it will be "inspiring and encouraging rather than defensive" (U.S.A.), and so that it will be a logical and clear presentation of the teaching role of the Church in this specific milieu.

8.2. Many bishops stress their conviction that a Catholic university must be excellent as a university if it is to be an effective partner in the dialogue with culture. They want the university to be a place of education and not of indoctrination. They stress the need for an effective and clear presentation of Catholic teaching in a way that will speak to today's world.

8.3. Responses from a wide variety of countries and cultures indicate a major preoccupation among the bishops that a more adequate pastoral care, in all its aspects, be provided within the Catholic university. One response suggested a separate Apostolic Constitution on this topic; many noted that pastoral care must be an integral part of the university itself and not something external to it or added on to it. They urged that this section of the draft schema be expanded and strengthened. "Requiere mayor énfasis, calidad y precisión en su naturaleza y finalidad como pastoral de la inteligencia, pastoral litúrgica y pastoral de estilo y ambiente de educación y vida cristiana" (Paraguay). "Gostaríamos de ver mais desenvolvida, no proêmio e nas normas, a matéria referente à pastoral universitária e à pastoral de inteligência, acentuando a ligação e a simbiose que devem ter com a vida das igrejas diocesanas e locais" (Portugal).

8.4. Responses from bishops suggested that the document could include a more complete discussion of ways in which the Catholic university can be of service to the Catholic community. Examples include the need to train lay people who can become Christian leaders in the future, and the need to deal with the urgent social problems of today.

8.5. Nearly all responses include a concern that the Catholic university present Catholic teaching as taught by the Magisterium of the Church, and they seem aware of their own responsibilities in seeing that this is done. But the responses are not uniform in suggesting how a pontifical document can assist them in achieving this goal.

8.5.1. Some responses speak very strongly in favor of the present draft schema as an effective instrument to help them exercise their responsibility, and a few indicate a desire to have even more direct control over Catholic universities than that indicated in the present draft.

8.5.2. Many responses from bishops do not speak explicitly about fidelity to the Magisterium in their responses, but their acceptance of the present draft is an implicit acceptance of the means contained in it.

8.5.3. The primary concern expressed in the responses of many bishops is pastoral rather than juridical; they seem sensitive to the delicate issue of the legitimate autonomy of the university and wish to exercise "vigilance" while at the same time respecting this autonomy. "La relación entre una universidad Catolica y la jerarquía no debe encuadrarse únicamente en una vinculación jurídica, que con frecuencia queda desprovisto de contenido y calor humanos, sino sobre todo en ligámenes personales, espirituales, de amistad y de presencia" (Peru). "L'Eglise doit reconnaître aux universités catholiques toute l'autonomie et toute la liberté dont ces dernières ont besoin pour exercer leurs fonctions universitaires" (Canada). Some bishops and episcopal conferences, including most of the responses from countries which have Catholic universities that are not canonically established, suggest that the "direct control" over Catholic universities contained in the present draft is neither possible nor desirable.

8.5.4. A suggestion contained in responses from bishops in all three of these groups is the same suggestion received from many others who responded: the norms developed in the final version of the schema should enunciate general principles; the development of more detailed norms could be left to episcopal conferences. "In view of the problems and dilemmas, I propose a *via media*, namely, that the Congregation for Education issue a document for Catholic universities akin to the *Ratio Fundamentalis* for seminaries. This would set forth the general norms. . . . Then each Episcopal Conference would draw up a program for its

Catholic [universities and other institutions of higher education] which, in turn, would require the approval of the Holy See. These programs would take into consideration the legal and cultural situation of specific countries and propose specific norms for universities which want to be considered Catholic" (U.S.A.).

PART III. COMMENTS AND QUESTIONS ARISING FROM THE RESPONSES

9. COMMENTS

9.1.   In general, the responses reveal a careful and detailed study of the Draft Schema. The suggestions are specific and they are helpful.

9.2.   There is general agreement with much that is contained in the present draft schema. The responses propose changes in *presentation* of this material: a more logical development, a more modest and realistic tone, avoidance of exclusively masculine terminology, clearer style, etc. This type of suggestion can easily be incorporated into the draft when it is revised.

9.3.   Other suggestions in the responses propose clarifications of statements that may be ambiguous or misleading. Here too, the proposals will help in the work of revision: misleading statements need to be clarified.

9.4.   Still other suggestions note points that have been omitted. While not every concern of every country can be included in the final document, some of these omissions are significant, and the revised draft will include as many of the suggestions as possible.

9.5.   Some suggestions in the responses are not sufficiently clear, or there is a lack of agreement in the responses about the way in which a problem should be treated. Further clarification of these points is needed before the material can be incorporated into a future revised draft.

10. QUESTIONS ARISING FROM THE RESPONSES

The points which need clarification can, perhaps, best be put into the form of questions. Without pretending to be a complete list, those below would seem to be some of the more important questions that arise from a study of the responses. The concern, of course, is to develop a general statement which is valid for Catholic universities and other institutions of higher education throughout the world.

10.1.   What is a brief but adequate descriptive definition of a university? Is it possible to give a reasonably short description (or collection of descriptions) of the various kinds of institutions that would normally be considered "post-secondary" or "tertiary" institutions? (This would include, for example, university faculties and post-secondary professional schools; it would probably not include institutions that provide vocational training or residences for students.) Is there a single expression that can be used to refer to all of these institutions?

10.2. How can the "search for truth" in a university be described? What elements make up this search?

10.3. What does "Catholic" add to "university"? Do the "characteristics" listed in §1 of the 1972 document *The Catholic University in the Modern World* give an adequate description of a Catholic institution of higher learning? Should there by any additions or changes in this description?

10.4. How can the Catholic nature of a Catholic institution of higher learning be manifested more clearly and more effectively?

10.5. What is the service that the Catholic institution of higher learning should be rendering *today* to the Church and to society?

10.6. How is academic freedom to be described or defined? What are the limitations to this "freedom"? When is it legitimate, and when is it possibly an abuse of the end that is intended?

10.7. Who is responsible for the Catholic nature of the institution? To what extent is this responsibility shared among the president/rector, the various directors or administrators, the deans, teachers, and others? To what extent are the local ordinary, the episcopal conference and the Holy See involved?

10.8. More generally, taking into account the different kinds of institutions (canonically established or not so established, etc.), what relationship should exist between a Catholic institution of higher learning and the local ordinary, the episcopal conference, and the Holy See? What are the responsibilities of each?

10.9. In theological teaching and research by a member of the Catholic faith, and also in the teaching and research in other areas of knowledge when these touch on faith and morals, how is academic freedom to be reconciled with fidelity to the Magisterium? What is the role and the responsibility of the Catholic university as an institution (e.g., in its statutes or methods of procedure—again taking into account the different kinds of institutions) in dealing with this tension between freedom and fidelity? What is the responsibility of other parties (e.g., other theologians, the local ordinary, the episcopal conferences, the Holy See)?

10.10.In a Catholic institution, the presence of members of other faiths can enrich the institution itself and also its dialogue with today's cultures. Recognizing this, and also recognizing the very different situations in different parts of the world, should any preferences be given to members of the Catholic Church in hiring teachers, directors, and administrators, and in admitting students? How can a Catholic institution ensure that members of other faiths (or of no faith) who work in the institution as teachers or directors share—or at least accept—its vision and purposes? 10.11.What constitutes adequate pastoral care in a Catholic university? In what ways does pastoral care enter into the various aspects of university life (including teaching and research)? What are the responsibilities of the local ordinary, and what are the responsibilities of the authorities in the institution, in providing this pastoral care? What responsibility does the university have in providing pastoral care for those teachers, staff, and students who are not members of the Catholic Church (i.e., a pastoral care that includes opportunities for them to grow in their own faith and religious commitment)?

CONCLUSION

The summary presented on these pages could not include all of the suggestions or all of the points raised. It has tried to highlight the major concerns in the more important areas of the draft schema, and to present these in a way that is informative, but at the same time brief and readable.

Whatever their degree of acceptance of the present draft schema or their suggestions for its revision, the constant theme in the responses—from both the institutions and from bishops and others—is a strong and ongoing concern for the Catholic nature of these institutions joined to a desire to find ways to maintain and strengthen this Catholic nature.

A study of the summary can itself be of assistance in coming to a better knowledge of the Catholic institutions of higher education throughout the world and to a better understanding of the different problems to be faced in the different places where these institutions are located.

NOTES

1. A complete list of responses received from Catholic universities and other institutions of higher education, university associations, episcopal conferences, individual bishops, and religious congregations is given in an appendix.

2. This evaluation of the responses necessarily involves subjective judgments. It is sometimes not easy to decide whether the suggestions constitute "major substantive changes" or "basic agreement with some substantive suggestions." In the university responses, the division between "no document" and "needs major substantive changes" is not always a clear one.

3. A more complete summary of the concerns expressed in responses from episcopal conferences and individual bishops is given at the end of Part II.

4. The English language does not normally make the distinction, found in most other languages, between "teaching" and "education." This fact will need to be taken into account in the final version of the document.

5. In a letter of April 25, 1973 to Presidents of Catholic Universities and Directors of Catholic Institutions of Higher Learning, Cardinal Garrone (then Prefect of the Congregation for Catholic Education) said that the Plenary Assembly of the Congregation considers the document as "valid but needing improvement." The letter notes two points about which the document "is not sufficiently explicit," and cautions against its misuse.

6. A great many responses ask that the document insist more on the need for an adequate pastoral ministry at a Catholic university. This is a special concern of bishops throughout the world, as will be seen.

7. Many responses from Spain and from other countries in Latin America also use the expression "a university of Christian inspiration" to refer to Catholic universities which are not canonically established. Some of these responses assume that the present draft schema does not apply to such universities, and so are approving of the schema with only minor changes; others assume that it does, and so ask for substantial changes in the document.

Revised Draft Schema for a Pontifical Document on Catholic Higher Education

November 8, 1988

INTRODUCTION

(1) Catholic universities and other Catholic institutions of higher education, through scholarly research, teaching, and service to the community, contribute to the mission to teach all nations given by Christ to his Church.[1] Like all institutions of higher education, they are engaged in an ongoing search for the truth; because they are Catholic, they enrich and illumine this search with the light of the Christian message, thus helping to lead men and women to a fuller knowledge of Christ, who is the Truth.[2] Moreover, they help to bring the Gospel of Christ into dialogue with contemporary culture and the cultures of specific groups of people, contributing to the progress of culture and enabling the Church to learn from culture.[3]

(2) These activities take on a particular importance and urgency today. Fundamental human values and the very meaning of human life are being called into question; religious concepts and ethical principles are often regarded as irrelevant in a world marked by increasing secularism; technological progress, used for material or political purposes, threatens to manipulate or even destroy humanity even while men and women everywhere are struggling for greater human dignity in a more just society. The search for solutions to these and other complex problems requires careful and highly specialized research carried on in an ethical and religious context, and a formation of students which joins rigorous professional training with a total humanistic, moral, and spiritual formation.

(3) The Church, therefore, while it recognizes with gratitude how much Catholic institutions of higher education have already contributed to the development of individuals and of society, asks these institutions

---

From the files of the Association of Catholic Colleges and Universities

to dedicate themselves to that ongoing renewal which will strengthen their ability to meet this contemporary challenge. Convinced that the union of faith and reason in both research and teaching offers the best hope of an adequate response, it asks them to become truly excellent both as educational centers and in their distinctively Catholic identity.

(4)   Catholic higher education is already aware of this call, and an ongoing renewal is already in process. Individual institutions have, for some years, been engaged in serious reflections on their identity and mission; regional, national, and international meetings have assisted in these reflections. Concrete results are evident in new areas of research and new ways of conducting this research, in new academic programs that integrate different areas of knowledge and join intellectual formation to human and religious formation, and in an increased attention given to the pastoral dimension of university life. There is also evidence of more frequent dialogue between the educational institutions and diocesan bishops, a dialogue which has benefited both the Church and the institutions. The International Federation of Catholic Universities has assisted in these efforts, and a series of meetings initiated by the Congregation for Seminaries and Educational Institutions resulted in the 1972 publication of *The Catholic University in the Modern World.*[4]

(5)   This present document builds on the results of these previous efforts in the light of the Second Vatican Council and the needs of today's world. Part One describes the nature of a Catholic institution of higher education and its role in the mission of the Church; norms developed from the Code of Canon Law (especially Canons 807 to 814) and other official Church documents are contained in Part Two. The faithful implementation of these norms will help to fulfill the hope of the Council Fathers, that "the Christian mind may achieve a public, persistent, and universal presence in the whole enterprise of advancing higher culture, and that the students of these institutions may become men and women truly outstanding in learning, ready to shoulder society's heavier burdens, and to witness the faith to the world.".[5] Thus Catholic institutions of higher education will continue to merit the trust put in them by the Church, the entire community of the faithful, and the whole of human society, and they will become ever "more effective in providing men and women with the content and dynamism of Catholic thought".[6]

(6)   Religious, political, and social conditions of the regions or nations in which they are located, together with the origins, traditions, and specific objectives of the institutions themselves, create great diversity among Catholic universities and other Catholic institutions of higher education. The diversity is found not only in their nature as educational institutions, but also in the ways in which they express their Catholic identity and the concrete ways in which they relate to Church authorities.

Nevertheless, the fact that they are all "Catholic" means that they will have certain characteristics in common, both in their identity and in their relationship to the Church. This document will speak of those common characteristics and define that relationship, while allowing for the distinctions and qualifications that may be necessary.

(7)   As far as possible, Catholic institutions of higher education are established in conformity with the civil laws of the region or country in which they are located so that, either of themselves or through another institution of which they form a part, they may award academic degrees that are civilly recognized. They are to be distinguished from ecclesiastical universities and faculties whose degrees, even though they also may have civil recognition, are awarded by the authority of the Holy See. Norms for these latter institutions, including those ecclesiastical faculties which form part of a Catholic university, are contained in the Apostolic Constitution *Sapientia Christiana*.[7]

PART I: THE IDENTITY AND MISSION
OF CATHOLIC HIGHER EDUCATION

A. THE DEVELOPMENT OF CATHOLIC HIGHER EDUCATION

(8)   God is present and active in all of creation, but especially in human history and the personal history of each individual. As a result, the basic human desire to know the truth, to understand the meaning of life and the meaning of the surrounding world, leads inevitably to a growing knowledge of God, while faith in God contributes to an understanding of the world and of the human person. Philosophers and scholars of many different cultures and religions have, through their search for truth, come to a knowledge of God, but this relationship has been realized most clearly within the Judaeo-Christian tradition. The Biblical narration of Israel's history is also the history of salvation; the prophets and the authors of the wisdom literature, by reflecting on historical events and on the human person, grew in their understanding of the nature and the will of God.

(9)   With the incarnation of Jesus Christ, God's presence in creation takes a new and more profound form. Jesus himself grew in wisdom;[8] he came in order that we might know the truth, and so become truly free.[9] His person and his teaching enable us to know the Father[10] and, at the same time, to come to a better understanding of human life. When the time came for him to return to the Father, he promised that the "Spirit of truth"[11] would remain with his followers, and he founded a Church to carry on his work, specifically charging that Church with the mission to teach all nations.[12]

(10) The Church has always known that its mission to teach must unite the commitment of faith with the search for truth, and that the one Truth is discovered both in revelation and in creation. Guided by the Spirit, and following the example of its model, Mary,[13] the Church has reflected on the message of Christ throughout its history in order to understand its meaning more deeply and express it more adequately; it has reflected on the world and on human events in order to see the hand of God at work, and in order to guide men and women in their lives on earth. Early Church scholars such as Athanasius, Basil, Augustine, and Gregory the Great, contributed to human knowledge while contributing to an understanding of the faith. The philosophical reflections of Plato and Aristotle assisted Peter Lombard and Thomas Aquinas in probing and explaining revelation. Though the relationship has not always been easy and smooth, the interaction of faith and reason has, throughout history, contributed to a more complete knowledge of truth, and of the one Truth.

(11) Intellectual life in the Church was embodied in scholastic centers as well as in persons. Alexandria and Antioch are a part of its early history; Christian monasteries of both East and West preserved and promoted human wisdom as well as the Scriptures and Christian writings. In time, the monasteries and cathedrals of the Western Church established schools to transmit this learning and, when different areas of human knowledge began to evolve into separate academic disciplines, these schools developed into the first European universities. Centers of learning took root in major cultural centers such as Bologna, Prague, and Paris, and soon appeared in other cities; the Church offered the support of its experience, guidance, and personnel, and provided cultural and economic resources. The Church, therefore, can truly be said to be responsible for the birth of the university in the West. Many of the academic practices and pedagogical methods that remain characteristic of today's universities, as well as the structure of the university itself and its integral formation based on the liberal arts, are a part of the heritage deriving from these early universities sponsored and guided by the Church.

(12) To fulfill the mission to "teach all nations," missionaries were sent from Europe to the Americas, India, and later to Africa, Asia, and Oceania. They brought learning along with faith, and they promoted the cultural development of the peoples to whom they preached the Gospel. To provide easier access to this learning these missionaries, nearly all members of religious congregations, founded schools which, before long, became the first universities in these countries of the "new world." Along with institutions founded by others, the education provided in these universities helped to deepen the faith of the people, gave an

opportunity for cultural advancement, and integrated new nations into world society. University centers in places such as Santo Domingo, Goa, Manila, and Georgetown contributed to the social, economic, political, cultural, and faith development of vast new human communities, and to the elevation and defense of human dignity among native peoples. Other university centers, especially in Asia and Africa, provided a point of contact between the Church and non-Christian cultures.

(13) In more recent times civil society has recognized the value and importance of universities for its well-being and growth and, in most countries, the civil government has assumed responsibility for large segments of higher education. While this has brought greater resources to humanistic and scientific research and has made university education accessible to larger numbers of people, it has at times led to a division, and even hostility, between secular and sacred studies; the separation of the university from the faith community in which it developed has been a deterrent to the dialogue between faith and culture. In some cases, the research and education in secular universities has been based on ideologies which attack the Church and the faith that it embraces and teaches.

(14) When the positive sciences developed their own distinctive methods and a scientific definition of truth, the result was often suspicion and antagonism between science and the Church. Scientific research, limiting itself to its own scientific methods, seemed to ignore the truths of faith; as a result the Church mistrusted science as a potential threat to the faith. While eminent Catholic scholars have contributed to the advancement of the natural and human sciences since their beginnings, many areas of study and research developed without taking account of the presence of God in the mystery of humanity, and some maintained that scientific truth is the only truth.

(15) Early in the nineteenth century, in order to reaffirm and strengthen the relationship between faith and reason in the one search for truth, and to bring faith and reason into an intellectually disciplined and constructive encounter, the Church began once again to establish universities linked to it by a formal bond and to give formal approval as Catholic to other universities desiring thus to participate more explicitly in the Church's teaching mission. Universities continued to be founded by religious congregations, and other Catholic institutions of higher education were founded to meet the specific needs of a local or regional community: research institutes, university colleges offering a basic liberal arts education, and professional schools for formation in pedagogy, law, medicine, and other fields.

B. CATHOLIC HIGHER EDUCATION TODAY

(16) Recent decades have witnessed rapid growth in the number, size, diversity, and complexity of universities and other institutions of higher education throughout the world, and Catholic institutions have shared in all aspects of this growth. In many countries, they continue to grow in size and complexity; in some countries, new Catholic institutions are still being established, or are being planned.

(17) Many Catholic institutions of higher education enjoy great prestige within their local or regional community for their formation and for the various services they offer; some are more widely recognized for the quality of their research and publications. Catholic institutions assist the Church through the formation of its members, through research in areas of vital concern to its bishops, and through the witness of Catholic thought and Catholic values they bring to the academic world and to society as a whole. They prepare men and women for leadership in professional life as well as for leadership in the Church, whether as scholars, teachers, catechists, active members of parish groups, committed laity in all walks of life, or founders of Christian families. Many who have received their education in these Catholic institutions offer a living witness to the quality of the academic and religious formation that was made available to them.

(18) In addition to the Catholic institutions, there are many individual Catholic scholars who combine dedicated research and teaching with outstanding Christian witness in life and work. They assist in the development of human knowledge and an understanding of revealed faith, and they contribute to the presence and growth of Catholic thought in society.

(19) At the same time, the contemporary world presents Catholic institutions, both as educational centers and as distinctively Catholic, with a number of serious challenges. In addition to external forces which condition and often restrict the freedom of these institutions, some trends in the current academic world can work against the traditional ideals of university education and, more specifically, can distort or cloud the Catholic character of the institution. Confronted with these challenges, they are called upon to be true educational centers which are fully integrated into the academic community and models of educational excellence, and at the same time to preserve their own distinctive identity within that community.

(20) There are countries in which existing Catholic universities were forcibly deprived of their Catholic character and the establishment of new Catholic institutions is not possible. In other countries, a variety

of social, ideological, and political factors prevent Catholic institutions from exhibiting their Catholic character openly. All too often, civil laws and public pressure restrict the freedom and autonomy proper to these institutions, determining priorities in research and imposing a course of studies based on pragmatic concerns. Where government financial support for private education does not exist or is insufficient, economic difficulties can influence educational priorities or even endanger the existence of Catholic institutions. Powerful factors, whether government or private, attempt to manipulate these educational institutions according to their own ideology and their own vision of the world and of the Church.

(21) Within the intellectual world, a narrow view of the legitimate autonomy of each academic discipline has at times joined forces with secularism in an effort to invalidate the dialogue between secular knowledge and Christian thought and to deny the relevance of the ethical principles which must always govern the search for truth. Pluralism of thought, which can assist in the search for truth through the presentation of different points of view, can also develop into conflicting ideologies or indifference to ethical principles, dividing the university community and making mature philosophical reflection impossible. An excessive preoccupation with professional formation or career training can restrict the possibilities for humanistic and spiritual development of the total person. The need for specialization within each academic discipline has at times overshadowed the search for integration among the disciplines, and fundamental issues concerning the relationship between knowledge and wisdom are ignored.

(22) As Catholic institutions strive for recognition in the academic world and are obliged to conform to official secular standards, preoccupation with quality in research and in teaching has sometimes meant that less attention is given to the Catholic identity of the institution and the life witness of the educational community. Some regard the legitimate rights of the Church with regard to Catholic institutions of higher education as interference in the legitimate autonomy of these institutions, while others ask whether all Catholic institutions today are maintaining sufficient fidelity to Church authorities and Church doctrine.

(23) Because it recognizes the vital importance of Catholic universities and other institutions of higher education, the Church wishes to offer its assistance in confronting these challenges. If they are to help in finding solutions to the urgent problems facing contemporary society, and help to lay the foundations for the building of a more perfect human society in the future, these Catholic institutions must excel in their academic quality, pursue understanding and wisdom as well as knowledge, offer

a total and integral formation to their students, and at the same time give evidence of a clear Catholic identity and a close relationship with the Church and its teaching mission.

(24) A long historical tradition establishes the right of the Church to establish institutions of higher education, whether through its hierarchy, its religious congregations, or its faithful. More particularly, this right is based on the natural right of parents to seek an education for their children that is in accord with their own religious and cultural convictions; that same natural right is extended to individuals as they reach maturity. The Church, because it has the mission to teach, has the right and duty to create and maintain its own educational system: to provide formation for its members and assist them to grow in the life of Christ, to preserve the bond between the scholarly search for truth and the light revealed through Christ, and to promote the full development of the human person for the welfare of society.[14]

C. THE NATURE OF A CATHOLIC INSTITUTION OF HIGHER EDUCATION

1. As an Educational Institution[15]

(25) A Catholic university, like every university, is an institution of higher learning: an academic community devoted to scholarly research, rigorous teaching and formation in the humanities and sciences, and to various educational services to the local, national, and international community; because it is Catholic, it inspires all its activities with the light of the Christian message. It will constantly seek greater excellence in all its educational activities, for its Catholic character safeguards rather than limits its university activity: it is a reminder that its task must be "catholic," or universal. "By vocation and radical requirement, [it] is open to the truth in all fields, to *all truth*."[16]

(26) As *universitas scientiarum*, it is a place where the various branches of human knowledge are represented by scholars who scrutinize reality in freedom, and with the methods proper to each branch,[17] and so contribute to the treasury of human knowledge. Individual disciplines are brought into dialogue with one another for their mutual enhancement and integration and in order to investigate the consistency of research in specific areas with the meaning and the transcendent destiny of life, of the human person, and of the world. While preserving its own integrity, each discipline contributes to an ordered vision of reality that encompasses the humanities, the sciences, philosophy, and theology. This search for truth is enriched because it is undertaken in the light of Christ, who is the Truth, and asks how Gospel values affect the discoveries of human

research and how these discoveries affect an understanding of the faith. Thus knowledge is put to the service of the whole human person and of human society, and the Church is helped to understand human reality more deeply.

(27) Its teachers and students, *universitas magistrorum et scholarium*, are dedicated to search for the truth together, in a spirit of honest and open dialogue; they develop a love for the truth that transforms truth into wisdom. The individual academic disciplines are taught and studied in a systematic manner, but are integrated in such a way that they offer a single unified system of formation.

(28) *University teachers* will unite true educational wisdom with competence in their respective disciplines. They communicate the objectives, methods, and results of research within the context of that coherent world vision which should always distinguish teaching in a Catholic university, and they assist students in the development of a critical judgment. Christians among the teachers are called to be "witnesses and educators of authentic Christian life, which evidences an attained integration between faith and culture, between professional competence and Christian wisdom."[18]

(29) *Students* are offered an education that combines the greatest possible excellence in humanistic and cultural formation with specialized professional training. With the help of philosophical and theological reflection they are elevated in spirit to an awareness of the values which enrich human life with dignity and meaning. They become aware of all that is human, are able to recognize beauty, and continue the search for truth throughout their lives. They are prepared to play an active role of leadership and influence in the world of today, devoted to the ethical practice of a professional life and at the same time dedicated to working for the good of individuals and the building of a more just society, guided and enlightened by Christian thought and Christian principles, "more spiritually mature, more aware of the dignity of their humanity, more responsible and more open to all others, more disposed to give and offer help to all."[19] For those able to respond, especially Catholic students, this will enable them to "acquire, or, if they have already done so to deepen, an authentically Christian life-style. They should realize the responsibility of their professional life, the enthusiasm of being the trained "leaders" of tomorrow, of being witnesses to Christ in whatever place they may exercise their profession."[20]

(30) As an *academic community*, it provides for the ongoing formation of all of its members in an atmosphere of dialogue and mutual respect which values the intellectual life, scholarly research, and religious values, and which is permeated with the spirit of the Gospel, for the freedom to search for the truth must be combined with humility, patience, and

respect for the differing ideas of others. The academic community is concerned with the larger community, offering its services as an academic institution to assist in making the growing body of human knowledge and a developing understanding of the Christian faith available to everyone. This university community includes, in addition to teachers and students, the directors and the nonacademic staff. Their dedication, wisdom, and witness are integral to the life of the university and the influence of the institution on Church and on society.

(31) Recognizing that the direct effect on a specific academic discipline or other university activity will vary with the nature of that activity, the members of the academic community bring the inspiration and light of the Christian message to all facets of research and the discovery of truth, to the transmission of that truth through teaching and through publications, and to all of the other various aspects of university life. University authorities are guided by Christian principles in all official policies and institutional concerns.

(32) The Catholic university has traditionally been a center in which Catholic lay people could exercise an apostolic role in the Church through research and teaching. That role takes on a particular importance today, when nearly all of the members of the academic community are lay, while lay men and women are, in increasing numbers, responsible for the direction of these institutions. In the contributions they make to the attainment of the university objectives, it is their vocation "to organize these affairs in such a way that they may always start out, develop, and continue according to Christ's mind, to the praise of the Creator and the Redeemer."[21]

(33) Catholic universities in many countries welcome members of other churches and religions, and those with no faith, as members of their academic communities. These men and women contribute their training and experience to the various academic disciplines or other university tasks; they provide a diversity of thought which contributes to the search for truth; many of them, recognizing its value, contribute positively to the distinctive Catholic identity of the institutions.

(34) A Catholic university has an institutional commitment to *service*: of the People of God and of the entire human community. It sees the search for truth as intrinsic to the nature of the human person and gives special emphasis, therefore, to those aspects of this search which will best foster human development, defend human rights, and promote human dignity.

(35) In summary, a Catholic university finds "its ultimate and profound significance in Christ, in his message of salvation that embraces the total human person, and in the teaching of the Church."[22] It brings men and women to a knowledge of the truth, which is their "deepest and noblest

aspiration,"[23] and gives clear witness to the Truth who is Christ: in the life of the university and in the life witness of the members of the university community.

2. Relationship to Civil Society

(36) A Catholic institution of higher education contributes to the good of individuals and of civil society; in its own traditions and structures it frequently reflects the nature of the civil society in which it is located and is, in some cases, actually an institution established or maintained by the civil government. While it retains the autonomy proper to all such institutions and cannot allow itself to be manipulated for political purposes, it respects civil laws concerning higher education and tries to ensure that its academic degrees receive civil recognition. It works in collaboration with other civil institutions, especially institutions of higher education, and is eager to cooperate with them for the common good and for the development of individuals and society. In today's profoundly pluralistic society, it respects the identity and freedom of these institutions and is enriched by dialogue with them.

(37) At the same time, the Catholic institution of higher education has it own distinctive identity and mission, and must be given the freedom, respect, and support by civil society that are necessary to maintain and foster this identity; it is only in this way that it can contribute to the good of society. Because of its distinctive identity, it can often have positive contributions to make to educational growth and to public legislation having to do with education.

3. Service of the Church

(38) Each Catholic institution of higher education, while retaining its proper autonomy, lives within the Church and assists the Church in its teaching mission. Each individual institution is most directly related to the local Church in which it is located; its activities and its character will depend on the location and the traditions of the institution. But every Catholic institution of higher education necessarily exercises a more universal influence which goes beyond its territorial limits and is therefore related to the Church as a whole, for both knowledge and faith are universal by their very nature.

(39) Because it is Catholic, it professes fidelity to the Christian message as taught by the Catholic Church, and respects the teaching authority of the Church.[24] This fidelity permeates institutional policy, teaching, research, pastoral activities, and the life witness of members of the university community. Catholic members of the community accept this

relationship and foster it; those in the community who are not members of the Catholic Church respect and honor the relationship as flowing from the institution's Catholic character.

(40) Catholic institutions, moreover, respond to the expectations of the people of God, who seek the intellectual and spiritual formation offered by these institutions to help them toward a mature and responsible living of their Christian vocation in the world. Parents entrust the formation of their children to these Catholic institutions of higher education; parishes look to them for assistance in the ongoing formation of their members; bishops seek their assistance in bringing Christian thought to bear on the problems of contemporary life and in helping to develop a language which will make the message of salvation comprehensible to contemporary men and women.

(41) Because of the contributions they make to the enrichment of human life and to the development of the faith, Catholic institutions of higher education have a right to the Church's encouragement and support. Bishops have a particular responsibility to assist these institutions in every possible way; bishops and priests, recognizing their value and importance for the Church, encourage all its members to become aware of the difficult and sensitive nature of the mission entrusted to these Catholic institutions and to support them in their educational efforts, as well as to help them maintain and protect their freedom in civil society. An ongoing dialogue should be fostered between Catholic institutions of higher education and the entire Church community, in which concerns and expectations are expressed, understanding grows, and the search for truth is facilitated. In many countries, Catholic institutions are also dependent on the economic support of the bishops and the Church community.

(42) Maintaining and promoting the Catholic character of the institution is primarily the responsibility of the academic community within the institution, a responsibility shared by all its members according to their different roles within the community. While it is clear that those in directive positions must have a clear awareness of the institution's distinct identity and a willingness to promote it, the shared responsibility for its Catholic character requires that active steps be taken to attract to the academic community those, especially Catholics, who will work positively to preserve its distinct identity, who will seek ways to clarify and promote it, and who will be conscious of the ways in which it affects their specific academic discipline or other educational task.

(43) Bishops, the "authentic teachers of the faith, that is, teachers endowed with the authority of Christ,"[25] also have a responsibility for the Catholic character of these institutions of higher education. The way in which this responsibility is exercised will depend on many different

factors, some of them cultural, others dependent on the way in which the university was established and whether or not a relationship between the institution and Church authorities is defined in the statutes or in some other equivalent document. In every case, however, a personal and pastoral relationship must exist between university authorities and Church authorities: a relationship which is characterized by mutual trust, close cooperation and ongoing dialogue. Even when they do not enter directly into the internal functioning of the university, bishops "should be seen not as external agents but as participants in the life of the Catholic university."[26]

(44) Every academic discipline contributes, according to its own nature, both to the development of society and to the total formation of the students; likewise, in ways that will differ with the different areas of knowledge, each discipline also contributes to an understanding and a building up of the faith. The Catholic identity of the institution implies fidelity to the Church, not only of the institution as a whole, but also within each academic discipline, whenever research or teaching within this discipline touches on doctrine or morality as taught by the Church. The same fidelity should be reflected in the lives of the individual members of the educational community. This fidelity is expected of Catholic members of the community; members of other churches and religions are expected to respect the Catholic character of the institution, and so respect its fidelity to the Church.

4. Theology in a Catholic Institution of Higher Education

(45) Theology has a particular importance among the academic disciplines. It is an internal, profound dimension of the institution itself, by which "the academic institution is, so to speak, specified and lived,"[27] for it extends the horizons of the search for truth to include a deeper and fuller understanding of revealed truth in the context of the one Truth. It serves the other academic disciplines by bringing a perspective and an orientation not contained within their own methodologies and by helping to investigate how their discoveries will affect individuals and society; it in turn is assisted by these disciplines to come to a better understanding of revelation. Theology, along with philosophy, exposes students to questions about life and its meaning and helps to integrate the knowledge they are acquiring. It can help to deepen their faith, or at least their appreciation of the faith of others.

(46) Theology, therefore, is an appropriate academic discipline in any university, but it is especially desirable that every Catholic university have a faculty or institute of theology, that every other Catholic institution of higher education at least have regular lectures given in theology,[28]

and that theology interact with the other disciplines in such a way that they can contribute to and learn from one another. As an academic discipline which brings a perspective to all other disciplines, theology courses are offered to all students, not only those who are Catholics, and all students are helped to investigate the religious and ethical aspects of the various professions which they are preparing for.

(47) The Church recognizes the freedom and responsibility of each academic discipline to search for truth in accordance with its own principles and proper methods;[29] theology, as a legitimate academic discipline, has the same freedom and responsibility. The search in theology, however, is for an understanding of revealed truth, whose authentic interpretation is entrusted to the bishops of the Church.[30] For a Catholic theologian, therefore, serving a community of faith, a reverence for Catholic doctrine and the teaching authority of the Church is an integral part of the academic discipline itself, and must be included within its principles and methods.

(48) This relationship between the theologian and the Church's teaching authority points to the importance of theology rather than to any restriction of its legitimate freedom. The church requires the theologians' search for understanding[31] just as the theologians require the authentic interpretation given by the Church. The tasks are distinct and complementary, and neither can be reduced to the other.[32] Theological research is essential if the faith is to be intelligible and relevant to people's lives; it explores facts and experiences in order to unfold new insight and understanding; while it must be based on a transmission of the truths of the Catholic faith, it must also probe that faith in order to come to a deeper understanding of its meaning and of its application to the specific questions raised by contemporary culture. Theology, therefore, assists the Church "by means of careful study of the faith, by searching out all ideas and notions which can lead to more accurate and fuller understanding of it and more suitable expressions in which to diffuse it, and finally by suggesting means of facilitating the art of teaching it, in ways which will more aptly demonstrate *what* is to be taught and *how* it is to be taught."[33] The task of harmonizing culture with Christian teaching can be a difficult one;[34] but that very difficulty makes the task more essential, for the Church today must make its faith intelligible to an increasingly educated human community.

(49) When engaged in research, the Catholic theologian has always had a responsibility to distinguish carefully between Catholic doctrine and efforts to justify, analyze, and clarify that doctrine. This includes the responsibility to distinguish between the search for an understanding of revealed truth and decisions about the pastoral consequences related to that truth. Because of the immediate and widespread publication of

university research in communications media, that responsibility takes on a new importance today. "The theologians' contribution will be enriching for the Church only if it takes into account the proper function of the bishops and the rights of the faithful,"[35] and these rights of the faithful include the right "not to be troubled by theories and hypotheses that they are not expert in judging or that are easily simplified or manipulated by public opinion for ends that are alien to the truth."[36]

(50) Many Catholic students today enter institutions of higher education without a clear knowledge of the content and reasoning of basic Christian truths; Catholic institutions of higher education, through appropriate courses in Scripture and Catholic doctrine which are presented in a challenging manner, can and should make up for this deficiency. The development of a critical judgment in the academic study of theology, whether as a preparation for adult Christian living or as a preparation for specialization in theology itself, will then be based on sound knowledge of the Catholic tradition and of Catholic doctrine.

D. THE CATHOLIC INSTITUTION
IN THE MISSION OF THE CHURCH

1. Education as an Evangelizing Mission

(51) Evangelization means "bringing the Good News into all the strata of humanity, and through its influence transforming humanity from within and making it new. . . . It is a question not only of preaching the Gospel in ever wider geographic areas or to ever greater numbers of people, but also of affecting and as it were upsetting, through the power of the Gospel, humanity's criteria of judgment, determining values, points of interest, lines of thought, sources of inspiration, and models of life, which are in contrast with the Word of God and the plan of salvation."[37]

(52) The task of evangelization, then, clearly requires a careful knowledge of the values, thoughts, and inspirations of men and women, and a thorough study of the cultural, scientific, and technological influences which determine so many of the models of life today. Since men and women are part of salvation history revealed to us by God, nothing which is human is outside the scope of the Christian understanding of reality.[38] It follows immediately that the Catholic institution of higher education, precisely through its research and teaching, is an important and necessary instrument of genuine evangelization. Research carried out in the light of the Christian message, putting new human discoveries at the service of individuals and society; formation done in a faith context that forms rational and critical persons conscious of the transcendent dignity of the human person; professional training that incorporates

ethical values and a sense of service to individuals and to society: all these activities "transform humanity from within and make it new," and therefore bring the university or other institution of higher education into a close relationship with the Church's evangelizing mission. "Precisely because it is more and more conscious of its salvific mission in this world, the Church wants to have these centers closely connected with it; it wants to have them present and operative in spreading the authentic message of Christ."[39]

2. The Dialogue with Culture

(53) The Catholic institution of higher education, through its search for truth, meaning, understanding, and wisdom, constitutes a public presence of the Church in the world of culture and, even more importantly, a place of dialogue between the Gospel and contemporary culture in which both are enriched.

(54) Every institution of higher education contributes to "forging an awareness of national identity" and "is naturally part of the cultural heritage of a people";[40] it enters into dialogue with culture, examines and evaluates its values, and contributes to its development. The Catholic institution brings to this cultural development and dialogue a belief in human transcendence, an awareness of God's activity in creation, and a set of ethical principles derived from the Word of God; while building culture it assists at the same time in the evangelization and transformation of culture.[41] "It is crucial that the Gospel should purify culture, uplift it, and orient it to the service of what is authentically human."[42]

(55) Each culture must be measured against the Gospel of Christ so that it can be strengthened, perfected, and restored in Christ.[43] A Catholic institution of higher education, therefore, in different ways that vary with the different academic disciplines, will analyze, assess, and discern both the positive and the negative aspects of the culture in which it operates; it will identity and criticize those elements of modern culture which are contrary to human and spiritual values.

(56) In developed nations, this dialogue with culture is more necessary and more urgent today because of the widespread emphasis on technology and consumerism. It has a special urgency in emerging nations, where men and women strive for human development not only in the face of the difficulties inherent in their own culture, but also threatened with the loss of traditional values by the economic might and ideological competition of developed nations.[44] Among many different peoples, there is a tendency toward a freedom of thought and action that has little or no reference to ethical principles, and a possible misuse or manipulation of the means of communication. Catholic institutions

of higher education, through their teaching and research, can help to preserve the values of local cultures and bring economic and political development into a context of true and total human development. At the same time they can promote a fruitful dialogue and understanding among different cultures, thus contributing to a spirit of solidarity and peace among nations.

(57) This dialogue with culture also provides the Church with the means to make the faith better understood by the men and women of a particular culture. While it is true that the Gospel cannot be identified with culture and transcends all cultures, it is also true that "the Kingdom which the Gospel proclaims is lived by men and women who are profoundly linked to a culture, and the building up of the Kingdom cannot avoid borrowing the elements of human culture or cultures."[45] Faith is expressed in the anthropological language and symbols of a particular culture; "a faith that places itself on the margin of what is human, of what is therefore culture, would be a faith unfaithful to the fullness of what the word of God manifests and reveals, a decapitated faith, worse still, a faith in the process of self-annihilation."[46]

3. The Dialogue between Faith and Reason

(58) Within the general dialogue between faith and culture is the more specific dialogue between faith and the knowledge gained by human reason and human research. Defining the relationship between faith and reason has been a concern of the Church throughout its history; at various times, especially in establishing the relationship between faith and the positive sciences, there has been more mistrust than dialogue between scholars and Church authorities. While that situation has improved,[47] the need for further clarification and dialogue remains.

(59) A real contradiction between the content of faith and the discoveries of the various types of human knowledge is not possible: although distinct methods are used in each of the academic disciplines, so that the resulting conclusions and discoveries are, in that sense, distinct levels of truth, all truth proceeds from a single source and must be ultimately one. "Methodical research within every branch of learning, when carried out in a truly scientific manner and in accord with moral norms, can never truly conflict with faith. For the things of the earth and the concerns of faith derive from the same God."[48]

(60) Since truth is ultimately one, the search for an integration or *synthesis* among the various branches of human knowledge, and a global vision which brings knowledge and faith into harmony, must be possible. The explosion of knowledge, its compartmentalization within individual academic disciplines, and diminished emphasis given to contributions of

philosophy in integrating knowledge make the process of integration increasingly difficult; in any case, it is evident that the task will never be completed. But the human quest for an understanding and a wisdom that go beyond factual knowledge—that ask for meaning, especially the meaning that is related to human life and human destiny—make it imperative that the search continue. Recognizing that the task will always remain incomplete, and preserving the distinction of method and content within the individual branches of knowledge, scholars in a Catholic university reflect on the legitimacy of the different approaches to truth, seek an understanding of the different levels of truth in the different disciplines and, in dialogue among these disciplines and aided by philosophical principles, search for the place and the meaning of new discoveries and new levels of understanding in the individual branches of knowledge within an overall picture of the world, the human person, and God who is the absolute Truth.

(61) This search for integration will be assisted by the presence of a faculty of theology actively interacting with philosophy and the other academic disciplines. In an ongoing dialogue between faith and reason, human knowledge encounters the mystery of existence, particularly as it is found within the mystery of the human person, and so recognizes the limits of human reason; spiritual values help to direct research in the various disciplines for the authentic good of humanity. Through faith, the gradual discovery of truth is seen as a reflection of God, the one eternal Truth, revealing Himself through human research. Faith, enriched by the new discoveries of human research, comes to a better understanding of the eternal truth and finds ways to express this truth in a manner more comprehensible to the men and women of today, living in changed historical and cultural conditions. Thus the dialogue between faith and reason can enrich theology along with the other academic disciplines, can enrich faith itself, and can facilitate the search for an integration of knowledge.

4. *The Promotion of Religious and Ethical Principles*

(62) In all its activities, both internally and in its services to the civil community and the mission of the Church, the Catholic institution of higher education acts in accord with, gives witness to, and promotes a sense of values or basic ethical and religious principles that are based on the transcendent nature of the human person both as an individual and as a member of the human community. Wisdom unites the true and the good, and scholarly research can never be separated from ethics. A Catholic institution of higher education, therefore, conducts an ongoing search for the ethical implications of new discoveries of research, for the

wisdom which is able to help men and women "measure according to criteria of truth the means to the ends, the projects to the ideals, the actions to the moral parameters which permit a balance of values to be established anew."[49]

(63) This close relationship between the search for truth and the promotion of religious principles has a particular application to scientific and technological research, for growth in scientific discoveries, without a corresponding growth in the human spirit, will inevitably lead to a misuse of science that can only diminish, and possibly destroy, humanity. In its own university activities and in its service of society, the Catholic institution of higher education values scientific and technological discoveries, but brings ethical values to bear on them so that "intelligence and conscience [control] those materialistic processes that threaten to destroy the value of the person and the meaning of life."[50] It encourages and supports all legitimate efforts to ensure that scientific and technological advances be used for development that is truly human, that is aware of the spiritual nature of the human person, whose destiny is communion with God. In what it says and what it does, the Catholic institution of higher education demonstrates that the person has primacy over things, and "to be" is more important than "to have."

5. The Progress of Peoples

(64) A Catholic institution of higher education, while it lives in close relationship with the Church, is deeply immersed in human society. It shares in all of the hopes and frustrations, the new discoveries and old traditions, the joys and difficulties of that society and of the individuals that compose it. Its research and teaching bring it into immediate contact with some of the crucial issues affecting society and its cultural growth today such as problems of life and its quality, a more just distribution of the world's riches, the search for peace and political stability, a new economic and political order that will promote the human community at an international level.

(65) A Catholic institution, committed to the following of Christ, cannot be blind to human needs and human development; a Catholic institution of higher education responds to probing the depths and complexity of these modern problems in order to discover their roots and their causes, by bringing the light of the Christian message and the principles of the Gospel to bear on proposals which will contribute to a solution, and by making all members of the academic community sensitive to these issues and their urgency.

(66) The Catholic institution of higher education, because it has an institutional commitment to be of service to the entire human family,

will be especially concerned with examining from a Christian point of view, and with the help of the social teachings of the Church, the values and norms which are predominant in modern society. It will try to communicate to society today those religious principles which give meaning to human life, and also give special attention to those problems which are of the most vital interest to the faith, to morality, and to the life of the Church in the contemporary world.[51] In this way, it will contribute to the development of a true Christian anthropology, whose source is the person of Christ, and which brings the reality and the dynamism of the creation and redemption to bear on the reality and the issues of contemporary life.[52]

(67) Of particular urgency in today's world are problems connected with social justice, promoting "the development of those peoples who are striving to escape from hunger, misery, endemic diseases, and ignorance; of those who are looking for a wider share in the benefits of civilization and a more active improvement of their human qualities; of those who are aiming purposefully at their complete fulfillment."[53] Just as every individual Christian, so also every Catholic institution of higher education has a duty to help promote development in emerging nations; of equal importance is that each Catholic institution of higher education, through means within its own competence as a center of learning, contribute to the progress of the specific society in which it is located.[54] It will be incarnated in the local culture, assuming it, healing it, elevating and transforming it according to the values and principles of the Gospel. The task of development is to remedy the causes of poverty, whether material, cultural, or spiritual. The Catholic Church has firmly committed itself to the integral growth of all men and women, basing its teaching on an ethical and cultural concept of human development.[55] Every Catholic institution of higher education will try to foster in its teachers, and develop in its students, this Christian spirit of service to others.

(68) In its attempts to assist in dealing with these complex issues that touch on so many different aspects of human experience, the Catholic institution of higher education will insist on cooperation among the different academic disciplines, each offering its own contribution in the search for solutions;[56] since the economic and personal resources of individual institutions are limited, cooperation among different Catholic institutions as well as cooperation with other private and governmental institutions of higher education, is essential, recognizing that the cooperation required by the search for truth involves disagreements and debates, and that this cooperation is not easily accomplished.

6. Ecumenism and Religious Dialogue

(69) A Catholic institution of higher education, committed by its very nature to the search for truth, can make an important contribution to ecumenism and, more generally, to a dialogue with other religions and with those who have no faith. While it must faithfully teach Catholic doctrine and morals in this as in all other areas, it can promote Christian unity, make the Church better understood, and help the Church come to a better understanding of the other great religions of the world in order to discover in them implications for a better understanding of the Catholic faith. Thus the Catholic institution can help to fulfill the responsibility of every Catholic to foster Christian unity.

(70) When the Catholic institution is located in a country with religious pluralism, the presence of professors and students of other churches and religions in an academic setting that promotes open dialogue in the search for truth can also promote ecumenical and inter-religious dialogue; it can help to bring about the understanding and acceptance that are essential for the beginnings of a movement toward unity and solidarity in serving the human family.

(71) Catholic institutions located in countries where the Catholic faith is little known and often misunderstood have a particular importance in the dialogue with other religions, beliefs, or ideologies. In their dialogue, while maintaining their Catholic identity, they will "acknowledge, preserve, and promote the spiritual and moral goods found among these men and women,"[57] helping to develop a local culture that may, in time, come to a better understanding and appreciation of the Christian faith.

E. PASTORAL MINISTRY

(72) Although the principal tasks of an educational institution are intellectual formation and the search for truth, many educational activities also have a pastoral dimension and are therefore, in a Catholic institution, related to the Church's pastoral mission as well as to its teaching mission. Exploring the ethical and social implications of new discoveries obtained through research, for example, has pastoral implications; a concern for the total formation of the students has a clear pastoral dimension, as do each of the contributions of a Catholic institution of higher education to the evangelizing mission of the Church. An academic community concerned with promoting the Catholic institution's distinctive character will be conscious of this pastoral dimension, and sensitive to the ways in which it can have an influence on its various educational activities. Furthermore, this same academic community, like any community, is itself in need of pastoral care.

(73) In order to assist the members of the academic community in discovering and developing the pastoral dimension of their educational work, as well as to provide the pastoral care that this community needs, every Catholic institution of higher education will need to have an office of pastoral ministry well integrated into the academic community, which means that the office is a part of the institutional structure and that pastoral activities are closely related to the educational activities of the institution.

(74) Those engaged in pastoral ministry must be men and women who combine unusual natural talent with an excellent professional training that is specifically designed to prepare them for pastoral care in a university setting. Their work, closely affecting the Catholic character of the institution, is of significant importance in promoting that distinctive character; at the same time, their work is difficult and complex. They combine pastoral concerns with educational concerns at a specialized level; they minister to professionally trained teachers, and at the same time to students in the process of integrating their academic formation with their personal and spiritual life in order to assume leadership roles in society. The number of those engaged in pastoral ministry at an institution will depend on its size and particular needs, but wherever possible the office of pastoral ministry should include priests, religious, and lay men and women because of the specific experience and witness that individuals within each of these groups can bring to this ministry.

(75) An office of pastoral ministry contributes to the *pastoral dimension of intellectual development* by assisting the academic community in the task of integrating learning with life. It works closely with theology and the other disciplines in promoting the dialogue with culture, and in investigating the ethical implications of new discoveries in the sciences and humanities. Through seminars and lectures, through personal counseling and preaching, those in pastoral ministry assist in combining intellectual growth with human and spiritual growth. In those Catholic institutions of education that have no faculty or institute of theology, the office of pastoral ministry may be entrusted with the task of offering the courses in Catholic doctrine and scripture that are needed, as well as courses which explore the ethical questions related to the various professions that students are preparing for. Because it is not related to any single academic discipline, it can assist students in integrating what they learn in the various distinct disciplines. It will assist both teachers and students to come to a better understanding of the social teachings of the Church, as well as to interpret current events in society, especially the local society in which the institution is situated, in the light of these social teachings.

(76) An office of pastoral ministry contributes to the formation of a *community* among all the individuals within the educational institution by helping its members to develop and express a common vision, a vision based on the shared educational goal of contributing to human dignity by promoting the development of individuals and society. As far as possible those in pastoral ministry, especially those who are priests, will promote the development of this community into a *community of faith* and a *worshipping community*. "The university community must know how to incarnate its faith within its own culture in a daily, existential way, with important moments of reflection and of prayer in order to recall the foundations of its faith, hope, and charity."[58] Even when the individuals within the academic community are members of several different churches and religions, opportunities can be provided for interreligious celebrations of a shared faith in God.

(77) Formation of community, especially if it is to become a worshipping community, involves a variety of different activities. They include activities which will promote a spirit of acceptance, understanding, and service of others among all individuals within the community; for those able to respond, they include opportunities for personal prayer, to study the Word of God, and to deepen an understanding of and commitment to Gospel values and Christian principles. Catholic members of the academic community will be encouraged to participate in and celebrate the sacraments, especially the Sacrament of Reconciliation and, above all, the Eucharist as the most perfect community act of worship.

(78) The faith community becomes apostolic by translating prayer and worship into action. The office of pastoral ministry will assist individuals in developing a commitment to help those in need, beginning within the academic community itself and reaching out to the larger community in society. It will promote a dedication to work for social justice as an implementation of the Gospel and the social teachings of the Church.

(79) Various associations or movements of apostolic life, especially those developed specifically for students, can be of great assistance both in developing the pastoral aspects of educational activities and in providing pastoral care to their members; it is the responsibility of the office of pastoral ministry to coordinate the activities of these movements in such a way that they unite rather than divide the community of faith.

(80) If the bishop as teacher is concerned with and related to the Catholic institutions of higher education in his diocese, the bishop as pastor will be even more closely related to the pastoral ministry in those institutions. Pastoral ministry in a Catholic institution of higher education should be carefully integrated into diocesan life as well as into the life of the educational center. Many of the pastoral ministry activities are

similar to the activities of a parish, and one of the goals of an effective pastoral ministry will be to help prepare students for an active participation in Church life. Close cooperation between pastoral ministry and parishes will contribute to the growth of both.

(81) Whatever the relationship between the Church and the individual Catholic institution of higher education, the diocesan bishop has a direct responsibility for pastoral activities, especially for liturgical celebrations. The bishop will work closely with institutional authorities in ensuring that pastoral ministry is effective and that the needed pastoral care is provided; the bishop, along with institutional authorities, will provide for the selection and adequate formation of those preparing to work in pastoral ministry; he will work with those already engaged in pastoral ministry in order to promote cooperation between those pastoral activities within the Catholic educational institution and the various other pastoral activities in the diocese.

(82) The bishop necessarily has a concern for the pastoral care of everyone in his diocese, including those in the various universities and other institutions of higher education that are not Catholic.[59] Because of the close relationship between the educational and the pastoral, and the specialized needs of an educational institution, he will want to establish centers close to these institutions which are staffed by qualified and trained priests and others who can provide services similar to those of an office of pastoral ministry at a Catholic institution.

(83) In a Catholic institution of higher education, the responsibility for pastoral ministry cannot be restricted to the office of pastoral ministry alone. Qualified and trained specialists in pastoral ministry are needed; but pastoral ministry, like the Catholic identity of the institution, is the responsibility of the entire community and especially of the institution's directors. It is only when pastoral concerns are well integrated with educational concerns that the educational center can form men and women who will not tolerate a divorce between the faith that they profess and the lives that they lead, but rather will unite their human, professional, scientific, or technical efforts into a vital synthesis with their religious values.[60]

(84) As many teachers and students as possible should be involved, not only in promoting and participating in the various pastoral activities that are offered, but also by their active leadership in these activities, whether it be teachers who contribute the expertise of their academic area by participating in a seminar on current issues, students exploring together the relationship between their studies and their faith, or some group within the community helping to plan a liturgical celebration. Teachers who are active in pastoral ministry are effective witnesses, and become "multiplying agents" of those engaged more directly in pastoral

ministry: for one another, and especially for the students. Students can prepare for a life of service by engaging in a "peer ministry" with other students.

(85) Pastoral ministry is concerned with all those working at the institution: directors, teachers, students, and nonacademic staff, whether or not they are members of the Catholic Church. Members of other churches and religions should be given the opportunities and the challenges which will enable them to grow in their own commitment to God, and also to bring them into contact with the Catholic faith so that they can have an appreciation of the distinctive spirit and character of the institution and, with God's help, come to appreciate the Catholic faith itself. The activities of pastoral ministry can assist the efforts of the institution in promoting ecumenism.

F. CONCLUSION

(86) This first section has tried to describe the nature of a Catholic institution of higher education and its contribution to the mission of the Church. Recognizing the great diversity that exists among these institutions, each of them "must make a specific contributions to the Church and to society through high quality scientific research, in-depth study of problems, and a just sense of history, together with the concern to show the full meaning of the human person regenerated in Christ, thus favoring the complete development of the person. . . . [It] must train young men and women of outstanding knowledge who, having made a personal synthesis between faith and culture, will be both capable and willing to assume tasks in the service of the community and of society in general, and to bear witness to their faith before the world. And finally, to be what it ought to be, [it] must set up, among its teachers and students, a real community which bears witness to a living and operative Christianity, a community where sincere commitment to scientific research and study goes together with a deep commitment to authentic Christian living."[61]

(87) These are the institutions which will truly be able to contribute to the teaching mission of the Church and respond to the hopes and expectations of the Church community; these are the Catholic educational centers which, in their search for truth, will contribute to the solution of the urgent and pressing problems of contemporary life.

(88) This development of their identity and mission is given with an awareness of the number of difficulties that these institutions must confront each day, but at the same time with great confidence and hope. There is ample proof of the dedication and the concern of everyone involved in these institutions, and also of the support of bishops and

the whole people of God to assist them in overcoming these difficulties. The directors, teachers, students and staffs of Catholic institutions of higher education, working in close collaboration with the bishops, will continue to ensure that Catholic higher education can respond to the needs of today and can bring the resources of truth and wisdom to the building of a better society tomorrow. The more they can excel, both as educational institutions and as Catholic, the more it will become true that "the future is no longer a destiny to be accepted but a project and a duty to accomplish together, with the light of God that penetrates the secret of the dynamism proper to every Catholic university and allows the undivided acceptance of the Gospel of Christ and the generous and intelligent service of his Church."[62]

(89) In order to assist in this ongoing development of their identity and mission, the orientations and principles for Catholic institutions of higher education which have been developed in this first section are put into more concrete form in the norms which follow in Part II of this document. In addition, each Catholic institution of higher education will have more specific activities, in response to the particular needs of the culture in which it lives and the local Church which it serves. Bishops, episcopal conferences, and assemblies of Catholic hierarchy, in dialogue with these institutions, are encouraged to develop statements complementary to this one which can clarify these local and regional concerns, and enable the institutions to accomplish their goals more perfectly. Moreover, bishops and educational institutions are urged to continue and even intensify their mutual dialogue in order to determine the ways in which this document and complementary local documents can be translated into the life and activity of the institutions.

(90) Because they bring Christ and the Christian message into union with the development of the human person, Catholic institutions of higher education "show concretely that intelligence is never diminished, but is on the contrary stimulated and strengthened by that inner source of deep understanding which is the Word of God, and by the hierarchy of values derived from it. . . . In its unique way, the Catholic university contributes to manifesting the superiority of the spirit, which can never, under pain of being lost, agree to put itself at the service of anything other than the search for truth."[63]

NOTES

1. Cf. Mt 28:18–20.

2. Cf. Jn 14:6.

3. "The word 'culture' in its general sense indicates all those factors by which a person refines and unfolds his or her manifold spiritual and bodily

qualities. It means the effort to bring the world itself under control through human knowledge and human labor. It includes the fact that by improving customs and institutions, social life is rendered more human both within the family and in the civic community. Finally, it is a feature of culture that throughout the course of time people express, communicate, and conserve in their works great spiritual experiences and desires, so that these may be of advantage to the progress of many, even of the whole human family." (*Gaudium et Spes*, n. 53.) The plural "cultures" reflects the sociological and ethnological ways in which culture develops among specific groups of people. (Cf. ibid.)

4. The official text is the French original, *L'Université Catholique dans le monde moderne, Document final de 2éme Congrès des Délégués des Universités Catholiques*, Rome, 20–29 novembre, 1972. This document is hereafter abbreviated UCMM.

5. Vatican Council II, Declaration on Catholic Education (*Gravissimum Educationis*), n. 10, *AAS* 58 (1966), p. 737.

6. John Paul II, Address to the Presidents and Rectors of Jesuit Universities, November 9, 1985.

7. *Sapientia Christiana* was issued on April 15, 1979; cf. *AAS* 71 (1979), pp. 469–521.

8. Cf. Luke 2:52.

9. Cf. Jn 8:32.

10. Cf. Jn 14:8–11.

11. Cf. Jn 14:17.

12. Cf. Mt 28:18–20.

13. Cf. Lk 2:19, 51.

14. Cf. *Gravissimum Educationis*, n. 3, and *Dignitatis Humanae*, n. 4.

15. This first section, describing the educational institution as such, speaks explicitly of the Catholic *university* because it is the university that most fully embodies the concept of an academic center of higher learning. Other Catholic institutions of higher learning have more specific academic and professional goals; at the same time, because they share some or all of the qualities of a university, the description given, in whole or in part, refers also to these other Catholic institutions.

16. John Paul II, Address to the University Community of Leuven, Belgium, May 20, 1985, n. 4.

17. "Academic freedom" is the guarantee given to those involved in teaching and research that, within their specific specialized branch of knowledge, they may search for the truth wherever analysis and evidence leads them, according to the methods proper to that specific area.

18. John Paul II, Address to the Students and Teachers of the Catholic Universities of Mexico, January 31, 1979, n. xx.: *AAS* 71 (1979), I, 236.

19. Cf. Pope John Paul II, encyclical letter *Redemptor Hominis*, n. 15.

20. Paul VI, Address to the Rectors and Presidents of Jesuit Universities, August 6, 1975, n. 4: *AAS* 67 (1975), 533.

21. Vatican II Apostolic constitution on the Church *Lumen Gentium*, n. 31. Cf. the Decree on the Apostolate of the Laity (*Apostolicam Actuositatem*), *passim*.

22. John Paul II, Address to the Students and Teachers of the Catholic Universities of Mexico, January 31, 1979, n. 2: *AAS* 71 (1979), I, 236.

23. Cf. John Paul II, Address to University Personnel at the Catholic University of America, Washington, D.C., October 6, 1979, n. 4.

24. Cf. UCMM § 15.

25. Vatican Council II, Dogmatic Constitution on the Church (*Lumen Gentium*), n. 25. *AAS* 57 (1965), pp. 29–42.

26. John Paul II, Address to Leaders of Catholic Higher Education, Xavier University of Louisiana, U.S.A., September 12, 1987.

27. John Paul II to the Students and Professors of the Catholic University of Mexico n. 2 (January 31, 1979): *AAS* 71 (1979, I), 237.

28. Cf. *Gravissimum Educationis*, n. 10.

29. Cf. *Gaudium et Spes*, n. 59.

30. Cf. *Lumen Gentium*, n. 25.

31. Cf. Address of Paul VI to the Theological Commission, October 11, 1973, n. 4.

32. Cf. the Address of John Paul II to the professors of sacred theology in Aliötting, Germany, November 18, 1980, n. 5.

33. Address of Paul VI to the Theological Commission, October 6, 1969. Cf. also John Paul II, Address to the University Community of Leuven, Belgium, May 20, 1985, n. 7.

34. Cf. *Gaudium et Spes*, n. 62.

35. John Paul II, Address to University Personnel at the Catholic University of America, October 6, 1979.

36. Ibid.

37. Paul VI, encyclical letter *Evangelii Nuntiandi*, nn. 18f.

38. Cf. UCMM § 6.

39. Paul VI, Address to the Presidents and Rectors of Universities of the Society of Jesus, August 6, 1975, n. 2: *AAS* 67 (1975), 533.

40. John Paul II, Address to university students and intellectuals at Kinshasa, Zaire, May 4, 1980, n. 2.

41. Cf. *Evangelii Nuntiandi*, n. 19.

42. John Paul II, Address to the Leaders of Catholic Higher Education, Xavier University of Louisiana, September 12, 1987.

43. Cf. *Gaudium et Spes*, n. 58.

44. Cf. John Paul II, encyclical letter *Sollicitudo Rei Socialis*, nn. 19ff.

45. Paul VI, *Evangelii Nuntiandi*, n. 20.

46. John Paul II, Address to the intellectuals and university students and staff in Medellin, Colombia, July 5, 1986, n. 3. Cf. also *Gaudium et Spes*, n. 58.

47. "The Church recognizes more clearly today the distinction between Revelation and scientific theories regarding the universe. Scientists have become more sensitive to the ethical dimension of their research and to the search for the Universal and the Absolute." John Paul II, Address to a group of recipients of the Nobel Prize, May 9, 1983. (*Osservatore Romano*, May 9–10, 1983.)

48. Vatican Council II, Pastoral Constitution on the Church in the Modern World (*Gaudium et Spes*), n. 36: *AAS* 58 (1966), p. 1054. Pope John Paul II adds that "while reason and faith surely represent two distinct orders of knowledge, each autonomous with regard to its own methods, the two must finally converge in the discovery of a single whole reality which has its origin in God." (John Paul II, Address given on May 9, 1983, to the meeting on Galileo, n. 3: *AAS* 75 [1983], 690.)

49. John Paul II, Address to the participants at the Second National Congress of the Church Movement for Cultural Commitment, February 9, 1985, n. 4: *L'Osservatore Romano*, February 10, 1985.

50. Ibid., n. 5. Cf. *Redemptor Hominis*, n. 16: *AAS* 71 (1979, I), p. 290.

51. Cf. UCMM § 8.

52. Cf. John Paul II to the members of the Council of the International Federation of Catholic Universities, February 24, 1979. (*Insegnamenti*, II, 1 [1979], 446.)

53. Paul VI, *Populorum Progressio*, n. 1: *AAS* 59 (1967), p. 257. Quoted in UCMM § 44.

54. Cf. UCMM §§ 44f.

55. Cf. John Paul II, *Sollicitudo Rei Socialis*, December 30, 1987, nn. 27–34.

56. Cf. UCMM § 7.

57. Vatican Council II, Declaration on the Relationship of the Church to Non-Christian Religions (*Nostra Aetate*), n. 2.

58. John Paul II, Address to the University Community of Leuven, Belgium, May 20, 1985, n. 3.

59. Cf. Canon 813, CIC.

60. Cf. *Gaudium et Spes*, n. 43.

61. John Paul II, Address to the Teachers and Students of the Catholic Universities of Mexico, January 31, 1979, n. xx: *AAS* 71 (1979), I, 236. Quoted in the address of John Paul II to the Professors and Theologians at the Catholic University of America, Washington, D.C., U.S.A., October 7, 1979, n. 3.

62. John Paul II, Address to the Academic community of Louvain-la-Neuve, May 21, 1985, n. 6.

63. Paul VI, "New Tasks for Catholic Universities," address to the delegates of the International Federation of Catholic Universities, November, 1972.

PART II: NORMS FOR CATHOLIC UNIVERSITIES AND OTHER CATHOLIC INSTITUTIONS OF HIGHER EDUCATION

CHAPTER I: NATURE AND OBJECTIVES[1]

Art. 1 §1 A Catholic university, like every university, is a community of scholars representing the various branches of human knowledge. It is dedicated to research, higher education of its members, and various kinds of educational service.

§2 While preserving the proper nature and autonomy of these university activities, a Catholic university, as *Catholic*, inspires and informs them with the light of the Christian message as encountered within the spirit, tradition, and authentic teaching of the Catholic Church. It [promotes harmony between faith and reason and] assures in an institutional manner a Christian presence in the university world.[2]

§3 A Catholic university contributes to the teaching mission of the Catholic Church, and is related to the Church either by a formal constitutive and statutory bond or because of an institutional commitment made by those responsible for the university.

[*Art. 1 Alternate 1*: The Catholic Church, in fulfillment of its own mission and within the university tradition which it has helped to create, has the right and the duty to create universities through an act of the hierarchy or a religious institute, and to recognize as Catholic those which, by a commitment made by those responsible for the institution, wish to be regarded as such. All institutions which wish to be regarded as Catholic are to be guided by the following norms.]

[*Art. 1 Alternate 2*: The Catholic university, as Catholic, is an institution of the Church which has a stable bond with the Church hierarchy either by virtue of its constitution or by a common decision of those responsible for it; it animates academic teaching, scientific research, cultural expression, and all other university activities with a Catholic spirit.]

Art. 2 §1 A Catholic university, as Catholic, has the following essential *characteristics*:[3]

   a. a Christian inspiration not only of individuals but of the university community as such;
   b. a continuing reflection in the light of the Catholic faith upon the growing treasury of human knowledge, to which it seeks to contribute by its own research;
   c. fidelity to the Christian message as it comes to us through the Church and is interpreted by its living teaching office;[4]

   [*c. alternate 1*: fidelity to the Christian message as expressed in the Gospel and the tradition of the Catholic Church and taught by its Magisterium.]

   [*c. alternate 2*: fidelity to the Christian message as it comes to us through the Church in its role as teacher.]

   d. an institutional commitment as a university to the service of the people of God and of the human family in their pilgrimage on earth toward the transcendent goal which gives meaning to life.

§2 Taking into account the region or country in which it is located, a Catholic university strives for excellence in research, teaching, and all other areas of university activity.

[*Art. 2 alternate*:

§1 A Catholic university, while fulfilling the university tasks of research and higher education, gives specific attention to all aspects of the Catholic faith. It searches for theological knowledge and ethical values within the Catholic Church, and cultivates intellectual disciplines such as philosophy, humanities, science, and the arts. It tries to create an effective presence of the faith within culture and strives to make the faith have an influence on all areas of knowledge in the service of society.

§2 In fulfillment of its specific mission, the Catholic university lives and is inspired by a Christian inspiration of both individuals and the university community, a fidelity to the message of Christ as transmitted by the Catholic Church in its teaching office, and by an institutional commitment to dedicate itself to the service of the people of God and the human family in the attainment of their transcendent goal.

§3 The Catholic university must be an authentic community of teachers and students called to serve individuals and society.]

Art. 3 §1 University colleges, schools for the training of teachers, professional schools, research institutes, and various other institutions of higher education engage in university activities and include some or all of the qualities normally ascribed to a university. All such institutions of higher education are Catholic which, within academic variations that depend upon the purposes of the institution, satisfy the definitions given in Articles 1 and 2.

§2 These norms apply to all Catholic institutions of higher education, both universities and other institutions.[5] When the word "university" is used, the adaptations which will make the norm more directly applicable to other institutions are to be understood, unless the norm itself makes an explicit distinction between different types of institutions.

Art. 4 §1 All ecclesiastical faculties, including those established within a Catholic university, are governed by the Apostolic Constitution *Sapientia Christiana* and its annexed Norms, along with Canons 815 to 821 of the Code of Canon Law.[6]

§2 When an ecclesiastical faculty has been established within a Catholic university, those responsible for the university will ensure the coordination of all university activities so that, as far as possible, the entire university forms a single academic community.

Art. 5   The principal *objectives* distinctive of a Catholic university, by which it assists in the evangelizing mission of the Church and gives witness to Christ, are the following:[7]

§1 To encourage *scholarly research* in seeking and disseminating truth. For a Catholic university, this research includes:

a. the search for a synthesis to determine the place and meaning of the various disciplines and their new discoveries within the context of a vision of the human person and of the world that is enlightened by the Gospel;

> b. special attention to research in those areas which are related to faith, to morality, to the life of the Church in the contemporary world, and to the particular problems that face individuals and society today;
>
> c. a study of the various cultures and civilizations, in order to facilitate the dialogue between these cultures and the Gospel.

§2 To assist in the *formation* of men and women who will become leaders both for civil society and for the Church. This formation, in addition to humanistic education and professional training, offers the ethical teachings based on Gospel values that give meaning to life and enable students to become persons qualified to work with others for the good of human society [showing forth the love of God in the world].[8]

§3 To create a *university community*, all of whose members are helped to develop personally, spiritually, and professionally.

§4 To exercise a *critical function*, examining from a Christian point of view the values and norms which are predominant in contemporary society.

§5 To promote *ecumenism*, and a *dialogue* between the Christian faith and the religions [and cultures] of the world.

§6 To provide opportunities for *continuing education* and other educational services for the wider community, and especially for its own former students.

Art. 6   The university objectives listed in Article 5 are also the objectives of an individual faculty or school within a Catholic university and of a Catholic institution of higher education that is not a university. Academic variations will, however, qualify these objectives according to the specific purposes of the institution or faculty.

Art. 7   §1 Each Catholic university or other Catholic institution of higher education is to give an accurate description of its Catholic identity and of its relationship to the Catholic Church in its statutes or in some equivalent internal document.

§2 The document will specify the ways in which the characteristics in Article 2 are to be maintained and the objectives in Article 5 pursued. More generally, it will include a description of the ways in which the Catholic identity of the institution influences its life and various activities, and will contain appropriate instruments of self-regulation to ensure that this Catholic identity is preserved and protected.

§3   The document will also indicate clearly all that is prescribed in these norms, taking account of civil law and the social reality of the region in which the institution is located while at the same time preserving the freedom of the Church. This is without prejudice to conventions signed by the Holy See with various nations or with the institutions themselves.

CHAPTER II: VARIOUS TYPES OF CATHOLIC INSTITUTIONS OF HIGHER EDUCATION[9]

Art. 8   Because it has been given a mission to teach, the Church has the right and duty to establish and maintain Catholic universities.[10] It can also recognize as Catholic those universities established by religious institutes and other juridical persons, or by associations of lay people, whether public or private.[11]

Art. 9   §1   As far as possible, while preserving the freedom of the Church, account is to be taken of civil law in the establishment and promotion of Catholic universities, so that their academic degrees may receive civil recognition.

§2   Since they contribute to the fuller development of the human person and of society, Catholic universities have the right to receive treatment, from civil governments and others, equal to that accorded to all other similar institutions.

Art. 10 §1   No university, even if it is in fact Catholic, may have the phrase "Catholic University" in its official title except by consent of the competent ecclesiastical authority.[12]

§2   The "competent ecclesiastical authority," whenever the phrase is used in these norms, refers to that ecclesiastical authority which established the university or gave it formal approval. For a university not canonically established or approved, the competent ecclesiastical authority is the diocesan bishop of the place in which the principal seat of the university is located, unless the Holy See, in consultation with the bishop and the university, has determined otherwise.

Art. 11   §1   As a sign of a closer bond with the universal Church as it is expressed in the See of Peter, a Catholic university may be awarded the honorary title "Pontifical" by the Congregation for Seminaries and Educational Institutions. The criteria for such an award are established on an individual basis.

§2   Within the context of the region or country in which it is located, a university honored with the title "Pontifical" will strive to be outstanding both in its qualities as a university and in the quality of its Catholic identity and witness.

A. Universities Established by the Holy See

Art. 12   §1   Those universities are Catholic which have been established or formally approved as such by the Holy See. [These have a special relationship to the universal Church, and give evidence of the Church's commitment to the academic and intellectual life.]

§2   Establishment or formal approval by the Holy See requires approval of the statutes by the Congregation for Seminaries and Educational Institutions and includes, ordinarily, the establishment of the office of Chancellor.[13]

Art. 13   §1   The Chancellor is the diocesan bishop of the place in which the principal seat of the university is located unless the Holy See, in consultation with the bishop and the university, has determined otherwise.

§2   If the Chancellor is not the diocesan bishop, the Chancellor and the bishop are to draw up written norms which will enable them to carry out their respective responsibilities in mutual accord; the norms will ensure that the rights of the diocesan bishop and of the episcopal conference or assembly of Catholic hierarchy, including all those indicated in these norms, are fully respected.

§3   When a university has extensions in several dioceses the norms prescribed in §2 are to include all of the diocesan bishops involved.

Art. 14   The authority and responsibilities of the Chancellor are described in the university statutes or equivalent internal document. Among these responsibilities, the Chancellor is to:

§1   represent the Holy See in its relations with the university and the university in its relations with the Holy See.

§2   defend and promote both the educational and the Catholic character of the university, and facilitate its communion with the local and universal Church.

§3   assist the chief executive officer[14] and other university officials in the preservation and progress of the university, and in a faithful observance of its statutes.

§4   promote pastoral ministry and, in particular, approve the appointment of those who will engage in pastoral ministry and the possible establishment of a university parish.[15]

[*Art. 14 additions*:

§ 5   facilitate close links of the university with the academic community and with society.

§ 6   grant the mandate to regular teachers of theological subjects.

§ 7   guarantee the effective Christian inspiration of all university teaching, as well as the academic and doctrinal quality of religious instruction, proposing or approving the teachers.

§ 8   ensure a sufficient number of persons for pastoral ministry in all parts of the university.

§ 9   promote liturgical life and pastoral activities within the university.

§10   resolve conflicts of authority between the Rector and the Academic Senate or other councils of the university.

§11   propose changes in the statutes to the Holy See and approve modifications in university regulations in accordance with the statutes.

§12   protect the patrimony when the university is the property of the Church.]

Art. 15   Where suitable the university may also have a Vice-Chancellor, whose authority and responsibilities are to be described in the statutes of the university or equivalent internal document.

Art. 16   Every five years, each Catholic university established or approved by the Holy See will send to the Congregation for Seminaries and Educational Institutions a statistical report along with information on its academic state, its educational and pastoral activities, and its Catholic identity as shown by its maintenance of the characteristics listed in Article 2 and its pursuit of the objectives listed in Article 5. This report is normally to be sent through the diocesan bishop [or Chancellor].

B. Universities Established by Other Ecclesiastical Bodies

Art. 17   §1   Those universities are Catholic which have been established or formally approved as such by an episcopal conference, an assembly of Catholic hierarchy, or a diocesan bishop, in accordance with norms which are to be approved by the Holy See.

            §2   Formal approbation is ordinarily to be given in the form of a written document. If the university will use the term "Catholic university" in its official title, the document is to include approval of that use.

Art. 18   §1   Those universities are Catholic which have been established by a religious institute or other juridical person[16] with the approval of the competent ecclesiastical authority.

            §2   Those universities are Catholic which, having been established or approved by an ecclesiastical authority, are administered by a religious institute or other juridical person.

Art. 19   A university of the type described in Article 17 or 18 may have a Chancellor or some equivalent person to represent the ecclesiastical authority in its relations with the university and the university in its relations with the ecclesiastical authority. The method for naming the Chancellor, together with his duties and responsibilities, are described in the statutes of the university or equivalent internal document.

Art. 20   Every five years, each university of the type described in Article 17 or 18 will send to the ecclesiastical authority or juridical person which established or administers the institution a report similar to that described in Article 16. A summary of this report is sent to the diocesan bishop, who will forward relevant information to the Congregation for Seminaries and Educational Institutions.

C. Other Catholic Universities

Art. 21   §1   Those universities are Catholic which are "Catholic in inspiration" by reason of an institutional commitment made by the authorities responsible for the institution; establishment of a university which is "Catholic in inspiration" must receive approval from the local bishop.

§2   Such institutions, though they have not been canonically established, are in communion with the Catholic Church; they are recognized as Catholic by their fulfillment of the definitions given in Articles 1 and 2 and by their observance of these norms.

Art. 22   Those universities and other institutions of higher education which are "Catholic in inspiration" will communicate information about their academic state and especially about their pastoral activities and their Catholic identity to the bishop of the diocese in which the principal seat of the institution is located, and to any religious institutes involved in the institution. The bishop will forward relevant information to the Congregation for Seminaries and Educational Institutions.

[*Alternate to replace Articles 12, 17.1, 18 and 21:*
§1   Those universities are Catholic which are established or approved as such by the Holy See, or by an episcopal conference or diocesan bishop according to norms approved by the Holy See.

§2   Those universities are also Catholic which depend on or are administered by a religious institute or other juridical person, or which accept in their statutes or equivalent document all that is prescribed in these norms.]

CHAPTER III: THE CATHOLIC
UNIVERSITY WITHIN THE CHURCH[17]

Art. 23   §1   A Catholic university possesses the administrative and academic autonomy necessary to perform its teaching and research functions effectively, so long as this autonomy is in accord with the proper pursuit of truth and the common good.[18]

§2   Each academic discipline is pursued according to its own proper methods and enjoys its own legitimate autonomy.[19] Freedom in research and teaching is recognized and respected, so long as the rights of the individual and of the community are preserved within the context of the common good.[20]

Art. 24   The Catholic university offers opportunities for lay Catholics to contribute their specific talents to the service of the Church and to exercise their proper apostolate.[21]

Art. 25   §1   Because a Catholic university contributes to the Church's teaching mission, it is closely related to both the local and the universal Church.

§2   Each Catholic university, of whatever type,[22] will maintain a close [personal and pastoral] relationship with the episcopal conference or assembly of Catholic hierarchy and with the diocesan bishops of the region or regions in which it is located; it respects and is faithful to these pastors of the Church in the exercise of their proper authority.

§3   This [personal and pastoral] relationship is to be fostered through mutual assistance and ongoing dialogue, which will both assist the Church and preserve and foster the identity of the Catholic university.[23]

Art. 26   Episcopal conferences, assemblies of Catholic hierarchy and diocesan bishops:

§1   have a concern for the welfare of the Catholic universities in their regions. They offer understanding, inspiration, encouragement, and support in order to help these institutions carry out their tasks.

§2   establish and foster close relationships that include mutual assistance with those religious institutes and other juridical persons engaged in the work of education in Catholic universities.

§3   assist priests, religious, and laity to understand the importance of Catholic universities; they encourage Catholic students to attend Catholic universities and encourage all Catholics to support the various activities of these institutions.

Art. 27   §1   The primary responsibility for maintaining and promoting the Catholic identity of the university rests with the university itself. While this responsibility is entrusted principally to university authorities, it is shared in varying degrees by all members of the university community.[24]

§2   Episcopal conferences, assemblies of Catholic hierarchy and diocesan bishops, working together with the Chancellor when one exists and also with the major superiors of any religious institutes that may be involved, have the duty and the right of ensuring that Catholic doctrine is faithfully taught and Catholic discipline is faithfully observed in the Catholic universities within their territories.[25]

Art. 28   §1   Should problems arise concerning the Catholic identity of the university, whether doctrinal, disciplinary, or pastoral, the ecclesiastical authority will confer with the university authorities, along with the major superiors of any religious institutes involved in the university, in order to find a satisfactory solution.

§2   If a satisfactory solution cannot be reached by dialogue, the ecclesiastical authority has the right and duty to intervene in order to protect the truth and integrity of the Christian message. The form which a possible intervention may take will vary in accordance with the type of Catholic institution involved, and will be conducted in a manner which takes into account the statutes and regulations of the institution [as well as accepted academic practices].

§3   Each episcopal conference or assembly of Catholic hierarchy, in consultation with the Catholic universities of its region, will establish procedures for such interventions, which are to be approved by the Holy See. These procedures will include a process by which the competent ecclesiastical authority can rescind its approval of the title "Catholic university" and can declare, for sufficiently grave reason, that a university is no longer Catholic in its identity. In all such procedures the university's right of appeal to the Holy See is to be preserved.[26]

Art. 29   Each episcopal conference or assembly of Catholic hierarchy is encouraged to create an episcopal commission to assist in promoting and fostering good relations with the Catholic universities of its region. Religious institutes engaged in the university apostolate and diocesan bishops who have Catholic universities within their dioceses may wish to establish similar commissions.

[*Art. 29 addition*:

§2   The Congregation for Seminaries and Educational Institutions will establish a commission, chosen from Catholic universities throughout the world, whose task it will be to promote cooperation among these universities as well as to promote their Catholic identity and their responsibilities toward the Church at an international level.]

CHAPTER IV: THE UNIVERSITY COMMUNITY[27]

Art. 30   §1   Except where the Article itself makes an exception, references to the Catholic faith, Catholic doctrine, or the promotion of the distinctive Catholic identity of the university in Articles 31 through 47 apply directly only to those in the university community who are members of the Catholic Church.

§2   University authorities, teachers, students, and non-academic staff who belong to other churches and religions are expected to recognize and respect the Catholic identity of the university; according to their different roles they are encouraged, while sustaining plurality of thought and religious freedom, to assist in maintaining and promoting this Catholic identity.

§3   In order that the university community may better understand the Catholic identity of the institution and thus be better able to promote it or at least respect it, programs of orientation and ongoing formation concerning this Catholic identity and its implications are to be provided for its members, especially university authorities and teachers.

Art. 31   §1   The university community is united by its common dedication to the service of the truth and by a common vision of the dignity and transcendent destiny of the human person as loved by God, revealed in the person and message of Christ.

§2   All members of this community will help to foster a genuine community spirit within the university, marked by charity, sincere dialogue, ethical values based on Gospel principles, respect for others, and a particular concern for those in need.

Art. 32   §1   Each member of the university community is, as an individual and as a member of various university bodies, responsible for the common good and for the development of the university. The degree of responsibility will vary in accord with the statutes and with the individual's position in the university.

§2   In ways that vary in accord with each one's individual responsibilities and role within the university, all members of the university community promote its Catholic identity by helping to maintain the characteristics of Article 2 and pursue the objectives listed in Article 5.

Art. 33   §1   Provision will be made in the statutes of the university or some equivalent internal document for all the members of the university community to participate in the formulation of university policy. The form of participation differs according to the individuals involved, and is not necessarily deliberative.[28]

§2   The rights and obligations of all members of the university community are to be clearly stated in appropriate university documents, and procedures established to deal with conflicts regarding these rights.[29]

A. University Authorities

Art. 34   §1   The chief executive officer of the institution[30] must have a thorough knowledge of higher education, proven administrative ability, a commitment to the distinctive identity and mission of the university both as a university and as Catholic, and an ability to promote this distinctive identity and mission.

§2   The way in which the chief executive officer is chosen and named, as well as the principal duties, the relation to the Chancellor when one exists, and procedures for termination of the chief executive officer when necessary, are all to be described in the university statutes.

§3   If the university has been canonically established or approved and has a Chancellor, the appointment or election of the chief executive officer is to be approved by that Chancellor. If the university has been established or approved by the Holy See, the appointment is also to be confirmed by the Holy See or by another ecclesiastical authority delegated by it.

Art. 35 §1 University authorities perform their duties in a spirit of service, paying special attention to the needs of the various individuals and groups within the institution, so that they may promote a genuine community spirit and a shared sense of responsibility for the educational quality and the Catholic identity of the institution.

§2 Appropriate means such as consultation of individuals, their participation in university councils and committees, and the creation of suitable associations within the university are to be used to make this sharing of responsibility more effective.

§3 All university authorities, within their own areas of responsibility, assist the chief executive officer not only in furthering the goals of the university as a university, but also in maintaining its distinctive character and promoting its distinctive objectives as Catholic.

Art. 36 §1 The specific duties of a board of trustees or equivalent body, when one exists, are described in the university statutes. These duties are to include a responsibility to assist the chief executive officer and other university authorities in maintaining and promoting the distinctive Catholic identity of the institution and in preserving a close relationship with the episcopal conference or assembly of Catholic hierarchy and with the local bishops.

§2 Members of such a board are ordinarily to be selected not only for their ability to promote the university as a university but also to promote its distinctive identity as Catholic.

Art. 37 The Catholic identity of the university is to be taken into consideration in any public activities with which the university or its authorities are associated, including official university recognition of individuals or of groups.

B. University Teachers

Art. 38 §1 Appointment of teachers in a Catholic university is carried out in accordance with its statutes.

§2   At the time of appointment, teachers are to be informed about the distinctive Catholic identity of the institution and its implications, and about their own responsibilities as teachers in a Catholic university.

Art. 39   Teachers initiate students in the knowledge and methods appropriate to the various academic disciplines, and at the same time they contribute to an education that joins total formation with sound morality. They assist each student to discover his or her own aptitudes and vocation in life and also help these students to acquire the motivation needed to contribute to the common good of society.[31]

Art. 40 §1   Since their life witness contributes to the formation of students and to the vitality of the university community, teachers in a Catholic university are distinguished not only in professional training, research potential, and pedagogical ability, but also in intellectual honesty, personal integrity, and uprightness of life.[32]

§2   In ways consistent with the different academic disciplines, teachers will be faithful to Catholic doctrine in their research and teaching.

Art. 41 §1   Because of their specific contribution to the dialogue between faith and reason, and their efforts to relate divine revelation to human knowledge and human endeavors, the research and the teaching of theologians are of significant importance in helping to achieve the objectives of a Catholic university.

§2   Catholic theologians recognize and accept the right of the bishops of the Church, as the authentic interpreters of Catholic doctrine, to judge the conformity of their theological research and teaching with authentic Catholicity and with divine revelation.[33]

§3   Those who teach theological subjects as regular teachers must have a mandate from the competent ecclesiastical authority.[34] A procedure for granting this mandate that takes account of the various types of Catholic institutions and their statutes is to be developed by episcopal conferences or assemblies of Catholic hierarchy, and approved by the Holy See.

Art. 42　§1　Norms for retention and promotion of teachers take into consideration not only professional competence in research and teaching, but also service to the university and its goals, including service to its distinctive characteristics and objectives as Catholic.

　　　　§2　The university statutes or some equivalent internal document include procedures for admonishing and, when necessary, disciplining those professors who are deficient in professional competence or behavior, or whose teaching or behavior is in conflict with the goals and objectives of the university. These procedures will, while respecting individual rights and accepted practices in the academic community of the country or region, make provision for the possible dismissal of teachers in cases of grave offense [and a lack of response to repeated warnings].[35]

Art. 43　§1　In their role as pastors of the Church, episcopal conferences, assemblies of Catholic hierarchy, and diocesan bishops will support and encourage all those who assist the Church through their teaching, research or other form of service in a Catholic university.

　　　　§2　Bishops have the right and duty of reprimanding or otherwise correcting members of the university community whose teaching or behavior is in conflict with Catholic doctrine or discipline. The procedures of Article 28, §3 are to include procedures for dealing with individual members of the university community, taking into account the type of institution, its statutes and regulations[, and accepted academic practices].

C. Students

Art. 44　§1　Students in a Catholic university are offered an education which will enable them to become critical and independent seekers of the truth, living according to the moral integrity that this truth demands, conscious of the rights of others within the university and in the larger human community.

　　　　§2　The education includes religious principles, taught in such a way that they lead to a commitment to live according to these principles. Catholic students are helped to become active witnesses of the Catholic faith.[36]

Art. 45   §1   All students are encouraged to acquire a sense of service to humanity. Catholic students are encouraged to serve humanity through service to the Church; other students are similarly encouraged to this service in ways that are in accord with their own beliefs.

§2   Special attention is given to students who are suited to research or university teaching, so that they may be encouraged to prepare themselves for service to the Church and society in a university or other institution of higher education.

§3   Likewise, those students who are suited to it will be encouraged to assist the Church as teachers in Catholic schools or through leadership in various parish activities.

Art. 46   Appropriate university documents are to describe the norms and procedures for student discipline, including grounds which will be sufficient for expulsion when this becomes necessary; the procedures will respect individual rights [and accepted academic practices].

D. Non-Academic Staff

Art. 47   §1   The non-academic staff are part of the university community, and contribute to its life and the service it renders.

§2   Non-academic staff members recognize the Catholic nature of the university and contribute to its within their own areas of responsibility. Their lives give witness to both human and Christian values.

§3   University practices and policies recognize the human dignity of all members of the university community, reflect the principles of social justice, and manifest Christian love.

§4   Suitable opportunities are provided to the non-academic staff for their continuing formation and for a deepening of their religious faith and witness.

CHAPTER V: UNIVERSITY ACTIVITIES

Art. 48   The Christian view of the world and of the human person is the background for all activities at a Catholic university; while respecting freedom of religion, Catholic teaching and practice influence both research and the formation of students.

Art. 49 §1 To the extent possible within its own specific purposes, each Catholic university or other institution of higher education gives special emphasis to interdisciplinary studies and to a formation that will enable students to understand the trends of modern culture and to bring the values of the Gospel to this culture.

§2 All students have an opportunity to study the social teachings of the Church and the application of these teachings to specific social issues. They will be encouraged to develop a commitment to a promotion of justice inspired by these teachings and by the ethical principles of the Gospel.

Art. 50 §1 As far as possible, every Catholic university or other institution of higher education is to have a faculty, an institute, or at least a chair of theology or religious studies.[37]

§2 If the university has been established or formally approved by an ecclesiastical authority, it is the responsibility of that authority to ensure that this faculty, institute, or chair is established.[38] If the institution is "Catholic in inspiration," the diocesan bishop and episcopal conference or assembly of Catholic hierarchy will encourage this establishment as a part of their pastoral responsibility for the Catholic identity of the institution.

Art. 51 §1 Courses in theology or religious studies are available to and recommended for all students, whether or not they are members of the Catholic Church.

§2 Courses in theology include the sources of the Christian faith, especially the Scriptures; attention is also given to other religions, including those that are not Christian.

§3 A Catholic university ensures that all Catholic students, either as a part of their theological formation or through other means, have an adequate knowledge of the basic truths taught by the Catholic Church.

Art. 52 §1 Either through theology courses or through other means, the Catholic university will ensure that theological issues related to the various disciplines are researched and taught.

§2 The program of studies for professional formation is to include courses in the ethics of that profession, so that students will be prepared to exercise their future profession in accord with ethical norms inspired by the Gospel.

Art. 53   Catholic universities, especially those located in pluralist cultures or countries whose culture include religions other than Christianity, promote dialogue on
ecumenical questions and with the various religions of
the world. In this dialogue, the norms of the Church
are to be followed.[39]

Art. 54   A Catholic university, through university policies and
through the life of the university community, is attentive
to the informal education of students provided by the
university environment.

[*Suggested additions to this section*:
1. As far as possible, each Catholic university will develop
institutes whose primary purpose is the promotion of intellectual research.
2. Courses in methods of teaching and of evaluation are made
available to university teachers, so that their work can obtain
the best possible results.]

CHAPTER VI: PLANNING AND COOPERATION

Art. 55   Each Catholic university is to be engaged in the planning needed to ensure financial viability, growing academic excellence, an increasing ability to achieve its
objectives, and an ever more effective Christian witness.

Art. 56   §1   As far as possible, Catholic universities or other types
of Catholic institutions of higher education are to be
established in those parts of the world where they do
not already exist. [In countries where it is appropriate,
these Catholic institutions can be joined into a federation with other private or public institutions.] Careful
and well-coordinated planning should ensure that these
Catholic institutions are well distributed, conveniently
located,[40] and able to meet the specific needs of a region
or culture.[41]

§2   Catholic institutions are to be distinguished for their
academic quality and Catholic nature rather than for
their number or the size of their enrollment.[42]

Art. 57 §1 It is the responsibility of episcopal conferences and assemblies of Catholic hierarchy, assisted by religious institutes and others involved in university education, as well as the Catholic universities themselves, to carry out the planning necessary for the establishment of new Catholic institutions of higher education.

[*Art. 57 addition*:

§2 Planning for new Catholic universities or other Catholic institutions of higher education will take into account the apostolic needs of the region and also the possibilities for economic support and the legal, social and political realities that may affect such institutions.]

Art. 58 Episcopal conferences, assemblies of Catholic hierarchy, bishops, and Catholic universities will take whatever steps are possible to ensure that Catholic universities are able to admit talented students with insufficient economic means. Students in developing countries can be assisted through international cooperation.

Art. 59 §1 Regional, national, and international cooperation is to be promoted among Catholic universities, both in research and in teaching, so that through mutual help the objectives listed in Article 5 may be more easily and more completely attained.[43] Cooperation is also to be promoted between Catholic universities and ecclesiastical universities and faculties.[44]

§2 Cooperation is facilitated by means such as sharing of information, exchange of teachers and students, interdisciplinary research centers, and academic conferences.

§3 This cooperation is especially necessary for research on problems of interest to the Church and society such as those related to social justice and the promotion of human culture.

Art. 60 §1 In order to facilitate cooperation and collaboration, associations of Catholic universities and of other Catholic institutions of higher education are to be encouraged on the regional, national, and international levels.

§2 Of particular importance is the International Federation of Catholic Universities, established by the Holy See in order to assist Catholic universities to collaborate more effectively in the attainment of their goals and objectives.[45]

Art. 61   §1   Cooperation is also to be encouraged with other universities, both private and governmental, through participation in university associations, common research projects, and other academic activities. [Catholic thought can, by these means, offer a contribution to the analysis of the problems of society and the correct use of scientific discoveries.]

§2   Catholic universities will, when possible and in accord with Catholic principles and doctrine, cooperate with government programs and other types of national and international organizations, so that the results of university research can be more easily applied to the good of the human person and of the human community.

Art. 62   Teachers and other university personnel are encouraged to join associations in their academic disciplines or areas of service and to participate in other programs which will promote cooperation.

Art. 63   The Congregation for Seminaries and Educational Institutions, assisted by experts, encourages and promotes planning and cooperation at the world level, working together with regional, national, and international university associations.

CHAPTER VII: PASTORAL MINISTRY[46]

Art. 64   §1   A Catholic university is attentive to the pastoral care of all members of the university community. While programs are adapted to the various needs of the members of the university community, priority is given to those means which will facilitate the integration of human and professional endeavors with religious values, in order to unite intellectual learning with religious living.[47]

§2   Particular attention is given to the pastoral care of university teachers. Their integration of the intellectual with the religious will enable them to be better guides and witnesses in the formation of students.

Art. 65   University authorities will ensure that a sufficient number of qualified priests and other persons are appointed to provide pastoral ministry for the university community, that adequate facilities are available for them to carry on their work, and that their place in the university structure is such that they are able to do their work effectively.

[*Suggested addition to Article 65*:
The Chancellor, where one exists, has a particular responsibility to promote pastoral ministry in the university.]

Art. 66　§1　While pastoral ministry in a university has its own specific identity and purpose, it is also a part of the Church's pastoral mission and is to be carried on in harmony and cooperation with the pastoral ministry of [other universities and with] the Church at the local and universal levels, under the guidance of the diocesan bishop.

　　　§2　University pastoral ministry is coordinated with parish ministry in such a way that Catholic students are prepared to become active leaders in parish life. Other students are similarly encouraged to become active in their own churches or religions.

Art. 67　§1　Diocesan bishops will cooperate with university authorities in promoting pastoral care within the university.[48] They will provide an adequate number of priests for this work, and help to ensure that all those engaged in pastoral ministry, whether priests, religious, or lay men and women, receive the training they need.

　　　§2　Diocesan bishops will also cooperate in the setting up of appropriate pastoral centers and residences for university students, and will establish a university parish whenever there is genuine need for one.[49]

　　　§3　Religious associations and movements, especially those established for university students, are to be encouraged for the assistance they can provide in pastoral care. They are to be approved by the diocesan bishop and their work coordinated by those responsible in the university for pastoral care.

[*Art. 67 addition*:
　　　§4　When the university has a Chancellor who is not the diocesan bishop, decisions about the setting up of associations or establishment of a university parish, along

with the naming of pastors, are made in collaboration with the Chancellor.]

Art. 68   §1   Those who will be engaged in pastoral ministry are appointed by the university after consultation with the diocesan bishop. Those who will exercise liturgical ministry are appointed jointly by university authorities and the diocesan bishop.[50]

§2   Those appointed are to be thoroughly trained in pastoral care, with specific training in the pastoral care of university teachers and students. They are to be men and women filled with apostolic zeal and capable of dialogue.

§3   Both teachers and students are to be invited to collaborate in pastoral activities, and to assist the work of pastoral ministry in whatever ways are possible.

Art. 69   §1   Those engaged in pastoral ministry will help to promote a genuine faith community within the university.

§2   Those members of the university community who belong to the Christian faith are encouraged to collaborate in efforts to make the university community a truly Christian one.

Art. 70   §1   Suitable opportunities such as lectures, seminars, and retreats are to be provided for at least the Catholic members of the university community to deepen their understanding of the Word of God and to prepare for and participate in the sacraments.

§2   The university community, at least in its Catholic members, is a worshipping community. Regular opportunities are available for the celebration of the sacraments of the Eucharist and Reconciliation. As occasion offers, the entire university community is asked to come together in prayer to worship God.

Art. 71   §1   The pastoral care of the university includes those members of the university community who are not members of the Catholic Church, and offers them any spiritual assistance they may need, at the same time respecting their freedom to maintain and express their own religious convictions and develop their own religious commitment.

§2   Representatives of other Churches and religions may be appointed to work in pastoral ministry in order to provide pastoral care for teachers and students who are members of those faiths.

§3   Professors and students who are not members of the Catholic Church will be offered opportunities to learn about the Catholic faith.

Art. 72 §1   Pastoral ministry also includes a concern for integrating the social teachings of the Church into university policies and the lives of the members of the university community.

§2   Those engaged in pastoral ministry encourage and assist students to help others in need, both within the university community and in society, and to develop a commitment to work for social justice, human development, and the promotion of human dignity.

§3   Vocations to the priesthood and religious life are to be fostered among Catholic students[; other students are encouraged to contribute to the welfare of their own churches or religions].

§4   Pastoral ministry will be especially alert to the specific needs of students from the economically deprived sectors of society, as well as students from other cultures present in the university community.

NOTES

1. Square brackets within the text indicate suggestions for alternate wording or suggested additions to the revision.

2. Cf. UCMM §§ 1f.

3. Cf. UCMM § 1.

4. Cf. *Dei verbum*, n. 10.

5. Cf. Canon 814, CIC.

6. Cf. Canons 816 and 817, CIC, and *Sapientia Christiana*, General Norms, Article 8. Ecclesiastical faculties are those which "have been canonically established or approved by the Apostolic See, foster and teach sacred doctrine and the sciences connected with it, and have the right to confer academic degrees by the authority of the Holy See" (*Sapientia Christiana*, General Norms, Article 2).

7. Cf. UCMM §§ 3–13.

8. Cf. Canon 795, CIC, and also *Gravissimum Educationis*, n. 10.

9. Cf. UCMM §§ 14–18.

10. Cf. Canon 807, CIC.

11. The meaning of the terms "juridical persons," and "public or private associations," is that given in Canon Law. Cf. Canons 113ff, 312ff, and 321ff, CIC.

12. Cf. Canon 808, CIC.

13. The "office of Chancellor" has different roles in different university contexts. The role in these norms is that determined by Articles 13 and 14.

14. The title of the chief executive officer varies, depending on the country and the type of institution. This title may be, for example, Rector, President, Director, or Principal.

15. Cf. Articles 67 § 2 and 68 § 1.

16. Cf. Canons 113–123, CIC.

17. Cf. UCMM §§ 50–60.

18. Cf. *Gaudium et Spes*, nn. 57 and 59; UCMM §§ 20f.

19. Cf. Canon 809, CIC.

20. Cf. *Gaudium et Spes*, n. 59; *Gravissimum Educationis*, n. 10.

21. Cf. *Apostolicam Actuositatem* and Canon 225, CIC.

22. See the various types of Catholic institutions in Chapter II of these norms.

23. Cf. also Article 27 § 2.

24. Cf. Chapter IV of these norms.

25. Canon 810 §2, CIC.

26. Cf. also Articles 41 § 3 and 43 § 2.

27. Cf. UCMM §§ 37–41.

28. Cf. UCMM §19.

29. Ibid.

30. Cf. Note 13.

31. Cf. *Gaudium et Spes*, n. 59.

32. Cf. Canon 810 §1, CIC.

33. Cf. Canon 218, CIC, *Dei Verbum*, n. 10, and UCMM §§ 53ff.

34. Cf. Canon 812, CIC.

35. Cf. Canon 810 §1, CIC.

36. Cf. *Gravissimum Educationis*, n. 10.

37. Canon 811 §1, CIC.

38. Ibid.

39. Cf. Canon 755, CIC, *The Ecumenical Directory*, Part II, and other documents of the Holy See and of local churches.

40. Cf. Canon 809, CIC, and *Gravissimum Educationis*, 10.

41. Cf. Canons 814 and 821, CIC.

42. Cf. *Gravissimum Educationis*, 10.

43. Cf. UCMM §§46–49.

44. Cf. Canon 820, CIC. Also see *Sapientia Christiana*, General Norms, Article 49.

45. Pius XII, The Apostolic Letter "Catholicas studiorum universitates," July 27, 1949. *AAS*, 42 (1950), p. 387.

46. Cf. UCMM §§42f.

47. Cf. *Gaudium et Spes*, n. 43.

48. Cf. Canon 813, CIC.

49. Ibid. Cf. also Article 14 § 4 when the university has a Chancellor.

50. Cf. canons 565 and 813, CIC. Cf. also Article 14 § 4 when the university has a Chancellor.

APPENDIX

RELATIONSHIP BETWEEN THE REVISED DRAFT AND THE
QUESTIONS LISTED IN THE SUMMARY OF RESPONSES

N.B.: In most cases, the suggested response to a question is treated
in many different parts of the revised draft. Only the principal
locations are indicated in this appendix.

1.   What is a brief but adequate description of a university?
            Part I: §§25–30
            Part II: Art. 1

       Is it possible to give a reasonably short description (or collec-
       tion of descriptions) of the various kinds of institutions that
       would normally be considered "post-secondary" or "tertiary"
       institutions?
            Part I: §§6, 7, 15
            Part II: Art. 3, 4, 6

       Is there a single expression that can be used to refer to all of
       these institutions?
            (The expressions used in Part I of the revised draft are
            "Catholic universities and other institutions of higher ed-
            ucation" or "Catholic institutions of higher education";
            these are occasionally abbreviated to "educational insti-
            tution" or "educational center." In Part II, the phrase
            "Catholic university" is used, modified by Article 3.)

2.   How can the "search for truth" in a university be described?
       What elements make up this search?
            Part I: §§ 1, 8–15, 35

3.   What does "Catholic" add to "university"?
            Part I: §§ 16–18, 25–30, 35 and *passim*
            Part II: Art. 1, Art. 48–54, and *passim*

       Do the "characteristics" listed in §1 of *The Catholic University
       in the Modern World* give an adequate description of a Catholic
       institution of higher learning? Should there be any additions or
       changes in this description?
            Part II: Art. 2

4.   How can the *Catholic* nature of a Catholic institution of higher
       learning be manifested more clearly and more effectively?
            Part I: §§ 3–5, 31, 86–90
            Part II: Art. 7 and *passim*

5.   What is the service that the Catholic institution of higher learning should be rendering *today* to the Church and to society?
Part I: §§2, 21–24, 36–38, 51–71
Part II: Art. 5, 44, 45

6.   How is academic freedom to be described or defined? What are the limitations to this "freedom"? When is it legitimate, and when is it possibly an abuse of the end that is intended?
Part I: §§ 21–23, 26, 47, 59–60
Part II: Art. 23

7.   Who is responsible for the Catholic nature of the institution? To what extent is this responsibility shared among the president/rector, the various directors or administrators, the deans, teachers, and others?
Part I: §§ 4, 31, 32, 39, 42, 44, 62, 65
Part II: Art. 27, 28, 31–40, 42, 44–46, 49

To what extent are the local ordinary, the episcopal conference, and the Holy See involved?
Part I: §§ 3, 5, 23, 24, 43
Part II: Art. 8, 10–22, 34

8.   More generally, taking into account the different kinds of institutions, what relationship should exist between a Catholic institution of higher learning and the local ordinary, the episcopal conference, and the Holy See? What are the responsibilities of each?
Part I: §§ 19, 24, 40, 41
Part II: Art. 25–29, 56–58, 63

9.   In theological teaching and research by a member of the Catholic faith, and also in the teaching and research in other areas of knowledge when these touch on faith and morals, how is academic freedom to be reconciled with fidelity to the Magisterium?
Part I: §§ 45–50, 61
Part II: Art. 41

What is the role and the responsibility of the Catholic university as an *institution* (e.g. in its statutes or methods of procedures—again taking into account the different kinds of institutions) in dealing with this tension between freedom and fidelity?
Part I: § 50
Part II: Art. 38, 42

What is the responsibility of other parties (e.g., other theologians, the local ordinary, the episcopal conference, the Holy See)?

> Part I: §§ 47, 48
> Part II: Art. 27–29, 43

10. In a Catholic institution, the presence of members of other faiths can enrich the institution itself and also its dialogue with today's cultures. Recognizing this, and also recognizing the very different situations in different parts of the world, should any preference be given to members of the Catholic Church in hiring teachers, directors, and administrators, and in admitting students? How can a Catholic institution ensure that members of other faiths (or of no faith) who work in the institution as teachers or directors share—or at least accept—its vision and purposes?

> Part I: §§ 33, 44, 70, 71
> Part II: Art. 30, 51, 54

11. What constitutes adequate pastoral care in a Catholic university? In what ways does pastoral care enter into the various aspects of university life (including teaching and research)?

> Part I: §§ 72–79
> Part II: Art. 64–66, 69–70, 72

What are the responsibilities of the local ordinary, and what are the responsibilities of the authorities in the institution, in providing this pastoral care?

> Part I: §§ 80–84
> Part II: Art. 66–68

What responsibility does the university have in providing pastoral care for those teachers, staff, and students who are not members of the Catholic Church (i.e., a pastoral care that includes opportunities for them to grow in their own faith and religious commitment)?

> Part I: § 85
> Part II: Art. 71

Recommendations from the Delegates of the International Meeting on Catholic Higher Education, Rome

April 25, 1989

These recommendations came out of the six groups and then were voted on in General Assembly. Most were unanimously accepted; the highest negative vote was 10. (Voters were ninety presidents and forty bishops).

Pre-Note: The full reports of the six working groups, containing their specific recommendations for the document will be distributed to the entire assembly and passed on to the Congregation. The following presupposes the contents of these six reports. For a fuller understanding of these summary recommendation, one must consult the full texts of the six reports.

1.   The document on the Catholic university should be positive, inspirational, and future-oriented. It should serve to encourage university people in the important mission of the Catholic university for the world and for the Church. It should be written according to academic standards and maintain a world perspective, sensitive to the richly diverse cultures that are the Catholic university's milieu. Whatever normative principles are included in the document should be few in numbers, general in nature, and interpreted and applied in accord with principles to be developed by regional bishops' conferences, taking into account regional laws and institutional status. (I, 9; III, 2, 4; IV, 1)

2.   A Catholic university must have the full autonomy necessary to develop its distinctive identity and pursue its mission of excellence. Freedom of research and teaching must be recognized and respected, so long as the rights of the individual and of the community are preserved within the context of the common good. (I, 3; III, 9)

From the files of the Association of Catholic Colleges and Universities.

3.   A clear distinction should be made between the mission of evangelization given by Christ to the Church through the apostles ("To teach all nations," Mt 28:18–20) and the teaching and research that constitute the mission of the Catholic university. While education and evangelization are related, the university should not be described simply as "an instrument of evangelization." (I, 7; III, 5; V, 5; VI, 8)

4.   When speaking of the Church, the document should reflect the vision of the Church as enunciated in *Lumen Gentium*. Care should be taken to distinguish the different meanings of:

   a) the Church as the realization of the Mystery of Grace,
   b) the Church as the people of God,
   c) the Church as hierarchy.

(II, 7; II, 8; VI, 1–4)

5.   The maintenance and strengthening of the Catholic identity of the university is primarily the responsibility of the university, a responsibility that calls for the attraction of faculty and staff who respect that identity and are both willing and able to promote it. (III, 15)

6.   In order not only to safeguard the freedom of the Church but also to guarantee that the statutes of Catholic universities, as they relate to the civil laws and state governments in each region, be fully respected, competent civil lawyers, as well as canon lawyers, designated by the bishops' conferences in each region, should review the whole document, but particularly its prescriptive norms, before its promulgation. In this context confer the recommendation of working group I on Article 7 of Part II. (I, 15 & 16)

7.   Given the unique importance of the Catholic university, as the place where the Church is present to and participates in the development of human cultures, bishops and episcopal conferences have a responsibility to promote and assist these institutions in maintaining their Catholic identity. Close personal and pastoral relationships should exist between university and Church authorities, characterized by mutual trust, cooperation, and continuing dialogue. Even when they do not enter directly into the internal governance of the university, bishops "should not be seen as external agents but as participants in the life of the Catholic university." (III, 16; I, 7)

8.   Assuming that all provisions of Canon Law regarding Catholic universities and their relations to legitimate ecclesiastical authority are to be fully and faithfully observed, nothing in the final document should extend the juridical meaning or scope of existing canons. In view of the existence of such canons and out of respect for Canon Law, no repetition of such pertinent canons is necessary or appropriate in this document. (IV, 4)

9.   The teaching of theology is of critical importance in a Catholic university, and the Catholic theology that is taught should be faithful to the magisterium of the Church. At the same time, research in theology is necessary and should be encouraged, if the doctrine of the Church is to be not only protected but better understood and communicated. The theological formation of lay persons becomes more important, in the light of the increasingly important role they play in the church, including theological teaching and research. Both philosophy and theology are crucial for that kind of interdisciplinary formation and research that is necessary for a greater integration of knowledge and a deeper comprehension of the human person. (IV, 7, 8, 9)

10.   La universidad católica aspira a ser una communidad participativa en que esten claras las funciones, deberes y derechos de cada estamento. Pretende loqar una formacion de las personans basada en la antropología cristiana y operante a traves del trabajo académico y del servicio en la institución y en la sociedad. Esto evitara cualquier riesgo de indoctrinación y proseltismo.

Así podrán formarse verdaderos lideres, católicos y otros, que esten presentes en todos los centros de creación de cultura, en medio de la civilización científico-técnica y del intercambio con los nuevos pueblos.

The Catholic university seeks to be a community of sharing, where the activities, responsibilities, and rights of each group are clearly defined. Its purpose is to achieve a personal formation that is based on a Christian anthropology and mediated through academic work and service of the institution and society. It thereby avoids all danger of indoctrination and proselytism.

In this way the university is able to form true leaders, both Catholic and non-Catholic, who will be engaged in all of the centers of the creation of culture, in the midst of the scientific–technological civilization as well as in emerging relationships with the new nations of the world. (II, 7; IV, 5, 9)

Address, Pope John Paul II to International Meeting on Catholic Higher Education

Rome
April 25, 1989

Venerable Brothers in the Episcopate, Dear Priests, Illustrious Professors and Teachers:

1.   It is a particular joy for me to be with you on this occasion—the Third International Meeting of Catholic Universities and other Institutions of Higher Education. If you will allow me to say something rather personal, I feel at home with you, since I spent several years in a Catholic university.

As Pastor of the Church, I would like to express my great appreciation for the work that you do in an area that is so important for the good both of humanity and of the Church. I am also grateful for what you have been doing *during these days*, in the course of this present meeting, whose participants include not only delegates of the Catholic universities, but also representatives of the episcopal conferences.

I know that the labor you have been engaged in here at Rome has been intense, but I believe that it has also been profitable work, very profitable for all of you. You have dealt with a theme which is dear to you, a theme which I have also discussed on many occasions, during the course of my visits to various Catholic universities around the world. You have been considering ways to give greater efficacy and a better expression to the two-poled entity "University—Catholic": an entity whose two poles complete and enrich one another, in which both poles must be maintained and brought to ever greater perfection in order to fulfill a task which remains always new and exciting. You must always

Unofficial English Translation from the files of the Association of Catholic Colleges and Universities keep in mind that it is *not only the Church* that looks to the Catholic universities and stands in need of them; *society too, throughout the world, looks to these universities and needs them. The expectations are twofold, convergent, and critical.*

*I*s this really true? Does the world *look to* and need *these universities?*

2.   Yes, because *there is a great deal that the world can receive from Catholic universities.* For the world today is confronted with a number of different challenges, challenges which are the result of its own progress and which today have assumed a universal—or as we often hear a global—dimension.

The tremendous economic development that has taken place in so many countries, a development inevitably tied to technological and scientific progress, has given men and women an awareness of their strengths and abilities, and has given them the capacity to overcome the scourges of hunger and sickness which have afflicted humanity for millennia. A problem which yesterday seemed to be insuperable, almost an impossibility, today has become, from a purely technical point of view, capable of being faced and solved. And yet many countries are still needy and underdeveloped; the same human person who is the artisan of so many new possibilities, all too frequently witnesses practical impossibilities, ones that he or she is not directly responsible for, but which prevent the benefits of development from becoming real. And development itself is often enough unilateral. Such contrasting situations need to be dealt with, and because the source of the difficulty lies within the human will, they must be faced with a strongly renewed moral commitment. We can become capable of this by reflecting once again on the *mystery of the human person*—so capable of greatness and at the same time so capable of misery—and by looking to the transcendent Fountain of justice.

All of us are aware of the fact that, while there can be no doubt that technological and scientific development bring great advantages to humanity, they also bring problematic and disturbing side effects which must be faced with committed and responsible ethical investigation. In addition, there is the crisis resulting from so many ideologies and models of conduct which are prevalent in the changing scene of today which have left men and women without identity and without any existential certainty.

This raises many questions—or, as I have said, many challenges.

3.   It is surely a fact that these challenges have had an effect on the world of the university. You experience them keenly in your own institutions, and they are common to all universities. It is for this reason that the purpose and the role of the university have been the object of study in recent years, in a search for appropriate responses. These studies

have taken place within individual countries, and also in international organizations such as UNESCO and the Council of Europe.

Approaches have been suggested and solutions proposed that are filled with rich and stimulating possibilities. Careful analysis has shown that the response is not to be sought only within a social ambience, as if it were enough to make the university more aware of society's needs and transform it into a training ground for a more efficient and productive work force; nor can the response be simply greater commitment on the level of organization and academic planning, such as multiplying departments, faculties, and specialized institutes. This may all be quite necessary, but it will not be sufficient; the challenge touches on more *basic questions*. What is at stake is *the very meaning of scientific and technological research*, of society, of culture; on a more profound level, what is at stake is *the very meaning of the human person*. Putting it in other words, and with a more general vision, we can say that the challenges have to do with the truth about the world with its laws which have to be discovered and put to use for the good of humanity; and the *truth about God*, the foundation of being, to whom all is to lead and who *alone* gives ultimate meaning to the human person and to the world.

4.   These are questions which are proper to the university world, and which universities must concern themselves with, since the proper role of the university is that of probing, going to the root of the problem. For the university is where the various branches of what can be known are the objects of teaching and of research. And teaching and research can only have the truth as their constant point of reference—their pole star. I am talking, therefore, about the truth as something researched, loved, taught, and promulgated. This is the heart and soul of the university, because it is the source of life for human reason: "Perfectio intellectus est verum"[1] says St. Thomas.

From this perspective we can understand that the university crisis which has developed since the Second World War, and for which remedies are still being sought, is not only organizational, but also spiritual and cultural. It is a crisis not so much of means as of identity, of purpose, and of values.

There is a common and widespread sense today that unity of knowledge has been lost in the area of university research; there is an increasing disparity among the various areas of academic progress which is the result of increasing specialization; there is no longer the search for that profoundly valid relationship among the various disciplines which will find a harmony in the results of their research and orient them to the true service of humanity within a framework of basic ethical principles. The university is meant to be a "living unity" of individual organisms dedicated to the research for truth, but unfortunately we now face the possibility that it will be reduced to a complex group of academic areas which produce only factual results which are, in the end, inarticulate and unrelated. If this is so, or when this is so, then the university will be able to offer an adequate professional formation, but it will no longer be useful for attaining the purposes of a rich and full human formation.

Therefore, it is necessary to work toward a higher synthesis of knowledge, in which alone lies the possibility of satisfying that *thirst for truth* which is profoundly inscribed on the heart of the human person. Augustine expresses this well: "Quid enim fortius desiderat anima quam veritatem?"[2] While all other creatures exist without any knowledge of the why, the intelligence of the human person is the protagonist of an ongoing search for this why. And I am not talking about something which is accidental or occasional. The "why" or the "whys" are ever-present within the fundamental questions of the human spirit. As the lungs need pure air, so the spirit of the human person needs to know the truth: a truth which is not manipulated and not distorted. And it is *this passionate* need *for the truth* which leads to a passionate search for the authentic good of humanity.

It is also within this perspective that the Catholic university can and should develop its own distinctive role within contemporary society, presenting itself as a convincing model of an institution in which research is joined to the search for solutions to fundamental human questions. As the second Christian millennium draws to a close, the Catholic university is presented with an opportunity which must not be missed.

5.   But *the Church also looks to the Catholic university and has need of the Catholic university.*

The challenges which I have referred to also have their effects within the Church, whose salvific mission embraces the total human person, in a concrete historical setting, with all of human problems. It is in this context, in the intertwining of these challenges, that the Church is called to fulfill its evangelical mission. You can understand, therefore, why it looks to the Catholic university, asking for the university's distinctively specific, positive, and enriching contribution toward a more effective accomplishment of the Church's own proper mission. Within the Catholic university *the evangelical mission of the Church and the university mission of research and of teaching* become *interrelated* and coordinated. For the response to these challenges must be developed culturally and scientifically, and the specific role of the Catholic university is to provide this perspective with adequate instruments and with the necessary professionalism. It is in this way that the university, while retaining its own proper nature as a university, will assist the Church in becoming sensitive to today's cultural needs and responding to them with adequate initiatives.

In fulfilling this role the means that the Catholic university uses are the same as those of any other university. However, in the conduct of its academic research, it can rely on a superior enlightenment which, without changing the nature of this research, purifies it, orients it, enriches it, and lifts it up. It is *the light of faith, the light of Christ* who has said "I am the Way, the Truth, and the Life."[3]

This light is not found *"outside"* of *rational research*, as a limitation or an impediment, but rather *"above"* it, as its elevation and an expansion of its horizons: the light of faith opens the way to the completion of truth, although it obviously does not dispense the Catholic university from the difficult and frustrating toil that research involves. It is a Light which aids and assists!

6.   Within the context of these needs which have already been indicated, the Catholic university must be willing to commit itself along certain specific lines:

a) Above all, a commitment in the dialogue with *science*: while it recognizes and promotes the value of knowledge, the Catholic university must be ever mindful of the limitations of science, and conduct itself in such a way that science is and always remains for the benefit of the human person and is never transformed into a destructive agent. This will be true only if the research and, more generally the scientific method, is always placed within a framework of ethical values.

b) Concerning social disparities, while the Catholic university will actively cooperate in the development of the technological means to overcome these disparities, it will never cease reminding the various social and political agents concerned that the problem of human development, beginning with those least fortunate, is much more an ethical problem than a technical one.[4]

c) The Catholic university must recognize the dignity and creativity within the various cultures of the world, but at the same time be committed to their purification and elevation through the light and active force of the Gospel—a process which in no way sacrifices what is authentically human; whatever is truly valid is developed and brought to complete and fruitful reality.[5] As I have written in my Exhortation *Christifideles laici*, "the Church asks lay people to be present, with outstanding courage and intellectual creativity, in the privileged posts of culture."[6]

d) And finally, in what concerns the *human person*, the Catholic university must inspire all of its activity with an integral humanistic vision so that all of its dimensions, including the spiritual, moral, and religious, are valued and cultivated. Only in such an anthropology will there be sufficient room for all of the existential demands of man.

7.   But the *supreme criterion*, in whose light the Catholic university must measure all its options, remains *Christ, the Incarnate Word* who

is the full Truth about the human person, the Teacher who lives within us, the universal Brother, in whom men and women find the meaning of life: the divine gift of solidarity and of fraternity; Christ, the Savior of all men and women of all times and every culture; Christ, the Son of God and at the same time the new Man, in whom subsists the fullness of divinity[7] with the fullness of humanity.

This Catholic character—perhaps Christocentric is a better expression—does not distort the university or restrict its legitimate autonomy as a place of moral formation and of free research; it recognizes and even confirms this autonomy, helping the university to realize its own true nature and to overcome the dangers of distortion.

It is precisely for this reason that the distinctive character of a Catholic university can become a *critical and prophetic voice* as it confronts a society which is becoming ever more characterized by a "persistent spreading of religious indifference and atheism in their various forms, especially in the form of secularism which is perhaps the most common form today."[8] On this subject it must have the courage to speak a truth which is not convenient, a truth which does not flatter, but a truth which is absolutely necessary in order to safeguard the true dignity of the human person. It must remind the world of culture that, while it is surely true that men and women can organize the world *without God,* without God it will, in the last analysis, be organized *against humanity.*[9]

8.   If, therefore, there is some urgency today in looking to the life of the Catholic university, it is not in order to weaken or distort it. Rather, the purpose is to deepen and strengthen its Catholic character, *on both the theoretical and the practical levels.* The expectations of today's society have become more vast and complex. It has today a function, or rather a mission, which goes far beyond the traditional role of establishing a *rapport between faith and reason,* a rapport which has to be deep-rooted in both research and in study, for both teachers and students. Its mission touches on and even embraces the vast and numerous areas of knowledge and, in a particular way, of scientific knowledge: which has seen vast new developments in today's world, which has opened up new horizons, which has been extended to new geographical areas and has reached new peoples. A Catholic university must become fully aware of its growing responsibility for verifying what is authentically moral and human in this progress and expansion. For experience has amply demonstrated the fact that *scientific* advancement is not always and necessarily equivalent to *moral and human* progress, balanced and shared.

Some of your universities also have non-Catholics within their communities, members of other Churches and religions, or those of no belief. These young people—men and women—can contribute a diversity of cultural and human experiences that should be acknowledged and are worthy of study. While it welcomes them and the contributions they bring, the Catholic university should also offer them the concrete possibility of knowing the genuine Christian message with its liberating and salvific strength. It is only right that, without any loss of respect for their freedom, these persons be given an opportunity to develop a Christian vision of the world and of life: this is a new opportunity which will be the more effective the more that the community of believers within the Catholic university are able to give witness, through a *coherent Christian life*, to the beauty and the greatness of the Gospel.

9.   With an awareness of these new responsibilities, delegates from Catholic universities throughout the world published a document in 1972 entitled "The Catholic University in the Modern World." In this document, at the very beginning, stress is laid on the fact that the adjective "Catholic" makes such a university distinctive through an institutional commitment. This must be a fundamental principle, involving the whole being of the university: in its organizational, directive, and academic structure, and also in its programs, in the ambience, and in the formation which is given to its students. The "Catholic" character must be visible and open. It will be expressly indicated in the statutes, or in some equivalent document, and, I repeat, must be translated into concrete decisions. But, more important than any written text or study plan, there is the question of a style and an atmosphere!

Seventeen years after the conclusion of the 1972 meeting, you have come together once again to reflect on this responsibility. The new element which characterizes this present meeting is the participation of representatives from the episcopates where Catholic universities are located, along with delegates of these universities and of other institutes of higher education, members of religious congregations which are responsible for Catholic universities, and also of some of the organizations of the Holy See. Such a presence indicates not only a wider interest in Catholic universities, but also a greater attention and sensitivity to the ecclesial values to be found in them. While the Catholic university is in society and in history, it is also in the Church.

It is apparent, therefore, that one question must inevitably be asked: *what kind of Catholic university is needed today?* A response to this question can only be given after we clarify a second question: *what ecclesial sense does the Catholic university have today?* And here our horizon is expanded by the need to reflect carefully on the two great Constitutions of the Second Vatican Council, *Lumen gentium* and *Gaudium et spes*, and, more specifically, on the Declaration *Gravissimum educationis*, nn. 7–10.

As we come to a deeper understanding, with the help of the Conciliar documents, of the *ecclesial function of the Catholic university*, we should become more clearly conscious of the role that the Magisterium of the Church has to play: a role of stimulus and encouragement, of enlightenment and guidance along a path which must always be directed toward the full truth. In this context, I would like to repeat what I said in a talk given at The Catholic University of America in October of 1979: "If your colleges and universities are institutionally joined to the Christian message, and if they are part of the Catholic evangelizing community, then it follows that they have an essential relationship with the hierarchy of the Church."[10]

10.   The fruit of such a deeper understanding should be a new "harmony": a closer and more faithful collaboration between the episcopate, the religious families, the ecclesial offices and the faithful on the one hand, and the universities and other Catholic institutions on the other; this will ensure that each activity undertaken within the ambience of these universities is in harmony with the Catholic nature of the institution. You and your universities should be proud of the title "Catholic," as suggested in the eloquent words of my predecessor Paul VI: "While equal to other universities in academic efforts and quality, and like them also in patterns and attainments, a Catholic university must not be afraid to be seen as different and original because of what can be called its baptism: this is a stimulus rather than a burden, which does not separate it from the world of culture, but rather enables it to enter this world with a more friendly and honest posture, not for vainglory but for the commitment of converting it."[11]

Such a mandate, given by this unforgettable Pontiff, remains valid today: if Christ is the Truth who illumines, frees, and gives meaning to life, if He is the complete response to the profound and persistent questioning of men and women, then *the truth which is Christ, the Truth which Christ has*, should be found within the Catholic university as a source of light for others, for the world. Jesus has said to us, "men do not light a lamp and then put it under a bushel basket. They set it on a stand where it gives light to all."[12]

Do not be afraid, then, beloved Brothers and illustrious Teachers, to profess the Catholicity of your institutions! A Catholic university and all those who work in it ought to be convinced that the Catholic character assists in the more complete and effective accomplishment of the mission of a university in the world of today.

Asking God to bless your commitment in an area that is so important for the life of the Church and of society, I impart to all of you here present and to all those who work with you, dedicating their energies in various locations throughout the world to such an important task, the most noble among all others, a special and comforting Apostolic Benediction.

NOTES

1. "Truth is the perfection of the intellect." *Contra Gentes*, III, 51.

2. "What is there that the soul desires more strongly than truth?" (*Tract. in Ioannem*, 26.5; PL 35, 1609.)

3. John 14:6.

4. Cf. the encyclical *Sollicitudo Rei Socialis*, 33.

5. Cf. the Pastoral Constitution (*Gaudium et Spes*), 58; the Apostolic Exhortation of Paul VI (*Evangelii Nuntiandi*), 20).

6. No. 44.

7. Cf. Col 2:9.

8. Apostolic Exhortation (*Christifideles laici*), 4.

9. Cf. Henri de Lubac, *The Drama of Atheistic Humanism*, p. 9.

10. Teachings of John Paul II, 1979 II, 2, p. 689.

11. Teachings of Paul VI, 1964, p. 237.

12. Mt 5:15

Revised Draft Schema for a Pontifical Document on Catholic Higher Education

July 1989

PART I: THE IDENTITY AND MISSION OF A CATHOLIC UNIVERSITY

(1)   A Catholic university[1] probes the mysteries of the universe and the human spirit in an ongoing search for truth; because it is Catholic, it enriches and illumines this search with the light of the Christian message. It undertakes specialized research in an ethical and religious professional training that is joined to humanistic, moral, and spiritual formation. While contributing to the progress of culture through its educational activities, it also finds in these activities an opportunity to bring the Gospel of Christ into dialogue with culture and the cultures of specific groups of people.[2]

(2)   The Church is grateful for these many services which Catholic universities offer to society and to the People of God. Convinced that the need for Catholic universities and their activities will become ever more essential in an increasingly complex world, it urges these institutions to preserve and strengthen their distinctive nature, so that "the Christian mind may achieve a public, persistent, and universal presence in the whole enterprise of advancing higher culture, and that the students of these institutions may become men and women truly outstanding in learning, ready to shoulder society's heavier burdens and to witness the faith to the world."[3] This document is written to encourage Catholic universities and their communities, and to assist them in preserving and strengthening their identity and renewing their dedication.

From the files of the Association of Catholic Colleges and Universities

A. The Identity of a Catholic University

1. Nature and Objectives

(3)   A Catholic university, as a *university*, is an academic community which, in a critical fashion, assists in the protection and advancement of a cultural heritage and of human dignity through research, teaching, and various services offered to the local, national, and international communities.[4] It is entrusted with that institutional autonomy necessary to perform its functions effectively and, so long as the rights of the individual and of the community are preserved within the context of the common good,[5] its members are guaranteed academic freedom.[6]

(4)   A Catholic university, as *Catholic*, has the following essential characteristics:

1. a Christian inspiration not only of individuals but of the university community as such;
2. a continuing reflection in the light of the Catholic faith upon the growing treasury of human knowledge, to which it seeks to contribute by its own research;
3. fidelity to the Christian message as it comes to us through the Church;
4. an institutional commitment to the service of the people of God and of the human family in their pilgrimage to the transcendent goal which gives meaning to life.[7]

(5)   A Catholic university, therefore, is a place where scholars *scrutinize reality* with the methods proper to each academic discipline, and so contribute to the treasury of human knowledge. The individual disciplines are studied and taught in a systematic manner, but are brought into dialogue, both in research and in teaching, for their mutual enhancement and integration.

(6)   Research is intimately linked to a concern for the *ethical and moral implications* involved both in the methods and in the discoveries of research, in order to enable men and women to "measure according to criteria of truth the means to the ends, the projects to the ideals, the actions to the moral parameters which permit a balance of values to be established anew."[8] This concern has a particular application to scientific and technological research, for growth in scientific knowledge without regard for its implications, and without a corresponding growth in the human spirit, will inevitably lead to a misuse of science that can only diminish, and possibly destroy, humanity.

(7)   In order that each discipline may contribute to an ordered vision of reality, university scholars are engaged in a constant search for an integration or *synthesis* among the various branches of human

knowledge, determining the place and meaning of the various disciplines within the context of a vision of the human person and the world that is enlightened by the Gospel.[9] The explosion of knowledge and its compartmentalization within the individual academic disciplines make the process of integration increasingly difficult, and the task will always remain incomplete. Nevertheless, convinced of its vital importance, a Catholic university gives priority to efforts directed toward an integration of knowledge, aided in this search for meaning by the specific and essential contributions of philosophy. Both philosophy and theology are crucial for that kind of interdisciplinary research that is necessary for a greater integration of knowledge and a deeper comprehension of the human person. "The university is meant to be a 'living union' of individual organisms dedicated to the search for the truth."[10]

(8) Its Christian inspiration gives the Catholic university a unique opportunity to promote the *dialogue between reason and faith*, showing that "methodical research within every branch of learning, when carried out in a truly scientific manner and in accord with moral norms, can never truly conflict with faith. For the things of the earth and the concerns of faith derive from the same God."[11] Scholars in the Catholic university pursue a wisdom which embraces and integrates reason with intuition, emotions, cultural traditions, and faith, demonstrating how the interaction of the two levels of truth, the truths of reason and the truths of faith, give fuller meaning to human life, contribute to a better understanding of the world, and lead to a greater love for truth, and for the one Truth who is their source.

(9) Theology has a particular importance among the academic disciplines. Research in theology is necessary and should be encouraged, if the doctrine of the Church is to be not only protected but better understood and communicated. Theological research probes the truths of faith in order to come to a deeper understanding of their meaning and of their application to the specific questions raised by contemporary culture. The results of this research serve the humanities and the human and positive sciences by bringing a perspective and an orientation not contained within their own methodologies and by helping them to investigate how their discoveries will affect individuals and society. Through dialogue with these other disciplines and their discoveries, theology in turn is enriched: it is helped to comprehend the world today, especially the scientific and technological world, and is thus better able to make its own theological research relevant and express the truths of faith in a way that can be understood.

(10) Academic research and university teaching are intimately related, so that the education offered to the students necessarily includes a concern for the ethical and moral dimension of what is being learned, and

stresses the need for an integration of knowledge. The philosophical and theological reflection that is a part of their education will enable students to develop a critical judgment in their search for meaning and bring them to an awareness of the Gospel values which enrich the meaning of human life and give it a new dignity. The teaching of theology is of critical importance in a Catholic university, and the Catholic theology that is taught should be faithful to the magisterium of the Church.

2. The University Community

(11) A Catholic university attains its objectives not only through academic pursuits but also through efforts at forming a genuine human community. This university community is animated by a spirit of freedom, charity, and respect for the particular character of the institution; it is characterized by mutual respect, sincere dialogue, protection of the rights of individuals, and a concern for those in need; its inspiration and source of unity flow from a common dedication to the truth, a common vision of the dignity of the human person and, ultimately, from the person and message of Christ.[12] Each member of the community helps to promote unity, and each one contributes, according to his or her role and capacity, toward decisions which affect the community, and toward maintaining and strengthening the Catholic character of the institution. (12) *University teachers* try to unite true educational wisdom with intellectual honesty and competence in their respective disciplines, and to communicate the objectives, methods, and results of research within the context of a coherent world vision. Christians among the teachers are called to be "witnesses and educators of authentic Christian life,"[13] which evidences an attained integration between faith and culture, between professional competence and Christian wisdom. (13) *Students* are challenged to pursue an education that combines excellence in humanistic and cultural formation with specialized professional training, and they are encouraged to form critical minds which will compel them to continue the search for truth and for meaning throughout their lives; they are guided and enlightened by Christian thought and Christian principles, so that they may become "more spiritually mature, more aware of the dignity of their humanity, more responsible and more open to all others, more disposed to give and offer help to all."[14] For those able to respond, especially Catholic students, this enables them to "acquire or, if they have already done so, to deepen an authentically Christian life-style. They should realize the responsibility of their professional life, the enthusiasm of being the trained 'leaders' of tomorrow, of being witnesses to Christ in whatever place they may exercise their profession."[15]

(14) The university community also includes *directors*, who promote the constant growth of the university and its community through a leadership of service, and the *non-academic staff*, whose dedication and witness are integral to the life of the university and its influence on Church and on society.

(15) The community in a Catholic university today is largely composed of lay men and women; in increasing numbers, they are assuming the direction of these institutions. These lay people have always exercised an apostolic role in the Church through their university activities; today these institutions are being entrusted to them by the Church with hope and with confidence, convinced that they will "organize these affairs in such a way that they may always start out, develop, and continue according to Christ's mind, to the praise of the Creator and the Redeemer."[16]

(16) In many countries, a Catholic university welcomes members of other churches, ecclesiastical communities, and religions, and also those with no faith, as a part of its university community. These men and women contribute their training and experience to the various academic disciplines or other university tasks; many of them, recognizing its value, contribute positively to the distinctive Catholic identity of the institution.

3. Pastoral Ministry

(17) Pastoral ministry is that dimension of the university which integrates religious and moral values into academic life, thus assisting in the total formation of the human person. A university community concerned with promoting the institution's Catholic character will be conscious of this pastoral dimension, and sensitive to the ways in which it can have an influence on its various educational activities. Pastoral ministry, therefore, will be well integrated both into the structure and into the community life of the university.

(18) The goal of pastoral ministry is helped by transforming the university community into a *community of faith* and a *worshipping community*.[17] Catholic members of the academic community are enabled to assimilate Catholic teaching and practice into their lives, and they are encouraged to participate in and celebrate the sacraments, especially the Sacrament of Reconciliation and above all, the Eucharist as the most perfect community act of worship. When the individuals within the academic community are members of several different churches, ecclesial communities, or religions, opportunities can be provided for ecumenical celebrations, or interreligious celebrations of a common belief in God.

(19) The faith community becomes apostolic by *translating prayer and worship into action*. Pastoral ministry assists individuals   to develop

a commitment to help those in need, beginning within the academic community itself and reaching out to the larger community in society. It promotes a dedication to work for social justice as an implementation of the Gospel and the social teachings of the Church.

(20) Various associations or movements of apostolic life, especially those developed specifically for students, can be of great assistance in developing the pastoral aspects of university life, but the activities of these movements within the university need to be coordinated in such a way that they unite rather than divide the university community.

(21) Finally, pastoral ministry can assist in developing and nurturing marriage and family life, and fostering vocations to the priesthood and to religious life; more generally, it is an important means by which students can be prepared for active participation in the life of the Church. Close cooperation between pastoral ministry and the parishes, under the guidance of the local bishop, will contribute to the growth of both.

B. The Catholic University in Society

(22) Every Catholic university is deeply immersed in human society, sharing in the hopes and frustrations, the joys and difficulties of that society and of the individuals that compose it at a given time in history. The university community is in constant dialogue with society in order to determine the needs which it can respond to through its educational activities.

(23) Its research and teaching bring it into immediate contact with some of the crucial issues affecting society and its cultural growth today; this will stimulate the Catholic university, always within its own competence as an educational institution, to be an effective instrument of progress for both society and individuals.[18] It will make all members of the academic community sensitive to the urgent need to seek solutions to current problems in areas such as the quality and dignity of human life, the family, the protection of nature, and a new economic and political order that will promote the human community at an international level. As an institution "in which research is joined to the search for solutions to fundamental human questions,"[19] it will probe the depths and complexity of these modern problems in order to discover their roots and their causes, to bring Gospel principles to bear on proposals which will contribute to a solution.

(24) A Catholic university will be especially concerned with examining from a Christian point of view, and with the help of the social teachings of the Church, the values and norms which are predominant in modern society. It will try to communicate to society today those religious principles which give meaning to human life. In this way, it will contribute

to the development of a true Christian anthropology, whose source is the person of Christ, and which brings the reality and the dynamism of the creation and redemption to bear on the reality and the issues of contemporary life.[20]

(25) Of particular urgency in today's world are problems connected with social justice such as a more just distribution of the world's riches and the search for peace and political stability, promoting "the development of those people who are striving to escape from hunger, misery, endemic diseases, and ignorance; of those who are looking for a wider share in the benefits of civilization and a more active improvement of their human qualities; of those who are aiming purposefully at their complete fulfillment."[21] Every Catholic university has a responsibility to help in promoting development in emerging nations; of equal importance is that each institution, through means within its own competence as a center of learning, contribute to the progress of the specific society in which it is located.[22] The Catholic Church has fully committed itself to the integral growth of all men and women, basing its teaching on an ethical and cultural concept of human development.[23] Every Catholic university will try to foster in its teachers, and develop in its students, this Christian spirit of service to others.

(26) In its attempts to assist in dealing with these complex issues that touch on so many different aspects of human experience, the Catholic university will insist on cooperation among the different academic disciplines, each offering its own distinct contribution in the search for solutions;[24] since the economic and personal resources of individual institutions are limited, cooperation in common research projects and common planning among different Catholic universities as well as cooperation with other private and governmental institutions is essential, even though not easily accomplished. In today's profoundly pluralistic society, the Catholic university respects the identity and freedom of institutions which are not Catholic, and is enriched by dialogue with them.

(27) Through programs of continuing education, and with the assistance of modern means of communication, the Catholic university assists in making the growing body of human knowledge and a developing understanding of the faith available to everyone, expanding the services of the university beyond its own university community.

(28) University authorities communicate regularly with civil authorities as a means of ensuring the institutional freedom and autonomy proper to an institution of higher learning. Together, they will look for ways to make university education available to everyone who can profit from it, especially the poor or members of minority groups who have traditionally been deprived of it.

C. The Catholic University in the Church

(29) Without losing its distinctive identity as a university, and without lessening its vital contact with society, every Catholic university is a part of the Church and has a close relationship with its pastors. Each individual institution derives some of its characteristics from the local Church in which it is situated and participates in the life of that local Church, but the same institution, because it is a university and therefore a part of the international community of scholarship and inquiry, necessarily exercises a more universal influence, contributing to the life of the universal Church.

(30) These Catholic institutions offer their intellectual and spiritual resources to the People of God, making scholarly discoveries available to them, assisting them in a mature and responsible living of their Christian vocation, and preparing men and women inspired by Christian principles who will be capable of assuming positions of responsibility in the Church and in society. They offer theological formation to lay persons, which becomes more important in the light of the increasingly important role they play in the Church, including theological teaching and research. Students, parents, parishes, and bishops look to them for assistance in bringing Christian thought to bear on the problems of contemporary life. They are one of the most important ways in which the Church is guaranteed a presence in the academic world and in the world of higher culture.

(31) Given this great importance of the Catholic university as a place where the Church is present to and participates in the development of human cultures, Catholic institutions of higher education have a right to the Church's encouragement and support. Bishops and priests, recognizing their value, encourage the entire People of God to support these institutions in their educational efforts, help them to maintain and protect their freedom in civil society, and try to assist in the establishment of new Catholic universities where they are needed. Religious congregations continue to give priority to these institutions in their apostolic work. In many countries, Catholic institutions are also dependent on the economic support of the bishops and the Church community.

(32) The university's fidelity to the Christian message includes a recognition of and adherence to the teaching authority of the Church in matters of faith and morals;[25] this inspiration permeates institutional policy, teaching, research, pastoral activities, and the life witness of members of the university community. Fidelity to the church is expected of Catholic members of the university community; while freedom of conscience and religious liberty are to be preserved, those in the university who are not Catholics are expected to respect the character of the institution, and so respect its fidelity to the Church.

(33) Bishops have a responsibility to assist these institutions in maintaining their Catholic identity. Close personal and pastoral relationships should exist between university and Church authorities, characterized by mutual trust, close cooperation, and continuing dialogue. Even when they do not enter directly into the internal governance of the university, bishops "should be seen not as external agents but as participants in the life of the Catholic university."[26]

(34) The Church recognizes the freedom and responsibility of each academic discipline to search for truth in accordance with its own principles and proper methods;[27] theology, as a legitimate academic discipline, has the same freedom and responsibility. This discipline, however, searches for an understanding of revealed truth, whose authentic interpretation is entrusted to the pastors of the Church.[28] This means that a Catholic theologian, serving a community of faith, assents to Catholic doctrine according to the degree of authority with which it is taught,[29] and maintains a reverence for the bishops as its authentic teachers, as an integral part of the principles and methods of the academic discipline itself, both in research and in teaching.[30]

(35) Members of the university community, like all the faithful, "have the right, indeed at times the duty, in keeping with their knowledge, competence, and position, to manifest to the sacred pastors their views on matters which concern the good of the Church."[31] This right includes the right to make their views known to others, "but in doing so they must always respect the integrity of faith and morals, show due reverence to the pastors and take into account both the common good and the dignity of individuals."[32] Because of the immediate and widespread publication of university research in communications media, that responsibility takes on new importance today.

(36) "In a Catholic university, therefore, Catholic ideals, attitudes, and principles penetrate and inform university activities in accordance with the proper nature and autonomy of these activities. In a word, being both a university and Catholic, it must be both a community of scholars representing various branches of human knowledge, and an academic institution in which Catholicism is vitally present and operative.[33]

D. THE MISSION OF THE CATHOLIC UNIVERSITY

1. Cultural and Religious Dialogue

(37) Every university "is naturally part of the cultural heritage of a people."[34] It develops culture through its research, transmits the local culture to each succeeding generation through its teaching, and assists cultures through its educational services. It is open to all human

experience, ready to dialogue with and learn from any individual and any culture. A Catholic university, inspired by the Christian message, brings a faith vision of the divine origin and the transcendent destiny of the human person to this dialogue. It constitutes a living witness to Christ and His message, so vitally important in cultures marked by secularism, or where Christ and His message are still virtually unknown. A Catholic university, therefore, is a primary and privileged place for the dialogue between faith and culture.

(38) Through this dialogue, carried on within and as part of its educational activities, the Catholic university seeks to know and understand the different cultures of society as well as various cultural traditions within the Church itself; it examines and evaluates cultural values and it examines its own values, identity, and specific characteristics in the light of these cultures. Interdisciplinary research measures cultures against the Gospel so that they can be strengthened, perfected, and restored in Christ.[35] In different ways that vary with the different academic disciplines, the Christian vision of the human person known through faith is translated into the language of human cultures and all authentic human values found in the various cultures are assumed and integrated into this vision. The Catholic university, finally, has a unique opportunity to promote fruitful dialogue and understanding among different cultures, thus contributing to a spirit of solidarity and peace among nations.

(39) The Catholic university assists the Church through this dialogue, helping it to relate to and be influenced by specific cultural values; it provides the Church with the means to make the faith better understood by the men and women of a particular culture.[36] "A faith that places itself on the margin of what is human, of what is therefore culture, would be a faith unfaithful to the fullness of what the word of God manifests and reveals, a decapitated faith, worse still, a faith in the process of self-annihilation.[37]

(40) Religious dialogue is an extension of this dialogue with culture. A Catholic university assists in analyzing, clarifying, and understanding the dynamics within other religions, and the relationship between faith and culture; without compromising its own identity, it is open to other religions in a recognition of their heritage and of their contributions to cultural development.

(41) The presence of professors and students of other churches and religions, and those with no belief, in an academic setting that promotes open dialogue in the search for truth, is particularly important for the promotion of ecumenical and inter-religious dialogue as well as dialogue with unbelief; this dialogue within the university can help to bring about the understanding an acceptance that are essential for the beginnings of

a movement toward unity among Christians and solidarity among all in serving the human family.

(42) Catholic institutions located in countries where the Catholic faith is little known and often misunderstood have a particular importance in the dialogue with the followers of other religions, beliefs, or ideologies. In their dialogue they will "acknowledge, preserve, and promote the spiritual and moral goods found among these men and women, as well as the values in their society and culture,"[38] helping to develop a local culture that may, in time, come to a better understanding and appreciation of the Christian faith.

2. Evangelization

(43) Evangelization is the primary and most fundamental work of the Church: to preach the Gospel in such a way that a relationship between faith and life is ensured both in the individual and in the socio-cultural context in which individuals live and act and communicate with one another. Evangelization, therefore, is much more than catechesis; it means "bringing the Good News into all the strata of humanity, and through its influence transforming humanity from within and making it new . . . . It is a question not only of preaching the gospel in ever wider geographic areas or to ever greater numbers of people, but also of affecting and as it were upsetting, through the power of the Gospel, humanity's criteria of judgment, determining values, points of interest, lines of thought, sources of inspiration, and models of life, which are in contrast with the Word of God and the plan of salvation."[39]

(44) While it is true that the educational mission of a Catholic university is and must remain distinct from the evangelizing mission of the Church, the description of the identity and role of the Catholic university given on these pages provides amble evidence of the important contribution that Catholic universities offer to the Church in its work of evangelization. Through the educational work of a Catholic university, the Church can come to a careful and precise knowledge of the values, thoughts, and aspirations of the men and women living in today's world, and can study the cultural, scientific, and technological influences which determine so many of the models of life today. Moreover, the basic activities of a Catholic university—research carried out in the light of the Christian message, putting new human discoveries at the service of individuals and society, formation done in a faith context that forms rational and critical persons conscious of the transcendent dignity of the human person, professional training that incorporates ethical values and a sense of service to individuals and to society—all "transform humanity from within and make it new." "Precisely because it is more and more

conscious of its salvific mission in this world, the Church wants to have these centers closely connected with it; it wants to have them present and operative in spreading the authentic message of Christ."[40]

(45) Because they bring Christ and the Christian message into union with the development of the human person, Catholic universities "show concretely that intelligence is never diminished, but is on the contrary stimulated and strengthened by that inner source of deep understanding which is the Word of God, and by the hierarchy of values derived from it.... In its unique way, the Catholic university contributes to manifesting the superiority of the spirit, which can never, under pain of being lost, agree to put itself at the service of anything other than the search for truth."[41]

(46) The description of the nature and mission of a Catholic university given in this first section is made more concrete in the general normative principles which follow in Part II; these *Normae Generales,"* necessary to maintain and strengthen the distinctive Catholic identity of the universities,[42] presuppose, and accordingly do not repeat, the Code of Canon Law (especially Canons 807 to 814) and other relevant Church legislation. The *Normae Generales* are to be applied at the local and regional levels in accord with principles to be developed by episcopal conferences and assemblies of Catholic hierarchy,[43] taking into account institutional statutes and, as far as possible, civil law; in addition, according to need, the principles to be developed should also be applicable to the other institutions of higher education in the region.[44] The work of the conferences and assemblies is to be submitted to the Holy See for its approval.

PART II: NORMAE GENERALES

Article 1 The Nature of a Catholic University.

§1 A Catholic university, as Catholic, is linked with the Church either by a formal, constitutive, and statutory bond, or by reason of an institutional commitment on the part of those responsible for it, animating its academic teaching, scientific research, and all other activities with a Catholic spirit.

§2 Every Catholic university will make known its Catholic identity, either in a mission statement or in some other appropriate public document, unless authorized otherwise by the competent ecclesiastical authority. It will provide its organization with the means to assure the expression and the preservation of this identity in a manner consistent with §1.

§3 A Catholic university possesses the autonomy necessary to develop its distinctive identity and pursue its proper mission. Freedom in research and teaching is recognized and respected, so long as the rights of the individual and of the community are preserved within the context of the common good.[45]

Article 2. The Establishment of a Catholic University.

§1 A Catholic university may be established or approved by the Holy See, by an episcopal conference or an assembly of Catholic hierarchy, by a diocesan bishop, or by a religious institute or other public juridical person with the consent of the diocesan bishop. In each case, the statutes of the university are to be approved by the ecclesiastical authority on whom the university depends.

§2 A Catholic university may also be established by other ecclesiastical or lay persons; such a university may call itself a "Catholic University" only with the consent of the competent ecclesiastical authority, with conditions which they shall agree upon.

Article 3. The University Community.

§1 The responsibility for maintaining and strengthening the Catholic identity of the university rests primarily with the university itself.[46] While this responsibility is entrusted principally to university authorities, it is shared in varying degrees by all members of the university community, and therefore calls for the selection of faculty and staff who respect that identity and are both willing and able to promote it.

§2 University authorities, teachers, students, and non-academic staff who belong to other churches and religions are expected to recognize and respect the character of the Catholic university.

§3 At the time of appointment, teachers are to be informed about the Catholic identity of the institution and its implications and their responsibility to respect and promote this identity, and about their own responsibilities with regard to Catholic doctrine and morals as teachers in a Catholic university.

Article 4. University Activities.

§1 While respecting freedom of religion, Catholic teaching and practice influence all university activities. The Catholic identity of the university is to be respected in any official university recognition of individuals or of groups.

§2 In ways appropriate to the different academic disciplines, teachers will be faithful to Catholic doctrine in their research and teaching. Catholic theologians are faithful to the Magisterium of the Church; they recognize and accept the right of the bishops of the Church, as the authentic interpreters of Catholic doctrine,[47] to judge the conformity of their theological research and teaching with authentic Catholicity and with divine revelation.[48]

§3 The education of students is to be integral, combining academic and professional formation with religious and moral principles and the social teachings of the Church; the programs of studies for each of the various professions is to include an appropriate ethical formation in that profession. Catholic students are to be given courses in Catholic doctrine and helped to become active witnesses of the Catholic faith.[49]

Article 5. Pastoral Ministry.

§1 A Catholic university is to be attentive to the pastoral care of all members of the university community. Priority is to be given to those means which will facilitate the integration of human and professional endeavors with religious values in the light of Catholic doctrine, in order to unite intellectual learning with religious living.[50]

§2 A sufficient number of priests and other qualified persons are to be appointed to provide pastoral ministry for the university community, carried on in harmony and cooperation with the pastoral ministry of the local Church under the guidance of the diocesan bishop.[51] Both teachers and students are to be invited to collaborate in pastoral activities, and to assist the work of pastoral ministry in whatever ways are possible.

Article 6. Cooperation.

§1 Regional, national, and international cooperation is to be promoted, both in research and in teaching: among Catholic universities, between Catholic universities and ecclesiastical universities and faculties,[52] and also with other universities, both private and governmental.

§2 Catholic universities will, when possible and in accord with Catholic principles and doctrine, cooperate with government programs and the programs of other national and international organizations.

Article 7. The Catholic University within the Church.

§1 The university is to maintain close contact with the local Church, and in particular with the diocesan bishops of the region or regions in which it is located. In ways consistent with its nature as a university, it collaborates actively in the work of evangelization.

§2 Each diocesan bishop has a responsibility to promote the welfare of the Catholic universities in his region and has the right and duty to watch over the preservation and strengthening of their Catholic character. If problems should arise concerning this Catholic character, the bishop is to resolve the matter by working with authorities on whom the university depends in accordance with established procedures which, for universities of article 2 §1, are to be in the university statutes approved by the ecclesiastical authority and, for other Catholic universities, are to be determined by episcopal conferences or assemblies of Catholic hierarchy.

§3 Periodically, each Catholic university of Article 2 §1 is to send relevant information about the university and its activities to the ecclesiastical authority on which it depends. Other Catholic universities are to communicate this information to the bishop of the diocese in which the principal seat of the institution is located.

NOTES

1. In addition to Catholic universities, there are many other types of Catholic institutions of higher education; depending on their own nature and objectives, they share some or all of the qualities of a university. While this document speaks explicitly of a Catholic university, it can be applied to all Catholic institutions of higher education by making the adaptations and qualifications necessary for each specific kind of institution.

2. "The word 'culture' in its general sense indicates all those factors by which a person refines and unfolds his or her manifold spiritual and bodily qualities. It means the effort to bring the world itself under control through human knowledge and human labor. It includes the fact that by improving customs and institutions, social life is rendered more human both within the family and in the civic community. Finally, it is a feature of culture that throughout the course of time people express, communicate, and conserve in their works great spiritual experiences and desires, so that these may be of advantage to the progress of many, even the whole family." (Vatican Council II, Pastoral Constitution on the Church in the Modern World (*Gaudium et Spes*), n. 53: *AAS* 58 [1966], p. 1075.) The plural "cultures" reflects the sociological and ethnological ways in which culture develops among specific groups of people. (Cf. ibid.)

3. Vatican Council II, Declaration on Catholic Education (*Gravissimum Educationis*), n. 10: *AAS* 58 (1966), p. 737.

4. Cf. *The Magna Carta of European Universities*, Bologna, Italy, September 18, 1988, "Fundamental Principles."

5. Cf. *Gaudium et Spes*, nn. 57 and 59: *AAS* 58 (1966), pp. 1078–1080; *Gravissimum Educationis*, n. 10: *AAS* 58 (1966), p. 737.

6. "Institutional autonomy" means that the governance of an academic institution is and remains internal to the institution; "Academic freedom" is the guarantee given to those involved in teaching and research that, within their specific specialized branch of knowledge, and according to the methods proper to that specific area, they may search for the truth wherever analysis and evidence leads them, and may teach and publish the results of this search.

7. Cf. *L'Université Catholique dans le monde moderne. Document final du 2ème Congrès des Délégués des Universités Catholiques,* Rome, 20–29 novembre, 1972, §1. This text is hereafter abbreviated UCMM.

8. John Paul II, Address to the participants at the Second National Congress of the Church Movement for Cultural Commitment, February 9, 1985, n. 4: *Insegnamenti* VII, 1 (1985), p. 456.

9. Cf. UCMM §3.

10. John Paul II, Address at the International Meeting on Catholic Higher Education, April 25, 1989, n. 4. *L'Osservatore Romano,* April 26, 1989.

11. *Gaudium et Spes,* n. 36: *AAS* 58 (1966), p. 1054. Pope John Paul adds that "while reason and faith surely represent two distinct orders of knowledge, each autonomous with regard to its own methods, the two must finally converge in the discovery of a single whole reality which has its origin in God." (John Paul II, Address to the meeting of Galileo. May 9, 1983, n. 3: *AAS* 75 [1983], p. 690.)

12. Cf. UCMM §37.

13. John Paul II, Address to the Students and Teachers of the Catholic Universities of Mexico, January 31, 1979, n. 2c.: *AAS* 71 (1979), I, p. 236.

14. John Paul II, encyclical letter *Redemptor hominis,* n. 15: *AAS* 7 (1979), p. 288.

15. Paul VI, Address to the Rectors and Presidents of Jesuit Universities, August 6, 1975, n. 4: *AAS* 67 (1975), p. 533.

16. Vatican Council II, Apostolic Constitution on the Church (*Lumen Gentium*), n. 31: *AAS* 57 (1965), pp. 37–38. Cf. Vatican Council II, Decree on the Apostolate of the Laity (*Apostolicam Actuositatem*), passim: *AAS* 58 (1966), pp. 837ff.

17. "The university community must know how to incarnate its faith within its own culture in a daily, existential way, with important moments of reflection and or prayer in order to recall the foundations of its faith, hope, and charity." John Paul II, Address to the University Community of Louvain, Belgium, May 20, 1985, n. 3: *Insegnamenti* VIII, 1 (1985), p. 1592.

18. Cf. UCMM §44.

19. John Paul II, Address at the International Meeting on Higher Education, April 25, 1989, n. 4. *L'Osservatore Romano,* April 26, 1989.

20. Cf. John Paul II to the members of the Council of the International Federation of Catholic Universities, February 24, 1979. *Insegnamenti* II, 1 (1979), p. 446.

21. Paul VI, encyclical letter *Populorum Progressio,* n. 1: *AAS* 59 (1967), p. 257. Quoted in UCMM §44.

22. Cf. UCMM §§44f.

23. Cf. John Paul II, encyclical letter *Sollicitudo rei socialis,* nn. 27–34: *AAS* 80 (1988), pp. 547–560.

24. Cf. UCMM §7.

25. Cf. UCMM §15.

26. John Paul II, Address to Leaders of Catholic Higher Education, Xavier University of Louisiana, U.S.A., September 12, 1987, n. 4: *AAS* 80 (1988), p. 764.

27. Cf. *Gaudium et Spes*, n. 59: *AAS* 58 (1966), p. 1080.

28. Cf. Vatican Council II Dogmatic Constitution on the Church (*Lumen Gentium*), n. 25: *AAS* 57 (1965), p. 29.

29. Cf. *Lumen Gentium*, n. 25; Canon 752, CIC.

30. Cf. the address of John Paul II to the professors of sacred theology in Altötting, Germany, November 18, 1980, n. 3: *AAS* 73 (1981), pp. 103–104.

31. Canon 212 §3, CIC.

32. Ibid.

33. UCMM §1.

34. John Paul II, Address to University Students and Intellectuals at Kinshasa, Zaire, May 4, 1980, n. 2: *AAS* 72 (1980), p. 455.

35. Cf. *Gaudium et Spes*, n. 58: *AAS* 58 (1966), p. 1079.

36. While it is true that the Gospel cannot be identified with culture and transcends all cultures, it is also true that "the Kingdom which the Gospel proclaims is lived by men and women who are profoundly linked to a culture, and the building up of the Kingdom cannot avoid borrowing the elements of human culture or cultures." Paul VI, Apostolic Exhortation *Evangelii Nuntiandi*, n. 20: *AAS* 68 (1976), p. 18. Cf. the letter of Pope John Paul II creating the Pontifical Council for Culture, May 20, 1982: *AAS* 74 (1983), pp. 683–688.

37. John Paul II, Address to the Intellectuals and University Students and Staff in Medellín, Colombia, July 5, 1986, n. 3: *AAS* 79 (1987), p. 99. Cf. *Gaudium et Spes*, n. 58: *AAS* 58 (1966), p. 741.

38. Vatican Council II Declaration on the Relationship of the Church to Non-Christian Religions *Nostra Aetate*, n. 2: *AAS* 58 (1966), p. 741.

39. *Evangelii Nuntiandi*, nn. 18f: *AAS* 68 (1970), pp. 17–18.

40. Paul VI, Address to the Presidents and Rectors of Universities of the Society of Jesus, August 6, 1975, n. 2: *AAS* 67 (1975), p. 533. Pope John Paul II, in speaking to the participants at the International Meeting on Catholic Higher Education, April 25, 1989, adds (n. 5), "Within the Catholic university the evangelical mission of the Church and the university mission of research and teaching become *interrelated and coordinated.*" *L'Osservatore Romano*, April 26, 1989.

41. Paul VI, "New Tasks for Catholic Universities," Address to the delegates of the International Federation of Catholic Universities, November 27, 1972: *AAS* 64 (1972), p. 770.

42. Ecclesiastical universities and faculties, which have the right to confer academic degrees by the authority of the Holy See, are governed by the norms of the Apostolic Constitution *Sapientia Christiana*: *AAS* 71 (1979), pp. 469–521.

43. Episcopal conferences have been established in the Latin Rite; other Rites have assemblies of Catholic hierarchy.

44. Cf. Canon 814, CIC.

45. *Gaudium et Spes*, nn. 57 and 59: *AAS* 58 (1966), pp. 1078–1080, *Gravissimum Educationis*, n. 10 *AAS* 58 (1966), p. 737.

46. See also Article 7 §2.

47. Cf. *Lumen Gentium*, n. 25: *AAS* 57 (1965), p. 29.

48. Cf. Canon 218, CIC; *Dei Verbum*, n. 10: *AAS* 58 (1966), p. 822.

49. Cf. *Gravissimum Educationis*, n. 10: *AAS* 58 (1966), p. 737.

50. Cf. *Gaudium et Spes*, n. 43: *AAS* 58 (1966), p. 1062–1064.

51. Cf. Canon 813, CIC.

52. Cf. Canon 820, CIC. Also see *Sapientia Christiana*, General Norms, Article 49: *AAS* 71 (1979), p. 512.

Ex Corde Ecclesiae John Paul II

August 15, 1990

INTRODUCTION

1.   Born from the heart of the church, a Catholic university is located in that course of tradition which may be traced back to the very origin of the University as an institution. It has always been recognized as an incomparable center of creativity and dissemination of knowledge for the good of humanity. By vocation, the *universitas magistrorum et scholarium* is dedicated to research, to teaching, and to the education of students who freely associate with their teachers in a common love of knowledge.[1] With every other university it shares that *gaudium de veritate*, so precious to Saint Augustine, which is that joy of searching for, discovering, and communicating truth in every field of knowledge.[2] A Catholic university's privileged task is "to unite existentially by intellectual effort two orders of reality that too frequently tend to be placed in opposition as though they were antithetical: the search for truth and the certainty of already knowing the fount of truth."[3]

2.   For many years I myself was deeply enriched by the beneficial experience of university life: the ardent search for truth and its unselfish transmission to youth and to all those learning to think rigorously, so as to act rightly and to serve humanity better.

Therefore, I desire to share with everyone my profound respect for Catholic universities and to express my great appreciation for the work that is being done in them in the various spheres of knowledge. In a particular way, I wish to manifest my joy at the numerous meetings which the Lord has permitted me to have in the course of my apostolic journeys with the Catholic university communities of various continents.

The official document, *Constitutio Apostolica de Universitatibus Catholicis* was published by Libreria Editrice Vaticana in 1990. This version is based on an English version published by Libreria Editrice Vaticana and distributed by the Sacred Congregation for Catholic Education. It also appears in *Origins* 20, no. 17 (October 4, 1990) 265–276.

They are for me a lively and promising sign of the fecundity of the Christian mind in the heart of every culture. They give me a well-founded hope for a new flowering of Christian culture in the rich and varied context of our changing times, which certainly face serious challenges but which also bear so much promise under the action of the Spirit of truth and of love.

It is also my desire to express my pleasure and gratitude to the very many Catholic scholars engaged in teaching and research in non-Catholic universities. Their task as academics and scientists, lived out in the light of the Christian faith, is to be considered precious for the good of the universities in which they teach. Their presence, in fact, is a continuous stimulus to the selfless search for truth and for the wisdom that comes from above.

3.   Since the beginning of this pontificate, I have shared these ideas and sentiments with my closest collaborators, the cardinals, with the Congregation for Catholic Education, and with men and women of culture throughout the world. In fact, the dialogue of the church with the cultures of our times is that vital area where "the future of the church and of the world is being played out as we conclude the twentieth century."[4] There is only one culture: that of man, by man, and from man.[5] And thanks to her Catholic universities and their humanistic and scientific inheritance, the church, expert in humanity, as my predecessor Paul VI expressed it at the United Nations,[6] explores the mysteries of humanity and of the world, clarifying them in the light of revelation.

4.   It is the honor and responsibility of a Catholic university to consecrate itself without reserve to the cause of truth. This is its way of serving at one and the same time both the dignity of man and the good of the church, which has "an intimate conviction that truth is (its) real ally . . . and that knowledge and reason are sure ministers to faith."[7] Without in any way neglecting the acquisition of useful knowledge, a Catholic university is distinguished by its free search for the whole truth about nature, man, and God. The present age is in urgent need of this kind of disinterested service, namely of proclaiming the meaning of truth, that fundamental value without which freedom, justice, and human dignity are extinguished. By means of a kind of universal humanism, a Catholic university is completely dedicated to the research of all aspects of truth in their essential connection with the supreme Truth, who is God. It does this without fear, but rather with enthusiasm, dedicating itself to every path of knowledge, aware of being preceded by him who is "the Way, the Truth, and the Life,"[8] the Logos, whose Spirit of intelligence and love enables the human person with his or her own intelligence to find the ultimate reality of which he is the source and end

and who alone is capable of giving fully that wisdom without which the future of the world would be in danger.

5.   It is in the context of the impartial search for truth that the relationship between faith and reason is brought to light and meaning. The invitation of Saint Augustine, "*Intellege ut credas; crede ut intellegas,*"[9] is relevant to Catholic universities that are called to explore courageously the riches of revelation and of nature so that the united endeavor of intelligence and faith will enable people to come to the full measure of their humanity, created in the image and likeness of God, renewed even more marvelously, after sin, in Christ, and called to shine forth in the light of the Spirit.

6.   Through the encounter which it establishes between the unfathomable richness of the salvific message of the Gospel and the variety and immensity of the fields of knowledge in which that richness is incarnated by it, a Catholic university enables the church to institute an incomparably fertile dialogue with people of every culture. Man's life is given dignity by culture, and, while he finds his fullness in Christ, there can be no doubt that the Gospel which reaches and renews him in every dimension is also fruitful for the culture in which he lives.

7.   In the world today, characterized by such rapid developments in science and technology, the tasks of a Catholic university assume an ever greater importance and urgency. Scientific and technological discoveries create an enormous economic and industrial growth, but they also inescapably require the correspondingly necessary search for meaning in order to guarantee that the new discoveries be used for the authentic good of individuals and of human society as a whole. If it is the responsibility of every university to search for such meaning, a Catholic university is called in a particular way to respond to this need: Its Christian inspiration enables it to include the moral, spiritual, and religious dimension in its research and to evaluate the attainments of science and technology in the perspective of the totality of the human person.[10]

In this context, Catholic universities are called to a continuous renewal, both as "universities" and as "Catholic." For, "What is at stake is the very meaning of scientific and technological research, of social life and of culture, but, on an even more profound level, what is at stake is the very meaning of the human person." Such renewal requires a clear awareness that, by its Catholic character, a university is made more capable of conducting an impartial search for truth, a search that is neither subordinated to nor conditioned by particular interests of any kind.

8.   Having already dedicated the apostolic constitution *Sapientia Christiana* to ecclesiastical faculties and universities,[11] I then felt obliged

to propose an analogous document for Catholic universities as a sort of *magna carta*, enriched by the long and fruitful experience of the church in the realm of universities and open to the promise of the future achievements that will require courageous creativity and rigorous fidelity.

9.   The present document is addressed especially to those who conduct Catholic universities, to the respective academic communities, to all those who have an interest in them, particularly the bishops, religious congregations, and ecclesial institutions, and to the numerous laity who are committed to the great mission of higher education. Its purpose is that "the Christian mind may achieve, as it were, a public, persistent, and universal presence in the whole enterprise of advancing higher culture and that the students of these institutions become people outstanding in learning, ready to shoulder society's heavier burdens and to witness the faith to the world."[12]

10.   In addition to Catholic universities, I also turn to the many Catholic institutions of higher education. According to their nature and proper objectives, they share some or all of the characteristics of a university, and they offer their own contribution to the church and to society, whether through research, education, or professional training. While this document specifically concerns Catholic universities, it is also meant to include all Catholic institutions of higher education engaged in instilling the Gospel message of Christ in souls and cultures.

Therefore, it is with great trust and hope that I invite all Catholic universities to pursue their irreplaceable task. Their mission appears increasingly necessary for the encounter of the church with the development of the sciences and with the cultures of our age.

Together with all my brother bishops who share pastoral responsibility with me, I would like to manifest my deep conviction that a Catholic university is without any doubt one of the best instruments that the church offers to our age which is searching for certainty and wisdom. Having the mission of bringing the good news to everyone, the church should never fail to interest herself in this institution. By research and teaching, Catholic universities assist the church in the manner most appropriate to modern times to find cultural treasures both old and new, "*nova et vetera*," according to the words of Jesus.[13]

11.   Finally, I turn to the whole church, convinced that Catholic universities are essential to her growth and to the development of Christian culture and human progress. For this reason, the entire ecclesial community is invited to give its support to Catholic institutions of higher education and to assist them in their process of development and renewal. It is invited in a special way to guard the rights and freedom of these institutions in civil society, and to offer them economic aid, especially in

those countries where they have more urgent need of it, and to furnish assistance in founding new Catholic universities wherever this might be necessary.

My hope is that these prescriptions, based on the teaching of Vatican Council II and the directives of the Code of Canon Law, will enable Catholic universities and other institutions of higher studies to fulfil their indispensable mission in the new advent of grace that is opening up to the new millennium.

I. IDENTITY AND MISSION

THE IDENTITY OF A CATHOLIC UNIVERSITY

1. Nature and Objectives

12.   Every Catholic university, as a university, is an academic community which, in a rigorous and critical fashion, assists in the protection and advancement of human dignity and of a cultural heritage through research, teaching, and various services offered to the local, national, and international communities.[14] It possesses that institutional autonomy necessary to perform its functions effectively and guarantees its members academic freedom, so long as the rights of the individual person and of the community are preserved within the confines of the truth and the common good.[15]

13.   Since the objective of a Catholic university is to assure in an institutional manner a Christian presence in the university world confronting the great problems of society and culture,[16] every Catholic university, as Catholic, must have the following essential characteristics:

> 1. A Christian inspiration not only of individuals but of the university community as such.
> 2. A continuing reflection in the light of the Catholic faith upon the growing treasury of human knowledge, to which it seeks to contribute by its own research.
> 3. Fidelity to the Christian message as it comes to us through the Church.
> 4. An institutional commitment to the service of the people of God and of the human family in their pilgrimage to the transcendent goal which gives meaning to life."[17]

14.   "In the light of these four characteristics, it is evident that besides the teaching, research, and services common to all universities, a Catholic university, by institutional commitment, brings to its task the inspiration and light of the Christian message. In a Catholic university, therefore,

Catholic ideals, attitudes, and principles penetrate and inform university activities in accordance with the proper nature and autonomy of these activities. In a word, being both a university and Catholic, it must be both a community of scholars representing various branches of human knowledge, and an academic institution in which Catholicism is vitally present and operative."[18]

15.   A Catholic university, therefore, is a place of research, where scholars scrutinize reality with the methods proper to each academic discipline, and so contribute to the treasury of human knowledge. Each individual discipline is studied in a systematic manner; moreover, the various disciplines are brought into dialogue for their mutual enhancement.

In addition to assisting men and women in their continuing quest for the truth, this research provides an effective witness, especially necessary today, to the church's belief in the intrinsic value of knowledge and research.

In a Catholic university, research necessarily includes (a) the search for an integration of knowledge, (b) a dialogue between faith and reason, (c) an ethical concern, and (d) a theological perspective.

16.   Integration of knowledge is a process, one which will always remain incomplete; moreover, the explosion of knowledge in recent decades, together with the rigid compartmentalization of knowledge within individual academic disciplines, makes the task increasingly difficult. But a university, and especially a Catholic university, "has to be a 'living union' of individual organisms dedicated to the search for truth.... It is necessary to work towards a higher synthesis of knowledge, in which alone lies the possibility of satisfying that thirst for truth which is profoundly inscribed on the heart of the human person."[19] Aided by the specific contributions of philosophy and theology, university scholars will be engaged in a constant effort to determine the relative place and meaning of each of the various disciplines within the context of a vision of the human person and the world that is enlightened by the Gospel, and therefore by a faith in Christ, the Logos, as the center of creation and of human history.

17.   In promoting this integration of knowledge, a specific part of a Catholic university's task is to promote dialogue between faith and reason, so that it can be seen more profoundly how faith and reason bear harmonious witness to the unity of all truth. While each academic discipline retains its own integrity and has its own methods, this dialogue demonstrates that "methodical research within every branch of learning, when carried out in a truly scientific manner and in accord with moral norms, can never truly conflict with faith. For the things of the earth and the concerns of faith derive from the same God."[20] A vital interaction of

two distinct levels of coming to know the one truth leads to a greater love for truth itself, and contributes to a more comprehensive understanding of the meaning of human life and of the purpose of God's creation.

18.   Because knowledge is meant to serve the human person, research in a Catholic university is always carried out with a concern for the ethical and moral implications both of its methods and of its discoveries. This concern, while it must be present in all research, is particularly important in the areas of science and technology. "It is essential that we be convinced of the priority of the ethical over the technical, of the primacy of the person over things, of the superiority of the spirit over matter. The cause of the human person will only be served if knowledge is joined to conscience. Men and women of science will truly aid humanity only if they preserve the 'sense of the transcendence of the human person over the world and of God over the human person.' "[21]

19.   Theology plays a particularly important role in the search for a synthesis of knowledge as well as in the dialogue between faith and reason. It serves all other disciplines in their search for meaning, not only by helping them to investigate how their discoveries will affect individuals and society, but also by bringing a perspective and an orientation not contained within their own methodologies. In turn, interaction with these other disciplines and their discoveries enriches theology, offering it a better understanding of the world today, and making theological research more relevant to current needs. Because of its specific importance among the academic disciplines, every Catholic university should have a faculty, or at least a chair, of theology.[22]

20.   Given the close connection between research and teaching, the research qualities indicated above will have their influence on all teaching. While each discipline is taught systematically and according to its own methods, interdisciplinary studies, assisted by a careful and thorough study of philosophy and theology, enable students to acquire an organic vision of reality and to develop a continuing desire for intellectual progress. In the communication of knowledge, emphasis is then placed on how human reason in its reflection opens to increasingly broader questions, and how the complete answer to them can only come from above through faith. Furthermore, the moral implications that are present in each discipline are examined as an integral part of the teaching of that discipline so that the entire educative process be directed toward the whole development of the person. Finally, Catholic theology, taught in a manner faithful to Scripture, tradition, and the church's magisterium, provides an awareness of the Gospel principles which will enrich the meaning of human life and give it a new dignity.

Through research and teaching the students are educated in the various disciplines so as to become truly competent in the specific sectors in which they will devote themselves to the service of society and of the church, but at the same time prepared to give the witness of their faith to the world.

2. The University Community

21.   A Catholic university pursues its objectives through its formation of an authentic human community animated by the spirit of Christ. The source of its unity springs from a common dedication to the truth, a common vision of the dignity of the human person, and, ultimately, the person and message of Christ which gives the institution its distinctive character. As a result of this inspiration, the community is animated by a spirit of freedom and charity; it is characterized by mutual respect, sincere dialogue, and protection of the rights of individuals. It assists each of its members to achieve wholeness as human persons; in turn, everyone in the community helps in promoting unity, and each one, according to his or her role and capacity, contributes toward decisions which affect the community, and also toward maintaining and strengthening the distinctive Catholic character of the institution.

22.   University teachers should seek to improve their competence and endeavor to set the content, objectives, methods, and results of research in an individual discipline within the framework of a coherent world vision. Christians among the teachers are called to be witnesses and educators of authentic Christian life, which evidences an attained integration between faith and life, and between professional competence and Christian wisdom. All teachers are to be inspired by academic ideals and by the principles of an authentically human life.

23.   Students are challenged to pursue an education that combines excellence in humanistic and cultural development with specialized professional training. Most especially, they are challenged to continue the search for truth and for meaning throughout their lives, since "the human spirit must be cultivated in such a way that there results a growth in its ability to wonder, to understand, to contemplate, to make personal judgments, and to develop a religious, moral, and social sense."[23] This enables them to acquire or, if they have already done so, to deepen a Christian way of life that is authentic. They should realize the responsibility of their professional life, the enthusiasm of being the trained 'leaders' of tomorrow, of being witness to Christ in whatever place they may exercise their profession.

24.   Directors and administrators in a Catholic university promote the constant growth of the university and its community through a leadership of service; the dedication and witness of the non-academic staff are vital for the identity and life of the university.

25. Many Catholic universities were founded by religious congregations and continue to depend on their support; those religious congregations dedicated to the apostolate of higher education are urged to assist these institutions in the renewal of their commitment, and to continue to prepare religious men and women who can positively contribute to the mission of a Catholic university.

Laypeople have found in university activities a means by which they too could exercise an important apostolic role in the church and, in most Catholic universities today, the academic community is largely composed of laity; in increasing numbers, lay men and women are assuming important functions and responsibilities for the direction of these institutions. These lay Catholics are responding to the church's call "to be present, as signs of courage and intellectual creativity, in the privileged places of culture, that is, the world of education—school and university."[24] The future of Catholic universities depends to a great extent on the competent and dedicated service of lay Catholics. The church sees their developing presence in these institutions both as a sign of hope and as a confirmation of the irreplaceable lay vocation in the church and in the world, confident that laypeople will, in the exercise of their own distinctive role, "illumine and organize these (temporal) affairs in such a way that they always start out, develop, and continue according to Christ's mind, to the praise of the Creator and the Redeemer."[25]

26. The university community of many Catholic institutions includes members of other Churches, ecclesial communities and religions, and also those who profess no religious belief. These men and women offer their training and experience in furthering the various academic disciplines or other university tasks.

3. The Catholic University in the Church

27. Every Catholic university, without ceasing to be a university, has a relationship to the church that is essential to its institutional identity. As such, it participates most directly in the life of the local church in which it is situated; at the same time, because it is an academic institution and therefore a part of the international community of scholarship and inquiry, each institution participates in and contributes to the life and the mission of the universal church, assuming consequently a special bond with the Holy See by reason of the service to unity which it is called to render to the whole church. One consequence of its essential relationship to the church is that the institutional fidelity of the university to the Christian message includes a recognition of and adherence to the teaching authority of the church in matters of faith and morals. Catholic members of the university community are also called to a personal

fidelity to the church with all that this implies. Non-Catholic members are required to respect the Catholic character of the university, while the university in turn respects their religious liberty.[26]

28.   Bishops have a particular responsibility to promote Catholic universities, and especially to promote and assist in the preservation and strengthening of their Catholic identity, including the protection of their Catholic identity in relation to civil authorities. This will be achieved more effectively if close personal and pastoral relationships exist between university and church authorities characterized by mutual trust, close and consistent cooperation, and continuing dialogue. Even when they do not enter directly into the internal governance of the university, bishops "should be seen not as external agents but as participants in the life of the Catholic university."[27]

29.   The church, accepting "the legitimate autonomy of human culture and especially of the sciences," recognizes the academic freedom of scholars in each discipline in accordance with its own principles and proper methods,[28] and within the confines of the truth and the common good.

Theology has its legitimate place in the university alongside other disciplines. It has proper principles and methods which define it as a branch of knowledge. Theologians enjoy this same freedom so long as they are faithful to these principles and methods.

Bishops should encourage the creative work of theologians. They serve the church through research done in a way that respects theological method. They seek to understand better, further develop, and more effectively communicate the meaning of Christian revelation as transmitted in Scripture and tradition and in the church's magisterium. They also investigate the ways in which theology can shed light on specific questions raised by contemporary culture. At the same time, since theology seeks an understanding of revealed truth whose authentic interpretation is entrusted to the bishops of the church,[29] it is intrinsic to the principles and methods of their research and teaching in their academic discipline that theologians respect the authority of the bishops and assent to Catholic doctrine according to the degree of authority with which it is taught.[30] Because of their interrelated roles, dialogue between bishops and theologians is essential; this is especially true today, when the results of research are so quickly and so widely communicated through the media.[31]

B. THE MISSION OF SERVICE OF A CATHOLIC UNIVERSITY

30.   The basic mission of a university is a continuous quest for truth through its research, and the preservation and communication of knowledge for the good of society. A Catholic university participates in this mission with its own specific characteristics and purposes.

1. Service to Church and Society

31. Through teaching and research, a Catholic university offers an indispensable contribution to the church. In fact, it prepares men and women who, inspired by Christian principles and helped to live their Christian vocation in a mature and responsible manner, will be able to assume positions of responsibility in the church. Moreover, by offering the results of its scientific research, a Catholic university will be able to help the church respond to the problems and needs of this age.

32. A Catholic university, as any university, is immersed in human society; as an extension of its service to the church, and always within its proper competence, it is called on to become an ever more effective instrument of cultural progress for individuals as well as for society. Included among its research activities, therefore, will be a study of serious contemporary problems in areas such as the dignity of human life, the promotion of justice for all, the quality of personal and family life, the protection of nature, the search for peace and political stability, a more just sharing in the world's resources, and a new economic and political order that will better serve the human community at a national and international level. University research will seek to discover the roots and causes of the serious problems of our time, paying special attention to their ethical and religious dimensions.

If need be, a Catholic university must have the courage to speak uncomfortable truths which do not please public opinion, but which are necessary to safeguard the authentic good of society.

33. A specific priority is the need to examine and evaluate the predominant values and norms of modern society and culture in a Christian perspective, and the responsibility to try to communicate to society those ethical and religious principles which give full meaning to human life. In this way a university can contribute further to the development of a true Christian anthropology, founded on the person of Christ, which will bring the dynamism of the creation and redemption to bear on reality and on the correct solution to the problems of life.

34. The Christian spirit of service to others for the promotion of social justice is of particular importance for each Catholic university, to be shared by its teachers and developed in its students. The church is firmly committed to the integral growth of all men and women.[32] The Gospel, interpreted in the social teachings of the church, is an urgent call to promote "the development of those peoples who are striving to escape from hunger, misery, endemic diseases, and ignorance; of those who are looking for a wider share in the benefits of civilization and a more active improvement of their human qualities; of those who are aiming purposefully at their complete fulfillment."[33] Every Catholic university feels responsible to contribute concretely to the progress of the society

within which it works: For example it will be capable of searching for ways to make university education accessible to all those who are able to benefit from it, especially the poor or members of minority groups who customarily have been deprived of it. A Catholic university also has the responsibility, to the degree that it is able, to help to promote the development of the emerging nations.

35.   In its attempts to resolve these complex issues that touch on so many different dimensions of human life and of society, a Catholic university will insist on cooperation among the different academic disciplines, each offering its distinct contribution in the search for solutions; moreover, since the economic and personal resources of a single institution are limited, cooperation in common research projects among Catholic universities, as well as with other private and governmental institutions, is imperative. In this regard, and also in what pertains to the other fields of the specific activity of a Catholic university, the role played by various national and international associations of Catholic universities is to be emphasized. Among these associations the mission of the International Federation of Catholic Universities, founded by the Holy See,[34] is particularly to be remembered. The Holy See anticipates further fruitful collaboration with this federation.

36.   Through programs of continuing education offered to the wider community, by making its scholars available for consulting services, by taking advantage of modern means of communication, and in a variety of other ways, a Catholic university can assist in making the growing body of human knowledge and a developing understanding of the faith available to a wider public, thus expanding university services beyond its own academic community.

37.   In its service to society, a Catholic university will relate especially to the academic, cultural, and scientific world of the region in which it is located. Original forms of dialogue and collaboration are to be encouraged between the Catholic universities and the other universities of a nation on behalf of development, of understanding between cultures, and of the defense of nature in accordance with an awareness of the international ecological situation.

Catholic universities join other private and public institutions in serving the public interest through higher education and research; they are one among the variety of different types of institutions that are necessary for the free expression of cultural diversity, and they are committed to the promotion of solidarity and its meaning in society and in the world. Therefore they have the full right to expect that civil society and public authorities will recognize and defend their institutional autonomy and academic freedom; moreover, they have the right to the financial support that is necessary for their continued existence and development.

2. Pastoral Ministry

38.   Pastoral ministry is that activity of the university which offers the members of the university community an opportunity to integrate religious and moral principles with their academic study and nonacademic activities, thus integrating faith with life. It is part of the mission of the church within the university, and is also a constitutive element of a Catholic university itself, both in its structure and in its life. A university community concerned with promoting the institution's Catholic character will be conscious of this pastoral dimension and sensitive to the ways in which it can have an influence on all university activities.

39.   As a natural expression of the Catholic identity of the university, the university community should give a practical demonstration of its faith in its daily activity, with important moments of reflection and of prayer. Catholic members of this community will be offered opportunities to assimilate Catholic teaching and practice into their lives and will be encouraged to participate in the celebration of the sacraments, especially the eucharist as the most perfect act of community worship. When the academic community includes members of other churches, ecclesial communities, or religions, their initiatives for reflection and prayer in accordance with their own beliefs are to be respected.

40.   Those involved in pastoral ministry will encourage teachers and students to become more aware of their responsibility towards those who are suffering physically or spiritually. Following the example of Christ, they will be particularly attentive to the poorest and to those who suffer economic, social, cultural, or religious injustice. This responsibility begins within the academic community, but it also finds application beyond it.

41.   Pastoral ministry is an indispensable means by which Catholic students can, in fulfillment of their baptism, be prepared for active participation in the life of the church; it can assist in developing and nurturing the value of marriage and family life, fostering vocations to the priesthood and religious life, stimulating the Christian commitment of the laity, and imbuing every activity with the spirit of the Gospel. Close cooperation between pastoral ministry in a Catholic university and the other activities within the local church, under the guidance or with the approval of the diocesan bishop, will contribute to their mutual growth.

42.   Various associations or movements of spiritual and apostolic life, especially those developed specifically for students, can be of great assistance in developing the pastoral aspects of university life.[35]

3. Cultural Dialogue

43.   By its very nature, a university develops culture through its research, helps to transmit the local culture to each succeeding generation through its teaching, and assists cultural activities through its educational services. It is open to all human experience and is ready to dialogue with and learn from any culture. A Catholic university shares in this, offering the rich experience of the church's own culture. In addition, a Catholic university, aware that human culture is open to revelation and transcendence, is also a primary and privileged place for a fruitful dialogue between the Gospel and culture.
44.   Through this dialogue a Catholic university assists the church, enabling it to come to a better knowledge of diverse cultures, discern their positive and negative aspects, to receive their authentically human contributions, and to develop means by which it can make the faith better understood by men and women of a particular culture.[36] While it is true that the Gospel cannot be identified with any particular culture and transcends all cultures, it is also true that "the kingdom which the Gospel proclaims is lived by men and women who are profoundly linked to a culture, and the building up of the kingdom cannot avoid borrowing the elements of human culture or cultures."[37] "A faith that places itself on the margin of what is human, of what is therefore culture, would be a faith unfaithful to the fullness of what the word of God manifests and reveals, a decapitated faith, worse still, a faith in the process of self-annihilation."[38]
45.   A Catholic university must become more attentive to the cultures of the world of today, and to the various cultural traditions existing within the church in a way that will promote a continuous and profitable dialogue between the Gospel and modern society. Among the criteria that characterize the values of a culture are above all, the meaning of the human person, his or her liberty, dignity, sense of responsibility, and openness to the transcendent. To a respect for persons is joined the preeminent value of the family, the primary unit of every human culture.

Catholic universities will seek to discern and evaluate both the aspirations and the contradictions of modern culture, in order to make it more suited to the total development of individuals and peoples. In particular, it is recommended that by means of appropriate studies, the impact of modern technology and especially of the mass media on persons, the family, and the institutions and whole of modern culture be studied deeply. Traditional cultures are to be defended in their identity, helping them to receive modern values without sacrificing their own heritage, which is a wealth for the whole of the human family. Universities, situated within the ambience of these cultures, will seek to harmonize local cultures with the positive contributions of modern cultures.

46. An area that particularly interests a Catholic university is the dialogue between Christian thought and the modern sciences. This task requires persons particularly well versed in the individual disciplines and who are at the same time adequately prepared theologically, and who are capable of confronting epistemological questions at the level of the relationship between faith and reason. Such dialogue concerns the natural sciences as much as the human sciences which posit new and complex philosophical and ethical problems. The Christian researcher should demonstrate the way in which human intelligence is enriched by the higher truth that comes from the Gospel: "The intelligence is never diminished, rather, it is stimulated and reinforced by that interior fount of deep understanding that is the word of God, and by the hierarchy of values that results from it. . . . In its unique manner, the Catholic university helps to manifest the superiority of the spirit, that can never, without the risk of losing its very self, be placed at the service of something other than the search for truth."[39]

47. Besides cultural dialogue, a Catholic university, in accordance with its specific ends, and keeping in mind the various religious-cultural contexts, following the directives promulgated by competent ecclesiastical authority, can offer a contribution to ecumenical dialogue. It does so to further the search for unity among all Christians. In interreligious dialogue it will assist in discerning the spiritual values that are present in the different religions.

4. Evangelization

48. The primary mission of the church is to preach the Gospel in such a way that a relationship between faith and life is established in each individual and in the socio-cultural context in which individuals live and act and communicate with one another. Evangelization means "bringing the good news into all the strata of humanity, and through its influence transforming humanity from within and making it new. . . . It is a question not only of preaching the Gospel in ever wider geographic areas or to ever greater numbers of people, but also of affecting and, as it were, upsetting, through the power of the Gospel, humanity's criteria of judgment, determining values, points of interest, lines of thought, sources of inspiration, and models of life, which are in contrast with the word of God and the plan of salvation."[40]

49. By its very nature, each Catholic university makes an important contribution to the church's work of evangelization. It is a living institutional witness to Christ and his message, so vitally important in cultures

marked by secularism, or where Christ and his message are still virtually unknown. Moreover, all the basic academic activities of a Catholic university are connected with and in harmony with the evangelizing mission of the church: research carried out in the light of the Christian message which puts new human discoveries at the service of individuals and society; education offered in a faith-context that forms men and women capable of rational and critical judgment and conscious of the transcendent dignity of the human person; professional training that incorporates ethical values and a sense of service to individuals and to society; the dialogue with culture that makes the faith better understood, and the theological research that translates the faith into contemporary language. "Precisely because it is more and more conscious of its salvific mission in this world, the church wants to have these centers closely connected with it; it wants to have them present and operative in spreading the authentic message of Christ."[41]

II. GENERAL NORMS

ARTICLE 1. THE NATURE OF THESE GENERAL NORMS

1. These general norms are based on, and are a further development of, the Code of Canon Law[42] and the complementary church legislation, without prejudice to the right of the Holy See to intervene should this become necessary. They are valid for all Catholic universities and other Catholic institutes of higher studies throughout the world.

2. The general norms are to be applied concretely at the local and regional levels by episcopal conferences and other assemblies of Catholic hierarchy[43] in conformity with the Code of Canon Law and complementary church legislation, taking into account the statutes of each university or institute and, as far as possible and appropriate, civil law. After review by the Holy See,[44] these local or regional "ordinances" will be valid for all Catholic universities and other Catholic institutes of higher studies in the region, except for ecclesiastical universities and faculties. These latter institutions, including ecclesiastical faculties which are part of a Catholic university, are governed by the norms of the apostolic constitution *Sapientia Christiana*.[45]

3. A university established or approved by the Holy See, by an episcopal conference or another assembly of Catholic hierarchy, or by a diocesan bishop is to incorporate these general norms and their local regional applications into its governing documents, and conform its existing statutes both to the general norms and to their applications, and submit them for approval to the competent ecclesiastical authority. It is contemplated that other Catholic universities, that is, those not

established or approved in any of the above ways, with the agreement of the local ecclesiastical authority, will make their own the general norms and their local and regional applications, internalizing them into their governing documents, and, as far as possible, will conform their existing statutes both to these general norms and to their applications.

ARTICLE 2. THE NATURE OF A CATHOLIC UNIVERSITY

1. A Catholic university, like every university, is a community of scholars representing various branches of human knowledge. It is dedicated to research, to teaching, and to various kinds of service in accordance with its cultural mission.

2. A Catholic university, as Catholic, informs and carries out its research, teaching, and all other activities with Catholic ideals, principles and attitudes. It is linked with the church either by a formal, constitutive and statutory bond or by reason of an institutional commitment made by those responsible for it.

3. Every Catholic university is to make known its Catholic identity, either in a mission statement or in some other appropriate public document, unless authorized otherwise by the competent ecclesiastical authority. The university, particularly through its structure and its regulations, is to provide means which will guarantee the expression and the preservation of this identity in a manner consistent with Section 2.

4. Catholic teaching and discipline are to influence all university activities, while the freedom of conscience of each person is to be fully respected.[46] Any official action or commitment of the university is to be in accord with its Catholic identity.

5. A Catholic university possesses the autonomy necessary to develop its distinctive identity and pursue its proper mission. Freedom in research and teaching is recognized and respected according to the principles and methods of each individual discipline, so long as the rights of the individual and of the community are preserved within the confines of the truth and the common good.[47]

ARTICLE 3. THE ESTABLISHMENT OF A CATHOLIC UNIVERSITY

1. A Catholic university may be established or approved by the Holy See, by an episcopal conference or another assembly of Catholic hierarchy, or by a diocesan bishop.

2. With the consent of the diocesan bishop, a Catholic university may also be established by a religious institute or other public juridical person.

3. A Catholic university may also be established by other ecclesiastical or lay persons; such a university may refer to itself as a Catholic

university only with the consent of the competent ecclesiastical authority, in accordance with the conditions upon which both parties shall agree.[48]

4. In the cases of Sections 1 and 2, the statutes must be approved by the competent ecclesiastical authority.

ARTICLE 4. THE UNIVERSITY COMMUNITY

1. The responsibility for maintaining and strengthening the Catholic identity of the university rests primarily with the university itself. While this responsibility is entrusted principally to university authorities (including, when the positions exist, the chancellor and/or a board of trustees or equivalent body), it is shared in varying degrees by all members of the university community, and therefore calls for the recruitment of adequate university personnel, especially teachers and administrators, who are both willing and able to promote that identity. The identity of a Catholic university is essentially linked to the quality of its teachers and to respect for Catholic doctrine. It is the responsibility of the competent authority to watch over these two fundamental needs in accordance with what is indicated in canon law.[49]

2. All teachers and all administrators, at the time of their appointment, are to be informed about the Catholic identity of the institution and its implications, and about their responsibility to promote, or at least to respect, that identity.

3. In ways appropriate to the different academic disciplines, all Catholic teachers are to be faithful to, and all other teachers are to respect, Catholic doctrine and morals in their research and teaching. In particular, Catholic theologians, aware that they fulfill a mandate received from the church, are to be faithful to the magisterium of the church as the authentic interpreter of sacred Scripture and sacred tradition.[50]

4. Those university teachers and administrators who belong to other churches, ecclesial communities, or religions, as well as those who profess no religious belief, and also all students, are to recognize and respect the distinctive Catholic identity of the university. In order not to endanger the Catholic identity of the university or institute of higher studies, the number of non-Catholic teachers should not be allowed to constitute a majority within the institution, which is and must remain Catholic.

5. The education of students is to combine academic and professional development with formation in moral and religious principles and the social teachings of the church; the program of studies for each of the various professions is to include an appropriate ethical formation in that profession. Courses in Catholic doctrine are to be made available to all students.[51]

ARTICLE 5. THE CATHOLIC UNIVERSITY WITHIN THE CHURCH

1. Every Catholic university is to maintain communion with the universal church and the Holy See; it is to be in close communion with the local church and in particular with the diocesan bishops of the region or nation in which it is located. In ways consistent with its nature as a university, a Catholic university will contribute to the church's work of evangelization.

2. Each bishop has a responsibility to promote the welfare of the Catholic universities in his diocese and has the right and duty to watch over the preservation and strengthening of their Catholic character. If problems should arise concerning this Catholic character, the local bishop is to take the initiatives necessary to resolve the matter, working with the competent university authorities in accordance with established procedures[52] and, if necessary, with the help of the Holy See.

3. Periodically, each Catholic university to which Article 3, Section 1 and 2 refers is to communicate relevant information about the university and its activities to the competent ecclesiastical authority. Other Catholic universities are to communicate this information to the bishop of the diocese in which the principal seat of the institution is located.

ARTICLE 6. PASTORAL MINISTRY

1. A Catholic university is to promote the pastoral care of all members of the university community, and to be especially attentive to the spiritual development of those who are Catholics. Priority is to be given to those means which will facilitate the integration of human and professional education with religious values in the light of Catholic doctrine, in order to unite intellectual learning with the religious dimension of life.

2. A sufficient number of qualified people—priests, religious, and lay persons—are to be appointed to provide pastoral ministry for the university community, carried on in harmony and cooperation with the pastoral activities of the local church under the guidance or with the approval of the diocesan bishop. All members of the university community are to be invited to assist the work of pastoral ministry, and to collaborate in its activities.

ARTICLE 7. COOPERATION

1. In order better to confront the complex problems facing modern society, and in order to strengthen the Catholic identity of the institutions, regional, national, and international cooperation is to be promoted in research, teaching, and other university activities among all Catholic universities, including ecclesiastical universities and faculties.[53] Such

cooperation is also to be promoted between Catholic universities and other universities, and with other research and educational institutions, both private and governmental.

2. Catholic universities will, when possible and in accord with Catholic principles and doctrine, cooperate with government programs and the programs of other national and international organizations on behalf of justice, development, and progress.

TRANSITIONAL NORMS

ARTICLE 8

The present constitution will come into effect on the first day of the academic year 1991.

ARTICLE 9

The application of the constitution is committed to the Congregation for Catholic Education, which has the duty to promulgate the necessary directives that will serve toward that end.

ARTICLE 10

It will be the competence of the Congregation for Catholic Education, when with the passage of time circumstances require it, to propose changes to be made in the present constitution in order that it may be adapted continuously to the needs of Catholic universities.

ARTICLE 11

Any particular laws or customs presently in effect that are contrary to this constitution are abolished. Also, any privileges granted up to this day by the Holy See whether to physical or moral persons that are contrary to this present constitution are abolished.

CONCLUSION

The mission that the church, with great hope, entrusts to Catholic universities holds a cultural and religious meaning of vital importance because it concerns the very future of humanity. The renewal requested to Catholic universities will make them better able to respond to the task of bringing the message of Christ to man, to society, to various cultures: "Every human reality, both individual and social, has been liberated by Christ: persons, as well as the activities of men and women, of which culture is the highest and incarnate expression. The salvific action of the church on cultures is achieved, first of all, by means of persons, families and educators. . . . Jesus Christ, our Savior, offers his light and his hope to all those who promote the sciences, the arts, letters, and the numerous fields developed by modern culture. Therefore, all the sons and daughters of the church should become aware of their mission and discover how the strength of the Gospel can penetrate and regenerate the mentalities and dominant values that inspire individual cultures, as well as the opinions and mental attitudes that are derived from it."[54]

It is with fervent hope that I address this document to all the men and women engaged in various ways in the significant mission of Catholic higher education.

Beloved brothers and sisters, my encouragement and my trust go with you in your weighty daily task that becomes ever more important, more urgent, and necessary on behalf of evangelization for the future of culture and of all cultures. The church and the world have great need of your witness and of your capable, free, and responsible contribution.

Given in Rome, at Saint Peter's, on August 15, the Solemnity of the Assumption of the Blessed Virgin Mary into heaven, in the year 1990, the twelfth of the pontificate.

Pope John Paul II

NOTES

1. Cf. The letter of Pope Alexander IV to the University of Paris, April 14, 1255, Introduction, *Bullarum Diplomatrum . . .*, vol. 3, (Turin 1858), p. 602.

2. St. Augustine, *Confessions*, X, xxiii, 33, "In fact, the blessed life consists in *the joy that comes from the truth*, since this joy comes from you who are truth, God my light, salvation of my face, my God," *Patrologia Latina* 32, pp. 793–794. Cf. St. Thomas Aquinas, *De Malo*, IX, 1: "It is actually natural to man to strive for knowledge of the truth."

3. John Paul II, Discourse to the Catholic Institute of Paris, June 1, 1980: *Insegnamenti di Giovanni Paolo II*, vol. 3/1 (1980), p. 1581.

4. John Paul II, Discourse to the Cardinals, Nov. 10, 1979: *Insegnamenti di Giovanni Paolo II*, vol. 2/2 (1979), p. 1096; cf. Discourse to UNESCO, Paris, June 2, 1980: *Acta Apostolicae Sedis* 72 (1980), pp. 735–752.

5. Cf. John Paul II, Discourse to the University of Coimbra, May, 15, 1982: *Insegnamenti di Giovanni Paolo II*, vol. 5/2 (1982), p. 1692.

6. Paul VI, Allocution to Representatives of States, October 4, 1965: *Insegnamenti di Paolo VI*, vol. 3 (1965), p. 508.

7. Cardinal John Henry Newman, *The Idea of a University* (London: Longmans, Green and Company, 1931), p. XI.

8. *Jn.* 14:6.

9. Cf. St. Augustine, *Sterm.* 43, 9: PL 38, 258. Cf. also St. Anselm, *Proslogion*, Ch. I: PL 158, p. 227.

10. Cf. John Paul II, Allocution to the International Congress on Catholic Universities, April 25, 1989, no. 3: *AAS* 18 (1989), p. 1218.

11. Ibid., *Sapientia Christiana*, Apostolic Constitution Concerning the Ecclesiastical Universities and Faculties, April 15, 1979: *AAS* 17 (1979), pp. 469–521.

12. Vatican Council II, Declaration on Catholic Education (*Gravissimum Educationis*), 10: *AAS* 58 (1966), p. 737.

13. Mt. 13:52

14. Cf. *The Magna Carta of the European Universities*, Bologna, Italy, September 18, 1988, "Fundamental Principles."

15. Cf. Vatican Council II, Pastoral Constitution on the Church in the Modern World (*Gaudium et Spes*), 59: *AAS* 58 (1966), p. 1080; *Gravissimum Educationis*, 10: *AAS* 58 (1966), p. 737. *Institutional autonomy* means that the governance of an academic institution is and remains internal to the institution; *academic freedom* is the guarantee given to those involved in teaching and research that, within their specific specialized branch of knowledge and according to the methods proper to that specific area, they may search for the truth wherever analysis and evidence lead them, and may teach and publish the results of this search, keeping in mind the cited criteria, that is, safeguarding the rights of the individual and of society within the confines of the truth and the common good.

16. There is a two-fold notion of *culture* used in the document: the *humanistic* and the *socio-historical*. "The word *culture* in its general sense indicates all those factors by which man refines and unfolds his manifold spiritual and bodily qualities. It means his effort to bring the world itself under his control by his knowledge and his labor. It includes the fact that by improving customs and institutions he renders social life more human both within the family and in the civic community. Finally, it is a feature of culture that throughout the course of time man expresses, communicates, and conserves in his works great spiritual experiences and desires, so that these may be of advantage to the progress of many, even of the whole human family. Hence it follows that human culture necessarily has a historical and social aspect and that the word culture often takes on a sociological and ethnological sense" *Gaudium et Spes*, 53.

17. "The Catholic University in the Modern World," final document of the Second International Congress of Delegates of Catholic Universities, Rome, Nov. 20–29, 1972, sec. 1.

18. Ibid.

19. John Paul II, Allocution to the International Congress of Catholic Universities. CF. also *Gaudium et Spes*, 61. Cardinal Newman observes that a university "professes to assign to each study which it receives, its proper place and its just boundaries; to define the rights, to establish the mutual relations and to effect the intercommunion of one and all" (*The Idea of a University*, p. 457).

20. *Gaudium et Spes*, 36. To a group of scientists I pointed out that "while reason and faith surely represents two distinct orders of knowledge, each autonomous with regard to its own methods, the two must finally converge in the discovery of a single whole reality which has its origin in God" (John Paul II, Address at the Meeting on Galileo, May 9, 1983, no. 3: *AAS* 75 [1983], p. 690).

21. John Paul II, Address at UNESCO, 22. The last part of the quotation uses words directed to the Pontifical Academy of Sciences, Nov. 10, 1979: *Insegnamenti di Giovanni Paolo II*, vol. 2/2 (1979), p. 1109.

22. Cf. *Gravissimum Educationis*, 10.

23. *Gaudium et Spes*, 59. Cardinal Newman describes the ideal to be sought in this way: "A habit of mind is formed which lasts through life, of which the attributes are freedom, equitableness, calmness, moderation, and wisdom" (*The Idea of a University*, pp. 101–102).

24. John Paul II, apostolic exhortation *Christifideles Laici*, Dec. 30, 1988, no. 44: *AAS* 81 (1989), p. 479.

25. Vatican Council II, Dogmatic Constitution on the Church (*Lumen Gentium*), 31: *AAS* 57 (1965), pp. 37–38. Cf. Decree on the Apostolate of the Laity (*Apostolican Actuositatem*), passim: *AAS* 58 (1966), pp. 837 ff. Cf. also *Gaudium et Spes*, 43.

26. Cf. ibid., Declaration on Religious Liberty (*Dignitatis Humanae*), 2: *AAS* 58 (1966), pp. 930–931.

27. John Paul II, Address to Leaders of Catholic Higher Education, Xavier University of Louisiana, September 12, 1987, no. 4: *AAS* 80 (1988), p. 764.

28. *Gaudium et Spes*, 59.

29. Cf. Vatican Council II, Dogmatic Constitution on Divine Revelation (*Dei Verbum*), nos. 8–10: *AAS* 58 (1966), pp. 820–822.

30. Cf. *Lumen Gentium*, 25.

31. Cf. Congregation for the Doctrine of the Faith, Instruction on the Ecclesial Vocation of the Theologian, May 24, 1990.

32. Cf. John Paul II, encyclical *Sollicitudo Rei Socialis*, 27–34: *AAS* 80 (1988), pp. 547–560.

33. Paul VI, encyclical *Populorum Progressio*, 1: *AAS* 59 (1967), p. 257.

34. "Therefore, in that there has been a pleasing multiplication of centers of higher learning, it has become apparent that it would be opportune for the faculty and the alumni to unite in common association which, working in reciprocal understanding and close collaboration, and based upon the authority of the supreme pontiff, as father and university doctor, they might more efficaciously

spread and extend the light of Christ" (Pius XII, apostolic letter *Catholicas Studiorum Universitates*, with which the International Federation of Catholic Universities was established: *AAS* 42 [1950], p. 386).

35. The Code of Canon Law indicates the general responsibility of the bishop toward university students: "The diocesan bishop is to have serious pastoral concern for students by erecting a parish for them or by assigning a priest for this purpose on a stable basis, he is also to provide for Catholic university centers at universities, even non-Catholic ones, to give assistance, especially spiritual to young people" (Canon 813).

36. "Living in various circumstances during the course of time, the church, too has used in her preaching the discoveries of different cultures to spread and explain the message of Christ to all nations, to probe it and more deeply understand it, and to give it better expression in liturgical celebrations and in the life of the diversified community of the faithful" (*Gaudium et Spes*, 58).

37. Paul VI, apostolic exhortation *Evangelii Nuntiandi*, 20: *AAS* 68 (1976), p. 18. Cf. *Gaudium et Spes*, 58.

38. John Paul II, Address to Intellectuals, Students, and University Personnel, July 5, 1986, n. 3: *AAS* 79 (1987), p. 99. Also *Gaudium et Spes*, 58.

39. Paul VI, Address to Delegates of the International Federation of Catholic Universities, Nov. 27, 1972: *AAS* 46 (1972), p. 770.

40. Paul VI, *Evangelii Nuntiandi*, 18ff.

41. Paul VI, Address to Presidents and Rectors of the Universities of the Society of Jesus, August 6, 1975, no. 2: *AAS* 67 (1975), p. 553. Speaking to the participants of the International Congress on Catholic Universities, April 25, 1989, I added (no. 5): "Within a Catholic university the evangelical mission of the church and the mission of research and teaching become interrelated and coordinated."

42. Cf. in particular the chapter of the code: "Catholic Universities and Other Institutes of Higher Studies" (Canon 807–814).

43. Episcopal conferences were established in the Latin rite. Other rites have other assemblies of Catholic hierarchy.

44. Cf. Canon 455.2

45. Cf. *Sapientia Christiana*. Ecclesiastical universities and faculties are those that have the right to confer academic degrees by the authority of the Holy See.

46. Cf. *Dignitatis Humanae*, 2.

47. Cf. *Gaudium et Spes*, 57 and 59; *Gravissimum Educationis*, 10.

48. Both the establishment of such a university and the conditions by which it may refer to itself as a Catholic university are to be in accordance with the prescription issued by the Holy See, episcopal conference, or other assembly of Catholic hierarchy.

49. Canon 810 of the Code of Canon Law specifies the responsibility of the competent authorities in this area: Section 1: "It is the responsibility of

the authority who is competent in accord with the statutes to provide for the appointment of teachers to Catholic universities who, besides their scientific and pedagogical suitability, are also outstanding in their integrity of doctrine and probity of life; when those requisite qualities are lacking they are to be removed from their positions in accord with the procedure set forth in the statutes. Section 2: The conference of bishops and the diocesan bishops concerned have the duty and right of being vigilant that in these universities the principles of Catholic doctrine are faithfully observed." Cf. also Article 5.2 ahead in these norms.

50. *Lumen Gentium*, 25; *Dei Verbum*, 8–10; cf. Canon 812: "It is necessary that those who teach theological disciplines in any institute of higher studies have a mandate from the competent ecclesiastical authority."

51. Cf. Canon 811.2.

52. For universities to which Article 3, Secs. 1 and 2 refer, these procedure are to be established in the university statutes approved by the competent ecclesiastical authority; for other Catholic universities, they are to be determined by episcopal conferences or other assemblies of Catholic hierarchy.

53. Cf. Canon 820. Cf. also *Sapientia Christiana*, "norms of application," Article 49.

54. John Paul II, Address to the Pontifical Council for Culture, Jan. 13, 1989, no. 2: *AAS* 81 (1989), pp. 857–858.

Index

Abbreviations of documents as employed in the index: ACCU86—Synthesis of Responses Received from U.S. Catholic College and University Presidents; CHEP—*Catholic Higher Education and the Pastoral Ministry of the Church*; CMFF—Empowered by the Spirit: Campus Ministry Faces the Future; CUMW—The Catholic University in the Modern World; ECE90—*Ex Corde Ecclesiae*; JPII87—Address, Pope John Paul II, September 12, 1987; JPII89—Address, Pope John Paul II, April 25, 1989; LOL—Land O'Lakes Statement; NCEAPP—Relations of American Catholic Colleges and Universities with the Church, NCEA Position Paper; RDS88—Revised Draft Schema (1988); RDS89—Revised Draft Schema (1989); RECDEL89—Recommendations from the Delegates (1989); RS—Rome Statement (1969); SPLC86—Statements of Presidents of Leading Catholic Universities of North America; SR86—Synthesis of Responses (1986); SR88—Summary of Responses (1988).